STUDIES IN PUBLIC COMMUNICATION

A. William Bluem, General Editor

MASS MEDIA AND THE SUPREME COURT

The Legacy of the Warren Years

STUDIES IN PUBLIC COMMUNICATION

STUDIES IN PUBLIC COMMUNICATION

MASS MEDIA
AND THE
SUPREME COURT

The Legacy of the Warren Years

EDITED, WITH COMMENTARIES
AND SPECIAL NOTES BY
KENNETH S. DEVOL, Ph.D.

COMMUNICATION ARTS BOOKS

HASTINGS HOUSE, PUBLISHERS, NEW YORK

For Shirley,
Sharon and Randall

Library of Congress Catalog Card Number: 70–165459

Cloth Edition ISBN: 8038–4659–2
Paper Edition ISBN: 8038–4661–4

Published simultaneously in Canada
by Saunders of Toronto, Ltd., Don Mills, Ontario

PRINTED IN THE UNITED STATES OF AMERICA
DESIGNED BY AL LICHTENBERG

CONTENTS

TABLE OF CASES

PREFACE

A newly aroused interest in the Supreme Court emerged during the 1960s—and continued into the early 1970s—largely because of the Justices' willingness to speak out on a series of First Amendment questions. With the democratic concept of majority rule as a foundation, the Warren Court turned its attention to the protection of minority rights, and included among these was freedom of expression—freedom to profess unorthodox and unpopular views. The Warren Court, for example, undertook questions of obscenity, motion picture censorship, libel, right of privacy and trial by television—questions largely ignored prior to the 16 years of the Warren era. This new legal activism increases the importance of the Court to those interested in the mass media, political science, sociology and other disciplines devoted to the changing patterns of our social fabric.

Constitutional law is not static. It is ever-evolving, ever-changing. It is significant, therefore, that excerpts from major concurrences and dissents are included. A Justice's dissent today may later become a majority view. The great issues of the First Amendment deserve more than a mere recounting of name, date and definition. Indeed, some of the issues—obscenity is one—have escaped adequate legal definition in spite of all of man's trying.

It might be helpful to the reader to note certain limits drawn by the editor. No attempt was made to review cases dealing with freedom of speech or assembly *per se*. Only questions concerning the mass media were included. Nor were cases included which deal primarily with business aspects of the media, such as anti-trust violations. Deletions in the opinions and articles were made only where indicated by ellipses, except for certain footnotes, case citations, legal jargon and other occasional references which, in the view of the editor, tended to impede reading for the layman. Major citations remain in the text and appear in the table of cases. More detailed citations may be found in the casebooks.

The editor, of course, is deeply indebted to those authors and publishing houses which allowed the use of material already under copyright. These interpretations of the Court's role added immeasurably to the value of this volume. Full credit is given to these scholars and publishers in footnotes which accompany the beginning of each article.

Legal opinions are stereotyped as being verbose, ponderous and boring. While this may be true more often than not, the pens of our leading jurists have recorded expressions of great power and wisdom. It is hoped that some of these moments have been captured in this volume of readings, along with some of the drama, the struggles of mind and matter which confronted these Justices over the years.

K.S.D.
Northridge, California
August, 1971

INTRODUCTION

In these days of campus activism, teachers of Public Communication may wish to consider anew Mr. Justice Frankfurter's observation that "the soil on which the Bill of Rights grew was not a soil of arid pedantry." Such a verity hardly suggests that we must employ leading rock groups to sing paeans to various constitutional amendments in our classrooms, but it does reflect a simple truth about transmitting respect for law and legal institutions to students—that if a teacher will not trouble to make his subject interesting, someone with less admirable motives will do it for him.

It is nearly certain that simplistic, emotional sloganeering will always win the day over dull legal casebooks. Yet we cannot yield to this situation, for it leaves us with two equally unnerving visions of the future. The first is of a "turned-off" civilization, desensitized to the point of dull non-involvement and indifferent toward everyone's rights and responsibilities, including—most tragically—their own. And if this Woodstockian spectre is not sufficiently chilling, there is its opposite; a future civilization dominated by mob-advocacy—by antirational hysteria born of intellectual over-amplification. Those who would prescribe massive doses of "Commitment, Relevance, and Social Concern" as essential educational antidotes to youthful non-involvement might be disconcerted by this forecast of British economist E. I. Mishan:

> If the present trends in mass education continue, there is every likelihood of millions of dissatisfied ex-students milling about American cities, their frail expertise unwanted (how many sociologists can the nation employ?), unable or unwilling to fit into the uninspiring niches provided by industry and government, and inevitably forming a sort of intellectual *Lumpenproletariat* that will go far toward aggravating general unrest, dissent and desperation.

One finally wonders whether the teacher of communications can really hope to define those reasonable essences which lie between the extremes of passivity and of over-commitment for an impatient, energetic rising generation.

Perhaps, like Kipling's *Gods of The Copybook Headings*, we can do no better than "limp up to explain it once more"—asking the help of young people in a battle which we did not begin, and which they most certainly will not finish. But somehow this seems too little. We are still obliged to continue the search for fresh, stimulating ways to bring the young to fuller comprehension of what is treasured by all men—freedom, safety and peace under just laws.

This obligation is shared by Kenneth S. Devol. The parameters of *Studies in Public Communication* hardly limit the series to publication of volumes which are useful as classroom texts, but it is a most happy and ideal circumstance, in my view, when the dedicated scholar produces a work which at once provides a fresh and stimulating teaching instrument for his colleagues as well as compelling and jargon-free reading for the student. Dr. Devol has produced such a volume, and we are fortunate that it comes at a time when concern over these matters is at a national peak.

A. WILLIAM BLUEM
Professor of Media Studies
Syracuse University

CHAPTER I

THE ROLE OF THE SUPREME COURT

Historians usually look at the development of the United States in terms of presidential administrations. Yet decisions rendered by the Supreme Court often surpass administrative programs in their impact on the American scene. Active, literate Justices, such as Warren, Marshall, Holmes, Brandeis, Hughes, Frankfurter, Brennan, and Black, all have woven into the democratic fabric significant and lasting patterns. Without these men and their less familiar colleagues the United States would be a far different nation. Perhaps only a handful of presidents have influenced public life more than these Supreme Court justices.

The 16 years of the Warren Court, 1953–69, have been termed the most dynamic since the 34-year tenure of Chief Justice Marshall in the early 1800s. The Court set national patterns and standards for race relations, representative government, freedom of the press and civil rights, including treatment of criminal suspects. In these decisions and others, the Warren Court changed the direction of national life.

Chief Justice Earl Warren, a former three-term governor and attorney general of California, was appointed to the bench by President Eisenhower following the death of Chief Justice Vinson. The following year he wrote the Court's opinion in its unanimous decision ordering desegregation of public schools, Brown v. Board of Education. Separate but equal, he wrote, cannot be tolerated in public education. This decision, in 1954, has been heralded as the beginning of the civil rights movement as a national commitment. The decision which the Chief Justice himself has said was most important during his tenure was the "one man, one vote" decision on legislative reapportionment.

But for all of its landmark decisions, the Court during Chief Justice Warren's tenure has been one of the most divided and controversial in history. There have been several non-majority decisions (some involving the media, e.g. Estes). The nation has not accepted nor has it implemented without foot-dragging many of the Court's major pronouncements (e.g. desegregation), has risen up in disbelief at some (e.g. outlawing required prayer and Bible reading in public schools), has expressed anger at others (e.g. setting higher standards for treatment of criminal suspects), and has experienced frustration due to still others (e.g. limiting obscenity prosecutions generally to hard-core pornography).

It has been charged that the major weakness of the Warren Court is its impreciseness, thereby causing confusion and frustration among the lower courts and police, as well as the general public, and its lack of what Justice Frankfurter called "judicial restraint." But the Court's lack of "judicial restraint" is applauded by the Court's supporters, who also are legion.

A criticism aimed specifically at Chief Justice Warren was that he was more a statesman than a jurist. He bonded the Court, it is claimed, more by personal warmth than by judicial logic. But this may have been the precise reason he was appointed to the bench and almost certainly was a factor in his appointment to head the President's Commission investigating the assassination of President Kennedy. Still, Senators fumed publicly, law enforcement officers complained, and ultra-right wing groups erected "Impeach Earl Warren" signs along America's highways. The criticism—and the praise—also seems to stem more from political or personal philosophy than from constitutional or legal grounds.

Another problem of the Warren Court was the huge workload it had accepted. The case volume had tripled since the days of the Hughes Court. Many areas, such as invasion of privacy, previously left to the states, became Supreme Court issues. Others, such as the relationship of motion pictures to the First Amendment and desegregation of public schools, were reversals of earlier decisions. Still others reflected an attempt to come to grips with major questions ignored or just touched upon previously, such as with libel and obscenity.

The era of Chief Justice Warren—some claim that it should not be labeled the "Warren Court" but the "Black Court" because of the great influence of the liberal Justice Hugo Black—came to an end with the close of the term in summer of 1969. But the departure of the Chief Justice alone did not close the era. Justice Black, usually considered the leader of the liberal wing, was 83 at the time of Chief Justice Warren's retirement. Justice Douglas was 70 and in troublesome health, as was Justice Harlan, also 70. The close of the era also saw the first Negro to assume a seat on the high court, Justice Thurgood Marshall, former Solicitor General, appointed two years before Chief Justice Warren's retirement.

Some have noted a move toward more conservative opinions as the era closed. Certainly, Justice Black had disappointed some of his supporters with several mid-1960 decisions. Also, the Court was under heavy fire from politicians who had counted their letters from home and found much criticism of some of the Court's major decisions. Indeed, some polls indicated that the public in 1969 failed to support the Court in its efforts, and public support of the Court is necessary to offset political pressures forthcoming from the Congress and the White House. Yet this support appeared to wane in the 1960s.

Symbolic of this unrest was Chief Justice Warren's announced retirement. President Johnson nominated Justice Abe Fortas, appointed to an Associate Justice seat in 1965, as Chief Justice Warren's successor. This nomination was immediately criticized by conservative members of the Senate, which must confirm presidential nominations to the bench. In public hearings, Justice Fortas was subjected to unprecedented questioning and confrontation. In face of mounting criticism, his nomination was withdrawn.

At issue were his voting record while sitting on the bench, his apparent liberalism countering a national conservative trend, his friendship with the then lame-duck President, and his constitutional philosophy. The seeds of a controversial Warren Court were bearing bitter fruit for his chosen successor. But the withdrawal of Justice Fortas's nomination as Chief Justice did not silence his critics nor the critics of the Court. In the closing months of the Warren Court, following disclosure of what some described as a conflict of interest and questionable business associations, Justice Fortas resigned from the Court. The Warren Court at its termination in June 1969, then, saw only eight of its nine chairs occupied. Justice Harry Blackmun finally took the Fortas seat in 1970 following Senate rejections of two of President Nixon's nominees, Judges Haynsworth and Carswell.

Chief Justice Warren's last official act was to introduce his successor, Chief Justice Warren Burger, a widely respected judge of the U.S. District Court of Appeals who was nominated by President Nixon and swiftly confirmed by the Senate. His appointment was seen by some to signalize the end of the Warren era as well as the Warren Court. He was considered a "strict constitutionalist," a conservative judicial position generally in keeping with the position of the Nixon administration and with political moderates and conservatives. But following the 16 years of "judicial activism" by the Warren Court, the philosophic leaning of the Burger Court—if, indeed, it is to be known by that name—is far from certain.

The tradition of an active, forceful Court did not begin with Chief Justice Warren. It was instituted by Chief Justice John Marshall, the fourth appointed to lead the High Court. He was named in 1801 by President John Adams and served during 34 of the most fateful years in American history. These years were filled with political struggle, threat of impeachment and, in the end, victory for the Marshall viewpoint. At stake, for example, was the concept of a strong federal government. Jefferson, one of the Court's leading adversaries, believed in a "weak" federal judiciary and in stronger state responsibility. Chief Justice Marshall argued for a strong federal system. Historians note that if the Marshall concept had lost, the Constitution might have become a weak document, somewhat similar to the Articles of Confederation. Chief Justice Marshall, for his role in strengthening the document, has been called the "Second Father of the Constitution."

The Marshall Court, then, helped establish a strong federal system, under which federal power must outweigh that of the states in time of direct conflict. Chief Justice Marshall also firmly established in Marbury v. Madison, decided two years after his appointment, the right of "judicial review," i.e. the right of the Court to review laws enacted by the legislative branch and to pass on their constitutionality. There is nothing in the Constitution which gives this power to the Supreme Court, yet this principle is accepted today as fundamental. Marbury v. Madison made Supreme Court opinions the "law of the land" and insured balancing strengths among the three branches of government, legislative, executive and judicial. It guaranteed that proper "checks and balances" would be available.

Chief Justice Marshall assumed his chair at a time when the Court was suffering from weakness, disrespect and uncertainty. The three Chief Justices before him, for example, served a total of only nine years. One, Justice Rutledge, was appointed by President Washington, but was not confirmed by the Senate.

Chief Justice Marshall had little formal schooling, but enjoyed extensive political experience in the Virginia Legislature, in the Congress and as Secretary of State. He and Madison led the debate in Virginia for ratification of the new U.S. Constitution. But this same strength and determination which led him to insure the strong federal legal system, judicial review, and checks and balances among the three branches of government also led to his unpopularity among many leading politicians of the day and to threats of his impeachment. Similar controversies were to surround active Chief Justices in the future, including Chief Justices Hughes and Warren. But before they were to enter the public arena, another era developed which was to introduce the philosophy of two Associate Justices, Holmes and Brandeis.

Oliver Wendell Holmes, Jr., is best remembered for his enunciation of the "clear and present danger" concept. He said that the First Amendment, which establishes freedom of the press, was to prevent "previous restraint" upon the press and that no such governmental prohibition on publication should take place without there being a "clear and present danger" to society. This concept was introduced in Schenck v. United States, 249 U.S. 47 (1919), in the following opinion:

SCHENCK V. UNITED STATES
249 U.S. 47 (1919)

MR. JUSTICE HOLMES *delivered the opinion of the Court.*

This is an indictment in three counts. The first charges a conspiracy to violate the Espionage Act of June 15, 1917, . . . by causing and attempting to cause insubordination, etc., in the military and naval forces of the United States, and to obstruct the recruiting and enlistment service of the United States, when the United States was at war with the German Empire; to wit, that the defendant willfully conspired to have printed and circulated to men who had been called and accepted for military service under the Act of May 18, 1917, a document set forth and alleged to be calculated to cause such insubordination and obstruction. The court alleges overt acts in pursuance of the conspiracy, ending in the distribution of the document set forth. The second count alleges a conspiracy to commit an offense against the United States; to wit, to use the mails for the transmission of matter declared to be non-mailable by title 12, section 2, of the Act of June 15, 1917, to wit, the above-mentioned document, with an averment of the same overt acts. The third count charges an unlawful use of the mails for the transmission of the same matter and otherwise as above. The defendants were found guilty on all the counts. They set up the First Amendment to the Constitution, forbidding Congress to make any law abridging the freedom of speech or of the press, and, bringing the case here on that ground, have argued some other points also of which we must dispose.

It is argued that the evidence, if admissible, was not sufficient to prove that the defendant Schenck was concerned in sending the documents. According to the testimony Schenck said he was general secretary of the Socialist party and had charge of the Socialist headquarters from which the documents were sent. He identified a book found there as the minutes of the executive committee of the party. The book showed a resolution of August 13, 1917, that 15,000 leaflets should be printed on the other side of one of them in use, to be mailed to men who had passed exemption boards, and for distribution. Schenck personally attended to the printing. . . . He said that he had about fifteen or sixteen thousand printed. There were files of the circular in question in the inner office which he said were printed on the other side of the one-sided circular and were there for distribution. Other copies were proved to have been sent through the mails to drafted men. Without going into confirmatory details that were proved, no reasonable man could doubt that the defendant Schenck was largely instrumental in sending the circulars about. . . .

The document in question, upon its first printed side, recited the 1st section of the 13th Amendment, said that the idea embodied in it was violated by the Conscription Act, and that a conscript is little better than a convict. In impassioned language it intimated that conscription was despotism in its worst form and a monstrous wrong against humanity, in the interest of Wall Street's chosen few. It said: "Do not submit to intimidation," but in form at least confined itself to peaceful measures, such as a petition for the repeal of the act. The other and later printed side of the sheet was headed, "Assert Your Rights." It stated reasons for alleging that anyone violated the Constitution when he refused to recognize "your right to assert your opposition to the draft," and went on: "If you do not assert and support your rights, you are helping to deny or disparage rights which it is the solemn duty of all citizens and residents of the United States to retain." It described the arguments on the other side as coming from cunning politicians and a mercenary capitalist press, and even silent consent to the Conscription Law as helping to support an infamous conspiracy. It denied the power to send our citizens away to foreign shores to shoot up the people of other lands, and added that words could not express the condemnation such cold-blooded ruthlessness deserves, etc., etc., winding up, "You must do your share to maintain, support, and uphold the rights of the people of this country." Of course the document would not have been sent unless it had been intended to have some effect, and we do not see what effect it could be expected to have upon persons subject to the draft except to influence them to obstruct the carrying of it out. The defendants do not deny that the jury might find against them on this point.

But it is said, suppose that that was the tendency of this circular, it is protected by the First Amendment to the Constitution. Two of the strongest expressions are said to be quoted respectively from well-known public men. It well may be that the prohibition of laws abridging the freedom of speech is not confined to previous restraints, although to prevent them may have been the main purpose, as intimated in *Patterson v. Colorado*, 205 U.S. 454, 462. We admit that in many places and in ordinary times the defendants, in saying all that was said in the circular, would have been within their constitutional rights. But the character of every act depends upon the circumstances in which it is done. The most stringent protection of free speech would not protect a man in falsely shouting fire in a theater, and causing a panic. It does not even protect a man from an injunction against uttering words that may have all the effect of force. The question in every case is whether the words used are used in such circumstances and are of such a nature as to create a clear and present danger that they will bring about the substantive evils that Congress has a right to prevent. It is a question of proximity and degree. When a nation is at war many things that might be said in time of peace are such a hindrance to its effort that their utterance will not be endured so long as men fight, and that no court could regard them as protected by any constitutional right. It seems to be admitted that if an actual obstruction of the recruiting service were proved, liability for words that produced that effect might be enforced. The Statute of 1917, in sec. 4, punishes conspiracies to obstruct as well as actual obstruction. If the act (speaking, or circulating a paper), its tendency and the intent with which it is done, are the same, we perceive no ground for saying that success alone warrants making the act a crime. . . .

*   *   *

The evolving status and definition of "clear and present danger," which had been debated by the Court for more than 30 years, reached a major plateau in 1951 with a 6-2 decision to uphold the conviction under the Smith Act of Eugene Dennis and ten others on charges of conspiracy to teach and advocate the overthrow of the United States government by force and violence. Dennis v. United States, 341 U.S. 494 (1951). The plateau was somewhat of a pragmatic compromise between the Holmes-Brandeis "clear and present danger" principle and the "dangerous tendency" concept followed in Gitlow. Added was the principle of balancing various interests.

It should be noted that the petitioners were convicted for conspiracy and advocacy, not with actual violence nor with an overt attempt to overthrow the government, and that the decision came during the Korean conflict that threatened to spread to a wider war. The majority held that the state cannot be expected to withhold preventative action until the actual moment of the putsch and that obstructions to free speech and press might be necessary in order to prevent an even greater evil to society.

The decision, in effect, allows legislatures the freedom to act against probable danger, but not by indiscriminate trampling of the rights of the individual. There was no real consensus of the Court (five separate opinions written by the eight Justices taking part). However, a generally accepted sliding scale incorporating "gravity" or "probable danger" was applied to the "clear and present danger" test, though it is not universally accepted that the Court really rejected the Holmes-Brandeis concept. In addition to the importance of the case itself and the acceptance of a more pragmatic approach to the problem of seditious utterances, the five opinions give keen insights into the philosophic conflicts in which the Court finds itself when dealing with free speech and press.

DENNIS V. UNITED STATES
341 U.S. 494 (1951)

MR. CHIEF JUSTICE VINSON *announced the judgment of the Court and an opinion in which Mr. Justice Reed, Mr. Justice Burton and Mr. Justice Minton join.*

Petitioners were indicted in July, 1948, for violation of the conspiracy provisions of the Smith Acts . . .

Sections 2 and 3 of the Smith Act, 54 State 670, 671, ch 439, 18 USC (1946 ed) sec. 10, 11 (see present 18 USC sec. 2385), provide as follows:

"Sec. 2.

"(a) It shall be unlawful for any person—

"(1) to knowingly or willfully advocate, abet, advise, or teach the duty, necessity, desirability, or propriety of overthrowing or destroying any government in the United States by force or violence, or by the assassination of any officer of such government;

"(2) with the intent to cause the overthrow or destruction of any government in the United States, to print, publish, edit, issue, circulate, sell, distribute, or publicly display any written or printed matter advocating, advising, or teaching the duty, necessity, desirability, or propriety of overthrowing or destroying any government in the United States by force or violence;

"(3) to organize or help to organize any society, group, or assembly of persons who teach, advocate, or encourage the overthrow or destruction of any government in the United States by force or violence; or to be or become a member of, or affiliate with, any such society, group, or assembly of persons, knowing the purposes thereof.

"(b) For the purposes of this section, the term 'government in the United States' means the Government of the United States, the government of any State, Territory, or possession of the United States, the government of the District of Columbia, or the government of any political subdivision of any of them.

"Sec. 3. It shall be unlawful for any person to attempt to commit, or to conspire to commit, any of the acts prohibited by the provisions of . . . this title." . . .

The very language of the Smith Act negates the interpretation which petitioners would have us impose on that Act. It is directed at advocacy, not discussion. Thus, the trial judge properly charged the jury that they could not convict if they found that petitioners did "no more than pursue peaceful studies and discussions or teaching and advocacy in the realm of ideas." He further charged that it was not unlawful "to conduct in an American college and university a course explaining the philosophical theories set forth in the books which have been placed in evidence." Such a charge is in strict accord with the statutory language, and illustrates the meaning to be placed on those words. Congress did not intend to eradicate the free discussion of political theories, to destroy the traditional rights of Americans to discuss and evaluate ideas without fear of governmental sanction. Rather Congress was concerned with the very kind of activity in which the evidence showed these petitioners engaged. . . .

We pointed out in *Douds*, 339 U.S. 382, that the basis of the First Amendment is the hypothesis that speech can rebut speech, propaganda will answer propaganda, free debate of ideas will result in the wisest governmental policies. It is for this reason that this Court has recognized the inherent value of free discourse. An analysis of the leading cases in this Court which have involved direct limitations on speech, however, will demonstrate that both the majority of the Court and the dissenters in particular cases have recognized that this is not an unlimited, unqualified right, but that the societal value of speech must, on occasion, be subordinated to other values and considerations.

No important case involving free speech was decided by this Court prior to *Schenck v. United States*, 249 U.S. 47. Indeed, the summary treatment accorded an argument based upon an individual's claim that the First Amendment protected certain utterances indicates that the Court at earlier dates placed no unique emphasis upon that right. It was not until the classic dictum of Justice Holmes in the *Schenck* case that speech *per se* received that emphasis in a majority opinion. . . .

Nothing is more certain in modern society than the principle that there are no absolutes, that a name, a phrase, a standard has meaning only when associated with the considerations which gave birth to the nomenclature. . . .

In this case we are squarely presented with the application of the "clear and present danger" test, and must decide what that phrase imports. . . .

Obviously, the words cannot mean that before the Government may act, it must wait until the *putsch* is about to be executed, the plans have been laid and the signal is awaited. If Government is aware that a group aiming at its overthrow is attempting to indoctrinate its members and to commit them to a course whereby they will strike when the leaders feel the circumstances permit, action by the Government is required. The argument that there is no need for Government to concern itself, for Government is strong, it possesses ample powers to put down a rebellion, it may defeat the revolution with ease needs no answer. For that is not the question. Certainly an attempt to overthrow the Government by force, even though doomed from the outset because of inadequate numbers or power of the revolutionists, is a sufficient evil for Congress to prevent. . . .

Chief Judge Learned Hand, writing for the majority below, interpreted the phrase as follows: "In each case [courts] must ask whether the gravity of the 'evil,' discounted by its improbability, justifies such invasion of free speech as is necessary to avoid the danger." We adopt this statement of the rule. As articulated by Chief Judge Hand, it is as succinct and inclusive as any other we might devise at this time. It takes into consideration those factors which we deem relevant, and relates their significances. More we cannot expect from words. . . .

MR. JUSTICE FRANKFURTER, *concurring in affirmance of the judgment.*

. . . Just as there are those who regard as invulnerable every measure for which the claim of national survival is invoked, there are those who find in the Constitution a wholly unfettered right of expression. Such literalness treats the words of the Constitution as though they were found on a piece of outworn parchment instead of being words that have called into being a nation with a past to be preserved for the future. The soil in which the Bill of Rights grew was not a soil of arid pedantry. The historic antecedents of the First Amendment preclude the notion that its purpose was to give unqualified immunity to every expression that touched on matters within the range of political interest. The Massachusetts Constitution of 1780 guaranteed free speech; yet there are records of at least three convictions for political libels obtained between 1799 and 1803. The Pennsylvania Constitution of 1790 and the Delaware Constitution of 1792 expressly imposed liability for abuse of the right of free speech. Madison's own State put on its books in 1792 a statute confining the abusive exercise of the right of utterance. And it deserves to be noted that in writing to John Adams' wife, Jefferson did not rest his condemnation of the Sedition Act of 1798 on his belief in unrestrained utterance as to political matter. The First Amendment, he argued, reflected a limitation upon Federal power, leaving the right to enforce restrictions on speech to the States.

The language of the First Amendment is to be read not as barren words found in a dictionary but as symbols of historic experience illumined by the presuppositions of those who employed them. Not what words did Madison and Hamilton use, but what was it in their minds which they conveyed? . . .

"The law is perfectly well settled," this Court said over fifty years ago, "that the first ten Amendments to the Constitution, commonly known as the Bill of Rights, were not intended to lay down any novel principles of government, but simply to embody certain guaranties and immunities which we had inherited from our English ancestors, and which had from time immemorial been subject to certain well-recognized exceptions arising from the necessities of the case. In incorporating these principles into the fundamental law there was no intention of disregarding the exceptions, which continued to be recognized as if they had been formally expressed." *Robertson v. Baldwin*, 165 U.S. 275, 281. That this represents the authentic view of the Bill of Rights and the spirit in which it must be construed has been recognized again and again in cases that have come here within the last fifty years. Absolute rules would inevitably lead to absolute exceptions, and such exceptions would eventually corrode the rules. The demands of free speech in a democratic society as well as the interest in national security are better served by candid and informed weighing of the competing interests, within the confines of the judicial process, than by announcing dogmas too inflexible for the non-Euclidian problems to be solved. . . .

MR. JUSTICE JACKSON, *concurring.*

This prosecution is the latest of never-ending, because never successful, quests for some legal formula that will secure an existing order against revolutionary radicalism. It requires us to reappraise, in the light of our own times and conditions, constitutional doctrines devised under other circumstances to strike a balance between authority and liberty. . . .

If we must decide that this Act and its application are constitutional only if we are convinced that petitioner's conduct creates a "clear and present danger" of violent overthrow, we must appraise imponderables, including international and national phenomena which baffle the best informed foreign offices and our most experienced politicians. We would have to foresee and predict the effectiveness of Communist propaganda, opportunities for infiltration, whether, and when, a time will come that they consider propitious for action, and whether and how fast our existing government will deteriorate. And we would have to speculate as to whether an approaching Communist *coup* would not be anticipated by a nationalistic fascist movement. No doctrine can be sound whose application requires us to make a prophecy of that sort in the guise of a legal decision. The judicial process simply is not adequate to a trial of such far-flung issues. The answers given would reflect our own political predilections and nothing more. . . .

MR. JUSTICE BLACK *dissenting.*

. . . These petitioners were not charged with an attempt to overthrow the Government. They were not charged with overt acts of any kind designed to overthrow the Government. They were not even charged with saying anything or writing anything designed to overthrow the Government. The charge was that they agreed to assemble and to talk and publish certain ideas at a later date: The indictment is that they conspired to organize the Communist Party and to use speech or newspapers and other publications in the future to teach and advocate the forcible overthrow of the Government. No matter how it is worded, this is a virulent form of prior censorship of speech and press, which I believe the First Amendment forbids. . . .

So long as this Court exercises the power of judicial review of legislation, I cannot agree that the First Amendment permits us to sustain laws suppressing freedom of speech and press on the basis of Congress' or our

own notions of mere "reasonableness." Such a doctrine waters down the
First Amendment so that it amounts to little more than an admonition to
Congress. The Amendment as so construed is not likely to protect any but
those "safe" or orthodox views which rarely need its protection. . . .

MR. JUSTICE DOUGLAS, *dissenting.*

If this were a case where those who claimed protection under the First
Amendment were teaching the techniques of sabotage, the assassination of
the President, the filching of documents from public files, the planting of
bombs, the art of street warfare, and the like, I would have no doubts. . . .
Petitioners, however, were not charged with a "conspiracy to overthrow"
the Government. They were charged with a conspiracy to form a party and
groups and assemblies of people who teach and advocate the overthrow of
our Government by force or violence and with a conspiracy to advocate and
teach its overthrow by force and violence. It may well be that indoctrina-
tion in the techniques of terror to destroy the Government would be in-
dictable under either statute. But the teaching which is condemned here is
of a different character.

So far as the present record is concerned, what petitioners did was to
organize people to teach and themselves teach the Marxist-Leninist doctrine contained chiefly in four books: *Foundations of Leninism* by Stalin
(1924), *The Communist Manifesto* by Marx and Engels (1848), *State
and Revolution* by Lenin (1917), *History of the Communist Party of the
Soviet Union* (B) (1939).

Those books are to Soviet Communism what *Mein Kampf* was to
Nazism. If they are understood, the ugliness of Communism is revealed,
its deceit and cunning are exposed, the nature of its activities becomes apparent, and the chances of its success less likely. That is not, of course,
the reason why petitioners chose these books for their classrooms. They are
fervent Communists to whom these volumes are gospel. They preached the
creed with the hope that some day it would be acted upon.

The opinion of the Court does not outlaw these texts nor condemn
them to the fire, as the Communists do literature offensive to their creed.
But if the books themselves are not outlawed, if they can lawfully remain
on library shelves, by what reasoning does their use in a classroom become
a crime? It would not be a crime under the Act to introduce these books
to a class, though that would be teaching what the creed of violent overthrow of the government is. The Act, as construed, requires the element
of intent—that those who teach the creed believe in it. The crime then
depends not on what is taught but on who the teacher is. That is to make
freedom of speech turn not on *what is said*, but on the intent with which
it is said. Once we start down that road we enter territory dangerous to the
liberties of every citizen.

There was a time in England when the concept of constructive treason
flourished. Men were punished not for raising a hand against the king but

for thinking murderous thoughts about him. The Framers of the Constitution were alive to that abuse and took steps to see that the practice would not flourish here. Treason was defined to require overt acts—the evolution of a plot against the country into an actual project. The present case is not one of treason. . . .

Intent, of course, often makes the difference in the law. An act otherwise excusable or carrying minor penalties may grow to an abhorrent thing if the evil intent is present. We deal here, however, not with ordinary acts but with speech, to which the Constitution has given a special sanction. . . .

The First Amendment provides that "Congress shall make no law . . . abridging the freedom of speech." The Constitution provides no exception. This does not mean, however, that the Nation need hold its hand until it is in such weakened condition that there is no time to protect itself from incitement to revolution. Seditious conduct can always be punished. But the command of the First Amendment is so clear that we should not allow Congress to call a halt to free speech except in the extreme case of peril from the speech itself. The First Amendment makes confidence in the common sense of our people and in their maturity of judgment the great postulate of our democracy. Its philosophy is that violence is rarely, if ever, stopped by denying civil liberties to those advocating resort to force. The First Amendment reflects the philosophy of Jefferson "that it is time enough for the rightful purposes of civil government for its officers to interfere when principles break out into overt acts against peace and good order." The political censor has no place in our public debates. Unless and until extreme and necessitous circumstances are shown, our aim should be to keep speech unfettered and to allow the processes of law to be invoked only when the provacateurs among us move from speech to action.

Vishinsky wrote in 1948 in *The Law of the Soviet State*, "In our state, naturally there can be no place for freedom of speech, press, and so on for the foes of socialism."

Our concern should be that we accept no such standard for the United States. Our faith should be that our people will never give support to these advocates of revolution, so long as we remain loyal to the purposes for which our Nation was founded.

*   *   *

The question of the degree of Justice Holmes' civil libertarianism has continued to today. Much of the legislation he supported was done to improve social conditions, but generally he was not considered a "reformer." His liberalism was more intellectual than political, possibly. Nonetheless, his pronouncements pointed the way for future libertarians.

Appointed to the Court in 1902 and serving for 29 years, Justice Holmes saw law as developing along with society and not as a stagnant pronounce-

ment based on platitudes and absolutes. He attempted to consider the broad picture of society as a whole. His ringing phrases have caused him to be called as much a philosopher as a jurist, and his strong dissents—some of which later were to become majority opinions—have caused him to be known as the "Great Dissenter." While he was not a Chief Justice, he and his colleague, Justice Brandeis, the first Jew to be named to the Court, cut as influential a path as the Court has ever seen.

It was not, however, until the Court sat under Chief Justice Charles Evans Hughes that the Holmes-Brandeis concept of "clear and present danger" was accepted as the legal test relating to censorship of unpopular ideas. Chief Justice Hughes served for 11 years beginning in 1930 and was a firm supporter of civil liberties, a view reflected in the decisions of his Court. The major freedom of expression decisions came as reactions to prior restraint by government. The landmark Near decision in 1931 held that prior restraint as a tool of suppression by government was to be eliminated in all but the most extreme cases. The Grosjean decision in 1936 removed from government the privilege of "taxing to destroy" a newspaper. And in the 1938 Lovell decision, the Court held circulation to be an integral part of freedom of the press. The final significant contribution of the Hughes Court to freedom of expression came in 1941 with the decision in Bridges. There it applied the "clear and present danger" principle to out-of-court contempt cases.

These major decisions gave new significance and clarity to First Amendment phrases. But the 1930s were not solely a time of debate within the chamber. The high court came under increasing attack by supporters of President Franklin D. Roosevelt who saw the Court as standing in the way of progress urgently needed to fulfill the promise of the New Deal. The Hughes Court had held many of the President's reforms unconstitutional. In 1937 President Roosevelt sent to the Congress a judicial reorganization proposal which, among other things, would have allowed the President to appoint additional Supreme Court justices when those on the bench reached the age of 70 and chose not to retire. The total number of Supreme Court Justices, under the proposal, could not exceed 15. This led to the hotly debated "Supreme Court packing" charge. The President felt that older justices had too narrow a view of social needs and were unable to adapt to the changing times and requirements of a nation in distress. Opponents charged the administration with "tampering" with the balance-of-power concept and with political interference of the Court's function. The bill was defeated, but within seven years death and retirement left only two non-Roosevelt appointees on the bench.

Chief Justice Hughes, a former governor of New York, was first appointed to the bench as Associate Justice in 1910, but he resigned to run for the presidency in 1916, losing narrowly to Woodrow Wilson. He was appointed Chief Justice in 1930 following more than a decade of public service. He was considered to be the greatest Chief Justice since Chief Justice Marshall. Historians will tell us whether this label will continue to stand under the impact of Chief Justice Warren. Certainly, both were embroiled in controversy, both were dedicated to human liberties, both were active leaders and both developed strong political foes.

The First Amendment

"Congress shall make no law," says the First Amendment to the Constitution of the United States, ". . . abridging the freedom of speech, or of the press. . . ." The framers of the Constitution did not interpret "freedom," leaving that task for the courts. At first reading, the statement appears to be clear. It says "no law." This is the firm interpretation placed upon it by "absolutists" of the United States Supreme Court, who in the Warren Court included Justices Black and Douglas. Yet the history of the Court's interpretation of the First Amendment is far from absolute. Whereas the first Ten Amendments to the Constitution, the Bill of Rights, were written to end uncertainty, several of those amendments have been encased in controversy which has tended to harden in recent years. Such fundamental concepts as free speech and press, fair trial, the right to keep and bear arms, separation of church and state, the right to dissent, self-incrimination, protection against illegal searches and seizures, and due process of law all have come under increasing public scrutiny during the Warren years.

The adoption of the first Ten Amendments was to put at ease those who noted that the original Constitution contained no guarantee of "human" or "natural" rights. This opposition was strong enough to present a clear threat to the ratification of the larger document. The Bill of Rights, then, was adopted by the First Congress and ratified by the states in order to set aside the fears of those who foresaw a return to the more autocratic English approach to government. Even though Constitutions of most of the 13 states contained individual rights guarantees, the adoption by the Congress of these same guarantees at the federal level insured ratification of the national Constitution.

But ratification did not end debate over the First Amendment's wording. Following Jefferson's lead, some urged that the freedoms mentioned in the First Amendment should be considered "natural human rights." Others talked in terms of "liberty versus license," i.e. in terms of degree. The Supreme Court prior to the 1930s suspended free speech and press if the expressions constituted a "reasonable tendency" to endanger society. Restraints in the 1930s were limited to only those expressions which created a "clear and present danger" to society.

This same period saw the revival of the historic concept of "prior" or "previous restraint." The Court with the landmark Near case of 1931 attempted to define freedom of the press as prohibiting government from restraining a publication prior to its distribution unless it was determined that the contents of that publication constituted a "clear and present danger" to society or that the expression did not fall within the bounds of First Amendment protection. In the years that followed, Justices have echoed the view that the goal of the framers of the First Amendment was indeed to guard against "prior restraint" by government, but they have disagreed as to when exceptions to this rule are constitutionally valid. More recently, the Court has been more inclined to consider the rights of the individual weighed against the rights of society, i.e. the "balancing interests" concept. And, of course, the Court has continued to rule that the First Amendment is not absolute and that certain expressions by their very nature do not fall within its protection, e.g. obscenity. Each of these theories—"prior restraint," "human rights," "liberty vs. license," "reasonable tendency," "clear and present danger," "balancing interests"—has had "its day in court."

The success of the Court in fulfilling the promise of the First Amendment, therefore, is debatable at best. Within a decade after the adoption of the Bill of Rights, the Congress passed the first in a series of laws to restrict speech and writing, the Alien and Sedition Acts of 1798. These short-lived laws were passed much to the anguish of citizens who forecast a return to "sovereign rule" from which they had intended to divorce themselves. The acts imposed fines and imprisonment on persons who wrote or spoke in a manner so as to arouse discontent with the government. The basic question then—and to this day—is whether the framers of the First Amendment meant to guarantee to the citizens the absolute right to comment upon and to criticize their government, i.e. whether the framers meant "no law" in a literal and absolute sense. Does the Constitution protect all speech or just "approved" speech? This debate is the history of the Supreme Court in its role as interpreter of the First Amendment.

In civil cases, such as libel and invasion of privacy, the Warren Court has noted that the purpose of free speech and press guarantees of the First Amendment and applied to the states by the Fourteenth Amendment (Gitlow v. New York) is to encourage open and diverse debate as necessary to any political or social change desired by a free society. The debate, the Supreme Court has ruled, may be robust, unpopular, diverse, unpleasant, caustic, sharp, and even untruthful. Only compelling interests by the state, therefore, have been accepted by the Court when questions of restricted public debate have come before it.

The pull and tug of judicial philosophy must be expected to continue unless one adopts the "absolutist" theory, i.e. that the "no law" wording of the First Amendment means just that—"no law." But this has not been the prevailing view. So, the tone of the nine-member panel can be expected to vary with the decades, with the events of the day, with presidential appointments and with changes within the Justices themselves.

THE COURT'S CONSTITUTIONAL ROLE

By WILLIAM R. BISHIN *

The Supreme Court of the United States has always posed a dilemma for students of American democratic theory. The court—through its power to declare legislative and executive action unconstitutional—is the most powerful judicial tribunal known to us. Yet it is immune—except in the most extraordinary cases—from any effective control by current popular majorities.

When the court flies in the face of important bodies of public opinion— as it has tended to do increasingly in the last quarter of a century—the paradox of its power, in a nation which styles itself democratic, is too much for many whom its decisions adversely affect.

With the aid of those who have always viewed the court's power as illegitimate in a democracy, and also of those ever-ready to exploit or instigate popular unrest for their own political interests, they can mount quite a furious campaign against the court's power and prestige.

The court's power ultimately stems from its independence. But its independence cannot be viewed as a contradiction of the scheme or spirit of the American democracy, for it is protected by the very document which defines the nature of that democracy.

It is Article III of the U.S. Constitution which creates the Supreme Court—the only court, incidentally, which the Constitution does specifically provide for. And it is Article III, not some self-serving judicial statement, which provides the justices with tenure for life and prohibits the diminution of their salaries.

The independence of the judges exists, among other reasons, to insure that the Supreme Court *cannot* be forced to reflect the will of current, transitory majorities. For such majorities are always prone to look only at immediate goals, to harbor unexamined prejudices which blind them to the impact of their actions on the values and ideals to which their society is committed.

As one chief justice said 34 years ago, the court's job is to exercise "the sober second thought" of the community. It can do this only if it is independent of political pressure.

Thus the cry that the court has gone against some current majority—

* William R. Bishin. "The Court's Constitutional Role." *Los Angeles Times*, September 24, 1968. Used with permission of the author, a professor of law at the University of Southern California.

even when true—is simply irrelevant. To be law, to be enforceable, that majority's desire must be consistent with the fundamental legal rules enshrined in the U.S. Constitution.

The last observation is an elementary fact of our constitutional life, yet it is dismaying how few of our citizens are aware of it, and how many of our political leaders exploit this ignorance when it suits their purposes.

Many persons will concede the court's power to thwart a current majority's will but insist that recently it has abused this power. The court's authority, they argue, is to interpret the Constitution, to apply the law, not to create its own personal Constitution. In short, the charge goes, the court has been making law, it has been guilty of "judicial legislation."

Yet any reasonably well-educated student of constitutional law knows that the words of the Constitution do not provide automatic answers to constitutional questions.

The First Amendment, for example, prohibits Congress from abridging the freedom of speech. One judge may find that this protects a man who reveals military secrets to a foreign power, since all the man did was speak. Another judge will say that, even though there is no exception in the Amendment itself, this is not the kind of speech which it protects. He finds the man guilty of espionage.

Which of these judges has made law? Which has been guilty of judicial legislation? If we must choose, it is surely the second judge who has taken liberties with the Constitution's literal terms. And yet, I venture to predict, virtually every serious student of constitutional law would say that the second judge was right, that he had properly carried out his judicial responsibilities—even if this did involve judicial legislation of an obvious sort.

The literal meaning is often the wrong meaning once we examine the particular constitutional provisions in light of surrounding provisions, and in the context of the history and current practices of this society. Thus, it is up to the judge to decide whether it is the literal meaning or some other which shall guide his decision. A man who has the power to make that choice is one who has the power to make law.

This may be a little difficult for the layman to swallow—although it has been confirmed repeatedly by modern linguists, semanticists and philosophers. What is dismaying—and distressing—is that many lawyers do not seem to know it, that many law schools persist in training their students in the myth of literal interpretation.

Yet even those lawyers, judges, and legal scholars who know very well that there is no simple, unimpeachable answer to problems of legal meaning continue to use the terms which their own experience has discredited. "Judicial legislation" or "judicial lawmaking" have become dirty names, hauled out whenever someone wishes to imply that a decision they disapprove is not simply disagreeable to them, not simply wrong, but somehow an abuse of judicial authority.

When the insights of modern language theory have become part of the general education of the entire citizenry, this irresponsible namecalling will surely disappear. In the meantime, however, it serves as a demagogic device which misleads the best-intentioned layman and unfairly places our courts in a defensive posture.

The fact that judges must make law, that interpretation necessarily means creation, has led some to think that the courts are thereby possessed of unlimited freedom to do as they choose, to follow their own personal, capricious whims. Since there can be no absolutely certain answer to a legal question, some people conclude that one answer is as justifiable as another. They therefore feel free to judge judicial decisions by their own notions of what is good for society and for the individual.

The answer to these people—in law as well as in other fields which depend on language—is that there are guides which help us arrive at reasonably successful answers. In constitutional law one can consult prior cases, surrounding constitutional provisions, the traditions and customs of the society, the political and social history of the nation.

These and other sources of information and insight limit, although they cannot completely control, a judge's discretion. They make it possible for courts to work out decisions which can be sincerely put forth as the meaning of a given Constitutional statement.

In the context of a given case the job of putting these factors together is always extremely difficult. It requires sensitivity, judgment, perception, analytical power. It requires a good deal of knowledge—of law, of history, of government, of how human beings think and act. It is a field that requires expertise. And like such fields, it may come up with answers that do not always comport with common sense.

But common sense is so often, as Einstein said, the *uneducated, unreflective, prejudiced* sense. It can be the sense of those who do not have the inclination to study the matter or the courage to face unpleasant facts.

That is why the furor of criticism—so loud, so nasty, so righteously indignant—is also mystifying. The people who level the charges almost always know nothing of the considerations which must enter the judicial decisions they attack. They are simply not qualified to have an opinion on the matter, let alone pass on the competence and conduct of the judges.

No doubt there is much to be desired in the decisions the Supreme Court turns out. They are too often intellectually deficient. There is need for better methods of selecting our justices—methods that will yield us more men who have the intellectual power and erudition necessary for the problems constitutional law poses.

On the other hand, it is hard to think of another institution of government which performs its task with the same devotion to duty, which carries out its duties with greater honesty, and which has the courage to face the wrath of the people and its leaders in the service of what it conceives to be its constitutional responsibility.

CHAPTER 2

PRIOR RESTRAINT

A fundamental difference between the system of government employed in the United States and that of many other countries is found in the Supreme Court's interpretation of constitutional prohibition against government censorship, i.e. against restraint prior to publication. Autocratic rulers historically have stifled dissent by requiring government approval through licensing or prepublication review of all broadcasts, books and periodicals. The United States Supreme Court has affirmed that "whatever a man publishes, he publishes at his peril," but at the same time the Court has banished any system of "prior restraint" or "previous restraint" in all but extreme cases. The Court has continued to hold that the First Amendment is not absolute and that under certain circumstances pre-publication restraint may be justified, but these cases usually have been restricted to film censorship, obscenity (both covered in later chapters) or sedition.

The Court has not stood still for thinly veiled attempts of various state and local legislative bodies to restrict the press through passage of certain nefarious laws, such as anti-litter legislation, prejudicial taxation schemes or "public nuisance" ordinances. Any law which tends to restrict constitutionally protected expressions must be accompanied by strict safeguards against misuse, the Court has ruled. These safeguards against prior restraint, however, in no way conflict with the possibility of punishment or legal redress subsequent to publication.

Such guarantees of freedom were not always the case in this country. The first newspaper to be published in America, Benjamin Harris's Publick Occurrences, was suspended after its first issue appeared in 1690 when the colonial Governor found contents not to his liking. He issued a statement declaring that the publication had been printed without authority, that it was not to be circulated and that all such future publications were to secure a license before going to press. Nearly half a century later, in the 1730s, John Peter Zenger was jailed and tried for seditious libel after a series of attacks on a colonial Governor in his New York Weekly Journal. His trial— and acquittal—resulted in the first major victory for freedom of the press in the American colonies. The case, because of its many technical peculiarities, had more symbolic than legal precedence. Still it was heralded as the tide of the future by those opposed to "establishment" rule of the colonies.

The landmark case dealing with "prior restraint" came in 1931 with Near v. Minnesota (283 U.S. 697), which came six years after the Court ruled that the free speech and press principles of the First Amendment applied to the states through the Fourteenth Amendment (Gitlow v. New York). Sidestepping the "clear and present danger" question, the Supreme Court focused instead on "prior restraint," a principle which had not been defined by the Court. Near, publisher of the Saturday Press, challenged a Minnesota law which authorized abatement as a public nuisance of publications deemed "malicious, scandalous, and defamatory." Near appealed that such action would violate the Fourteenth Amendment in that it would deny him freedom to publish without due process of law. Chief Justice Hughes, who spoke for the 5-4 majority, agreed, terming the Minnesota statute suppression rather than punishment. He further noted that other avenues of legal redress, e.g. libel action, still were open to those who sought to punish the publisher for alleged wrongdoing. In his publication, Near had severely attacked public officials and had alleged dishonesty and racketeering. Pre-publication censorship, the Court ruled, clearly was not philosophically compatible with the First Amendment.

NEAR V. MINNESOTA
283 U.S. 697 (1931)

MR. CHIEF JUSTICE HUGHES *delivered the opinion of the Court.*

. . . This statute, for the suppression as a public nuisance of a newspaper or periodical, is unusual, if not unique, and raises questions of grave importance transcending the local interests involved in the particular action. It is no longer open to doubt that the liberty of the press and of speech is within the liberty safeguarded by the due process clause of the 14th Amendment from invasion by state action. . . . The limits of this sovereign power must always be determined with appropriate regard to the particular subject of its exercise. . . .

First. The statute is not aimed at the redress of individual or private wrongs. Remedies for libel remain available and unaffected. . . .

Second. The statute is directed not simply at the circulation of scandalous and defamatory statements with regard to private citizens, but at the continued publication by newspapers and periodicals of charges against public officers of corruption, malfeasance in office, or serious neglect of duty. . . .

Third. The object of the statute is not punishment, in the ordinary sense, but suppression of the offending newspaper or periodical. The reason for the enactment, as the state court has said, is that prosecution to enforce penal statutes for libel do not result in "efficient repression or suppression of the evils of scandal." . . . Under this statute, a publisher of a newspaper or periodical, undertaking to conduct a campaign to expose and to censure official derelictions, and devoting his publication principally to that purpose, must face not simply the possibility of a verdict against him in a suit or prosecution for libel, but a determination that his newspaper or periodical is a public nuisance to be abated, and that this abatement and suppression will follow unless he is prepared with legal evidence to prove the truth of the charges and also to satisfy the court that, in addition to being true, the matter was published with good motives and for justifiable ends.

This suppression is accomplished by enjoining publication and that restraint is the object and effect of the statute.

Fourth. The statute not only operates to suppress the offending newspaper or periodical but to put the publisher under an effective censorship. When a newspaper or periodical is found to be "malicious, scandalous and defamatory," and is suppressed as such, resumption of publication is punishable as a contempt of court by fine or imprisonment. . . .

If we cut through mere details of procedure, the operation and effect of the statute in substance is that public authorities may bring the owner or publisher of the newspaper or periodical before a judge upon a charge of conducting a business of publishing scandalous and defamatory matter—in particular that the matter consists of charges against public officers of official dereliction—and unless the owner or publisher is able and disposed to bring competent evidence to satisfy the judge that the charges are true and are published with good motives and for justifiable ends, his newspaper or periodical is suppressed and further publication is made punishable as a contempt. This is of the essence of censorship. . . .

The statute in question cannot be justified by reason of the fact that the publisher is permitted to show, before injunction issues, that the matter published is true and is published with good motives and for justifiable ends. If such a statute, authorizing suppression and injunction on such a basis, is constitutionally valid, it would be equally permissible for the legislature to provide that at any time the publisher of any newspaper could be brought before a court, or even an administrative officer (as the constitutional protection may not be regarded as resting on mere procedural details) and required to produce proof of the truth of his publication, or of what he intended to publish, and of his motives, or stand enjoined. . . . The recognition of authority to impose previous restraint upon publication in order to protect the community against the circulation of charges of misconduct, and especially of official misconduct, necessarily would carry with it the admission of the authority of the censor against which the constitutional barrier was erected. . . .

Equally unavailing is the insistence that the statute is designed to prevent the circulation of scandal which tends to disturb the public peace and to provoke assaults and the commission of crime. Charges of reprehensible conduct, and in particular of official malfeasance, unquestionably create a public scandal, but the theory of the constitutional guaranty is that even a more serious public evil would be caused by authority to prevent publication. . . .

For these reasons we hold the statute, so far as it authorized the proceedings in this action . . . to be an infringement of the liberty of the press guaranteed by the Fourteenth Amendment. We should add that this decision rests upon the operation and effect of the statute, without regard to the question of the truth of the charges contained in the particular periodical. . . .

MR. JUSTICE BUTLER, *dissenting*.

The decision of the court in this case declares Minnesota and every other state powerless to restrain by injunction the business of publishing and circulating among the people malicious, scandalous and defamatory periodicals that in due course of judicial procedure has been adjudged to be a public nuisance. It gives to freedom of the press a meaning and a scope not heretofore recognized and construes "liberty" in the due process clause of the Fourteenth Amendment to put upon the states a Federal restriction that is without precedent. . . .

The record shows and it is conceded that defendants' regular business was the publication of malicious, scandalous and defamatory articles concerning the principal public officers, leading newspapers of the city, many private persons and the Jewish race. It also shows that it was their purpose at all hazards to continue to carry on the business. In every edition slanderous and defamatory matter predominates to the practical exclusion of all else. Many of the statements are so highly improbable as to compel a finding that they are false. The articles themselves show malice. . . .

The Minnesota statute does not operate as a previous restraint on publication within the proper meaning of that phrase. It does not authorize administrative control in advance such as was formerly exercised by the licensers and censors but prescribes a remedy to be enforced by a suit in equity. In this case there was previous publication made in the course of the business of regularly producing malicious, scandalous and defamatory periodicals. The business and publications unquestionably constitute an abuse of the right of free press. The statute denounces the things done as a nuisance on the ground, as stated by the state supreme court, that they threaten morals, peace and good order. There is no question of the power of the state to denounce such transgressions. The restraint authorized is only in respect of continuing to do what has been duly adjudged to constitute a nuisance. . . . There is nothing in the statute purporting to prohibit publications that have not been adjudged to constitute a nuisance. . . .

It is well known, as found by the state supreme court, that existing libel laws are inadequate effectively to suppress evils resulting from the kind of business and publications that are shown in this case. The doctrine that measures such as the one before us are invalid because they operate as previous restraints to infringe freedom of press exposes the peace and good order of every community and the business and private affairs of every individual to the constant and protracted false and malicious assaults of any insolvent publisher who may have purpose and sufficient capacity to contrive and put into effect a scheme or program for oppression, blackmail or extortion.

*   *   *

Five years after Near, the Court struck down what it held to be an unreasonable and inequitable tax on newspapers, but at the same time held that newspapers were not immune from fair taxation to support normal governmental functions. Grosjean v. American Press, 297 U.S. 233 (1936). At issue was a 1934 Louisiana tax of two per cent placed on all newspapers and magazines with weekly circulations of more than 20,000. The tax has been described as retaliatory against those publications which were opposed to the actions of Huey Long. A unanimous Supreme Court held the tax to be discriminatory, unusual and a means of control and, therefore, invalid. "Normal" taxation to support government services was not ruled out, however. The Court in Grosjean relied upon Near, but interpreted the First Amendment's free press philosophy as more encompassing than simply "prior restraint."

GROSJEAN V. AMERICAN PRESS
297 U.S. 233 (1936)

MR. JUSTICE SUTHERLAND *delivered the opinion of the Court.*

This suit was brought by appellees, nine publishers of newspapers in the State of Louisiana, to enjoin the enforcement against them of the provisions of sec. 1 of the act of the legislature of Louisiana known as Act No. 23, passed and approved July 12, 1934, as follows:

> That every person, firm, association or corporation, domestic or foreign, engaged in the business of selling, or making any charge for,

advertising or for advertisements, whether printed or published, or to be printed or published, in any newspaper, magazine, periodical or publication whatever having a circulation of more than 20,000 copies per week, or displayed and exhibited, or to be displayed and exhibited by means of moving pictures, in the State of Louisiana, shall, in addition to all other taxes and licenses levied and assessed in this State, pay a license tax for the privilege of engaging in such business in this State of two per cent (2%) of the gross receipts of such business.

The nine publishers who brought the suit publish thirteen newspapers; and these thirteen publications are the only ones within the State of Louisiana having each a circulation of more than 20,000 copies per week, although the lower court finds there are four other daily newspapers each having a circulation of "slightly less than 20,000 copies per week" which are in competition with those published by appellees both as to circulation and as to advertising. In addition, there are 120 weekly newspapers published in the state, also in competition, to a greater or less degree, with the newspapers of appellees. The revenue derived from appellees' newspapers comes almost entirely from regular subscribers or purchasers thereof and from payments received for the insertion of advertisements therein. . . .

That freedom of speech and of the press are rights of the same fundamental character, safeguarded by the due process of law clause of the Fourteenth Amendment against abridgment by state legislation, has likewise been settled by a series of decisions of this court, beginning with *Gitlow v. New York*, 268 U.S. 652, and ending with *Near v. Minnesota*, 283 U.S. 697. The word "liberty" contained in that amendment embraces not only the right of a person to be free from physical restraint, but the right to be free in the enjoyment of all his faculties as well.

Appellant contends that the Fourteenth Amendment does not apply to corporations; but this is only partly true. A corporation, we have held, is not a "citizen" within the meaning of the privileges and immunities clause. But a corporation is a "person" within the meaning of the equal protection and due process of law clauses, which are the clauses involved here.

The tax imposed is designated a "license tax for the privilege of engaging in such business"—that is to say, the business of selling, or making any charge for, advertising. As applied to appellees, it is a tax of two per cent on the gross receipts derived from advertisements carried in their newspapers when and only when, the newspapers of each enjoy a circulation of more than 20,000 copies per week. It thus operates as a restraint in a double sense. First, its effect is to curtail the amount of revenue realized from advertising, and, second, its direct tendency is to restrict circulation. This is plain enough when we consider that, if it were increased to a high degree, as it could be if valid, it well might result in destroying both advertising and circulation. . . .

. . . [I]n the adoption of the English newspaper stamp tax and the tax on advertisements, revenue was of subordinate concern; and that the dominant and controlling aim was to prevent, or curtail the opportunity for, the acquisition of knowledge by the people in respect to their governmental affairs. It is idle to suppose that so many of the best men of England would for a century of time have waged, as they did, stubborn and often precarious warfare against these taxes if a mere matter of taxation had been involved. The aim of the struggle was not to relieve taxpayers from a burden, but to establish and preserve the right of the English people to full information in respect to the doings or misdoings of their government. . . .

In 1785, only four years before Congress had proposed the First Amendment, the Massachusetts legislature, following the English example, imposed a stamp tax on all newspapers and magazines. The following year an advertisement tax was imposed. Both taxes met with such violent opposition that the former was repealed in 1786, and the latter 1788: Duniway, *Freedom of the Press in Massachusetts*, pp. 136, 137. . . .

In the light of all that has now been said, it is evident that the restricted rules of the English law in respect of the freedom of the press in force when the Constitution was adopted were never accepted by the American colonists, and that by the First Amendment it was meant to preclude the national government, and by the Fourteenth Amendment to preclude the states, from adopting any form of previous restraint upon printed publications, or their circulation, including that which had theretofore been effected by these two well known and odious methods.

This court had occasion in *Near v. Minnesota*, to discuss at some length the subject in its general aspect. The conclusion there stated is that the object of the constitutional provisions was to prevent previous restraints on publication; and the court was careful not to limit the protection of the right to any particular way of abridging it. Liberty of the press within the meaning of the constitutional provision, was broadly said (p. 716), meant "principally although not exclusively, immunity from previous restraints or [from] censorship." . . .

It is not intended by anything we have said to suggest that the owners of newspapers are immune from any of the ordinary forms of taxation for support of the government. But this is not an ordinary form of tax, but one single in kind, with a long history of hostile misuse against the freedom of the press.

The predominant purpose of the grant of immunity here invoked was to preserve an untrammeled press as a vital source of public information. The newspapers, magazines and other journals of the country, it is safe to say, have shed and continue to shed, more light on the public and business affairs of the nation than any other instrumentality of publicity; and since informed public opinion is the most potent of all restraints upon misgovernment, the suppression or abridgment of the publicity afforded by a free press cannot be regarded otherwise than with grave concern. The tax here involved is bad not because it takes money from the pockets of the appellees. If that were all, a wholly different question would be presented. It is bad because, in the light of its history and of its present setting, it is seen to be a deliberate and calculated device in the guise of a tax to limit the circulation of information to which the public is entitled in virtue of the constitutional guaranties. A free press stands as one of the great interpreters between the government and the people. To allow it to be fettered is to fetter ourselves. . . .

*   *   *

The Court also ruled that constitutional guarantees of freedom of the press included the right to distribute a publication as well as freedom to print it. Lovell v. Griffin, 303 U.S. 444 (1938). Similarly, the Court held in Martin v. Struthers that the citizen has a right to receive printed matter. Circulation, said the Court, is essential to the concept of publishing.

In Lovell, the Court looked at an ordinance of the City of Griffin, Ga., which prohibited the distribution of circulars, advertising or literature of any type unless written permission was first obtained from the city manager. This prohibition was challenged under the First and Fourteenth Amendments as abridging free press guarantees. Chief Justice Hughes, in a strongly worded opinion for the 8-0 majority, agreed. He noted the importance of pamphlets in the history of the nation and held, significantly, that free press guarantees included circulation and were not intended solely for newspapers, but for pamphlets and leaflets as well.

LOVELL V. GRIFFIN
303 U.S. 444 (1938)

MR. CHIEF JUSTICE HUGHES *delivered the opinion of the Court.*

. . . Freedom of speech and freedom of the press, which are protected by the First Amendment from infringement by Congress, are among the fundamental personal rights and liberties which are protected by the Fourteenth Amendment from invasion by state action. It is also well settled that municipal ordinances adopted under state authority constitute state action and are within the prohibition of the amendment.

The ordinance in its broad sweep prohibits the distribution of "circulars, handbooks, advertising, or literature of any kind." It manifestly applies to pamphlets, magazines and periodicals. The evidence against appellant was that she distributed a certain pamphlet and a magazine called the "Golden Age." Whether in actual administration the ordinance is applied, as apparently it could be, to newspapers does not appear. The City Manager testified that "everyone applies to me for a license to distribute literature in this City. None of these people (including defendant) secured a permit from me to distribute literature in the City of Griffin." The ordinance is not limited to "literature" that is obscene or offensive to public morals or that advocates unlawful conduct. There is no suggestion that the pamphlet and magazine distributed in the instant case were of that character. The ordinance embraces "literature" in the widest sense.

The ordinance is comprehensive with respect to the method of distribution. It covers every sort of circulation "either by hand or otherwise." There is thus no restriction in its application with respect to time or place. It is not limited to ways which might be regarded as inconsistent with the maintenance of public order, or as involving disorderly conduct, the molestation of the inhabitants, or the misuse or littering of the streets. The ordinance prohibits the distribution of literature of any kind at any time, at any place, and in any manner without a permit from the City Manager.

We think that the ordinance is invalid on its face. Whatever the motive which induced its adoption, its character is such that it strikes at the very foundation of the freedom of the press by subjecting it to license and censorship. The struggle for the freedom of the press was primarily directed against the power of the licensor. It was against that power that John Milton directed his assault by his "Appeal for the Liberty of Unlicensed Printing." And the liberty of the press became initially a right to publish *without* a license what formerly could be published only *with* one." . . .

The liberty of the press is not confined to newspapers and periodicals. It necessarily embraces pamphlets and leaflets. These indeed have been historic weapons in the defense of liberty, as the pamphlets of Thomas Paine and others in our own history abundantly attest. The press in its historic connotation comprehends every sort of publication which affords a vehicle of information and opinion. What we have had recent occasion to say with respect to the vital importance of protecting this essential liberty from every sort of infringement need not be repeated.

The ordinance cannot be saved because it relates to distribution and not to publication. "Liberty of circulating is as essential to that freedom as liberty of publishing; indeed, without the circulation, the publication would be of little value." *Ex Parte Jackson*, 96 U.S. 727. . . .

*   *   *

The question of prohibiting election editorials on election day came before the Warren Court on appeal from James E. Mills, editor of the Birmingham (Ala.) Post-Herald. He had been convicted under Alabama law for a 1962 election-day editorial urging voters to abandon the city's commissioner form of government in favor of a mayor-council plan. The change was approved. At issue were the principles of freedom of speech and press and the state's police power to set standards of conduct for orderly elections. The Court in a 1966 decision held the Alabama law to be unconstitutional.

MILLS V. ALABAMA
384 U.S. 214 (1966)

MR. JUSTICE BLACK delivered the opinion of the Court.

The question squarely presented here is whether a State, consistently with the United States Constitution, can make it a crime for the editor of a daily newspaper to write and publish an editorial *on election day* urging people to vote a certain way on issues submitted to them. . . .

. . . The First Amendment, which applies to the States through the Fourteenth, prohibits laws "abridging the freedom of speech, or of the press." The question here is whether it abridges freedom of the press for a State to punish a newspaper editor for doing no more than publishing an editorial on election day urging people to vote a particular way in the election. We should point out that once that this question in no way involves the extent of a State's power to regulate conduct in and around the polls in order to maintain peace, order and decorum there. The sole reason for the charge that Mills violated the law is that he wrote and published an editorial on election day which urged Birmingham voters to cast their votes in favor of changing their form of government.

Whatever differences may exist about interpretations of the First Amendment, there is practically universal agreement that a major purpose of that Amendment was to protect the free discussion of governmental affairs. This of course includes discussions of candidates, structures and forms of government, the manner in which government is operated or should be operated, and all such matters relating to political processes. The Constitution specifically selected the press, which includes not only newspapers, books, and magazines, but also humble leaflets and circulars, to play an important role in the discussion of public affairs. Thus the press serves and was designed to serve as a powerful antidote to any abuses of power by governmental officials and as a constitutionally chosen means for keeping officials elected by the people responsible to all the people whom they were selected to serve. Suppression of the right of the press to praise or criticize governmental agents and to clamor and contend for or against change, which is all that this editorial did, muzzles one of the very agencies the Framers of our Constitution thoughtfully and deliberately selected to improve our society and keep it free. The Alabama Corrupt Practices Act by providing criminal penalties for publishing editorials such as the one here silences the press at a time when it can be most effective. It is difficult to conceive of a more obvious and flagrant abridgment of the constitutionally guaranteed freedom of the press.

. . . The state statute leaves people free to hurl their campaign charges up to the last minute of the day before election. The law held valid by the Alabama Supreme Court then goes on to make it a crime to answer those "last minute" charges on election day, the only time they can be effectively answered. Because the law prevents any adequate reply to these charges, it is wholly ineffective in protecting the electorate "from confusive last-minute charges and countercharges." We hold that no test of reasonableness can save a state law from invalidation as a violation of the First Amendment when that law makes it a crime for a newspaper editor to do no more than urge people to vote one way or another in a publicly held election. . . .

* * *

Severe challenges to the Near philosophy surfaced in the early 1970s. This new threat of prior restraint came in the form of subpoena and injunction. The year 1970, in fact, has been labeled by journalists "the year of the subpoena." There is little disagreement among journalists that a continuation of this subpoena action would have a serious "chilling effect" on newsmen as they attempted to perform their "watchdog" function over government and that support of these subpoena actions by the courts would be disastrous to the public's right to know. The first such action to receive national notice came in 1970 with a Federal Grand Jury subpoena of New York Times newsman Earl Caldwell in an apparent attempt to force him to reveal his sources of information for stories dealing with the Black Panther organization. Several states have "shield laws" which protect newsmen from being forced to reveal their sources of news, but there is no such Federal law. The U.S. Court of Appeals dismissed a contempt citation against Caldwell, who had refused to appear before the Grand Jury, but the matter was appealed to the Supreme Court, which agreed to hear the case. Additional subpoenas have been issued to newsmen in New York, Chicago, Detroit and Los Angeles. The question of the relationship between the newsman's subpoena and the First Amendment appears to have arrived.

A second major confrontation between the subpoena powers of the Federal Government and freedom of the press occurred early in 1971, this time involving the Congress rather than the courts. A House subcommittee headed by Rep. Staggers subpoenaed CBS notes and "outtakes" involved in the production of the network documentary "The Selling of the Pentagon." Outtakes are materials gathered in connection with the production of the program, but not actually used over the air. They include unused film and tape. The documentary presented evidence that the Defense Department was spending tens of millions of dollars in public relations allocations each year solely to "sell" the Vietnam war to the public and that news coming out of the Pentagon was so tightly controlled that the military was easily able to hide its mistakes. CBS President Frank Stanton declined to make notes and outtakes available to the subcommittee, claiming congressional harassment and incompatibility with the First Amendment. The charges made in the documentary were not the focal point of the subpoena. At issue were news judgments and editing which were alleged to have resulted in distortion. Dr. Stanton pointed out that since the Federal Government licenses broadcasters, such subpoena actions, if allowed to stand, would have a particularly "chilling effect" upon broadcast journalism. Following his appearance before the subcommittee and his refusal to supply notes and outtakes, Dr. Stanton was threatened by Chairman Staggers with contempt of Congress. Dr. Stanton earlier had stated that he would take the question to the Supreme Court if necessary. The Congress, however, rejected the contempt move.

Finally, and in what some believe to be the most serious threat to a free press in decades, the Justice Department brought suit in June of 1971 to halt publication by the New York Times—and later the Washington Post and other newspapers—of the "Pentagon Papers," secret government documents detailing the history of the U.S. involvement in the Vietnam War. The New York Times published three installments, but suspended a fourth when the Federal Court at the request of the government issued a temporary order halting further publication of the material. New York Times attorney and Yale Law Professor Alexander M. Bickel claimed that successful efforts by the government to restrain newspapers prior to publication had never happened before in the history of the Republic. It was, he said, a classic case of censorship. The government claimed threats to the national security. The newspaper denied such threats and claimed that a free, democratic society is best served by the public's right to know, that embarrassment to the Pentagon—not national security—was the real reason behind the injunctive action, and that such restraints prior to publication are repugnant to the national interest and the Constitution. Separate Federal Courts of Appeal decided differently in the two early cases brought to them. In New York, the Times was given permission to resume publication of the series, but only those portions deemed by the government not detrimental to national security. In Washington, the Post was given permission to resume full publication. The question went immediately to the Supreme Court, which was about to adjourn for the summer recess.

The Supreme Court heard oral arguments June 26, 1971, in an unusual Saturday session and announced its decision just four days later and 15 days after the injunction was first ordered against the Times. In a 6-3 decision, the Justices rejected the Government's claim that the national security would be imperiled by publication of the documents. The order freeing the newspapers to print the documents in full was given in a brief, unsigned opinion. Each Justice, then, added a separate opinion. Dissenting were Chief Justice Burger and Justices Blackmun and Harlan, all of whom were critical of the speed with which they were called upon to reach a judgment.

The action of the Court disappointed both sides. The Government, of course, lost its bid to keep the documents secret. In addition, Congress had begun hearings into possible revisions of the procedures used in classification of materials allegedly sensitive to national security. But the media were disappointed also, for the division of the Court, as revealed by the nine separate opinions, held out the possibility that prior restraint by the Government at some future time would be acceptable to a majority of the Justices. The opinion did not close the door on prior restraint, as some had hoped it would. Indeed, the Government was successful—if only temporarily—in its first known attempt at "censorship through injunction." Still, the message was clear: the First Amendment demands that with any attempt at prior restraint by government, the burden of proving grave danger to the nation would be a heavy burden indeed. The Near principle stood the test, though questions remained as to the effect the decision would have on future similar actions by government or the media.

The unsigned opinion appears in its entirety, followed by edited versions of each of the nine Justices' separate opinions.

NEW YORK TIMES V. UNITED STATES

UNITED STATES V. WASHINGTON POST
(Announced June 30, 1971)

Per curiam.

We granted certiorari in these cases in which the United States seeks to enjoin the *New York Times* and the *Washington Post* from publishing the contents of a classified study entitled "History of U.S. Decision-Making Process on Vietnam Policy."

"Any system of prior restraints of expression comes to this court bearing a heavy presumption against its constitutional validity." *Bantam Books, Inc. v. Sullivan,* 372 U.S. 58, 70 (1963); see also *Near v. Minnesota,* 283 U.S. 697 (1931). The Government "thus carries a heavy burden of showing justification for the enforcement of such restraint." *Organization for a Better Austin v. Keefe* (1971). The District Court for the Southern District of New York in the *New York Times* case and the District Court for the District of Columbia and the Court of Appeals for the District of

Columbia Circuit in the *Washington Post* case held that the Government had not met that burden. We agree.

The judgment of the Court of Appeals for the District of Columbia Circuit is therefore affirmed. The order of the Court of Appeals for the Second Circuit is reversed and the case is remanded with directions to enter a judgment affirming the judgment of the District Court for the Southern District of New York. The stays entered June 25, 1971, by the court are vacated. The mandates shall issue forthwith.

So ordered.

MR. JUSTICE BLACK, *with whom Mr. Justice Douglas joins, concurring.*

. . . I believe that every moment's continuance of the injunctions against these newspapers amounts to a flagrant, indefensible and continuing violation of the First Amendment. . . . In my view it is unfortunate that some of my brethren are apparently willing to hold that the publication of news may sometimes be enjoined. Such a holding would make a shambles of the First Amendment. . . .

. . . Now, for the first time in the 182 years since the founding of the Republic, the Federal Courts are asked to hold that the First Amendment does not mean what it says, but rather means that the Government can halt the publication of current news of vital importance to the people of this country.

In seeking injunctions against these newspapers and in its presentation to the Court, the Executive Branch seems to have forgotten the essential purpose and history of the First Amendment. When the Constitution was adopted, many people strongly opposed it because the document contained no Bill of Rights to safeguard certain basic freedoms. They especially feared that the new powers granted to a central government might be interpreted to permit the Government to curtail freedom of religion, press, assembly and speech. In response to an overwhelming public clamor, James Madison offered a series of amendments to satisfy citizens that these great liberties would remain safe and beyond the power of government to abridge. . . . The amendments were offered to curtail and restrict the general powers granted to the Executive, Legislative, and Judicial Branches two years before in the original Constitution. The Bill of Rights changed the original Constitution into a new charter under which no branch of government could abridge the people's freedoms of press, speech, religion and assembly. Yet the Solicitor General argues and some members of the Court appear to agree that the general powers of the Government adopted in the original Constitution should be interpreted to limit and restrict the specific and emphatic guarantees of the Bill of Rights adopted later. I can imagine no greater perversion of history. . . .

. . . The press was to serve the governed, not the governors. The Government's power to censor the press was abolished so that the press would remain forever free to censure the Government. The press was protected so that it could bare the secrets of government and inform the people. Only a free and unrestrained press can effectively expose deception in government. And paramount among the responsibilities of a free press is the duty to prevent any part of the government from deceiving the people and sending them off to distant lands to die of foreign fevers and foreign shot and shell. In my view, far from deserving condemnation for their courageous reporting, the *New York Times*, the *Washington Post* and other newspapers should be commended for serving the purpose that the Founding Fathers saw so clearly. In revealing the workings of government that led to the Vietnam war, the newspapers nobly did precisely that which the Founders hoped and trusted they would do. . . .

MR. JUSTICE DOUGLAS, *with whom Mr. Justice Black joins, concurring.*

. . . It should be noted at the outset that the First Amendment provides that "Congress shall make no law . . . abridging the freedom of speech or of the press." That leaves, in my view, no room for governmental restraint on the press.

There is, moveover, no statute barring the publication by the press of the material which the *Times* and *Post* seek to use. . . .

Thus Congress has been faithful to the command of the First Amendment in this area. . . .

These disclosures may have a serious impact. But that is no basis for sanctioning a previous restraint on the press. . . .

The dominant purpose of the First Amendment was to prohibit the widespread practice of governmental suppression of embarrassing information. It is common knowledge that the First Amendment was adopted against the widespread use of the common law seditious libel to punish the dissemination of material that is embarrassing to the powers-that-be. . . . The present cases will, I think, go down in history as the most dramatic illustration of that principle. A debate of large proportions goes on in the nation over our posture in Vietnam. That debate antedated the disclosure of the contents of the present documents. The latter are highly relevant to the debate in progress.

Secrecy in government is fundamentally anti-democratic, perpetuating bureaucratic errors. Open debate and discussion of public issues are vital to our national health. On public questions there should be "open and robust debate." . . .

MR. JUSTICE BRENNAN, *concurring.*

. . . So far as I can determine, never before has the United States sought to enjoin a newspaper from publishing information in its possession. . . .

The error which has pervaded these cases from the outset was the granting of any injunctive relief whatsoever, interim or otherwise. The entire thrust of the government's claim throughout these cases has been that publication of the material sought to be enjoined "could," or "might," or "may" prejudice the national interest in various ways. But the First Amendment tolerates absolutely no prior judicial restraints of the press predicated upon surmise or conjecture that untoward consequences may result. Our cases, it is true, have indicated that there is a single, extremely narrow class of cases in which the First Amendment's ban on prior judicial restraint may be overridden. Our cases have thus far indicated that such cases may arise only when the nation "is at war," *Schenck v. United States,* 249 U.S. 47, 52 (1919), during which times "no one would question but that a government might prevent actual obstruction to its recruiting service or the publication of the sailing dates of transports or the number and location of troops." *Near v. Minnesota,* 283 U.S. 697, 716 (1931). Even if the present world situation were assumed to be tantamount to a time of war, or if the power of presently available armaments would justify even in peacetime the suppression of information that would set in motion a nuclear holocaust, in neither of these actions has the government presented or even alleged that publication of items from or based upon the material at issue would cause the happening of an event of that nature. . . . In no event may mere conclusions be sufficient: for if the Executive Branch seeks judicial aid in preventing publication, it must inevitably submit the basis upon which that aid is sought to scrutiny by the judiciary. And therefore, every restraint issued in this case, whatever its form, has violated the First Amendment—and none the less so because that restraint was justified as necessary to afford the Court an opportunity to examine the claim more thoroughly. Unless and until the government has clearly made out its case, the First Amendment commands that no injunction may issue.

MR. JUSTICE STEWART, *with whom Mr. Justice White joins, concurring.*

. . . In the absence of the governmental checks and balances present in other areas of our national life, the only effective restraint upon executive policy and power in the areas of national defense and international affairs may lie in an enlightened citizenry—in an informed and critical public opinion which alone can here protect the values of democratic government. For this reason, it is perhaps here that a press that is alert, aware, and free most vitally serves the basic purpose of the First Amendment. For without an informed and free press there cannot be an enlightened people.

Yet it is elementary that the successful conduct of international diplomacy and the maintenance of an effective national defense require both confidentiality and secrecy. Other nations can hardly deal with this nation in an atmosphere of mutual trust unless they can be assured that their confidences will be kept. . . . In the area of basic national defense the frequent need for absolute secrecy is, of course, self-evident.

I think there can be but one answer to this dilemma, if dilemma it be. The responsibility must be where the power is. If the Constitution gives the Executive a large degree of unshared power in the conduct of foreign affairs and the maintenance of our national defense, then under the Constitution the Executive must have the largely unshared duty to determine and preserve the degree of internal security necessary to exercise that power successfully. It is an awesome responsibility, requiring judgment and wisdom of a high order. I should suppose that moral, political, and practical consideration would dictate that a very first principle of that wisdom would be an insistence upon avoiding secrecy for its own sake.

For when everything is classified, then nothing is classified, and the system becomes one to be disregarded by the cynical or the careless, and to be manipulated by those intent on self-protection or self-promotion. I should suppose, in short, that the hallmark of a truly effective internal security system would be the maximum possible disclosure, recognizing that secrecy can best be preserved only when credibility is truly maintained. . . .

MR. JUSTICE WHITE, *with whom Mr. Justice Stewart joins, concurring.*

I concur in today's judgments, but only because of the concededly extraordinary protection against prior restraints enjoyed by the press under our constitutional system. I do not say that in no circumstances would the First Amendment permit an injunction against publishing information about Government plans or operations. Nor, after examining the materials the Government characterizes as the most sensitive and destructive, can I deny that revelation of these documents will do substantial damage to public interests. Indeed, I am confident that their disclosure will have that result. But I nevertheless agree that the United States has not satisfied the very heavy burden which it must meet to warrant an injunction against publication in these cases, at least in the absence of express and appropriately limited congressional authorization for prior restraints in circumstances such as these.

The Government's position is simply stated: the responsibility of the Executive for the conduct of the foreign affairs and for the security of the nation is so basic that the President is entitled to an injunction against publication of a newspaper story whenever he can convince a court that the information to be revealed threatens "grave and irreparable" injury to the public interest; and the injunction should issue whether or not the material to be published is classified, whether or not publication would be lawful under relevant criminal statutes enacted by Congress and regardless of the circumstances by which the newspaper came into possession of the information.

At least in the absence of legislation by Congress, based on its own investigations and findings, I am quite unable to agree that the inherent powers of the Executive and the courts reach so far as to authorize remedies having such sweeping potential for inhibiting publications by the press. . . .

. . . The fact of a massive breakdown in security is known, access to the documents by many unauthorized people is undeniable and the efficacy of equitable relief against these or other newspapers to avert anticipated damage is doubtful at best.

What is more, terminating the ban on publication of the relatively few sensitive documents the Government now seeks to suppress does not mean that the law either requires or invites newspapers or others to publish them or that they will be immune from criminal action if they do. Prior restraints require an unusually heavy justification under the First Amendment; but failure by the Government to justify prior restraints does not measure its constitutional entitlement to a conviction for criminal publication. . . .

MR. JUSTICE MARSHALL, *concurring.*

. . . The issue is whether this court or the Congress has the power to make law. . . .

. . . It may be more convenient for the Executive if it need only convince a judge to prohibit conduct rather than to ask the Congress to pass a law and it may be more convenient to enforce a contempt order than seek a criminal conviction in a jury trial. Moreover, it may be considered politically wise to get a court to share the responsibility for arresting those who the Executive has probable cause to believe are violating the law. But convenience and political considerations of the moment do not justify a basic departure from the principles of our system of government.

In this case we are not faced with a situation where Congress has failed to provide the Executive with broad power to protect the nation from disclosure of damaging state secrets. Congress has on several occasions given extensive consideration to the problem of protecting the military and strategic secrets of the United States. This consideration has resulted in the enactment of statutes making it a crime to receive, disclose, communicate, withhold, and publish certain documents, photographs, instruments, appliances and information. . . .

Thus it would seem that in order for this Court to issue an injunction it would require a showing that such an injunction would enhance the already existing power of the government to act. . . . Here there has been no attempt to make such a showing. The Solicitor General does not even mention in his brief whether the Government considers there to be probable cause to believe a crime has been committed or whether there is a conspiracy to commit future crimes. . . .

Even if it is determined that the Government could not in good faith bring criminal prosecutions against the *New York Times* and the *Washington Post*, it is clear that Congress has specifically rejected passing legislation that would have clearly given the President the power he seeks here and made the current activities of the newspapers unlawful. When Congress specifically declines to make conduct unlawful it is not for this Court to redecide those issues—to overrule Congress.

On at least two occasions Congress has refused to enact legislation that would have made the conduct engaged in here unlawful and given the President the power that he seeks in this case. In 1917 during the debate over the original Espionage Act, still the basic provisions of (sec.) 793 [of U.S. Code Title 18], Congress rejected a proposal to give the President in time of war or threat of war authority to directly prohibit by proclamation the publication of information relating to national defense that might be useful to the enemy. . . .

In 1957 the U.S. Commission on Government Security found that "airplane journals, scientific periodicals, and even the daily newspaper have featured articles containing information and other data which should have been deleted in whole or in part for security reasons." In response to this problem the commission, which was chaired by Sen. Cotton, proposed that "Congress enact legislation making it a crime for any person willfully to disclose without proper authorization, for any purpose whatever, information classified 'secret' or 'top secret,' knowing, or having reasonable grounds to believe, such information to have been so classified." After substantial floor discussion on the proposal, it was rejected. If the proposal that Sen. Cotton championed on the floor had been enacted, the publication of the documents involved here would certainly have been a crime. Congress refused, however, to make it a crime. The Government is here asking this Court to remake that decision. This Court has no such power. . . .

MR. CHIEF JUSTICE BURGER, *dissenting.*

So clear are the constitutional limitations on prior restraint against expression, that from the time of *Near v. Minnesota,* 283 U.S. 697 (1931), until recently in *Organization for a Better Austin v. Keefe* (1971), we have had little occasion to be concerned with cases involving prior restraints against news reporting on matters of public interest. There is, therefore, little variation among the members of the Court in terms of resistance to prior restraints against publication. Adherence to this basic constitutional principle, however, does not make this case a simple one. In this case, the imperative of a free and unfettered press comes into collision with another imperative, the effective functioning of a complex modern government and specifically the effective exercise of certain constitutional powers of the Executive. Only those who view the First Amendment as an absolute in all circumstances—a view I respect, but reject—can find such a case as this to be simple or easy. . . .

. . . A great issue of this kind should be tried in a judicial atmosphere conducive to thoughtful, reflective deliberation, especially when haste, in terms of hours, is unwarranted in the light of the long period the *Times,* by its own choice, deferred publication.

It is not disputed that the *Times* has had unauthorized possession of the documents for three to four months, during which it has had its expert analysts studying them, presumably digesting them and preparing the material for publication. During all of this time, the *Times,* presumably in its capacity as trustee of the public's "right-to-know," has held up publication for purposes it considered proper and thus public knowledge was delayed. No doubt this was for a good reason; the analysis of 7,000 pages of complex material drawn from a vastly greater volume of material would inevitably take time and the writing of good news stories takes time. But why should the United States Government, from whom this information was illegally acquired by someone, along with all the counsel, trial judges and appellate judges be placed under needless pressure? . . .

Would it have been unreasonable, since the newspaper could anticipate the Government's objections to release of secret material, to give the Government an opportunity to review the entire collection and determine whether agreement could be reached on publication? . . .

With such an approach—one that great newspapers have in the past practiced and stated editorially to be the duty of an honorable press—the newspapers and Government might well have narrowed the area of disagreement as to what was and was not publishable, leaving the remainder to be resolved in orderly litigation if necessary. To me it is hardly believable that a newspaper long regarded as a great institution in American life would fail to perform one of the basic and simple duties of every citizen with respect to the discovery or possession of stolen property or secret government documents. That duty, I had thought—perhaps naively—was to report forthwith, to responsible public officers. This duty rests on taxi drivers, justices and the *New York Times.* If the action of the judges up to now has been correct, that result is sheer happenstance. . . .

MR. JUSTICE HARLAN, *with whom the Chief Justice and Mr. Justice Blackmun join, dissenting.*

. . . With all respect, I consider that the court has been almost irresponsibly feverish in dealing with these cases. . . .

This frenzied train of events took place in the name of the presumption against prior restraints created by the First Amendment. Due regard for the extraordinarily important and difficult questions involved in these litigations should have led the Court to shun such a precipitate timetable. . . .

These are difficult questions of fact, of law, and of judgment; the potential consequences of erroneous decision are enormous. The time which has been available to us, to the lower courts, and to the parties has been wholly inadequate for giving these cases the kind of consideration they deserve. . . .

Forced as I am to reach the merits of these cases, I dissent from the opinion and judgments of the Court. Within the severe limitations imposed by the time constraints under which I have been required to operate, I can only state my reasons in telescoped form, even though in different circumstances I would have felt constrained to deal with the cases in the fuller sweep indicated above. . . .

. . . It is plain to me that the scope of the judicial function in passing upon the activities of the Executive Branch of the Government in the field of foreign affairs is very narrowly restricted. This view is, I think, dictated by the concept of separation of powers upon which our constitutional systems rests. . . .

The power to evaluate the "pernicious influence" of premature disclosure is not, however, lodged in the Executive alone. I agree that, in performance of its duty to protect the values of the First Amendment against political pressures, the judiciary must review the initial Executive determination to the point of satisfying itself that the subject matter of the dispute does lie within the proper compass of the President's foreign relations power. Constitutional considerations forbid "a complete abandonment of judicial control." . . .

Even if there is some room for the judiciary to override the Executive determination, it is plain that the scope of review must be exceedingly narrow. I can see no indication in the opinions of either the District Court or the Court of Appeals in the *Post* litigation that the conclusions of the Executive were given even the deference owing to an administrative agency, much less that owing to a coequal branch of the Government operating within the field of its constitutional prerogative.

Accordingly, I would vacate the judgment of the Court of Appeals for the District of Columbia Circuit on this ground and remand the case for further proceedings in the District Court. Before the commencement of such further proceeding, due opportunity should be afforded the Government for procuring from the Secretary of State or the Secretary of Defense or both an expression of their views on the issue of national security. . . .

Pending further hearings in each case conducted under the appropriate ground rules, I would continue the restraints on publication. . . .

MR. JUSTICE BLACKMUN.

. . . At this point the focus is on only the comparatively few documents specified by the Government as critical. So far as the other material

—vast in amount—is concerned, let it be published and published forth-with if the newspapers, once the strain is gone and the sensationalism is eased, still feel the urge to do so.

But we are concerned here with the few documents specified from the 47 volumes. . . .

The *New York Times* clandestinely devoted a period of three months examining the 47 volumes that came into its unauthorized possession. Once it had begun publication of material from those volumes, the New York case now before us emerged. It immediately assumed, and ever since has maintained, a frenetic pace and character. Seemingly, once publication started, the material could not be made public fast enough. Seemingly from then on, every deferral or delay, by restraint or otherwise, was ab-horrent and was to be deemed violative of the First Amendment and of the public's "right immediately to know." Yet that newspaper stood be-fore us at oral argument and professed criticism of the Government for not lodging its protest earlier than by a Monday telegram following the initial Sunday publication.

The District of Columbia case is much the same.

. . . The country would be none the worse off were the cases tried quickly, to be sure, but in the customary and properly deliberative man-ner. The most recent of the material, it is said, dates no later than 1968, already about three years ago, and the *Times* itself took three months to formulate its plan of procedure and, thus, deprived its public for that period.

The First Amendment, after all, is only one part of an entire Con-stitution. Article II of the great document vests in the Executive Branch primary power over the conduct of foreign affairs and places in that branch the responsibility for the nation's safety. Each provision of the Constitution is important, and I cannot subscribe to a doctrine of unlimited absolutism for the First Amendment at the cost of downgrading other provisions. . . .

. . . What is needed here is a weighing, upon properly developed stan-dards, of the broad right of the press to print and of the very narrow right of the government to prevent. Such standards are not yet developed. The parties here are in disagreement as to what those standards should be. But even the newspapers concede that there are situations where restraint is in order and is constitutional. . . .

I therefore would remand these cases to be developed expeditiously, of course, but on a schedule permitting the orderly presentation of evi-dence from both sides, with the use of discovery, if necessary, as authorized by the rules, and with the preparation of briefs, oral argument and court opinions of a quality better than has been seen to this point. . . .

I strongly urge, and sincerely hope, that these two newspapers will be fully aware of their ultimate responsibilities to the United States of America. . . . I hope that damage already has not been done. If, however,

damage has been done, and if, with the Court's action today, these newspapers proceed to publish the critical documents and there results therefrom "the death of soldiers, the destruction of alliances, the greatly increased
difficulty of negotiation with our enemies, the inability of our diplomats to
negotiate," to which list I might add the factors of prolongation of the
war and of further delay in the freeing of United States prisoners, then the
nation's people will know where the responsibility for these sad consequences rests.

FREEDOM OF SPEECH AS I SEE IT

By Zechariah Chafee, Jr.*

Speech should be fruitful as well as free. Our experience introduces this qualification into the classical argument of Milton and John Stuart Mill, that only through open discussion is truth discovered and spread. In their simpler times, they thought it enough to remove legal obstacles like the censorship and sedition prosecutions. Mill assumed that if men were only left alone, their reasoning powers would eventually impel them to choose the best ideas and the wisest course of action. To us this policy is too exclusively negative. For example what is the use of telling an unpopular speaker that he will incur no criminal penalties by his proposed address, so long as every hall owner in the city declines to rent him space for his meeting and there are no vacant lots available? There should be municipal auditoriums, school houses out of school hours, church forums, parks in summer, all open to thresh out every question of public importance, with just as few restrictions as possible, for otherwise the subjects that most need to be discussed will be the very subjects that will be ruled out as unsuitable for discussion.

We must do more than remove the discouragements to open discussion. We must exert ourselves to supply active encouragements.

Physical space and lack of interference alone will not make discussion fruitful. We must take affirmative steps to improve the methods by which discussion is carried on. Of late years the argument of Milton and Mill has been questioned, because truth does not seem to emerge from a controversy in the automatic way their logic would lead us to expect. For one thing, reason is less praised nowadays than a century ago; instead, emotions conscious and unconscious are commonly said to dominate the conduct of men. Is it any longer possible to discover truth amidst the clashing blares of advertisements, loud speakers, gigantic billboards, party programs, propaganda of a hundred kinds? To sift the truth from all these half truths seems to demand a statistical investigation beyond the limits of anybody's time and money. So some modern thinkers despairingly conclude that the great mass of voters cannot be trusted to detect the fallacies in emotional arguments by Communists and hence must be prevented from hearing them. Even the intellectuals don't seem to do much better in reaching

* From Zechariah Chafee, Jr. "Freedom of Speech as I See It Today." *Journalism Quarterly*, Vol. 18 (June 1941), p. 158. Used with permission of the *Journalism Quarterly*. The author was a professor of law at Harvard University.

Truth by conflicting arguments. For example, take controversies between professors. They talk and talk, and at the end each sticks to his initial position. On which side does Truth stand? We still do not know. Then too, the emergencies seem greater and more pressing than of yore. We are less willing to await the outcome of prolonged verbal contests. Perhaps Truth will win in the long run; but in the long run, as Walter Lippmann says, we shall all be dead—and perhaps not peacefully in our beds either. Debating is only fiddling while Rome burns. Away with all this talk, let's have action—now.

Nevertheless, the main argument of Milton and Mill still holds good. All that this disappointment means is that friction is a much bigger drag on the progress of Truth than they supposed. Efforts to lessen that friction are essential to the success of freedom of speech. It is a problem, not for law, but for education in the wide sense that includes more than schools and youngsters. The conflict of oral evidence and arguments can be made increasingly profitable by wise improvements in technique. . . . Journalists and other writers value accuracy of facts far more than formerly—we can expect even more from them in future. None of us can get rid of our emotions, but we can learn to drive them in harness. As for blazing propaganda on both sides, young Americans can be trained to keep alive the gumption which comes down to us from Colonial farmers; this will make them distrust all men who conceal greed or a lust for power behind any flag, whether red or red-white-and-blue.

Reason is more imperfect than we used to believe. Yet it still remains the best guide we have, better than our emotions, better even than patriotism, better than any single human guide, however exalted his position.

A second point deserves renewed emphasis. The effect of suppression extends far beyond the agitators actually put in jail, far beyond the pamphlets physically destroyed. A favorite argument against free speech is that the men who are thus conspicuously silenced had little to say that was worth hearing. Concede for the moment that the public would suffer no serious loss if every Communist leaflet were burned or if some prominent pacifist were imprisoned, as perhaps he might be under the loose language of the unprecedented federal sedition law passed last spring, for discouraging drafted men by his talk about plowing every fourth boy under. Even so, my contention is that the pertinacious orators and writers who get hauled up are merely extremist spokesmen for a mass of more thoughtful and more retiring men and women, who share in varying degrees the same critical attitude toward prevailing policies and institutions. When you put the hot-heads in jail, these cooler people don't get arrested—they just keep quiet. And so we lose things they could tell us, which would be very advantageous for the future course of the nation. Once the prosecutions begin, then the hush-hush begins too. Discussion becomes one-sided and artificial. Questions that need to be threshed out don't get threshed out. . . .

The Supreme Court, though much more anxious to support liberty of speech than it was twenty years ago, can do nothing to keep discussion open during an emergency. Cases of suppression will get to Washington long after the emergency is over. What counts is what the local United States judges do. Still more important is the attitude of the prosecutors and police, because they can stifle free speech by breaking up meetings by arrests and confiscating pamphlets, and then not bothering to bring many persons to trial. Above all, the maintenance of open discussion depends on all of you, on the great body of unofficial citizens. If a community does not respect liberty for unpopular ideas, it can easily drive such ideas underground by persistent discouragement and sneers, by social ostracism, by boycotts of newspapers and magazines, by refusal to rent halls, by objections to the use of municipal auditorium and school houses, by discharging teachers and professors and journalists, by mobs and threats of lynching. On the other hand an atmosphere of open and unimpeded controversy may be made as fully a part of the life of a community as any other American tradition. The law plays only a small part in either suppression or freedom. In the long run the public gets just as much freedom of speech as it really wants.

This brings me to my final argument for freedom of speech. It creates the happiest kind of country. It is the best way to make men and women love their country. Mill says:

> A state which dwarfs its men, in order that they may be more docile instruments in its hands even for beneficial purposes, will find that with small men no great thing can really be accomplished.

And Arthur Garfield Hays tells the story of a liberated slave who met his former master on the street. The master asked, "Are you as well off as before you were free?" The Negro admitted that his clothes were frayed, his house leaked, and his meals were nothing like the food on the old plantation. "Well, wouldn't you rather be a slave again?" "No, massa. There's a sort of a looseness about this here freedom that I likes."

Doubtless it was an inspiring sight to see the Piazza Venezia in Rome full of well-drilled blackshirts in serried ranks cheering Mussolini or to watch Nuremberg thronged with hundreds of thousands of Nazis raising their arms in perfect unison at the first glimpse of Hitler. In contrast our easy-going crowds seem sloppy and purposeless, going hither and thither about their own tasks and amusements. But we do not have the other side of the picture—when every knock on the door may mean that the father of the family is to be dragged off to a concentration camp from which no word returns; great newspapers reduced to mere echoes of the master's voice; the professorships of universities that once led the world filled as we fill third-class postmasterships; the devoted love of young men and women broken up by racial hatreds; the exiles; the boycotts; and what is perhaps worst of all, those who conform to the will of the men in power in order to avoid financial ruin or worse, and yet, even while holding their jobs, live days and nights in the uneasy fear of calamity and the shameful consciousness that they have had to sell out their minds and souls. Once commit ourselves to the ideal of enforced national unanimity, and all this logically and easily follows.

Behind the dozens of sedition bills in Congress last session, behind teachers' oaths and compulsory flag salutes, is a desire to make our citizens loyal to their government. Loyalty is a beautiful idea, but you cannot create it by compulsion and force. A government is at bottom the officials who carry it on, legislators and prosecutors, school superintendents and police. If it is composed of legislators who pass short-sighted sedition laws by overwhelming majorities, of narrow-minded school superintendents who oust thoughtful teachers of American history and eight-year old children whose rooted religious convictions prevent them from sharing in a brief ceremony, a government of snoopers and spies and secret police, how can you expect love and loyalty? You make men love their government and country by giving them the kind of government and the kind of country that inspire respect and love, a country that is free and unafraid, that lets the discontented talk in order to learn the causes for their discontent and end those causes, that refuse to impel men to spy on their neighbors, that protects its citizens vigorously from harmful acts while it leaves the remedies for objectionable ideas to counter-argument and time.

Plutarch's Lives were the favorite reading of men who framed and ratified our Constitution. There they found the story of Timoleon who saved his native city of Syracuse from the Carthaginian tyrants. In later years young hot-heads used to get up in the public assembly and abuse Timoleon as an old fossil. His friends urged him just to say the word, and they would soon silence his detractors. But Timoleon insisted on letting the vituperative youngsters have their say. "He had taken all the extreme pains and labor he had done, and had passed so many dangers, in order that every citizen and inhabitant of Syracuse might frankly use the liberty of their laws. He thanked the gods that they had granted him the thing he had so oft requested of them in his prayers, which was, that he might some day see the Syracusans have full power and liberty to say what they pleased."

It is such a spirit that makes us love the United States of America. With all the shortcomings of economic organization, with all the narrowness and ignorance of politicians, we know that we are still immeasurably freer than we should be in Italy, Germany or Russia to say what we think and write what we believe and do what we want. "There's a looseness about this here freedom that I likes."

Let us not in our anxiety to protect ourselves from foreign tyrants imitate some of their worst acts, and sacrifice in the process of national defense the very liberties which we are defending.

THE FIRST AMENDMENT IS AN ABSOLUTE

By Alexander Meiklejohn *

. . . Apart from the First Amendment itself, the passages of the Constitution which most directly clarify its meaning are the Preamble, the Tenth Amendment, and sec. 2 of Article I. All four provisions must be considered in their historical setting, not only in relation to one another but, even more important, in relation to the intention and structure of the Constitution as a whole. Out of such consideration the following principles seem to emerge:

1. All constitutional authority to govern the people of the United States belongs to the people themselves, acting as members of a corporate body politic. They are, it is true, "the governed." But they are also "the governors." Political freedom is not the absence of government. It is self-government.

2. By means of the Constitution, the people establish subordinate agencies, such as the legislature, the executive, the judiciary, and delegate to each of them such specific and limited powers as are deemed necessary for the doing of its assigned governing. These agencies have no other powers.

3. The people do not delegate all their sovereign powers. The Tenth Amendment speaks of powers that are reserved "to the people," as well as of powers "reserved to the States."

4. Article I, sec. 2, speaks of a reserved power which the people have decided to exercise by their own direct activity: "The House of Representatives shall be composed of members chosen every second year by the people of the several States. . . ." Here is established the voting power through which the people, as an electorate, actively participate in governing both themselves, as subjects of the laws, and their agencies, as the makers, administrators, and interpreters of the laws. In today's government, the scope of direct electoral action is wider than the provisions made when Article I, sec. 2, was adopted, but the constitutional principle or intention is the same.

5. The revolutionary intent of the First Amendment is, then, to deny to all subordinate agencies authority to abridge the freedom of the electoral power of the people.

---

* From Alexander Meiklejohn. "The First Amendment Is an Absolute." *The Supreme Court Review*. Chicago: University of Chicago Press, 1961, at p. 253. Used with permission of the University of Chicago Press and Philip B. Kurland, editor. Copyright 1961 by the University of Chicago. The author was president of Amherst College.

For the understanding of these principles it is essential to keep clear the crucial difference between "the rights" of the governed and "the powers" of the governors. And at this point, the title "Bill of Rights" is lamentably inaccurate as a designation of the first ten amendments. They are not a "Bill of Rights" but a "Bill of Powers and Rights." The Second through the Ninth Amendments limit the powers of the subordinate agencies in order that due regard shall be paid to the private "rights of the governed." The First and Tenth Amendments protect the governing "powers" of the people from abridgment by the agencies which are established as their servants. In the field of our "rights," each one of us can claim "due process of law." In the field of our governing "powers," the notion of "due process" is irrelevant.

THE FREEDOM OF THOUGHT AND COMMUNICATION BY WHICH WE GOVERN

The preceding section may be summed up thus: The First Amendment does not protect a "freedom to speak." It protects the freedom of those activities of thought and communication by which we "govern." It is concerned, not with a private right, but with a public power, a governmental responsibility.

In the specific language of the Constitution, the governing activities of the people appear only in terms of casting a ballot. But in the deeper meaning of the Constitution, voting is merely the external expression of a wide and diverse number of activities by means of which citizens attempt to meet the responsibilities of making judgments, which that freedom to govern lays upon them. That freedom implies and requires what we call "the dignity of the individual." Self-government can exist only insofar as the voters acquire the intelligence, integrity, sensitivity, and generous devotion to the general welfare that, in theory, casting a ballot is assumed to express.

The responsibilities mentioned are of three kinds. We, the people who govern, must try to understand the issues which, incident by incident, face the nation. We must pass judgment upon the decisions which our agents make upon those issues. And, further, we must share in devising methods by which those decisions can be made wise and effective or, if need be, supplanted by others which promise greater wisdom and effectiveness. Now it is these activities, in all their diversity, whose freedom fills up "the scope of the First Amendment." These are the activities to whose freedom it gives its unqualified protection. And it must be recognized that the literal text of the Amendment falls far short of expressing the intent and the scope of that protection. I have previously tried to express that inadequacy:

> We must also note that, though the intention of the Amendment is sharp and resolute, the sentence which expresses that intention is

awkward and ill-constructed. Evidently, it was hard to write and is, therefore, hard to interpret. Within its meaning are summed up centuries of social passion and intellectual controversy, in this country and in others. As one reads it, one feels that its writers could not agree, either within themselves or with each other, upon a single formula which would define for them the paradoxical relation between free men and their legislative agents. Apparently, all that they could make their words do was to link together five separate demands which had been sharpened by ages of conflict and were being popularly urged in the name of the "Freedom of the People." And yet, those demands were, and were felt to be, varied forms of a single demand. They were attempts to express, each in its own way, the revolutionary idea which, in the slowly advancing fight for freedom, has given to the American experiment in self-government its dominating significance for the modern world.

What I have said is that the First Amendment, as seen in its constitutional setting, forbids Congress to abridge the freedom of a citizen's speech, press, peaceable assembly, or petition, whenever those activities are utilized for the governing of the nation. In these respects, the Constitution gives to all "the people" the same protection of freedom which, in Article I, sec. 6(1), it provides for their legislative agents: "and for any speech or debate in either House, they shall not be questioned in any other place." Just as our agents must be free in their use of their delegated powers, so the people must be free in the exercise of their reserved powers.

What other activities, then, in addition to speech, press, assembly, and petition, must be included within the scope of the First Amendment? First of all, the freedom to "vote," the official expression of a self-governing man's judgment on issues of public policy, must be absolutely protected. None of his subordinate agencies may bring pressure upon him to drive his balloting this way or that. None of them may require him to tell how he has voted; none may inquire by compulsory process into his political beliefs or associations. In that area, the citizen has constitutional authority and his agents have not.

Second, there are many forms of thought and expression within the range of human communications from which the voter derives the knowledge, intelligence, sensitivity to human values: the capacity for sane and objective judgment which, so far as possible, a ballot should express. These, too, must suffer no abridgment of their freedom. I list four of them below.

1. Education, in all its phases, is the attempt to so inform and cultivate the mind and will of a citizen that he shall have the wisdom, the independence, and, therefore, the dignity of a governing citizen. Freedom of education is, thus, as we all recognize, a basic postulate in the planning of a free society.

2. The achievements of philosophy and the sciences in creating knowledge and understanding of men and their world must be made available, without abridgment, to every citizen.

3. Literature and the arts must be protected by the First Amendment. They lead the way toward sensitive and informed appreciation and response to the values out of which the riches of the general welfare are created.

4. Public discussions of public issues, together with the spreading of information and opinion bearing on those issues, must have a freedom unabridged by our agents. Though they govern us, we, in a deeper sense, govern them. Over our governing, they have no power. Over their governing we have sovereign power.

A PARADOX

Out of the argument thus far stated, two apparently contradictory statements emerge. Congress may, in ways carefully limited, "regulate" the activities by which the citizens govern the nation. But no regulation may abridge the freedom of those governing activities. I am sure that the two statements are not contradictory. But their combination is, to say the least, paradoxical. It is that paradox that I must now face as I try to respond to Professor Kalven's challenge. As a non-lawyer, I shall not discuss in detail the difficulties and puzzlements with which the courts must deal. I can only suggest that, here and there, seeming contradictions are not real.

First. A distinction must be drawn between belief and communication in their relations to Congressional authority. A citizen may be told when and where and in what manner he may or may not speak, write, assemble, and so on. On the other hand, he may not be told what he shall or shall not believe. In that realm each citizen is sovereign. He exercises powers that the body politic reserves for its own members. In 1953, testifying before the Senate Committee on Constitutional Rights, I said:

> . . . our First Amendment freedom forbids that any citizen be required, under threat of penality, to take an oath, or make an affirmation, as to beliefs which he holds or rejects. Every citizen, it is true, may be required and should be required, to pledge loyalty, and to practice loyalty, to the nation. He must agree to support the Constitution. But he may never be required to *believe* in the Constitution. His loyalty may never be tested on grounds of adherence to, or rejection of, any *belief*. Loyalty does not imply conformity of opinion. Every citizen of the United States has Constitutional authority to approve or to condemn any laws enacted by the Legislature, any actions taken by the Executive, any judgments rendered by the judiciary, any principles established by the Constitution. All these enactments which, as men who are governed, we must obey, are subject to our approval or disapproval, as we govern. With respect to all of them we, who are

free men, are sovereign. We are "The People." We govern the United States.

However far our practice falls short of the intention expressed by those words, they provide the standard by which our practice must be justified or condemned.

Second. We must recognize that there are many forms of communication which, since they are not being used as activities of governing, are wholly outside the scope of the First Amendment. Mr. Justice Holmes has told us about these, giving such vivid illustrations as "persuasion to murder" and "falsely shouting fire in a theatre and causing a panic." And Mr. Justice Harlan, referring to Holmes and following his lead, gave a more extensive list: "libel, slander, misrepresentation, obscenity, perjury, false advertising, solicitation of crime, complicity by encouragement, conspiracy. . . ." Why are these communications not protected by the First Amendment? Mr. Justice Holmes suggested an explanation when he said of the First Amendment in *Schenck:* "It does not even protect a man from an injunction against uttering words that may have all the effect of force."

Now it may be agreed that the uttering of words cannot be forbidden by legislation, nor punished on conviction, unless damage has been done by them to some individual or to the wider society. But that statement does not justify the imputation that all "words that may have all the effect of force" are denied the First Amendment's protection. The man who falsely shouts "Fire!" in a theatre is subject to prosecution under validly enacted legislation. But the army officer who, in command of a firing squad, shouts "Fire!" and thus ends a life, cannot be prosecuted for murder. He acts as an agent of the government. And, in fact, all governing communications are intended to have, more or less directly, "the effect of force." When a voter casts his ballot for a tax levy, he intends that someone shall be deprived of property. But his voting is not therefore outside the scope of the First Amendment. His voting must be free.

The principle here at stake can be seen in our libel laws. In cases of private defamation, one individual does damage to another by tongue or pen; the person so injured in reputation or property may sue for damages. But, in that case, the First Amendment gives no protection to the person sued. His verbal attack has no relation to the business of governing. If, however, the same verbal attack is made in order to show the unfitness of a candidate for governmental office, the act is properly regarded as a citizen's participation in government. It is, therefore, protected by the First Amendment. And the same principle holds good if a citizen attacks, by words of disapproval and condemnation, the policies of the government, or even the structure of the Constitution. These are "public" issues concerning which, under our form of government, he has authority, and is assumed to have competence, to judge. Though private libel is subject to legislative control, political or seditious libel is not. . . .

Fifth. In the current discussions as to whether or not "obscenity" in literature and the arts is protected by the First Amendment, the basic principle is, I think, that literature and the arts are protected because they have a "social importance" which I have called a "governing" importance. For example, the novel is at present a powerful determinative of our views of what human beings are, how they can be influenced, in what directions they should be influenced by many forces, including, especially, their own judgments and appreciations. But the novel, like all the other creations of literature and the arts, may be produced wisely or unwisely, sensitively or coarsely, for the building up of a way of life which we treasure or for tearing it down. Shall the government establish a censorship to distinguish between "good" novels and "bad" ones? And, more specifically, shall it forbid the publication of novels which portray sexual experiences with a frankness that, to the prevailing conventions of our society, seems "obscene"?

The First Amendment seems to me to answer that question with an unequivocal "no." Here, as elsewhere, the authority of citizens to decide what they shall write and, more fundamental, what they shall read and see, has not been delegated to any of the subordinate branches of government. It is "reserved to the people," each deciding for himself to whom he will listen, whom he will read, what portrayal of the human scene he finds worthy of his attention. And at this point I feel compelled to disagree with Professor Kalven's interpretation of what I have tried to say. In his recent article on obscenity, he wrote:

> The classic defense of John Stuart Mill and the modern defense of Alexander Meiklejohn do not help much when the question is why the novel, the poem, the painting, the drama, or the piece of sculpture falls within the protection of the First Amendment. Nor do the famous opinions of Hand, Holmes, and Brandeis. The emphasis is all on truth winning out in a fair fight between competing ideas. The emphasis is clearest in Meiklejohn's argument that free speech is indispensable to the informed citizenry required to make democratic self-government work. The people need free speech because they vote. As a result his argument distinguishes sharply between public and private speech. Not all communications are relevant to the political process. The people do not need novels or dramas or paintings or poems because they will be called upon to vote. Art and belles-lettres do not deal in such ideas—at least not good art or belles-lettres. . . .

In reply to that friendly interpretation, I must, at two points, record a friendly disavowal. I have never been able to share the Miltonian faith that in a fair fight between truth and error, truth is sure to win. And if one had that faith, it would be hard to reconcile it with the sheer stupidity of the policies of this nation—and of other nations—now driving humanity to the very edge of final destruction. In my view, "the people need free speech" because they have decided, in adopting, maintaining and interpreting their Constitution, to govern themselves rather than to be governed by others. And, in order to make that self-government a reality rather than an illusion, in order that it may become as wise and efficient as its responsibilities require, the judgment-making of the people must be self-educated in the ways of freedom. That is, I think, the positive purpose to which the negative words of the First Amendment gave a constitutional expression. Moreover, as against Professor Kalven's interpretation, I believe, as a teacher, that the people do need novels and dramas and paintings and poems, "because they will be called upon to vote." The primary social fact which blocks and hinders the success of our experiment in self-government is that our citizens are not educated for self-government. We are terrified by ideas, rather than challenged and stimulated by them. Our dominant mood is not the courage of people who dare to think. It is the timidity of those who fear and hate whenever conventions are questioned. . . .

CHAPTER 3

POSTAL CENSORSHIP

The Congress traditionally has held that the widest possible dissemination of information is in the best interest of an open, democratic society. This is reflected in its establishment of post offices and post roads and in its authorization of lower postal rates to publications through second-class mailing permits. However, the right to use the postal facilities may be denied to those who circulate matters deemed harmful to the general public or matter not constitutionally protected, i.e. obscene, seditious or lottery material.

President Washington argued for the establishment of an efficient postal service as necessary to a democratic government. There were fears, however, that a strong federal postal branch would result in government surveillance and possible control of content of the mail. The Continental Congress in 1775 named the renowned publisher and statesman Benjamin Franklin America's first Postmaster General. It was common for colonial postmasters also to be publishers.

In 1782 the Continental Congress prohibited the inspection of sealed mail, such as first class letters. This inspection was undertaken in early colonial days as a means of ascertaining disloyalty to the king. Nearly a century later, in 1878, the Supreme Court in Ex parte Jackson ruled that freedom of the press has little meaning without freedom to distribute, but that inspection of unsealed printed matter, such as newspapers, did not interfere with this freedom.

Justice Holmes once said an adequate postal distribution service is as important to free written expression as a tongue is to free speech. While newspapers, books, magazines and educational material all may be mailed at reduced rates, this privilege has resulted in censorial practices by various postmasters. The warnings of colonialists who feared that a federal postal service would result in government interference of mail were fully realized with the rise of Anthony Comstock, who waged through the Post Office the nation's most nefarious one-man anti-obscenity campaign. Postmasters in the mid-1800s ruled on postal acceptability of printed matter submitted to the Post Office for mailing. In 1913 the Supreme Court in Lewis Publishing Co. v. Morgan, authorized the Post Office Department to uphold standards set by the Congress in granting second-class permits.

In Milwaukee Publishing Co. v. Burleson the Court upheld refusal of postal services under the Espionage Act of 1917, but more importantly the case furnished an opportunity for strong dissents by Justices Brandeis and Holmes, whose views were to become the majority view in Hannegan v. Esquire a quarter of a century later. 327 U.S. 146 (1946). The censorial rights of the postmaster were terminated with the landmark Hannegan decision. Postmaster General Hannegan had acted to revoke the second-class permit of Esquire Magazine as "morally improper" and not devoted to the public good. He cited as his authority the Postal Classification Act of 1879. The Court, Justice Douglas voicing the 8-0 opinion, disagreed.

HANNEGAN V. ESQUIRE
327 U.S. 146 (1946)

MR. JUSTICE DOUGLAS *delivered the opinion of the Court.*

Congress has made obscene material nonmailable, and has applied criminal sanctions for the enforcement of that policy. It has divided mailable matter into four classes, periodical publications constituting the second-class. And it has specified four conditions upon which a publication shall be admitted to the second-class. The Fourth condition, which is the only one relevant here, provides:

> Except as otherwise provided by law, the conditions upon which a publication shall be admitted to the second-class are as follows . . . Fourth. It must be originated and published for the dissemination of information of a public character, or devoted to literature, the sciences, arts, or some special industry, and having a legitimate list of subscribers. Nothing herein contained shall be so construed as to admit to the second-class rate regular publications designed primarily for advertising purposes, or for free circulation, or for circulation at nominal rates.

Respondent is the publisher of *Esquire Magazine,* a monthly periodical which was granted a second-class permit in 1933. In 1943 . . . a citation was issued to respondent by the . . . Postmaster General . . . to show cause why that permit should not be suspended or revoked. A hearing was held before a board designated by the then Postmaster General. The board recommended that the permit not be revoked. Petitioner's predecessor took a different view. He did not find that *Esquire Magazine* contained obscene material and therefore was nonmailable. He revoked its second-class permit because he found that it did not comply with the Fourth condition. The gist of his holding is contained in the following excerpt from his opinion:

> The plain language of this statute does not assume a publication must in fact be 'obscene' within the intendment of the postal obscenity statutes before it can be found not to be 'originated and published for the dissemination of information of a public character, or devoted to literature, the sciences, arts, or some special industry.'
>
> Writings and pictures may be indecent, vulgar, and risque and still not be obscene in a technical sense. Such writings and pictures may be in that obscure and treacherous borderland zone where the average person hesitates to find them technically obscene, but still may see ample proof that they are morally improper and not for the public welfare and the public good. When such writings or pictures occur in isolated instances their dangerous tendencies and malignant qualities may be considered of lesser importance.
>
> When, however, they become a dominant and systematic feature they most certainly cannot be said to be for the public good, and a publication which uses them in that manner is not making the 'special contribution to the public welfare' which Congress intended by the Fourth condition.
>
> A publication to enjoy these unique mail privileges and special preferences is bound to do more than refrain from disseminating material which is obscene or bordering on the obscene. It is under a positive duty to contribute to the public good and the public welfare. . . .

The issues of *Esquire Magazine* under attack are those for January to November inclusive of 1943. The material complained of embraces in bulk only a small percentage of those issues. Regular features of the magazine (called "The Magazine for Men") include articles on topics of current interest, short stories, sports articles or stories, short articles by men prominent in various fields of activities, articles about men prominent in the news, a book review department headed by the late William Lyon Phelps, a theatrical department headed by George Jean Nathan, a department devoted to lively arts by Gilbert Seldes, a department devoted to men's clothing, and pictoral features, including war action paintings, color photographs of dogs and water colors or etchings of game birds and reproductions of famous paintings, prints and drawings. There was very little in these features which was challenged. But petitioner's predecessor found that the objectionable items, though a small percentage of the total bulk, were regular recurrent features which gave the magazine its dominant tone or characteristic. These include jokes, cartoons, pictures, articles, and poems. They were said to reflect the smoking-room type of humor, featuring, in the main, sex. Some witnesses found the challenged items highly objectionable, calling them salacious and indecent. Others thought they were only racy and risque. Some condemned them as being merely in poor taste. Other witnesses could find no objection to them.

An examination of the items makes plain, we think, that the controversy is not whether the magazine publishes "information of a public character" or is devoted to "literature" or to the "arts." It is whether the contents are "good" or "bad." To uphold the order of revocation would, therefore, grant the Postmaster General a power of censorship. Such a power is so abhorrent to our traditions that a purpose to grant it should not be easily inferred. . . .

The policy of Congress has been clear. It has been to encourage the distribution of periodicals which disseminated "information of a public character" or which were devoted to "literature, the sciences, arts, or some special industry," because it was thought that those publications as a class contributed to the public good. The standards prescribed in the Fourth condition have been criticized, but not on the ground that they provide for censorship. As stated by the Postal Commission of 1911, H Doc 559, 62d Cong 2d Sess p. 142:

> The original object in placing on second-class matter a rate far below that on any other class of mail was to encourage the dissemination of news and current literature of educational value. This object has been only in part attained. The low rate has helped to stimulate an enormous mass of periodicals, many of which are of little utility for the cause of popular education. Others are of excellent quality, but the experience of the post office has shown the impossibility of making a satisfactory test based upon literary or educational values. To attempt to do so would be to set up a censorship of the press. Of necessity the words of the statute—"devoted to literature, the sciences, arts, or some special industry"—must have a broad interpretation.

We may assume that Congress has a broad power of classification and need not open second-class mail to publications of all types. The categories of publications entitled to that classification have indeed varied through the years. And the Court held in *Ex parte Jackson,* 96 U.S. 727, that Congress could constitutionally make it a crime to send fraudulent or obscene material through the mails. But grave constitutional questions are immediately raised once it is said that the use of the mails is a privilege which may be extended or withheld on any grounds whatsoever. See the dissents of Mr. Justice Brandeis and Mr. Justice Holmes in *United States ex rel. Milwaukee S. D. Pub. Co. v. Burleson,* 255 U.S. 407. Under that view the second-class rate could be granted on condition that certain economic or political ideas not be disseminated. The provisions of the Fourth condition would have to be far more explicit for us to assume that Congress made such a radical departure from our traditions and undertook to clothe the Postmaster General with the power to supervise the tastes of the reading public of the country.

It is plain, as we have said, that the favorable second-class rates were granted periodicals meeting the requirements of the Fourth condition, so that the public good might be served through a dissemination of the class of periodicals described. But that is a far cry from assuming that Congress had any idea that each applicant for the second-class rate must convince the Postmaster General that his publication positively contributes to the public good or public welfare. Under our system of government there is an accommodation for the widest varieties of tastes and ideas. What is good literature, what has educational value, what is refined public information, what is good art, varies with individuals as it does from one generation to another. There doubtless would be a contrariety of views concerning Cervantes' *Don Quixote*, Shakespeare's *Venus and Adonis*, or Zola's *Nana*. But a requirement that literature or art conform to some norm prescribed by an official smacks of an ideology foreign to our system. The basic values implicit in the requirements of the Fourth condition can be served only by uncensored distribution of literature. From the multitude of competing offerings the public will pick and choose. What seems to one to be trash may have for others fleeting or even enduring values. But to withdraw the second-class rate from this publication today because its contents seemed to one official not good for the public would sanction withdrawal of the second-class rate tomorrow from another periodical whose social or economic views seemed harmful to another official. The validity of the obscenity laws is recognition that the mails may not be used to satisfy all tastes, no matter how perverted. But Congress has left the Postmaster General with no power to prescribe standards for the literature or the art which a mailable periodical disseminates.

This is not to say that there is nothing left to the Postmaster General under the Fourth condition. It is his duty to "execute all laws relative to the Postal Service." Rev Stat sec. 396. For example, questions will arise as they did in *Houghton v. Payne*, 194 U.S. 88; *Bates & G. Co. v. Payne*, 194 U.S. 106; and *Smith v. Hitchcock*, 226 U.S. 53, whether the publication which seeks the favorable second-class rate is a periodical as defined in the Fourth condition or a book or other type of publication. And it may appear that the information contained in a periodical may not be of a "public character." But the power to determine whether a periodical (which is mailable) contains information of a public character, literature or art does not include the further power to determine whether the contents meet some standard of the public good or welfare.

Rulings of the Warren Court in the 1960s further extended First Amendment guarantees of distribution through the United States mails. In 1962 the Court overruled the Postmaster, who had refused to accept magazines he himself had judged to be obscene (Manual Enterprises v. Day) and three years later overturned Post Office practices of delaying unsealed mail from overseas (Lamont v. Postmaster General).

Postmaster General Day declared nonmailable certain magazines consisting largely of nude and seminude photographs of male models. The magazine also included photographers' names and addresses and advertisements telling how additional such material might be obtained. The Warren Court by a 6-1 majority declined to support the Postmaster General, but, despite the sizable majority, could not reach a consensus as to the reasons for their decision. Of importance to the study of postal censorship was the concurrence of Justice Brennan, who was joined by Chief Justice Warren and Justice Douglas. Their position was that the Postmaster is not given the authority to decide arbitrarily which publications are obscene and, therefore, nonmailable. A second element is of great importance to the general discussion of literary obscenity (see Chapters 5 and 6). Justice Harlan, joined by Justice Stewart, submitted an additional test to the "prurient interest" criterion of Roth (see Chapter 5). A work must be "patently offensive," they maintained, in order for it to be judged obscene. Even though there was no strong consensus by the Court, it appears clear that the Justices gave greater latitude to freedom of the press by further restricting attempts at governmental censorship.

MANUAL ENTERPRISES, INC. V. DAY
370 U.S. 478 (1962)

MR. JUSTICE HARLAN announced the judgment of the Court and an opinion in which Mr. Justice Stewart joins.

. . . Petitioners are three corporations respectively engaged in publishing magazines titled Manual, Trim, and Grecian Guild Pictorial. They have offices at the same address in Washington, D.C., and a common president, one Herman L. Womack. The magazines consist largely of photographs of nude, or near-nude, male models and give the names of each model and the photographer, together with the address of the latter. They also contain a number of advertisements by independent photographers offering nudist photographs for sale.

On March 25, 1960, six parcels containing an aggregate of 405 copies of the three magazines, destined from Alexandria, Virginia, to Chicago, Illinois, were detained by the Alexandria postmaster, pending a ruling by his superiors at Washington as to whether the magazines were "nonmail-able." After an evidentiary hearing before the Judicial Officer of the Post Office Department there ensued the administrative and court decisions now under review.

I

On the issue of obscenity, as distinguished from unlawful advertising, the case comes to us with the following administrative findings, which are supported by substantial evidence and which we, and indeed the parties, for the most part, themselves, accept: (1) the magazines are not, as asserted by petitioners, physical culture or "body-building" publications, but are composed primarily, if not exclusively, for homosexuals, and have no literary, scientific or other merit; (2) they would appeal to the "prurient interest" of such sexual deviates, but would not have any interest for sexually normal individuals; and (3) the magazines are read almost entirely by homosexuals, and possibly a few adolescent males; the ordinary male adult would not normally buy them. . . .

. . . These magazines cannot be deemed so offensive on their face as to affront current community standards of decency—a quality that we shall hereafter refer to as "patent offensiveness" or "indecency." Lacking that quality, the magazines cannot be deemed legally "obscene," and we need not consider the question of the proper "audience" by which their "prurient interest" appeal should be judged.

The words . . . "obscene, lewd, lascivious, indecent, filthy or vile" connote something that is portrayed in a manner so offensive as to make it unacceptable under current community mores. While in common usage the words have different shades of meaning, the statute since its inception has always been taken as aimed at obnoxiously debasing portrayals of sex. . . .

We come then to what we consider the dispositive question on this phase of the case. Are these magazines offensive on their face? . . .

We cannot accept in full the Government's description of these magazines which, contrary to *Roth* [see Chapter 5], tends to emphasize and in some respects overdraw certain features in several of the photographs, at the expense of what the magazines fairly taken as a whole depict. Our own independent examination of the magazines leads us to conclude that the most that can be said of them is that they are dismally unpleasant, uncouth, and tawdry. But this is not enough to make them "obscene." Divorced from their "prurient interest" appeal to the unfortunate persons whose patronage they were aimed at capturing (a separate issue), these portrayals of the male nude cannot fairly be regarded as more objectionable than many portrayals of the female nude that society tolerates. Of course not every portrayal of male or female nudity is obscene. . . .

II

There remains the question of the advertising. It is not contended that the petitioners held themselves out as purveyors of obscene material, or that the advertisements, as distinguished from the other contents of the magazines, were obscene on their own account. . . . The claim on this branch of the case rests, then, on the fact that some of the third-party advertisers were found in possession of what undoubtedly may be regarded as "hardcore" photographs, and that postal officials, although not obtaining the names of the advertisers from the lists in petitioners' magazines, received somewhat less offensive material through the mails from certain studios which were advertising in petitioners' magazines.

. . . Since publishers cannot practicably be expected to investigate each of their advertisers, and since the economic consequences of an order barring even a single issue of a periodical from the mails might entail heavy financial sacrifice, a magazine publisher might refrain from accepting advertisements from those whose own materials could conceivably be deemed objectionable by the Post Office Department. This would deprive such materials, which might otherwise be entitled to constitutional protection, of a legitimate and recognized avenue of access to the public. . . .

On these premises we turn to the record in this case. Although postal officials had informed petitioners' president, Womack, that their Department was *prosecuting* several of his advertisers for sending obscene matter through the mails, there is no evidence that any of this material was shown to him. He thus was afforded no opportunity to judge for himself as to its alleged obscenity. Contrariwise, one of the government witnesses at the administrative hearing admitted that the petitioners had deleted the advertisements of several photographic studios after being informed by the Post Office that the proprietors had been *convicted* of mailing obscene material. The record reveals that none of the postal officials who received allegedly obscene matter from some of the advertisers obtained their names from petitioners' magazines; this material was received as a result of independent test checks. Nor on the record before us can petitioners be linked with the material seized by the police. . . .

In conclusion, nothing in this opinon of course remotely implies approval of the type of magazines published by these petitioners, still less of the sordid motives which prompted their publication. All we decide is that on this record these particular magazines are not subject to repression. . . .

MR. JUSTICE BRENNAN, *with whom The Chief Justice and Mr. Justice Douglas join, concurring in the reversal.*

I agree that the judgment below must be reversed, though for a reason different from my Brother Harlan's. This is the first occasion on which the Court has given plenary review to a Post Office Department order holding matter "nonmailable" because obscene. . . .

Mr. Justice Holmes has said: "The United States may give up the Post Office when it sees fit, but while it carries it on the use of the mails is almost as much a part of free speech as the right to use our tongues, and it would take very strong language to convince me that Congress ever intended to give such a practically despotic power to any one man." *United States ex rel. Milwaukee S. D. Pub. Co. v. Burleson* (dissenting opinion).

Whether Congress, by its enactment or amendment of 18 USC sec. 1461 (a part of the Criminal Code), has authorized the Postmaster General to censor obscenity, is our precise question. . . . The area of obscenity is honeycombed with hazards for First Amendment guarantees, and the grave constitutional questions which would be raised by the grant of such a power should not be decided when the relevant materials are so ambiguous as to whether any such grant exists. . . .

We have sustained the criminal sanctions of sec. 1461 against a challenge of unconstitutionality under the First Amendment. *Roth v. United States.* We have emphasized, however, that the necessity for safeguarding First Amendment protections for non-obscene materials means that Government "is not free to adopt whatever procedures it pleases for dealing with obscenity . . . without regard to the possible consequences for constitutionally protected speech." *Marcus v. Search Warrant of Property.* . . . However, it is enough to dispose of this case that Congress has not, in sec. 1461, authorized the Postmaster General to employ any process of his own to close the mails to matter which, in his view, falls within the ban of that section. . . .

MR. JUSTICE CLARK, *dissenting.*

While those in the majority like ancient Gaul are split into three parts, the ultimate holding of the Court today, despite the clear Congressional mandate found in sec. 1461, requires the United States Post Office to be the world's largest disseminator of smut and Grand Informer of the names and places where obscene material may be obtained. The Judicial Officer of the Post Office Department, the District Court, and the Court of Appeals have all found the magazines in issue to be nonmailable on the alternative grounds that they are obscene and that they contain information on where obscene material may be obtained. The Court, however, says that these magazines must go through the mails. Brother Harlan, writing for himself and Brother Stewart, finds that the magazines themselves are unobjectionable because sec. 1461 is not so narrowly drawn as to prohibit the mailing of material "that incites immoral sexual conduct," and that the presence of information leading to obscene material does not taint the magazines because their publishers were unaware of the true nature of this information. Brother Brennan, joined by The Chief Justice and Brother Douglas, finds that sec. 1461 does not authorize the Postmaster General through administrative process to close the mails to matter included within its proscriptions. Since in my view the Postmaster General is required by sec. 1461 to reject nonmailable matter, I would affirm the judgment on the sole ground that the magazines contain information as to where obscene material can be obtained and thus are nonmailable. I, therefore, do not consider the question of whether the magazines as such are obscene. . . .

The content and direction of the magazines themselves are a tip-off as to the nature of the business of those who solicit through them. The magazines have no social, educational, or entertainment qualities but are designed solely as sex stimulants for homosexuals. . . . The publishers freely admit that the magazines are published to appeal to the male homosexual group. The advertisements and photographer lists in such magazines were quite naturally "designed so as to attract the male homosexual and to furnish him with names and addresses where nude male pictures in poses and conditions which would appeal to his prurient interest may be obtained." Moreover, the advertisements themselves could leave no more doubt in the publishers' minds than in those of the solicited purchasers. To illustrate: some captioned a picture of a nude or scantily attired young man with the legend "perfectly proportioned, handsome, male models, age 18–26." Others featured a photograph of a nude male with the area around the privates obviously retouched so as to cover the genitals and part of the pubic hair and offered to furnish an "original print of this photo." Finally, each magazine specifically endorsed its listed photographers and requested its readers to support them by purchasing their products. In addition, three of the four magazines involved expressly represented that they were familiar with the work of the photographers listed in their publications.

Turning to Womack, the president and directing force of all three corporate publishers, it is even clearer that we are not dealing here with a "Jack and Jill" operation. Mr. Womack admitted that the magazines were planned for homosexuals, designed to appeal to and stimulate their erotic interests. To improve on this effect, he made suggestions to photographers as to the type of pictures he wanted. For example, he informed one of the studios listed in his publications that "physique fans want their 'truck driver types' already cleaned up, showered, and ready for bed . . . [and] it is absolutely essential that the models have pretty faces and a personality not totally unrelated to sex appeal." Womack had also suggested to the photographers that they exchange customer names with the hope of compiling a master list of homosexuals. He himself had been convicted of selling obscene photographs via the mails. More recently he has pleaded not guilty by reason of insanity to like charges. Furthermore, he was warned in March, April, and July of 1959 that a number of his photographer advertisers were being prosecuted for mailing obscene matter and that he might be violating the law in transmitting through the mails their advertisements. However, he continued to disseminate such information through the mails, removing photographers from his lists only as they were convicted. Finally, through another controlled corporation not here involved, he filled orders for one of his advertisers sent in by the readers of his magazines. This material was found to be obscene and like all of the above facts and findings it is not contested here.

The corporate petitioners are chargeable with the knowledge of what they do, as well as the knowledge of their president and leader. How one can fail to see the obvious in the record is beyond my comprehension. In the words of Milton: "O dark, dark, dark amid the blaze of noon." For one to conclude that the above undisputed facts and findings are insufficient to show the required scienter, however stringently it may be defined, is in effect to repeal the advertising provisions of sec. 1461. To condition non-mailability on proof that the sender actually saw the material being sold by his advertisers is to portray the Congress as the "mother" in the jingle, "Mother, may I go out to swim? Yes, my darling daughter. Hang your clothes on a hickory limb and don't go near the water."

For these reasons I would affirm the decision below.

*   *   *

The Warren Court in 1965 decided in two cases that it was unconstitutional for postal officials to delay delivery of alleged Communist propaganda as authorized by a 1962 statute. Under the law, addressees, after being informed that the Post Office was holding unsealed matter deemed to be Communist propaganda, would have to specifically request that postal officials forward the matter being detained. It was charged that the Post Office compiled lists of those who requested the alleged propaganda and routinely made these lists available to other government agencies, such as the House Committee on Un-American Activities. The Court by an 8-0 vote held that the act was an unconstitutional infringement on free speech and press.

The steady trend since Hannegan, the landmark case in postal censorship, has been to restrict the powers of the postmaster in deciding what matter is nonmailable and what matter should be denied second-class postal privileges, which are essential to wide periodical circulation. This trend carried through the Warren Court and into the early 1970s under Chief Justice Burger. Other important mail cases, Ginzburg v. United States and United States v. Reidel, are more directly concerned with the Supreme Court's attitude toward obscenity per se and are covered in Chapter 6.

LAMONT V. POSTMASTER GENERAL

FIXA V. HEILBERG
381 U.S. 301 (1965)

MR. JUSTICE DOUGLAS *delivered the opinion of the Court.*

. . . The statute contains an exemption from its provisions for mail addressed to government agencies and educational institutions, or officials thereof, and for mail sent pursuant to a reciprocal cultural international agreement.

To implement the statute the Post Office maintains 10 or 11 screening points through which is routed all unsealed mail from the designated foreign countries. At these points the nonexempt mail is examined by Customs authorities. When it is determined that a piece of mail is "communist political propaganda," the addressee is mailed a notice identifying the mail being detained and advising that it will be destroyed unless the addressee requests delivery by returning an attached reply card within 20 days. . . .

We conclude that the Act as construed and applied is unconstitutional because it requires an official act (*viz.*, returning the reply card) as a limitation on the unfettered exercise of the addressee's First Amendment rights. As stated by Mr. Justice Holmes in *Milwaukee Pub. Co. v. Burleson* (dissenting): "The United States may give up the Post Office when it sees fit, but while it carries it on the use of the mails is almost as much a part of free speech as the right to use our tongues." . . .

. . . We do not have here, any more than we had in *Hannegan v. Esquire, Inc.*, any question concerning the extent to which Congress may classify the mail and fix the charges for its carriage. Nor do we reach the question whether the standard here applied could pass constitutional muster. Nor do we deal with the right of Customs to inspect material from abroad for contraband. We rest on the narrow ground that the addressee in order to receive his mail must request in writing that it be delivered. This amounts in our judgment to an unconstitutional abridgment of the addressee's First Amendment rights. The addressee carries an affirmative obligation which we do not think the Government may impose on him. This requirement is almost certain to have a deterrent effect, especially as respects those who have sensitive positions. Their livelihood may be dependent on a security clearance. Public officials, like schoolteachers who have no tenure, might think they would invite disaster if they read what the Federal Government says contains the seeds of treason. Apart from them, any addressee is likely to feel some inhibition in sending for literature which federal officials have condemned as "communist political propaganda." The regime of this Act is at war with the "uninhibited, robust, and wide-open" debate and discussion that are contemplated by the First Amendment. *New York Times Co. v. Sullivan.* . . .

MR. JUSTICE BRENNAN, *with whom Mr. Justice Goldberg joins, concurring.*

. . . It is true that the First Amendment contains no specific guarantee of access to publications. However, the protection of the Bill of Rights goes beyond the specific guarantees to protect from Congressional abridgment those equally fundamental personal rights necessary to make the express guarantees fully meaningful.

I think the right to receive publications is such a fundamental right. The dissemination of ideas can accomplish nothing if otherwise willing addressees are not free to receive and consider them. It would be a barren marketplace of ideas that had only sellers and no buyers. . . .

*   *   *

A key element in the federal government's anti-obscenity drive of the late 1960s was a law passed by Congress in 1967 and ruled upon by the post-Warren Court of 1970. It allowed persons to stop firms from continuing to send through the mails "pandering advertisements" which the recipients consider "erotically arousing or sexually provocative." When persons received such advertisements, they were to inform the Post Office, which, in turn, was to notify the sender to remove that person's name from his mailing lists. Three characteristics of the law should be emphasized. First, only unsolicited advertisements were involved. The law did not include, for example, magazines or other material desired by the addressee. Second, the addressee was to be the sole judge as to the "erotically arousing or sexually provocative" qualities of the advertisement. And third, action to stop the sending of the materials was to be initiated by the addressee, not the government.

Chief Justice Burger, writing for a unanimous Court in Rowan v. Post Office Dept., 397 U.S. 728 (1970), described the law as a new element in one's right of privacy. In challenging the law, mailers and publishers claimed their freedoms of speech, press, and distribution were being denied. The Chief Justice's answer was that "the asserted right of the mailer . . . stops at the outer boundary of every person's domain." A three-judge federal district court in Los Angeles had previously held the law constitutional. The Supreme Court agreed. Congress had acted in response to parents and others who had claimed their homes were being deluged with advertisements for *sexual material they found offensive. The Post Office had said that by 1970, complaints of such material being received through the mails had risen to more than 250,000 per year.*

ROWAN V. POST OFFICE DEPT.
397 U.S. 728 (1970)

MR. CHIEF JUSTICE BURGER *delivered the opinion of the Court.*

Appellants challenge the constitutionality of Title III of the Postal Revenue and Federal Salary Act of 1967, 81 Stat. 645, 39 U.S.C. sec. 4009 (Supp. IV, 1969), under which a householder may require that a mailer remove his name from its mailing lists and stop all future mailings to the householder. The appellants are publishers, distributors, owners, and operators of mail order houses, mailing list brokers, and owners and operators of mail service organizations whose business activities are affected by the challenged statute.

A brief description of the statutory framework will facilitate our analysis of the questions raised in this appeal. Title III of the Act is entitled "Prohibition of pandering advertisements in the mails." It provides a procedure whereby any householder may insulate himself from advertisements that offer for sale "matter which the addressee in his sole discretion believes to be erotically arousing or sexually provocative."

Subsection (b) mandates the Postmaster, upon receipt of a notice from the addressee specifying that he has received advertisements found by him to be within the statutory category, to issue on the addressee's request an order directing the sender and his agents or assigns to refrain from further mailings of such materials to the named addressees. Additionally, subsection (c) requires the Postmaster to order the affected sender to delete the name of the designated addressee from all mailing lists owned or controlled by the sender and prohibits the sale, rental, exchange, or other transactions involving mailing lists bearing the name of the designated addressee.

If the Postmaster has reason to believe that an order issued under this section has been violated, subsection (d) authorizes him to notify the sender by registered or certified mail of his belief and the reasons therefor, and grant him an opportunity to respond and have a hearing on whether a violation has occurred.

If the Postmaster thereafter determines that the order has been or is being violated, he is authorized to request the Attorney General to seek an order from a United States District Court directing compliance with the prohibitory order. Subsection (e) grants to the District Court jurisdiction to issue a compliance order upon application of the Attorney General.

Appellants initiated an action in the United States District Court for the Central District of California upon a complaint and petition for declaratory relief on the ground that 39 U.S.C. sec. 4009 is unconstitutional. They alleged that they have received numerous prohibitory orders pursuant to the provisions of the statute. Appellants contended that the section violates their rights of free speech and due process guaranteed by the First and Fifth Amendments to the United States Constitution. Additionally, appellants argued that the section is unconstitutionally vague, without standards and ambiguous. . . .

(1) Background and Congressional Objectives

Section 4009 was a response to public and congressional concern with use of mail facilities to distribute unsolicited advertisements that recipients found to be offensive because of their lewd and salacious character. Such mail was found to be pressed upon minors as well as adults who did not seek and did not want it. Use of mailing lists of youth organizations was part of the mode of doing business. At the congressional hearings it developed that complaints to the Postmaster General increased from 50,000 to 250,000 annually. The legislative history, including testimony of child psychology specialists and psychiatrists, reflected concern over the impact of the materials before the Committee on the development of children. A declared objective of Congress was to protect minors and the privacy of homes from such material and to place the judgment of what constitutes an offensive invasion of those interests in the hands of the addressee. . . .

It would be anomalous to read the statute to affect only similar material or advertisements and yet require the Postmaster General to order the sender to remove the addressee's name from all mailing lists in his actual or constructive possession. The section was intended to allow the addressee complete and unfettered discretion in electing whether or not he desired to receive further material from a particular sender. The impact of this aspect of the statute is on the mailer, not the mail. The interpretation of the statute that most completely effectuates that intent is one which prohibits any further mailings. Limiting the prohibitory order to similar materials or advertisements is open to at least two criticisms: (a) it would expose the householder to further burdens of scrutinizing the mail for objectionable material and possible harassment, and (b) it would interpose the Postmaster General between the sender and the addressee and, at the least, create the appearance if not the substance of governmental censorship. It is difficult to see how the Postmaster General could decide whether the materials were "similar" or possessing touting or pandering characteristics without an evaluation suspiciously like censorship. . . .

(2) First Amendment Contentions

The essence of appellants' argument is that the statute violates their constitutional right to communicate. One sentence in appellants' brief perhaps characterizes their entire position:

The freedom to communicate orally and by the written word and, indeed, in every manner whatsoever is imperative to a free and sane society.

Without doubt the public postal system is an indispensable adjunct of every civilized society and communication is imperative to a healthy social order. But the right of every person "to be let alone" must be placed in the scales with the right of others to communicate.

In today's complex society we are inescapably captive audiences for many purposes, but a sufficient measure of individual autonomy must survive to permit every householder to exercise control over unwanted mail. To make the householder the exclusive and final judge of what will cross his threshold undoubtedly has the effect of impeding the flow of ideas, information and arguments which, ideally, he should receive and consider. Today's merchandising methods, the plethora of mass mailings subsidized by low postal rates, and the growth of the sale of large mailing lists as an industry in itself have changed the mailman from a carrier of primarily private communications, as he was in a more leisurely day, and has made him an adjunct of the mass mailer who sends unsolicited and often unwanted mail into every home. It places no strain on the doctrine of judicial notice to observe that whether measured by pieces or pounds, Everyman's mail today is made up overwhelmingly of material he did not seek from persons he does not know. And all too often it is matter he finds offensive.

In *Martin v. Struthers*, Mr. Justice Black, for the Court, while supporting the "[f]reedom to distribute information to every citizen," acknowledged a limitation in terms of leaving "with the homeowner himself" the power to decide "whether distributors of literature may lawfully call at a home." Weighing the highly important right to communicate, but without trying to determine where it fits into constitutional imperatives, against the very basic right to be free from sights, sounds and tangible matter we do not want, it seems to us that a mailer's right to communicate must stop at the mailbox of an unreceptive addressee.

The Court has traditionally respected the right of a householder to bar, by order or notice, solicitors, hawkers, and peddlers from his property. In this case the mailer's right to communicate is circumscribed only by an affirmative act of the addressee giving notice that he wishes no further mailings from that mailer.

To hold less would tend to license a form of trespass and would make hardly more sense than to say that a radio or television viewer may not twist the dial to cut off an offensive or boring communication and thus bar its entering his home. Nothing in the Constitution compels us to listen to or view any unwanted communication, whatever its merit; we see no basis for according the printed word or pictures a different or more preferred status because they are sent by mail. The ancient concept that "a man's home is his castle" into which "not even the king may enter" has lost none of its vitality, and none of the recognized exceptions includes any right to communicate offensively with another.

Both the absoluteness of the citizen's right under sec. 4009 and its finality are essential; what may not be provocative to one person may well be to another. In operative effect the power of the householder under the statute is unlimited; he or she may prohibit the mailing of a dry goods catalog because he objects to the contents—or indeed the text of the language touting the merchandise. Congress provided this sweeping power not only to protect privacy but to avoid possible constitutional questions that might arise from vesting the power to make any discretionary evaluation of the material in a governmental official.

In effect, Congress has erected a wall—or more accurately permits a citizen to erect a wall—that no advertiser may penetrate without his acquiescence. The continuing operative effect of a mailing ban once imposed presents no constitutional obstacles; the citizen cannot be put to the burden of determining on repeated occasions whether the offending mailer has altered his material so as to make it acceptable. Nor should the householder be at risk that offensive material come into the hands of his children before it can be stopped.

We therefore categorically reject the argument that a vendor has a right under the Constitution or otherwise to send unwanted material into the home of another. If this prohibition operates to impede the flow of even valid ideas, the answer is that no one has a right to press even "good" ideas on an unwilling recipient. That we are often "captives" outside the sanctuary of the home and subject to objectionable speech and other sound does not mean we must be captives everywhere. The asserted right of a mailer, we repeat, stops at the outer boundary of every person's domain. . . .

*   *   *

Eight months after upholding the government's case in Rowan, the Supreme Court unanimously rejected as unconstitutional the administration's use of two other laws which had been used by the Post Office to block what it termed the flow of pornographic matter through the mails. Blount v. The Mail Box, announced January 14, 1971. One allowed the Post Office to deny mail and money orders to persons who, through administrative hearings, were deemed to be dealing in obscene matter. The other allowed for the discontinuance of mail delivery to these same persons while the proceedings were under way.

The opinion, by Justice Brennan, relied heavily on a 1965 film case, Freedman v. Maryland, in which the Court established that the First

Amendment (1) requires swift review by the courts, rather than simply
hearings by governmental agencies in questions of obscenity, and (2)
places the heavy burden of proof on the government rather than on the
accused. The Mail Box, run by Tony Rizzi of Los Angeles, distributed
so-called "girlie magazines," alleged by the Post Office to be obscene. The
Book Bin was a distribution firm in Atlanta. In these two cases, three-judge
federal courts ruled separately that the postal regulations in question
lacked constitutional safeguards. The Supreme Court, deciding both cases
together, agreed. Justice Black, long an advocate of the "absolutist" position relative to the First Amendment, concurred in the result, but did not
join in the opinion.

BLOUNT V. THE MAIL BOX

UNITED STATES V. THE BOOK BIN
400 U.S. 410 (1971)

MR. JUSTICE BRENNAN *delivered the opinion of the Court.*

Mail Box draws into question the constitutionality of 39 U.S.C. sec.
4006 (1964) under which the Postmaster General, following administrative hearings, may halt use of the mails and of postal money orders for
commerce in allegedly obscene materials. *Book Bin* also draws into question the constitutionality of 39 U.S.C. sec. 4007 (1964) under which the
Postmaster General may obtain a court order permitting him to detain the
defendant's incoming mail pending the outcome of sec. 4006 proceedings
against him. . . .

In *Mail Box* . . . [a] three-judge court was convened and held that
39 U.S.C. sec. 4006 "is unconstitutional on its face, because it fails to meet
the requirements of *Freedman v. Maryland* (1965) 380 U.S. 51. . . ." The
court, therefore, vacated the administrative order, directed the delivery
"forthwith" of all mail addressed to Mail Box, and enjoined any proceedings to enforce sec. 4006.

In *Book Bin* . . . [a] three-judge court was convened and held both
sections unconstitutional. It agreed with the three-judge court in *Mail Box*
that the procedures of sec. 4006 were fatally deficient under *Freedman v.
Maryland* and also held that the finding under sec. 4007 merely of "probable cause" to believe material was obscene was not a constitutionally sufficient standard to support a temporary mail detention order. . . .

Our discussion appropriately begins with Mr. Justice Holmes' frequently quoted admonition that, "The United States may give up the
Post Office when it sees fit, but while it carries it on the use of the mails

is almost as much a part of free speech as the right to use our tongues. . . ." *Milwaukee Social Democratic Pub. Co. v. Burleson*, 255 U.S. 407 (1921) (dissenting opinion). . . .

The procedure established by sec. 4006 and the implementing regulations omit those "sensitive tools" essential to satisfy the requirements of the First Amendment. The three-judge courts correctly held in these cases that our decision in *Freedman v. Maryland* compels this conclusion. . . .

The scheme has no statutory provision requiring governmentally initiated judicial participation in the procedure which bars the magazines from the mails, or even any provision assuring prompt judicial review. . . . [T]he fatal flaw of the procedure [is] in failing to require that the Postmaster General seek to obtain a prompt judicial determination of the obscenity of the material; rather, once the administrative proceedings disapprove the magazines the distributor "must assume the burden of instituting judicial proceedings and of persuading the courts that the . . . [magazines are] . . . protected expression." The First Amendment demands that the Government must assume this burden. . . .

Moreover, once a sec. 4006 administrative order has been entered against the distributor, there being no provision for judicial review, the Postmaster may stamp as "unlawful" and immediately return to the sender orders for purchase of the magazines addressed to the distributor, and prohibit the payment of postal money orders to him. . . .

The authority of the Postmaster General under sec. 4007 to apply to a district court for an order directing the detention of the distributor's incoming mail pending the conclusion of the sec. 4006 administrative proceedings and any appeal therefrom plainly does not remedy the defects in sec. 4006. . . . We agree with the three-judge court in *Book Bin* that to satisfy the demand of the First Amendment "it is vital that prompt judicial review on the issue of obscenity—rather than merely probable cause—be assured on the Government's initiative before the severe restrictions of sec. 4006, 4007 are invoked." . . .

The appellees here not only were not afforded "prompt judicial review" but they "can only get full judicial review on the question of obscenity . . . after lengthy administrative proceedings, and then only by [their] own initiative. During the interim, the prolonged threat of an adverse administrat[ive] order, will have a severe restriction on the exercise of [appellees'] First Amendment rights—all without a final judicial determination of obscenity." . . .

*   *   *

Another postal regulation aimed at obscenity was passed by the Congress in 1970 and became effective in February of 1971. Several questions as to the constitutionality of the law have been raised. Shortly after the effective date, a Los Angeles federal judge issued a temporary restraining order to prohibit the Post Office from enforcing the new regulations. It appears certain the Supreme Court will be handed yet another postal obscenity question.

The 1970 law allows a citizen who does not wish to receive "sexually oriented" material to place his name on a list maintained by the Post Office. Publishers and mailers of "sexually oriented" material must purchase these lists and subsequent monthly supplements. Mailings of "sexually oriented" matter to those on the lists would carry a heavy penalty for the mailer.

One of the constitutional problems, of course, is in trying to determine what type of material is legally "sexually oriented." See Ginzburg. Another is the supposed "chilling effect" such lists have on those in government or other sensitive jobs. See Lamont. Differences should be noted between this law and the 1967 law upheld by the Court in Rowan. The more recent law restrains the mailer prior to any distribution and calls upon him to make legal, definitive judgments in classifying his material. The 1967 law, on the other hand, requires the recipient to make the judgment as to what is offensive to him personally after he has had an opportunity to inspect the material sent to him from a publishing house. The Court, almost certainly, will have to decide whether these differences, and others, place significant restraints on constitutionally protected expression.

CHAPTER 4

CONTROL OF
BROADCASTING

The unique nature of broadcasting brings with it problems which do not concern the print media. First is the newness of the industry and its lack of legal precedent. Second, there are rapidly changing developments which alter the very core of electronic journalism, e.g. cable television (or CATV) and FM radio. Third, there is limited access to the broadcasting band, thereby requiring control of available airwaves. Fourth, there are interstate and international problems resulting from the fact that broadcast signals cannot be controlled at state or national borders. Finally, there is the over-riding philosophy in this country that the airwaves belong to the people and that commercial broadcasters are to use these "public properties" only in the public interest.

Early experiments in broadcasting began prior to World War I and increased rapidly following the Armistice. This growth was uncontrolled and led to broadcasting chaos involving overlapping signals and battles over location on the radio dial. The emerging industry soon asked for Federal assistance in establishing ground rules for broadcasters. The result was the Radio Act of 1927 in which the Congress authorized a five-man commission to regulate forms of radio communication. It was established under this Act that the airwaves were to remain public in nature and that licenses would be granted to private parties to broadcast in the "public interest, convenience, or necessity." These licenses would be renewable every three years. This commission in 1934 was expanded to seven members, given added responsibility and renamed the Federal Communications Commission.

The entry of television in the 1920s signalled new problems for the Commission. World War II held up development of commercial television, but the growth of the television industry in the last quarter century

probably has been greater than any in the history of industrial development. Though the FCC took steps to encourage independent stations and
to control networks, the networks became paramount, just as they did in
the development of radio. Coaxial cable and microwave relay resulted in
coast-to-coast broadcasting by 1951.

A decade before Chief Justice Warren donned his robes, the Supreme
Court received its first major broadcasting case. National Broadcasting Co.
v. United States, 319 U.S. 190 (1943). In its decision, the Court held that
denial of a broadcasting license by the FCC did not violate First Amendment guarantees of free speech.

NATIONAL BROADCASTING CO. V. UNITED STATES
319 U.S. 190 (1943)

MR. JUSTICE FRANKFURTER *delivered the opinion of the Court.*

. . . We come . . . to an appeal to the First Amendment. The Regulations, even if valid in all other respects, must fall because they abridge,
say the appellants, their right of free speech. If that be so, it would follow
that every person whose application for a license to operate a station is
denied by the Commission is thereby denied his constitutional right of
free speech. Freedom of utterance is abridged to many who wish to use
the limited facilities of radio. Unlike other modes of expression, radio inherently is not available to all. That is its unique characteristic, and that
is why, unlike other modes of expression, it is subject to governmental regulation. Because it cannot be used by all, some who wish to use it must
be denied. But Congress did not authorize the Commission to choose
among applicants upon the basis of their political, economic or social
views, or upon any other capricious basis. If it did, or if the Commission
by these Regulations proposed a choice among applicants upon some such
basis, the issue before us would be wholly different. The question here is
simply whether the Commission, by announcing that it will refuse licenses
to persons who engage in specified network practices (a basis for choice
which we hold is comprehended within the statutory criterion of "public
interest"), is thereby denying such persons the constitutional right of free
speech. The right of free speech does not include, however, the right to
use facilities of radio without a license. The licensing system established
by Congress in the Communications Act of 1934 was a proper exercise of
its power over commerce. The standard it provided for the licensing of
stations was the "public interest, convenience, or necessity." Denial of a
station license on that ground, if valid under the Act, is not a denial of
free speech. . . .

During the 16-year period of the Warren Court, legal questions regarding broadcasting began to increase just as they did in other types of public expression. With Chief Justice Warren writing the majority opinion, the Court in 1954 held that the popular "give away" programs did not constitute a lottery. Federal Communications Commission v. American Broadcasting Co. Eleven years later, the Chief Justice again spoke for the Court, which ruled in a much publicized case that television commercial tests generally must show what they purport to show. Federal Trade Commission v. Colgate-Palmolive Co.

As the Warren Court entered its final years, the broadcasting industry came under increasing pressure from the FCC, the Federal Trade Commission and the Congress. Proposals to place greater restrictions on broadcasters were introduced from various elements of public life. Among these proposals, aimed primarily at television, were those to restrict news reporting and programming, to investigate ownership practices and license renewal policies, to study the effects of televised violence, to ban cigarette advertising, to institute penalties for false and misleading advertising, and to consider the licensing of networks. Clearly, influential segments of society felt that television self-regulation was weak and largely ineffectual.

At the same time, the FCC signaled the possibility of a new era of activism in the public interest. The Commission required anti-smoking messages and later called for an outright ban on cigarette commercials on television. It also authorized a nation-wide system of pay (or subscription) television, launched a broad study of media ownership patterns, toughened fairness doctrine policies, limited network control of prime-time programming, and revoked the license of a major broadcaster (WHDH, Boston).

The Commission itself did not escape criticism during this turbulent period. It was chastised in 1969 for its renewal of the license to station WLBT, Jackson, Miss., a station accused of racial prejudice in its broadcasting policies. The question of the renewal was taken to court and, in a significant decision, the U.S. Court of Appeals vacated the license, implying broadly expanded powers in the public's attempts to challenge licensing decisions. The judge who wrote the unanimous three-man Appellate Court opinion was, significantly, to be Chief Justice Warren's successor, Chief Justice Warren Burger.

The Court of Appeals had ruled in 1966 that interested citizens must be given the right to participate in FCC hearings involving license renewal. The 1969 decision ruled that the FCC had conducted the hearing with prejudice and impropriety. The opinion also said the FCC erred by placing the burden of proof for license revocation on the challengers, whereas, the opinion said, it should be for the licensee to establish that renewal would be in the best public interest. A similar decision was reached by the U.S. Court of Appeals in 1971, overturning a 1970 FCC policy which favored the broadcaster over the challenger for the license.

It will be difficult in the 1970s for the courts and the FCC to ignore the directive of the Court of Appeals, especially in light of the subsequent ascendancy of the author of the earlier opinions to the highest legal chair in the United States. Also the Supreme Court in the final two years under Chief Justice Warren handed down three major decisions. The Court ruled that cable television (or CATV) falls under the jurisdiction of the FCC. United States v. Southwestern Cable Co. It held that CATV is not subject to copyright restrictions. Fortnightly Corp. v. United Artists Television, Inc. And it held without dissent that the fairness doctrine requirements are not a violation of the free speech of the broadcaster and, in addition, are in keeping with the proper role of the FCC as established by the Congress. Red Lion Broadcasting Co. v. Federal Communications Commission. Future such questions are waiting in the wings for the opening of the Burger era.

The popular "give away" radio and television programs of the 1950s came under Supreme Court scrutiny on appeal from the Federal Communications Commission. The question was whether these programs constituted a lottery and whether the FCC could deny a license to a station which participated in their broadcast. All agreed that the three necessary elements of a lottery were consideration, prize and chance. The Court, noting that contestants merely answered the phone and were not required to pay admission prices nor to make purchases, held that these programs were not lotteries and affirmed lower court decisions favoring the networks. The Court in the same decision ruled on similar cases involving the National Broadcasting Company and the Columbia Broadcasting System.

FEDERAL COMMUNICATIONS COMMISSION
V. AMERICAN BROADCASTING CO.
347 U.S. 284 (1954)

MR. CHIEF JUSTICE WARREN *delivered the opinion of the Court.*

These cases are before us on direct appeal from the decision of a three-judge District Court in the Southern District of New York, enjoining the Federal Communications Commission from enforcing certain provisions in its rules relating to the broadcasting of so-called "give-away" programs. The question presented is whether the enjoined provisions correctly interpret sec. 1304 of the United States Criminal Code, formerly sec. 316 of the Communications Act of 1934. This statute prohibits the broadcasting of ". . . any lottery, gift enterprise, or similar scheme, offering prizes dependent in whole or in part upon lot or chance. . . ."

All the parties agree that there are three essential elements of a "lottery, gift enterprise, or similar scheme": (1) the distribution of prizes; (2) according to chance; (3) for a consideration. They also agree that prizes on the programs under review are distributed according to chance, but they fall out on the question of whether the home contestant furnishes the necessary consideration. . . .

And so it is here. We find no decisions precisely in point on the facts of the cases before us. The courts have defined consideration in various ways, but so far as we are aware none has ever held that a contestant's listening at home to a radio or television program satisfies the consideration requirement. Some courts—with vigorous protest from others—have held that the requirement is satisfied by a "raffle" scheme giving free chances to persons who go to a store to register in order to participate in the drawing of a prize, and similarly by a "bank night" scheme giving free chances to persons who gather in front of a motion picture theater in order to participate in a drawing held for the primary benefit of the paid patrons of the theater. But such cases differ substantially from the cases before us. To be eligible for a prize on the "give-away" programs involved here, not a single home contestant is required to purchase anything or pay an admission price or leave his home to visit the promoter's place of business; the only effort required for participation is listening.

We believe that it would be stretching the statute to the breaking point to give it an interpretation that would make such programs a crime. . . .

It is apparent that these so-called "give-away" programs have long been a matter of concern to the Federal Communications Commission; that it believes these programs to be the old lottery evil under a new guise, and that they should be struck down as illegal devices appealing to cupidity and the gambling spirit. It unsuccessfully sought to have the Department of Justice take criminal action against them. Likewise, without success, it urged Congress to amend the law to specifically prohibit them. The Commission now seeks to accomplish the same result through agency regulations. In doing so, the Commission has overstepped the boundaries of interpretation and hence has exceeded its rule-making power. Regardless of the doubts held by the Commission and others as to the social value of the programs here under consideration, such administrative expansion of sec. 1304 does not provide the remedy. . . .

*   *   *

Tests, experiments and demonstrations used in television commercials, the Supreme Court said in 1965, must show what they purport to show. The Federal Trade Commission had charged the Colgate-Palmolive Co. and the Ted Bates Advertising agency with deception in the widely used "sandpaper shaving test" commercials. The Court upheld the FTC in a 7-2 decision, but authorized normal props where there were no tests, ex-

periments or demonstrations offering proof of product claims. In addition, the Court urged wide discretionary authority for the FTC in dealing with questions of product advertising.

FEDERAL TRADE COMMISSION V. COLGATE-PALMOLIVE CO.
380 U.S. 374 (1965)

MR. CHIEF JUSTICE WARREN *delivered the opinion of the Court.*

The basic question before us is whether it is a deceptive trade practice, prohibited by sec. 5 of the Federal Trade Commission Act, to represent falsely that a televised test, experiment, or demonstration provides a viewer with visual proof of a product claim, regardless of whether the product claim is itself true.

The case arises out of an attempt by respondent Colgate-Palmolive Company to prove to the television public that its shaving cream, "Rapid Shave," outshaves them all. Respondent Ted Bates & Company, Inc., an advertising agency, prepared for Colgate three one-minute commercials designed to show that Rapid Shave could soften even the toughness of sandpaper. Each of the commercials contained the same "sandpaper test." The announcer informed the audience that, "To prove Rapid Shave's super-moisturizing power, we put it right from the can onto this tough, dry sandpaper. It was apply . . . soak . . . and off in a stroke." While the announcer was speaking, Rapid Shave was applied to a substance that appeared to be sandpaper, and immediately thereafter a razor was shown shaving the substance clean. . . .

In reviewing the substantive issues in the case, it is well to remember the respective roles of the Commission and the courts in the administration of the Federal Trade Commission Act. When the Commission was created by Congress in 1914, it was directed by sec. 5 to prevent "[u]nfair methods of competition in commerce." Congress amended the Act in 1938 to extend the Commission's jurisdiction to include "unfair or deceptive acts or practices in commerce"—a significant amendment showing Congress' concern for consumers as well as for competitors. . . .

This statutory scheme necessarily gives the Commission an influential role in interpreting sec. 5 and in applying it to the facts of particular cases arising out of unprecedented situations. Moreover, as an administrative agency which deals continually with cases in the area, the Commission is often in a better position than are courts to determine when a practice is "deceptive" within the meaning of the Act. This Court has frequently stated that the Commission's judgment is to be given great weight by reviewing courts. This admonition is especially true with respect to allegedly deceptive advertising since the finding of a sec. 5 violation in this field rests so heavily on inference and pragmatic judgment. . . .

It has also been held a violation of sec. 5 for a seller to misrepresent to the public that he is in a certain line of business, even though the misstatement in no way affects the qualities of the product.

. . . And it has also been held that it is a deceptive practice to misappropriate the trade name of another.

Respondents claim that all these cases are irrelevant to our decision because they involve misrepresentations related to the product itself and not merely to the manner in which an advertising message is communicated. This distinction misses the mark for two reasons. In the first place, the present case is not concerned with a mode of communication, but with a misrepresentation that viewers have objective proof of a seller's product claim over and above the seller's word. Secondly, all of the above cases, like the present case, deal with methods designed to get a consumer to purchase a product, not with whether the product, when purchased, will perform up to expectations. . . .

We agree with the Commission . . . that the undisclosed use of plexiglass in the present commercials was a material deceptive practice, independent and separate from the other misrepresentation found. We find unpersuasive respondents' other objections to this conclusion. Respondents claim that it will be impractical to inform the viewing public that it is not seeing an actual test, experiment or demonstration, but we think it inconceivable that the ingenious advertising world will be unable, if it so desires, to conform to the Commission's insistence that the public be not misinformed. If, however, it becomes impossible or impractical to show simulated demonstrations on television in a truthful manner, this indicates that television is not a medium that lends itself to this type of commercial, not that the commercial must survive at all costs. Similarly unpersuasive is respondents' objection that the Commission's decision discriminates against sellers whose product claims cannot be "verified" on television without the use of simulations. All methods of advertising do not equally favor every seller. If the inherent limitations of a method do not permit its use in the way a seller desires, the seller cannot by material misrepresentation compensate for those limitations. . . .

The Court of Appeals has criticized the reference in the Commission's order to "test, experiment or demonstration" as not capable of practical interpretation. It could find no difference between the Rapid Shave commercial and a commercial which extolled the goodness of ice cream while giving viewers a picture of a scoop of mashed potatoes appearing to be ice cream. We do not understand this difficulty. In the ice cream case the mashed potato prop is not being used for additional proof of the product claim, while the purpose of the Rapid Shave commercial is to give the viewer objective proof of the claims made. If in the ice cream hypothetical the focus of the commercial becomes the undisclosed potato prop and the viewer is invited, explicitly or by implication, to see for himself the truth of the claims about the ice cream's rich texture and full color, and perhaps compare it to a "rival product," then the commercial has become similar to the one now before us. Clearly, however, a commercial which depicts happy actors delightedly eating ice cream that is in fact mashed potatoes or drinking a product appearing to be coffee but which is in fact some other substance is not covered by the present order.

The crucial terms of the present order—"test, experiment or demonstration . . . represented . . . as actual proof of a claim"—are as specific as the circumstances will permit. . . .

MR. JUSTICE HARLAN, *whom Mr. Justice Stewart joins, dissenting in part.*

. . . I do not see how such a commercial can be said to be "deceptive" in any legally acceptable use of that term. The Court attempts to distinguish the case where a "celebrity" has written a testimonial endorsing some product, but the original testimonial cannot be seen over television and a copy is shown over the air by the manufacturer. The Court states of this "hypothetical": "In respondents' hypothetical the objective proof of the product claim that is offered, the word of the celebrity or agency that the experiment was actually conducted, does exist; while in the case before us the objective proof offered, the viewer's own perception of an actual experiment, does not exist." *Ante,* at 917. But in both cases the viewer is told to "see for himself," in the one case that the celebrity has endorsed the product; in the other, that the product can shave sandpaper; in neither case is the viewer actually seeing the proof; and in both cases the objective proof does exist, be it the original testimonial or the sandpaper test actually conducted by the manufacturer. In neither case, however, is there a material misrepresentation, because what the viewer sees is an accurate image of the objective proof. . . .

*   *   *

The 16 years of the Warren Court saw the growth of a new concept of mass communications—cable television, or community antenna television (CATV). The future of CATV is not limited to normal television entertainment as we now know it. Predictions of its use as a totally new concept in electronic journalism have been generally accepted as inevitable. The prime advantages of CATV are the excellent quality of the picture attainable and the ability of the community antenna to pull in distant stations not normally available by the conventional rooftop antenna. Cable transmission is not bothered by normal interference, by tall obstructions such as buildings and mountains, nor by extreme weather conditions. By a 7-0 vote, the Supreme Court in 1968 placed jurisdiction of cable systems clearly in the hands of the FCC. Justice Harlan in his opinion noted that the Congress had given the FCC broad authority over broadcasting and that CATV systems should not expect to be immune.

UNITED STATES V. SOUTHWESTERN CABLE CO.

MIDWEST TELEVISION, INC. V. SOUTHWESTERN CABLE CO.
392 U.S. 157 (1968)

MR. JUSTICE HARLAN *delivered the opinion of the Court.*

. . . CATV systems receive the signals of television broadcasting stations, amplify them, transmit them by cable or microwave, and ultimately distribute them by wire to the receivers of their subscribers. CATV systems characteristically do not produce their own programming, and do not recompense producers or broadcasters for use of the programming which they receive and redistribute. Unlike ordinary broadcasting stations, CATV systems commonly charge their subscribers installation and other fees.

The CATV industry has grown rapidly since the establishment of the first commercial system in 1950. In the late 1950s, some 50 new systems were established each year; by 1959, there were 550 "nationally known and identified" systems serving a total audience of 1,500,000 to 2,000,000 persons. It has been more recently estimated that "new systems are being founded at a rate of more than one per day, and . . . subscribers signed on at the rate of 15,000 per month." By late 1965, it was reported that there were 1,847 operating CATV systems, that 758 others were franchised but not yet in operation, and that there were 938 applications for additional franchises. The statistical evidence is incomplete, but, as the [Federal Communications] Commission has observed, "whatever the estimate, CATV growth is clearly explosive in nature."

CATV systems perform either or both of two functions. First, they may supplement broadcasting by facilitating satisfactory reception of local stations in adjacent areas in which such reception would not otherwise be possible; and second, they may transmit to subscribers the signals of distant stations entirely beyond the range of local antennae. As the number and size of CATV systems have increased, their principal function has more ferquently become the importation of distant signals. In 1959, only 50 systems employed microwave relays, and the maximum distance over which signals were transmitted was 300 miles; by 1964, 250 systems used microwave, and the transmission distances sometimes exceeded 665 miles. . . . CATV systems, formerly no more than local auxiliaries to broadcasting, promise for the future to provide a national communications system, in which signals from selected broadcasting centers would be transmitted to metropolitan areas throughout the country.

. . . [T]he Commission has reasonably concluded that regulatory authority over CATV is imperative if it is to perform with appropriate effectiveness certain of its other responsibilities. Congress has imposed upon the

Commission the "obligation of providing a widely dispersed radio and television service," with a "fair, efficient, and equitable distribution" of service
among the "several States and Communities." The Commission has, for
this and other purposes, been granted authority to allocate broadcasting
zones or areas, and to provide regulations "as it may deem necessary" to
prevent interference among the various stations. The Commission has concluded, and Congress has agreed, that these obligations require for their
satisfaction the creation of a system of local broadcasting stations, such
that "all communities of appreciable size [will] have at least one television
station as an outlet for local self-expression." . . .

The Commission has reasonably found that the achievement of each
of these purposes is "placed in jeopardy by the unregulated explosive
growth of CATV." . . . Although CATV may in some circumstances
make possible "the realization of some of the [Commission's] most important goals," its importation of distant signals into the service areas of
local stations may also "destroy or seriously degrade the service offered by
a television broadcaster," and thus ultimately deprive the public of the
various benefits of a system of local broadcasting stations. In particular,
the Commission feared that CATV might, by dividing the available audiences and revenues, significantly magnify the characteristically serious financial difficulties of UHF and educational television broadcasters. The
Commission acknowledged that it could not predict with certainty the
consequences of unregulated CATV, but reasoned that its statutory responsibilities demand that it "plan in advance of foreseeable events, instead of waiting to react to them." We are aware that these consequences
have been variously estimated, but must conclude that there is substantial evidence that the Commission cannot "discharge its overall responsibilities without authority over this important aspect of television service." . . .

The Commission has been charged with broad responsibilities for the
orderly development of an appropriate system of local television broadcasting. The significance of its efforts can scarcely be exaggerated, for broadcasting is demonstrably a principal source of information and entertainment for a great part of the Nation's population. The Commission has
reasonably found that the successful performance of these duties demands
prompt and efficacious regulation of community antenna television systems. . . . [W]e therefore hold that the Commission's authority over "all
interstate . . . communication by wire or radio" permits the regulation of
CATV systems. . . .

*   *   *

*The second cable television ruling in two weeks came with a 5-1 deci-
sion that CATV systems may pick up distant broadcasts and deliver them*

by cable to their subscribers without violating the copyright of the original "performer." If the Southwestern Cable decision decided earlier was considered a setback for CATV, the Fortnightly decision was an unexpected—if only temporary—windfall. The immediate result was to allow CATV systems to offer their subscribers stations they could not normally receive. Justice Stewart in his majority opinion said that CATV did not "perform," but merely improved the viewer's "capacity to receive." The long-term effect might well be for the traditional broadcaster to get further into CATV and for the Congress to act on antiquated copyright statutes passed in 1909. The Congress had had before it various proposals to update the statutes, but several difficult questions, such as a definition of "fair use" of protected material, had prevented passage. Justice Fortas dissenting in Fortnightly chastised his colleagues for not allowing Congress to act first and for reversing, in his judgment, previous concepts dealing with copyright and "performance."

FORTNIGHTLY CORP. V. UNITED ARTISTS TELEVISION, INC.
392 U.S. 390 (1968)

MR. JUSTICE STEWART delivered the opinion of the Court.

The petitioner, Fortnightly Corporation, owns and operates community antenna television (CATV) systems in Clarksburg and Fairmont, West Virginia. There were no local television broadcasting stations in that immediate area until 1957. Now there are two, but, because of hilly terrain, most residents of the area cannot receive the broadcasts of any additional stations by ordinary rooftop antennas. Some of the residents have joined in erecting larger cooperative antennas in order to receive more distant stations, but a majority of the householders in both communities have solved the problem by becoming customers of the petitioner's CATV service.

The petitioner's systems consist of antennas located on hills above each city, with connecting coaxial cables, strung on utility poles, to carry the signals received by the antennas to the home television sets of individual subscribers. The systems contain equipment to amplify and modulate the signals received, and to convert them to different frequencies, in order to transmit the signals efficiently while maintaining and improving their strength.

During 1960, when this proceeding began, the petitioner's systems provided customers with signals of five television broadcasting stations, three located in Pittsburgh, Pennsylvania, one in Steubenville, Ohio, and one in Wheeling, West Virginia. The distance between those cities and Clarksburg and Fairmont ranges from 52 to 82 miles. The systems carried all the programming of each of the five stations, and a customer could choose any of the five programs he wished to view by simply turning the knob on his own television set. The petitioner neither edited the programs received nor originated any programs of its own. The petitioner's customers were charged a flat monthly rate regardless of the amount of time that their television sets were in use.

The respondent, United Artists Television, Inc., holds copyrights on several motion pictures. During the period in suit, the respondent (or its predecessor) granted various licenses to each of the five television stations in question to broadcast certain of these copyrighted motion pictures. Broadcasts made under these licenses were received by the petitioner's Clarksburg and Fairmont CATV systems and carried to its customers. At no time did the petitioner (or its predecessors) obtain a license under the copyrights from the respondent or from any of the five television stations. The licenses granted by the respondent to the five stations did not authorize carriage of the broadcasts by CATV systems, and in several instances the licenses specifically prohibited such carriage.

The respondent sued the petitioner for copyright infringement in a federal court, asking damages and injunctive relief. . . .

At the outset it is clear that the petitioner's systems did not "perform" the respondent's copyrighted works in any conventional sense of that term, or in any manner envisaged by the Congress that enacted the law in 1909. But our inquiry cannot be limited to ordinary meaning and legislative history, for this is a statute that was drafted long before the development of the electronic phenomena with which we deal here. In 1909 radio itself was in its infancy, and television had not been invented. We must read the statutory language of 60 years ago in the light of drastic technological change. . . .

The television broadcaster in one sense does less than the exhibitor of a motion picture or stage play; he supplies his audience not with visible images but only with electronic signals. The viewer conversely does more than a member of a theater audience; he provides the equipment to convert electronic signals into audible sounds and visible images. Despite these deviations from the conventional situation contemplated by the framers of the Copyright Act, broadcasters have been judicially treated as exhibitors, and viewers as members of a theater audience. Broadcasters perform. Viewers do not perform. Thus, while both broadcaster and viewer play crucial roles in the total television process, a line is drawn between them. One is treated as active performer; the other, as passive beneficiary.

When CATV is considered in this framework, we conclude that it falls on the viewer's side of the line. Essentially, a CATV system no more than enhances the viewer's capacity to receive the broadcaster's signals; it provides a well-located antenna with an efficient connection to the viewer's television set. It is true that a CATV system plays an "active" role in making reception possible in a given area, but so do ordinary television sets and antennas. CATV equipment is powerful and sophisticated, but the basic function the equipment serves is little different from that served by the equipment generally furnished by a television viewer. If an individual erected an antenna on a hill, strung a cable to his house, and installed the necessary amplifying equipment, he would not be "performing" the programs he received on his television set. The result would be no different if several people combined to erect a cooperative antenna for the same purpose. The only difference in the case of CATV is that the antenna system is erected and owned not by its users, but by an entrepreneur. . . .

MR. JUSTICE FORTAS, *dissenting.*

This case calls not for the judgment of Solomon but for the dexterity of Houdini. We are here asked to consider whether and how a technical, complex, and specific Act of Congress, the Copyright Law, which was drafted in 1909, applies to one of the recent products of scientific and promotional genius, CATV. The operations of CATV systems are based upon the use of other people's property. The issue here is whether, for this use, the owner of copyrighted material should be compensated.

. . . Our major object, I suggest, should be to do as little damage as possible to traditional copyright principles and to business relationships, until the Congress legislates and relieves the embarrassment which we and the interested parties face. . . .

*   *   *

Two significant principles regarding First Amendment freedoms and the broadcaster were announced by the Supreme Court in the Red Lion *decision of June 9, 1969, the last media decision to be handed down by the Warren Court. First, the Court held that the unique nature of broadcasting requires standards of First Amendment interpretation different from those applied to the print media. This, in effect, extended to broadcasting the Court's 1961* Times Film *principle, which applied separate standards of freedom of expression to motion pictures. The Radio Television News Directors Association and many individual broadcasters had argued for several years that free speech standards be applied uniformly to all media, electronic and print. The Court rejected that appeal. Second, and reflecting the principle mentioned above, the Court ruled that enforcement of the FCC's fairness doctrine does not violate First Amendment guarantees of the broadcaster. The thrust of the First Amendment, the Court said, is aimed at protecting the listening and viewing citizen rather than the licensed broadcaster. The fairness doctrine requires that when a person is attacked on radio or television he must be given an op-*

portunity to reply. The decision was 7-0. Justice Douglas did not take part because of absence during oral arguments, and Justice Fortas's resignation earlier that spring left the Court with one vacant seat at the time of the decision. Two years later, in June of 1971, the FCC announced its intention to review the fairness doctrine and asked interested persons to submit statements. The Commission said its goal was not to eliminate the fairness doctrine, but to see that it is producing the intended results.

RED LION BROADCASTING CO. V.
FEDERAL COMMUNICATIONS COMMISSION

UNITED STATES V.
RADIO TELEVISION NEWS DIRECTORS ASSN.
395 U.S. 367 (1969)

MR. JUSTICE WHITE *delivered the opinion of the Court.*

. . . *Red Lion* involves the application of the fairness doctrine to a particular broadcast, and *RTNDA* arises as an action to review the FCC's 1967 promulgation of the personal attack and political editorializing regulations, which were laid down after the *Red Lion* litigation had begun.
. . . The Red Lion Broadcasting Company is licensed to operate a Pennsylvania radio station, WGCB. On November 27, 1964, WGCB carried a 15-minute broadcast by Reverend Billy James Hargis as part of a "Christian Crusade" series. A book by Fred J. Cook entitled *Goldwater— Extremist on the Right* was discussed by Hargis, who said that Cook had been fired by a newspaper for fabricating false charges against city officials; that Cook had then worked for a Communist-affiliated publication; that he had defended Alger Hiss and attacked J. Edgar Hoover and the Central Intelligence Agency; and that he had now written a "book to smear and destroy Barry Goldwater." When Cook heard of the broadcast he concluded that he had been personally attacked and demanded free reply time, which the station refused. After an exchange of letters among Cook, Red Lion, and the FCC, the FCC declared that the Hargis broadcast constituted a personal attack on Cook; that Red Lion had failed to meet its obligation under the fairness doctrine. . . .
The [RTNDA] broadcasters challenge the fairness doctrine and its specific manifestations in the personal attack and political editorial rules on conventional First Amendment grounds, alleging that the rules abridge their freedom of speech and press. Their contention is that the First Amendment protects their desire to use their allotted frequencies continuously to broadcast whatever they choose, and to exclude whomever

they choose from ever using that frequency. No man may be prevented from saying or publishing what he thinks, or from refusing in his speech or other utterances to give equal weight to the views of his opponents. This right, they say, applies equally to broadcasters.

Although broadcasting is clearly a medium affected by a First Amendment interest, *United States v. Paramount Pictures, Inc.*, differences in the characteristics of new media justify differences in the First Amendment standards applied to them. *Joseph Burstyn, Inc. v. Wilson.* For example, the ability of new technology to produce sounds more raucous than those of the human voice justifies restrictions on the sound level, and on the hours and places of use, of sound trucks so long as the restrictions are reasonable and applied without discrimination. *Kovacs v. Cooper.*

Just as the Government may limit the use of sound amplifying equipment potentially so noisy that it drowns out civilized private speech, so may the Government limit the use of broadcast equipment. The right of free speech of a broadcaster, the user of a sound truck, or any other individual does not embrace a right to snuff out the free speech of others. *Associated Press v. United States.*

. . . Because of the scarcity of radio frequencies, the Government is permitted to put restraints on licensees in favor of others whose views should be expressed on this unique medium. But the people as a whole retain their interest in free speech by radio and their collective right to have the medium function consistently with the ends and purposes of the First Amendment. It is the right of the viewers and listeners, not the right of the broadcasters, which is paramount. It is the purpose of the First Amendment to preserve an uninhibited marketplace of ideas in which truth will ultimately prevail, rather than to countenance monopolization of that market, whether it be by the Government itself or a private licensee. . . . It is the right of the public to receive suitable access to social, political, esthetic, moral, and other ideas and experiences which is crucial here. . . .

In terms of constitutional principle, and as enforced sharing of a scarce resource, the personal attack and political editorial rules are indistinguishable from the equal-time provision of sec. 315, a specific enactment of Congress requiring stations to set aside reply time under specified circumstances and to which the fairness doctrine and these constituent regulations are important complements. That provision, which has been part of the law since 1927, Radio Act of 1927, has been held valid by this Court as an obligation of the licensee relieving him of any power in any way to prevent or censor the broadcast, and thus insulating him from liability for defamation. The constitutionality of the statute under the First Amendment was unquestioned.

Nor can we say that it is inconsistent with the First Amendment goal of producing an informed public capable of conducting its own affairs to require a broadcaster to permit answers to personal attacks occurring in the course of discussing controversial issues, or to require that the political opponents of those endorsed by the station be given a chance to communicate with the public. Otherwise, station owners and a few networks would have unfettered power to make time available only to the highest bidders, to communicate only their own views on public issues, people and candidates, and to permit on the air only those with whom they agreed. There is no sanctuary in the First Amendment for unlimited private censorship operating in a medium not open to all. . . .

In view of the prevalence of scarcity of broadcast frequencies, the Government's role in allocating those frequencies, and the legitimate claims of those unable without governmental assistance to gain access to those frequencies for expression of their views, we hold the regulations and ruling at issue here are both authorized by statute and constitutional. The judgment of the Court of Appeals in *Red Lion* is affirmed and that in *RTNDA* reversed and the causes remanded for proceedings consistent with this opinion.

ACCESS—THE ONLY CHOICE FOR THE MEDIA?

By Jerome A. Barron *

Red Lion and a Constitutional Right to Access

In the light of this new focus on concentration of power of the media, the Supreme Court's recent opinion in *Red Lion Broadcasting Company v. FCC* should be given particular attention. In my view, the Supreme Court's decision in *Red Lion* has greatly energized the legal stimulus for access to the media. Today the future of an access-oriented approach to the media and the First Amendment is in a more open-ended position than has ever been true in the history of American law. . . .

The prelude to the Supreme Court decision in *Red Lion* was dramatic. CBS and NBC had intervened with *amicus curiae* briefs bearing the names of distinguished lawyers, many of them academics with reputations as civil libertarians. The Supreme Court had never dealt directly with the constitutionality of the fairness doctrine. But broader issues were raised. What was the impact of a new technology on traditional First Amendment theory? Is the First Amendment to be interpreted as just a prohibition on governmental restraints on expression or as a command imposing affirmative obligations to ensure the interchange of opposing viewpoints? If such a command exists, does it apply to the print media as well as to the broadcast media?

Broadcast industry expectations with regard to the Court's ultimate decision in *Red Lion* were ambivalent. On the one hand, the broadcasters and the networks had become accustomed to the fairness doctrine during the past twenty years of its existence. On the other hand, the broadcasting industry wanted to believe its aging rhetoric that the imposition of affirmative obligations on broadcasters with regard to programming was a violation of freedom of speech and press. Rather than protecting the right of listeners or viewers, freedom in broadcasting in this view, was the freedom of the broadcaster. To anyone who knew the realities of broadcasting the rhetoric was fantastic. The vaunted freedom of the licensee consists mainly of his "opportunity" to become a network-affiliate and consign, he hoped, his most lucrative prime-time hours to network-originated programming. Similarly, the vaunted freedom of the press in many American communities

* From Jerome A. Barron. "Access—The Only Choice for the Media?" *Texas Law Review*, Vol. 48 (March 1970), p. 766, at p. 767. Used with permission of the holder of reprint rights, Fred B. Rothman & Co. The author is a professor of law at George Washington University.

permits newspaper chains to operate newspapers in distant cities on a policy of heavy reliance on wire service news and canned editorials and features. Nevertheless, it was, and still is, good box office for publishers to talk as broadcasters still do about freedom of the press. Yet freedom of the press in real terms too often means the property rights of the only newspaper in the community, which more often than not is owned by a newspaper chain.

Freedom of expression should no longer be defined by the legal immunities of publishers or broadcasters. Mr. Justice White in *Red Lion* makes it very clear that the imposition of duties on broadcasters accomplished by the FCC's fairness doctrine and personal attack rules "enhance[s] rather than abridge[s] the freedom of speech and press protected by the First Amendment."

Red Lion launches the Supreme Court on the path of an affirmative approach to freedom of expression that emphasizes the positive dimension of the First Amendment. In fact, the access-for-ideas rationale practically replaces the original legal justification for broadcast regulation—that broadcasting is a limited-access medium. This older view proceeded on the theory that since there were only so many frequencies to go around, some substantive criteria had to be improvised in order to have a rational allocation policy. This philosophy of broadcast regulation had been set down by Mr. Justice Frankfurter in the most important case on broadcasting policy prior to *Red Lion, NBC v. United States,* a case decided more than a quarter of a century ago.

Red Lion reveals an interplay between the older technical limited-access theory, which was justified on the basis of limitations in the spectrum, and the new First Amendment-based theory of access, which attempts to provide mechanisms for the interchange of ideas in the dominant media.

On its respectable or conventional level, the Supreme Court in *Red Lion* relied on the limitation-of-the-spectrum argument for its result. And it is that older face that the Court apparently prefers to put forward. On the other hand, the opinion is studded with observations that give it a radical undertone throughout and that display the constant tension in the opinion, and perhaps in the Court, between a rationale for broadcast regulation based on limitation of the spectrum and one based on maximizing opportunities for expression.

Essentially, the *Red Lion* case appears to challenge the future of the limitation-of-the-spectrum rationale. The broadcasters had argued that the frequencies were no longer limited and that therefore there was no need to insist that those holding views different from licensees should have direct access to broadcast facilities. The Court, of course, denied that the scarcity problem had disappeared. But the Court also stressed the advantage that the prestige or established media have in terms of status within the opinion process. The Court implied that this advantage required some counterbalance in order to equalize the opportunity for opposing viewpoints within the dominant broadcast media.

The Supreme Court noted that a new technology had replaced "atomized, relatively informal communication with mass media as a source of national cohesion." Freedom of expression in the context of the mass media in the third quarter of the twentieth century requires a more polycentric approach to freedom of expression than a theory that exalts the controller of the media and ignores all other participants in the communication process. The Supreme Court has responded to the need for more sensitive and subtle analysis of media problems to stimulate opportunities for intense and representative debate. The *Red Lion* case therefore finds the law of freedom of expression in mid-passage. Old and new theories of broadcast regulation walk into each other in the case.

Mr. Justice White says in *Red Lion* that it is not a first amendment purpose to countenance monopolization of the marketplace of ideas. For this proposition he cites a string of cases, many of them involving print media, particularly newspapers. My point is that *Red Lion* is not just a broadcast case. It is a media case. It represents a look at the first amendment in the light of new social realities of concentration of ownership and control in a few hands that has been produced by the twin developments of media oligopoly and technological change. It is in the background of these realities that the new first amendment right of access spoken of by Mr. Justice White should be understood. There is a remarkable sentence in *Red Lion*. It marks the recognition by the Supreme Court of a new constitutional right: "It is the right of the public to receive suitable access to social, political, esthetic, moral, and other ideas and experiences which is crucial here." . . .

THE PRESS AND THE BROADCAST MEDIA: THE LEGAL CONTRAST

I have pointed to the existence of a dual theme in *Red Lion:* the conventional limitation-of-the-spectrum theme and the theme of access played by the Court in the minor key. Access is a theme destined to gather much greater importance in the years ahead. Moreover, the Court, in an intriguing finale, makes it very clear that it recognizes the possibilities of an access-oriented approach to the press as well. In the American press, the number of dailies has steadily dwindled. Today less than 1,800 daily newspapers are published in this country. The economic cost of establishing a new newspaper is a financial challenge that even the most well-heeled dare not assume. The problem is technological as well. The technology that has bred the broadcast media has revolutionized the print media as well. The price of this new technology has been high.

In *Red Lion,* in a footnote at the very end of the case, the Court makes a comment that asks us to think beyond media problems presented by technological or even economic scarcity. The Court says there is another argument which remains to be considered:

Congress does not abridge freedom of speech or press by legislation directly or indirectly multiplying the voices and views presented
to the public through time sharing, fairness doctrines, or other devices
which limit or dissipate the power of those who sit astride the channels of communication with the general public.

This observation to me appears to constitute awareness by the Supreme Court that freedom of the press is something that can be provided
for by legislation. It is a recognition that the meaning of freedom of the
press is not exhausted by its undoubted and traditional function as the
guarantor against government censorship and restraint. The Court declared that it put this argument aside. But the decision to defer is full of
implication for the press.

Much more familiarity is needed with existing machinery for access in
broadcasting by the public. Much more sympathy is needed for these
mechanisms on the part of the Federal Communications Commission and
the broadcasting industry. But the point is that this machinery exists and
that it has been given a new constitutional benediction by the Supreme
Court. If the law is allowed to take its course, . . . opportunities for diversity of expression in broadcasting should be sharply increased. How
starkly different is the situation in the press. The American press may attack whom they choose no matter how unfairly or how persistently. Unlike broadcasters, newspaper publishers in most American jurisdictions are
totally without any legal obligation to afford opportunity for reply even in
a libel context. In 1964, in *New York Times v. Sullivan* the Supreme Court,
in the interests of "uninhibited, robust, and wide-open" debate, made it
far more difficult for newspapermen to be sued in libel. As a result, the
press are the beneficiaries of a new and wider freedom to libel than they
have ever enjoyed. All this was done in the interests of a debate that no
one bothered to secure.

In broadcasting, both the fairness doctrine and the right of reply to
groups and individuals attacked by the broadcast media have been held
constitutionally authorized. Clearly, as a matter of law, more social responsibility is presently demanded from the broadcast media than is demanded from the press. Since there are *more* broadcast outlets than newspapers, I find it hard to be persuaded by the traditional rationale that radio
and television, unlike the daily press, are limited-access media.

It was the essential philosophy of *New York Times v. Sullivan* that a
free press, engaged in public debate, should not have to live in fear of
prohibitive libel judgments. But what is the purpose of free debate? It is
free so that there shall really be free debate within the nation. If that is
true, then a necessary step to securing debate should have been to require
newspapers to provide the subjects of their attacks with an opportunity for
reply. This would have been a fair price to extract for the new relative

freedom from libel judgments. In many cases the same corporations or families own both television stations and newspapers, yet the responsibilities of these same people in the newspaper field are far less. Does not *Red Lion* present a sharp contrast to *New York Times v. Sullivan?* In reason, does it not seem absurd that both decisions could be correct? One of them, since it fails to provide the vital supplement of right to reply, is in error, and that one is *New York Times v. Sullivan.* . . .

ACCESS: INSTRUMENT OF DIVERSITY

Let me close with a recent example of the possibilities of the idea of access. In the fall of last year, a much celebrated suit, *Smothers Brothers v. Columbia Broadcasting System,* was filed in the United States District Court for the Central District of California. The Smothers Brothers' complaint in this case consists of a number of legal theories upon which the Smothers Brothers might seek legal redress from CBS. One of these theories illustrates the creative possibilities of an access approach to media restraints on freedom of expression. The Smothers Brothers accuse CBS of exercising censorship over what should be their constitutionally protected program scripts. The complaint says that no network justification for censorship over program content was offered by the network except that the Smothers Brothers' programs failed to comply with CBS "program practices."

What is the legal idea revealed in the Smothers Brothers' complaint? Obviously it cannot be that CBS has to contract with any independent producer that would like its material to be televised. But that is not the Smothers Brothers' contention. Rather the contention is that once a contract is entered into, once a producer has selected the network and the network the producer, the producer's program cannot be arbitrarily censored by vague network "program standards." This position confronts us with a powerful idea—an idea that tries to re-establish the autonomy of the various creative units in broadcasting. It attempts to afford some legal leverage against the vast capacity for private censorship that exists in network decisions. Is not the application of access theory here an attempt to effect decentralization and diversity in the transmission of ideas? It is this decentralization that is vital to the well-being and continuing freedom of the opinion-making process.

CONCLUSION: THE PREMISES OF DIALOGUE

Access can be realized under existing broadcasting law if that law is energized and enforced more vigorously than it has been in the past. Access can be realized in the press through legislation and judicial implementation of opportunities for expression and response. Through these means the dominant media may become more representative and responsive to the apparently desperate need in our society for participation in basic institutions such as the media. But these are not the only means of attempting to construct procedures to assure diversity of viewpoint and decentralization in the media. Proposals for local autonomous communications systems in planned communities to be operated by those communities are now being studied in several of the new planned cities that are developing throughout the nation. The use of community antenna television stations for the origination of programming, the rise of public or educational television, and the possibility of pay television are all alternatives to existing concentration in the broadcast media. In the print media, the future appears to contain less in the way of alternatives to the monopoly newspaper situation in American communities; therefore, I think the possibilities of opening up those newspapers through a right of access are especially necessary and urgent.

I have styled existing constitutional theory on the First Amendment as romantic in its assumptions. I have called it romantic because it builds a system of legal rights and duties on the assumption that there is a self-operating and self-correcting mechanism in the communication of ideas that is called somewhat hopefully the "marketplace of ideas." But there is no marketplace of ideas. Milton spoke long ago of letting truth and falsehood grapple. But unlike seventeenth century men we are not sure that we can identify truth although we are more than mindful that we recognize about us an abundance of falsehood. What has happened is that with the media, not only in the Western world but in the Communist world as well, we believe everything and we believe nothing. Operating on two levels, we constantly alternate between a massive credulity and an equally prevalent destructive and cynical skepticism.

A premise we live by, nonetheless, is that on the basis of the maximum available information, the members of a free society make the judgments that direct the path of that society. The suggestions and the approach that I have outlined are prompted out of a desire to provide a forum within the dominant media for the various contesting voices abroad in the land. The whole premise of this effort is predicated on the belief that if access to the media becomes a reality, then those who have been given opportunities to present their views will abide by the verdict of a majority of their countrymen. In honesty it must be conceded that this premise may itself be styled romantic. But with regard to this possibility I cannot improve on the words of Learned Hand uttered now so many years ago:

> However, neither exclusively, nor even primarily are the interests of the newspaper industry conclusive; for that industry serves one of the most vital of all general interests: the dissemination of news from many different sources, with as many different facets and colors as is possible. That interest is closely akin to, if indeed it is not the same

as, the interest protected by the First Amendment; it presupposes that right conclusions are more likely to be gathered out of a multitude of tongues. To many this is and always will be folly: but we have staked upon it our all.

Contemporary social realities call for new legal means to implement these words, but their bite and force is undiminished with the years. Learned Hand's brave optimism that "right conclusions are more likely to be gathered out of a multitude of tongues" is our contemporary challenge. How can we achieve an orderly and meaningful "multitude of tongues" within the media? Herbert Marcuse has written that we should no longer define a free society in terms of traditional economic, political, and intellectual liberties. He says these liberties have become too significant to be capable of continuing expression within traditional forms. He writes that "new modes of realization are needed, corresponding to the new capabilities of society." I am not sure that intellectual and political liberty of discussion is "a new capability of society" or even that it is in any ideal sense a capability. I have no confidence that Marcuse's vision of management of the media by intellectuals in behalf of some conception of the good would put us any farther ahead than we are now. Manipulative capacity is a talent that any power elite stands ready to learn. Operators of the media, whoever they are, will always have to resist the temptation not just to inform or to persuade opinion but to capture it.

But it is true that new forms for dialogue are necessary. What I propose is to implant these forms on an existing structure. I would not substitute government control of the media for their present private ownership. What I suggest is that the media be rendered more hospitable as a routine and legal matter to diversity of viewpoint.

Interchange of ideas will not arise naturally and without new procedures. Economic and technological factors have become such constraints on the life of ideas that the *laissez faire* Millsian approach to freedom of expression that was the natural accompaniment of the liberal free market economics of the nineteenth century is now a hopeless anachronism. But the democratic faith in reason—in judgments made by individual citizen decision-makers on the basis of information and reflection—is still the basic assumption of our institutions. Unless we are ready to discard this faith, we should give considerable attention to the idea of access and to attempts to realize that idea through new legislation and more intensive and sympathetic uses of existing law.

CHAPTER 5

OBSCENITY DEFINED

Man historically has attempted to ban as harmful those viewpoints and expressions he finds uncomfortable. This is best illustrated through the study of obscenity. Although there is no substantial body of evidence to establish a cause-and-effect relationship between exposure to salacious material and anti-social behavior, strong voices in this country have argued for more than a century that obscenity is not protected by constitutional guarantees of free speech and press. The Supreme Court has been among those voices. Conversely, there is some evidence to indicate that salacious material might tend to have the opposite effect, i.e. that it might be beneficial to society as a vicarious outlet or "escape valve." It is safe to say only that the record is not yet clear.

Critics of restrictive anti-obscenity legislation point to three other arguments which they say make such legislation almost impossible to understand or to enforce. First, even our most learned judges, legislators and philosophers cannot reach agreement as to what constitutes obscenity. Second, no other area of constitutional law is so dependent upon the temperament of the presiding judge or jury. And third, the area of obscenity is the most ill-defined body of law in American jurisprudence.

What is clear, however, is that a changing morality spread across the nation in the decades following World War II. This is reflected in advertising, motion pictures, the stage, magazines, books and personal patterns of behavior. Our forefathers were not confronted publicly with the dilemma we face today because of their puritan controls, the difficult agrarian life, lack of mass printing and distribution, low literacy rates and less leisure time, among other reasons. It is generally accepted that reading of salacious literature was accomplished in earlier times, but only by those of means, prominence and education, and without fanfare.

With the rise of the middle class and industrial technology in the mid-nineteenth century, Congress and state legislatures began to deal with censorship of alleged obscenity. The most significant of these was the famous "Comstock Law" of 1873, which meted out censorship with a heavy hand. Anthony Comstock, who had campaigned with the slogan "Books are Feeders for Brothels" (Ernst and Morris, Censorship: The Search for the Obscene, p. 30), directed his campaign at the Congress and the Post Office. Following the passage of strict anti-obscenity measures, Comstock was appointed special agent to the Post Office to assist in uncovering violations. State legislatures followed with similar restrictive laws. Meanwhile, in England, the 1868 "Hicklin rule" was enunciated by Lord Chief Justice Cockburn and was accepted both in England and the United States as the test for obscenity. A work was judged on isolated passages and on its estimated effect on the most susceptible person.

Comstock censorship and the "Hicklin test" stood until 1913, when it was challenged by publisher Mitchell Kennerly. Judge Learned Hand preferred to interpret obscenity as "the present critical point in the compromise between candor and shame at which the community may have arrived here and now." United States v. Kennerly. 209 F. 119.

The watershed case involving censorship was United States v. One Book called "Ulysses." 5 F. Supp. 182 (1933). Customs officials had denied the entry of James Joyce's novel into the United States, but Judge John M. Woolsey in a frequently quoted opinion ruled the book not obscene. He held that the test was to be based on a person with "average sex instincts," rather than the "most susceptible" person of the "Hicklin test." His views were sustained the following year in the Circuit Court of Appeals by jurists Learned and Augustus Hand. 72 F.2d 705 (1934). By the mid-1930s, then, books were judged as a whole, taking into consideration the average reader, the author's intent, and the relevance to the theme of the passages in question.

The first major case involving a question of obscenity to come to the Supreme Court was decided in 1948 (Winters v. New York). A bookseller had been convicted under a section of the New York Penal Law which made it a misdemeanor for anyone to sell or distribute obscene publications. Obscene publications included those "primarily made up of . . . criminal deeds of bloodshed, lust or crime." In holding the New York statute unconstitutional as too vague and indefinite, the 6-3 majority ruled that the first essential of due process is that men of common intelligence should not be required to guess at the meaning and interpretation of a law and that a citizen must be able to ascertain the courses of conduct he may lawfully pursue.

Following this "opening round" of obscenity tests, the Warren Court was drawn into the debate. It handed down 17 major decisions on obscenity and related censorship questions in the 16 years under Chief Justice Warren. The Roth decision of 1957 was the first attempt by the Court to define obscenity. That definition, with refinements covered in the next chapter, lasted through the Warren years.

In the first of two cases preliminary to the landmark Roth decision, the Warren Court emphasized that a statute must be reasonably related to the evil with which it is intended to deal. The Michigan Penal Code made it a misdemeanor to sell literary material which would corrupt the morals of youth or tend to incite them to violent, depraved, or immoral acts. The Court through Justice Frankfurter held unanimously that the statute violated the due process clause of the Fourteenth Amendment because the statute was not reasonably related to the evil with which it sought to deal. Rather it tended to reduce the reading level of the adult population to that of a child.

BUTLER V. MICHIGAN
352 U.S. 380 (1957)

MR. JUSTICE FRANKFURTER *delivered the opinion of the Court.*

This appeal from a judgment of conviction entered by the Recorder's Court of the City of Detroit, Michigan, challenges the constitutionality of the following provision, sec. 343, of the Michigan Penal Code:

> Any person who shall import, print, publish, sell, possess with the intent to sell, design, prepare, loan, give away, distribute or offer for sale, any book, magazine, newspaper, writing, pamphlet, ballad, printed paper, print, picture, drawing, photograph, publication or other thing, including any recordings, containing obscene, immoral, lewd or lascivious language, or obscene, immoral, lewd or lascivious prints, pictures, figures or descriptions, tending to incite minors to violent or depraved or immoral acts, manifestly tending to the corruption of the morals of youth, or shall introduce into any family, school or place of education or shall buy, procure, receive or have in his possession, any such book, pamphlet, magazine, newspaper, writing, ballad, printed paper, print, picture, drawing, photograph, publication or other thing, either for the purpose of sale, exhibition, loan or circulation, or with intent to introduce the same into any family, school or place of education, shall be guilty of a misdemeanor.

Appellant was charged with its violation for selling to a police officer what the trial judge characterized as "a book containing obscene, immoral, lewd, lascivious language, or descriptions, tending to incite minors to violent or depraved or immoral acts, manifestly tending to the corruption of the morals of youth." Appellant moved to dismiss the proceeding on the claim that application of sec. 343 unduly restricted freedom of speech as protected by the Due Process Clause of the Fourteenth Amendment in that the statute (1) prohibited distribution of a book to the general public on the basis of the undesirable influence it may have upon youth; (2) damned a book and proscribed its sale merely because of some isolated passages that appeared objectionable when divorced from the book as a whole; and (3) failed to provide a sufficiently definite standard of guilt. . . . Appellant was fined $100. . . .

It is clear on the record that appellant was convicted because Michigan, by sec. 343, made it an offense for him to make available for the general reading public (and he in fact sold to a police officer) a book that the trial judge found to have a potentially deleterious influence upon youth. The State insists that, by thus quarantining the general reading public against books not too rugged for grown men and women in order to shield juvenile innocence, it is exercising its power to promote the general welfare. Surely, this is to burn the house to roast the pig. Indeed, the Solicitor General of Michigan has, with characteristic candor, advised the Court that Michigan has a statute specifically designed to protect its children against obscene matter "tending to the corruption of the morals of youth." But the appellant was not convicted for violating this statute.

We have before us legislation not reasonably restricted to the evil with which it is said to deal. The incidence of this enactment is to reduce the adult population of Michigan to reading only what is fit for children. It thereby arbitrarily curtails one of those liberties of the individual, now enshrined in the Due Process Clause of the Fourteenth Amendment, that history has attested as the indispensable conditions for the maintenance and progress of a free society. We are constrained to reverse this conviction. . . .

*   *   *

The question of the constitutionality per se of an anti-obscenity law was resolved in 1957 with the Kingsley Books decision. The appellants were convicted under a New York obscenity statute and brought to the Court the question of whether such laws were constitutional at all. Appellants did not appeal the lower court finding that the publications were in fact, obscene, but raised only the question of the constitutionality of the statute. The Court, by a 5-4 margin, upheld the New York law, and, therefore approved the concept of anti-obscenity legislation in cases where these statutes were drawn carefully and with full legal procedural safeguards. Dissenting were Justices Warren, Douglas, Brennan, and Black. The decision was announced on the same day as Roth, but interestingly there was no hint as to the magnitude of the landmark decision which was to follow.

KINGSLEY BOOKS, INC. V. BROWN
354 U.S. 436 (1957)

MR. JUSTICE FRANKFURTER *delivered the opinion of the Court.*

In an unbroken series of cases extending over a long stretch of this Court's history, it has been accepted as a postulate that "the primary requirements of decency may be enforced against obscene publications." *Near v. Minnesota.* And so our starting point is that New York can constitutionally convict appellants of keeping for sale the booklets incontestably found to be obscene. . . .

If New York chooses to subject persons who disseminate obscene "literature" to criminal prosecution and also to deal with such books as deodands of old, or both, with due regard, of course, to appropriate opportunities for the trial of the underlying issue, it is not for us to gainsay its selection of remedies. Just as *Near v. Minnesota,* one of the landmark opinions in shaping the constitutional protection of freedom of speech and of the press, left no doubts that "Liberty of speech, and of the press, is also not an absolute right," it likewise made clear that "the protection even as to previous restraint is not absolutely unlimited." To be sure, the limitation is the exception; it is to be closely confined so as to preclude what may fairly be deemed licensing or censorship. . . .

MR. CHIEF JUSTICE WARREN, *dissenting.*

. . . This is not a criminal obscenity case. Nor is it a case ordering the destruction of materials disseminated by a person who has been convicted of an offense for doing so, as would be authorized under provisions in the laws of New York and other states. It is a case wherein the New York police, under a different state statute, located books which, in their opinion, were unfit for public use because of obscenity and then obtained a court order for their condemnation and destruction.

The majority opinion sanctions this proceeding. I would not. Unlike the criminal cases decided today, this New York law places the book on trial. There is totally lacking any standard in the statute for judging the book in context. The personal element basic to the criminal laws is entirely absent. In my judgment, the same object may have wholly different impact depending upon the setting in which it is placed. Under this statute, the setting is irrelevant.

It is the manner of use that should determine obscenity. It is the conduct of the individual that should be judged, not the quality of art or literature. To do otherwise is to impose a prior restraint and hence to violate the Constitution. Certainly in the absence of a prior judicial determination of illegal use, books, pictures and other objects of expression should not be destroyed. It savors too much of book burning.

I would reverse.

MR. JUSTICE DOUGLAS, *with whom Mr. Justice Black concurs, dissenting.*

. . . This provision is defended on the ground that it is only a little encroachment, that a hearing must be promptly given and a finding of obscenity promptly made. But every publisher knows what awful effect a decree issued in secret can have. We tread here on First Amendment grounds. And nothing is more devastating to the rights that it guarantees than the power to restrain publication before even a hearing is held. This is prior restraint and censorship at its worst.

. . . I think every publication is a separate offense which entitles the accused to a separate trial. Juries or judges may differ in their opinions, community by community, case by case. The publisher is entitled to that leeway under our constitutional system. One is entitled to defend every utterance on its merits and not to suffer today for what he uttered yesterday. Free speech is not to be regulated like diseased cattle and impure butter. The audience (in this case the judge or the jury) that hissed yesterday may applaud today, even for the same performance. . . .

*   *   *

The most important decision to come from the Supreme Court in the area of obscenity sprang from the Roth and Alberts cases, decided upon together. Never before had the Court faced so squarely the problem of trying to define obscenity. The background of the cases is relatively unimportant when weighed against the three important rules of law enunciated by Justice Brennan, speaking for the Court: (1) Obscenity is not protected by the First Amendment thereby eliminating the need to use the "clear and present danger" test; (2) the Court for the first time defined obscene material as matter "which deals with sex in a manner appealing to prurient interest," thereby separating obscenity from sex per se; and (3) the standard for judging obscenity is not by the effect of an isolated passage upon the most susceptible person, but "whether to the average person, applying contemporary community standards, the dominant theme of the material taken as a whole appeals to prurient interest," thereby laying to rest the old "Hicklin rule." The decision, as in Kingsley Books, decided the same day, was 5-4. Several refinements and augmentations were to come within the next decade, but the Court had for the first time faced the issue head-on and had attempted to hammer out a formula upon which to judge obscenity.

ROTH V. UNITED STATES

ALBERTS V. CALIFORNIA
354 U.S. 476 (1957)

MR. JUSTICE BRENNAN *delivered the opinion of the Court.*

The constitutionality of a criminal obscenity statute is the question in each of these cases. In *Roth*, the primary constitutional question is whether the federal obscenity statute violates the provision of the First Amendment that "Congress shall make no law . . . abridging the freedom of speech, or of the press. . . ." In *Alberts*, the primary constitutional question is whether the obscenity provisions of the California Penal Code invade the freedoms of speech and press as they may be incorporated in the liberty protected from state action by the Due Process Clause of the Fourteenth Amendment.

Other constitutional questions are: whether these statutes violate due process, because too vague to support conviction for crime; whether power to punish speech and press offensive to decency and morality is in the States alone, so that the federal obscenity statutes violates the Ninth and Tenth Amendments (raised in *Roth*); and whether Congress, by enacting the federal obscenity statute, under the power . . . to establish post offices and post roads, pre-empted the regulation of the subject matter (raised in *Alberts*).

Roth conducted a business in New York in the publication and sale of books, photographs and magazines. He used circulars and advertising matter to solicit sales. He was convicted by a jury in the District Court for the Southern District of New York upon 4 counts of a 26-count indictment charging him with mailing obscene circulars and advertising, and an obscene book, in violation of the federal obscenity statute. His conviction was affirmed by the Court of Appeals for the Second Circuit. We granted certiorari.

Alberts conducted a mail-order business from Los Angeles. He was convicted by the Judge of the Municipal Court of the Beverly Hills Judicial District (having waived a jury trial) under a misdemeanor complaint which charged him with lewdly keeping for sale obscene and indecent books, and with writing, composing and publishing an obscene advertisement of them, in violation of the California Penal Code. The conviction was affirmed by the Appellate Department of the Superior Court of the State of California in and for the County of Los Angeles. We noted the probable jurisdiction.

The dispositive question is whether obscenity is utterance within the area of protected speech and press. Although this is the first time the question has been squarely presented to this Court, either under the First Amendment or under the Fourteenth Amendment, expressions found in numerous opinions indicate that this Court has always assumed that obscenity is not protected by the freedoms of speech and press. . . .

In light of this history it is apparent that the unconditional phrasing of the First Amendment was not intended to protect every utterance. This phrasing did not prevent this Court from concluding that libelous utterances are not within the area of constitutionally protected speech. *Beauharnais v. Illinois.* At the time of the adoption of the First Amendment, obscenity law was not as fully developed as libel law, but there is sufficiently contemporaneous evidence to show that obscenity, too, was outside the protection intended for speech and press.

The protection given speech and press was fashioned to assure unfettered interchange of ideas for the bringing about of political and social changes desired by the people. . . .

All ideas having even the slightest redeeming social importance—unorthodox ideas, controversial ideas, even ideas hateful to the prevailing climate of opinion—have the full protection of the guaranties, unless excludable because they encroach upon the limited area of more important interests. But implicit in the history of the First Amendment is the rejection of obscenity as utterly without redeeming social importance. This rejection for that reason is mirrored in the universal judgment that obscenity should be restrained, reflected in the international agreement of over 50 nations, in the obscenity laws of all of the 48 States, and in the 20 obscenity laws enacted by the Congress from 1842 to 1956. This is the same judgment expressed by this Court in *Chaplinsky v. New Hampshire:*

> . . . There are certain well-defined and narrowly limited classes of speech, the prevention and punishment of which have never been thought to raise any Constitutional problem. These include the lewd and obscene. . . . It has been well observed that such utterances are no essential part of any exposition of ideas, and are of such slight social value as a step to truth that any benefit that may be derived from them is clearly outweighed by the social interest in order and morality. . . .

We hold that obscenity is not within the area of constitutionally protected speech or press.

It is strenuously urged that these obscenity statutes offend the constitutional guaranties because they punish incitation to impure sexual thoughts, not shown to be related to any overt antisocial conduct which is or may be incited in the persons stimulated to such thoughts. . . . It is insisted that the constitutional guaranties are violated because convictions may be had without proof either that obscene material will perceptibly create a clear and present danger of antisocial conduct, or will probably induce its recipients to such conduct. But, in light of our holding that obscenity is not protected speech, the complete answer to this argument is in the holding of this Court in *Beauharnais v. Illinois:*

> Libelous utterances not being within the area of constitutionally protected speech, it is unnecessary, either for us or for the State courts, to consider the issues behind the phrase 'clear and present danger.' Certainly no one would contend that obscene speech, for example, may be punished only upon a showing of such circumstances. Libel, as we have seen, is in the same class.

However, sex and obscenity are not synonymous. Obscene material is material which deals with sex in a manner appealing to prurient interest. The portrayal of sex, *e.g.*, in art, literature and scientific works, is not itself sufficient reason to deny material the constitutional protection of freedom of speech and press. Sex, a great and mysterious motive force in human life, has indisputably been a subject of absorbing interest to mankind through the ages; it is one of the vital problems of human interest and public concern. As to all such problems, this Court said in *Thornhill v. Alabama:*

> The freedom of speech and of the press guaranteed by the Constitution embraces at the least the liberty to discuss publicly and truthfully all matters of public concern without previous restraint or fear of subsequent punishment. The exigencies of the colonial period and the efforts to secure freedom from oppressive administration developed a broadened conception of these liberties as adequate to supply the public need for information and education with respect to the significant issues of the times. . . . Freedom of discussion, if it would fulfill its historic function in this nation, must embrace all issues about which information is needed or appropriate to enable the members of society to cope with the exigencies of their period.

The fundamental freedoms of speech and press have contributed greatly to the development and well-being of our free society and are indispensable to its continued growth. Ceaseless vigilance is the watchword to prevent their erosion by Congress or by the States. The door barring federal and state intrusion into this area cannot be left ajar; it must be kept tightly closed and opened only the slightest crack necessary to prevent encroachment upon more important interests. It is therefore vital that the standards for judging obscenity safeguard the protection of freedom of speech and press for material which does not treat sex in a manner appealing to prurient interest.

The early leading standard of obscenity allowed material to be judged merely by the effect of an isolated excerpt upon particularly susceptible persons. Some American courts adopted this standard but later decisions have rejected it and substituted this test: whether to the average person, applying contemporary community standards, the dominant theme of the material taken as a whole appeals to prurient interest. The *Hicklin* test, judging obscenity by the effect of isolated passages upon the most susceptible persons, might well encompass material legitimately treating with sex, and so it must be rejected as unconstitutionally restrictive of the freedoms of speech and press. On the other hand, the substituted standard provides safeguards adequate to withstand the charge of constitutional infirmity. . . .

MR. CHIEF JUSTICE WARREN, *concurring in the result.*

I agree with the result reached by the Court in these cases, but, because we are operating in a field of expression and because broad language used here may eventually be applied to the arts and sciences and freedom of communication generally, I would limit our decision to the facts before us and to the validity of the statutes in question as applied. . . .

That there is a social problem presented by obscenity is attested by the expression of the legislatures of the 48 states as well as the Congress. To recognize the existence of a problem, however, does not require that we sustain any and all measures adopted to meet that problem. The history of the application of laws designed to suppress the obscene demonstrates convincingly that the power of government can be invoked under them against great art or literature, scientific treatises, or works exciting social controversy. Mistakes of the past prove that there is a strong countervailing interest to be considered in the freedoms guaranteed by the First and Fourteenth Amendments.

The line dividing the salacious or pornographic from literature or science is not straight and unwavering. Present laws depend largely upon the effect that the materials may have upon those who receive them. It is manifest that the same object may have a different impact, varying according to the part of the community it reached. But there is more to these cases. It is not the book that is on trial; it is a person. The conduct of the defendant is the central issue, not the obscenity of a book or picture. The nature of the materials is, of course, relevant as an attribute of the defendant's conduct, but the materials are thus placed in context from which they draw color and character. A wholly different result might be reached in a different setting.

The personal element in these cases is seen most strongly in the requirement of scienter. Under the California law, the prohibited activity must be done "willfully and lewdly." The federal statute limits the crime to acts done "knowingly." In his charge to the jury, the district judge stated that the matter must be "calculated" to corrupt or debauch. The defendants in both these cases were engaged in the business of purveying textual or graphic matter openly advertised to appeal to erotic interest of their customers. They were plainly engaged in the commercial exploitation of the morbid and shameful craving for materials with prurient effect. I believe that the State and Federal Governments can constitutionally punish such conduct. That is all that these cases present to us, and that is all we need to decide. . . .

MR. JUSTICE HARLAN, *concurring in the result in* [Alberts] *and dissenting in* [Roth].

I regret not to be able to join the Court's opinion. I cannot do so because I find lurking beneath its disarming generalizations a number of problems which not only leave me with serious misgivings as to the future effect of today's decisions, but which also, in my view, call for different results in these two cases.

My basic difficulties with the Court's opinion are threefold. First, the opinion paints with such a broad brush that I fear it may result in a loosening of the tight reins which state and federal courts should hold upon the enforcement of obscenity statutes. Second, the Court fails to discriminate between the different factors which, in my opinion, are involved in the constitutional adjudication of state and federal obscenity cases. Third, relevant distinctions between the two obscenity statutes here involved, and the Court's own definition of "obscenity," are ignored.

In final analysis, the problem presented by these cases is how far, and on what terms, the state and federal governments have power to punish individuals for disseminating books considered to be undesirable because of their nature or supposed deleterious effect upon human conduct. . . . The Court seems to assume that "obscenity" is a peculiar genus of "speech and press," which is as distinct, recognizable, and classifiable as poison ivy is among other plants. On this basis the constitutional question before us simply becomes, as the Court says, whether "obscenity," as an abstraction, is protected by the First and Fourteenth Amendments, and the question whether a particular book may be suppressed becomes a mere matter of classification, of "fact," to be entrusted to a fact-finder and insulated from independent constitutional judgment. But surely the problem cannot be solved in such a generalized fashion. Every communication has an individuality and "value" of its own. The suppression of a particular writing or other tangible form of expression is, therefore, an individual matter, and in the nature of things every such suppression raises an individual constitutional problem, in which a reviewing court must determine for itself whether the attacked expression is suppressible within constitutional standards. Since those standards do not readily lend themselves to generalized definitions, the constitutional problem in the last analysis becomes one of particularized judgments which appellate courts must make for themselves. . . .

. . . Many juries might find that Joyce's *Ulysses* or Boccaccio's *Decameron* was obscene, and yet the conviction of a defendant for selling either book would raise, for me, the gravest constitutional problems, for no such verdict could convince me, without more, that these books are "utterly without redeeming social importance." In short, I do not understand how the Court can resolve the constitutional problems now before it without making its own independent judgment upon the character of the material upon which these convictions were based. I am very much afraid that the broad manner in which the Court has decided these cases will tend to obscure the peculiar responsibilities resting on state and federal courts in this field and encourage them to rely on easy labeling and jury verdicts as a substitute for facing up to the tough individual problems of constitutional judgment involved in every obscenity case. . . .

Quite a different situation is presented . . . where the Federal Government imposes the ban. The danger is perhaps not great if the people of one State, through their legislature, decide that *Lady Chatterley's Lover* goes so far beyond the acceptable standards of candor that it will be deemed offensive and non-sellable, for the State next door is still free to make its own choice. At least we do not have one uniform standard. But the dangers to free thought and expression are truly great if the Federal Government imposes a blanket ban over the Nation on such a book. The prerogative of the States to differ on their ideas of morality will be destroyed, the ability of States to experiment will be stunted. The fact that the people of one State cannot read some of the works of D. H. Lawrence seems to me, if not wise or desirable, at least acceptable. But that no person in the United States should be allowed to do so seems to me to be intolerable, and violative of both the letter and spirit of the First Amendment.

I judge this case, then, in view of what I think is the attenuated federal interest in this field, in view of the very real danger of deadening uniformity which can result from nation-wide federal censorship, and in view of the fact that the constitutionality of this conviction must be weighed against the First and not the Fourteenth Amendment. So viewed, I do not think that this conviction can be upheld. The petitioner was convicted under a statute which, under the judge's charge, makes it criminal to sell books which "tend to stir sexual impulses and lead to sexually impure thoughts." I cannot agree that any book which tends to stir sexual impulses and lead to sexually impure thoughts necessarily is "utterly without redeeming social importance." Not only did this charge fail to measure up to the standards which I understand the Court to approve, but as far as I can see, much of the great literature of the world could lead to conviction under such a view of the statute. Moreover, in no event do I think that the limited federal interest in this area can extend to mere "thoughts."

The Federal Government has no business, whether under the postal or commerce power, to bar the sale of books because they might lead to any kind of "thoughts."

It is no answer to say, as the Court does, that obscenity is not protected speech. The point is that this statute, as here construed, defines obscenity so widely that it encompasses matters which might very well be protected speech. I do not think that the federal statute can be constitutionally construed to reach other than what the Government has termed as "hard-core" pornography. Nor do I think the statute can fairly be read as directed only at persons who are engaged in the business of catering to the prurient minded, even though their wares fall short of hard-core pornography. Such a statute would raise constitutional questions of a different order. That being so, and since in my opinion the material here involved cannot be said to be hard-core pornography, I would reverse this case with instructions to dismiss the indictment.

MR. JUSTICE DOUGLAS, *with whom Mr. Justice Black concurs, dissenting.*

When we sustain these convictions, we make the legality of a publication turn on the purity of thought which a book or tract instills in the mind of the reader. I do not think we can approve that standard and be faithful to the command of the First Amendment, which by its terms is a restraint on Congress and which by the Fourteenth is a restraint on the States. . . .

By these standards punishment is inflicted for thoughts provoked, not for overt acts nor antisocial conduct. This test cannot be squared with our decisions under the First Amendment. Even the ill-starred *Dennis* case conceded that speech to be punishable must have some relation to action which could be penalized by government. *Dennis v. United States.* This issue cannot be avoided by saying that obscenity is not protected by the First Amendment. The question remains, what is the constitutional test of obscenity?

The tests by which these convictions were obtained require only the arousing of sexual thoughts. Yet the arousing of sexual thoughts, and desires, happens every day in normal life in dozens of ways. Nearly 30 years ago a questionnaire sent to college and normal school women graduates asked what things were most stimulating sexually. Of 409 replies, 9 said "music"; 18 said "pictures"; 29 said "dancing"; 40 said "drama"; 95 said "books"; and 218 said "man." Alpert, "Judicial Censorship of Obscene Literature," 52 Harv L Rev 40, 73. . . .

If we were certain that impurity of sexual thoughts impelled to action, we would be on less dangerous ground in punishing the distributors of this sex literature. But it is by no means clear that obscene literature, as so defined, is a significant factor in influencing substantial deviations from the community standards.

There are a number of reasons for real and substantial doubts as to the soundness of that hypothesis. (1) Scientific studies of juvenile delinquency demonstrate that those who get into trouble, and are the greatest concern of the advocates of censorship, are far less inclined to read than those who do not become delinquent. The delinquents are generally the adventurous type, who have little use for reading and other non-active entertainment. Thus, even assuming that reading sometimes has an adverse effect upon moral conduct, the effect is not likely to be substantial, for those who are susceptible seldom read. (2) Sheldon and Eleanor Glueck, who are among the country's leading authorities on the treatment and causes of juvenile delinquency, have recently published the results of a ten-year study of its causes. They exhaustively studied approximately 90 factors and influences that might lead to or explain juvenile delinquency, but the Gluecks gave no consideration to the type of reading material, if any, read by the delinquents. This is, of course, consistent with their finding that delinquents read very little. When those who know so much about the problem of delinquency among youth—the very group about whom the advocates of censorship are most concerned—conclude that what delinquents read has so little effect upon their conduct that it is not worth investigating in an exhaustive study of causes, there is good reason for serious doubt concerning the basic hypothesis on which obscenity censorship is defended. (3) The many other influences in society that stimulate sexual desire are so much more frequent in their influence, and so much more potent in their effect, that the influence of reading is likely, at most, to be relatively insignificant in the composite of forces that lead an individual into conduct deviating from the community sex standards. The Kinsey studies show the minor degree to which literature serves as a potent sexual stimulant. . . .

The absence of dependable information on the effect of obscene literature on human conduct should make us wary. It should put us on the side of protecting society's interest in literature, except and unless it can be said that the particular publication has an impact on action that the government can control.

As noted, the trial judge in the *Roth* case charged the jury in the alternative that the federal obscenity statute outlaws literature dealing with sex which offends "the common conscience of the community." That standard is, in my view, more inimical still to freedom of expression.

The standard of what offends "the common conscience of the community" conflicts, in my judgment, with the command of the First Amendment that "Congress shall make no law . . . abridging the freedom of speech, or of the press." Certainly that standard would not be an acceptable one if religion, economics, politics or philosophy were involved. How does it become a constitutional standard when literature treating with sex is concerned?

Any test that turns on what is offensive to the community's standards is too loose, too capricious, too destructive of freedom of expression to be squared with the First Amendment. Under that test, juries can censor, suppress, and punish what they don't like, provided the matter relates to "sexual impurity" or has a tendency "to excite lustful thought." This is community censorship in one of its worst forms. It creates a regime where in the battle between the literati and the Philistines, the Philistines are certain to win. If experience in this field teaches anything, it is that "censorship of obscenity has almost always been both irrational and indiscriminate." . . .

I can understand (and at times even sympathize) with programs of civic groups and church groups to protect and defend the existing moral standards of the community. I can understand the motives of the Anthony Comstocks who would impose Victorian standards on the community. When speech alone is involved, I do not think that government, consistently with the First Amendment, can become the sponsor of any of these movements. I do not think that government, consistently with the First Amendment, can throw its weight behind one school or another. Government should be concerned with antisocial conduct, not with utterances. Thus, if the First Amendment guarantee of freedom of speech and press is to mean anything in this field, it must allow protests even against the moral code that the standard of the day sets for the community. In other words, literature should not be suppressed merely because it offends the moral code of the censor. . . .

I do not think that the problem can be resolved by the Court's statement that "obscenity is not expression protected by the First Amendment." With the exception of *Beauharnais v. Illinois,* none of our cases has resolved problems of free speech and free press by placing any form of expression beyond the pale of the absolute prohibition of the First Amendment. Unlike the law of libel, wrongfully relied on in *Beauharnais,* there is no special historical evidence that literature dealing with sex was intended to be treated in a special manner by those who drafted the First Amendment. . . . I reject too the implication that problems of freedom of speech and of the press are to be resolved by weighing against the values of free expression, the judgment of the Court that a particular form of the expression has "no redeeming social importance." The First Amendment, its prohibition in terms absolute, was designed to preclude courts as well as legislatures from weighing the values of speech against silence. The First Amendment puts free speech in the preferred position. . . .

I would give the broad sweep of the First Amendment full support. I have the same confidence in the ability of our people to reject noxious literature as I have in their capacity to sort out the true from the false in theology, economics, politics, or any other field.

METAPHYSICS OF THE LAW OF OBSCENITY

By Harry Kalven, Jr.*

. . . The Brennan opinion [in *Roth*] invites three lines of consideration. First, is the two-level theory of free speech tolerable as doctrine?
Second, is there disclosed a weakness in the preoccupation of free-speech
theory with competition in the market place of ideas when we turn to art
and belles-lettres, which deal primarily with the imagination and not with
ideas in any strict sense? Finally, will the tendency of the Court's decision
be to relax or to make more restrictive the enforcement of the obscenity
laws?

The two-level speech theory, although it afforded the Court a states-
manlike way around a dilemma, seems difficult to accept as doctrine. It is
perhaps understandable in the context of *Chaplinsky*, where the speech in
question is nothing more complex than the utterance "son of a bitch,"
said rapidly. In connection with libel, as in *Beauharnais*, or obscenity, as
in *Roth*, however, it seems a strained effort to trap a problem. At one level
there are communications which, even though odious to the majority opinion of the day, even though expressive of the thought we hate, are entitled
to be measured against the clear-and-present-danger criterion. At another
level are communications apparently so worthless as not to require any extensive judicial effort to determine whether they can be prohibited. There
is to be freedom for the thought we hate, but not for the candor we deplore. The doctrinal apparatus is thus quite intricate. In determining the
constitutionality of any ban on a communication, the first question is
whether it belongs to a category that has any social utility. If it does not,
it may be banned. If it does, there is a further question of measuring the
clarity and proximity and gravity of any danger from it. It is thus apparent
that the issue of social utility of a communication has become as crucial
a part of our theory as the issue of its danger. Although the Court has
not yet made this clear it must be assumed that the Court's concern is
with the utility of a category of communication rather than with a particular instance. Thus, to go back to the pamphlet in *Gitlow*, presumably
the question, were the case to arise today, would be about the social utility
of revolutionary speech and not the utility of the particular pamphlet

* From Harry Kalven, Jr. "Metaphysics of the Law of Obscenity." *The Supreme Court
Review*. Chicago: University of Chicago Press, 1960, p. 1, at p. 10. Used with permission of the University of Chicago Press and Philip B. Kurland, editor. Copyright
1960 by the University of Chicago. The author is a professor of law at the University
of Chicago.

which so bored Mr. Justice Holmes. There is, to be sure, no quarrel with the premise that even odious revolutionary speech has value. If a man is seriously enough at odds with society to advocate violent revolution, his speech has utility not because advocating revolution is useful but because such serious criticism should be heard. No one advocates violent overthrow of government without advancing some premises in favor of his conclusion. It is the premises and not the conclusion that are worth protecting. This is in effect what Judge Hand meant in the *Dennis* case when he spoke of utterances which have a "double aspect: *i.e.*, when persuasion and instigation were inseparably confused." There is thus no contradiction in the concept of speech which presents a clear and present danger but which nevertheless has sufficient social utility to require close constitutional scrutiny. The difficulties are with the other half of the theory, with the categories of speech that have no social utility. Neither in *Beauharnais* nor in *Roth* has the Court spoken at any length about the concept of social utility. It has confined itself on each occasion to the historical point that these categories—libel and obscenity—have long been regarded as worthless speech subject to prohibition. But, if history alone is to be the guide, the same inference might better be drawn about the utility of revolutionary speech.

It is at this point that Mr. Justice Brennan's phrasing of "the dispositive question" bears strange fruit. It seems hardly fair to ask: what is the social utility of obscenity? Rather the question is: what is the social utility of excessively candid and explicit discussions of sex? Here too there is the problem of the mixed utterance. The well-known sexual passages in *Lady Chatterley's Lover* are integral to the possibly strange but indubitably serious view of English postwar life that Lawrence wished to portray. And even if they were not a part of a complex whole—which will be destroyed with them if the novel is held obscene, just as the critical premises of the revolutionary would disappear—they would appear to have some value in their own right as a lyrical view of the potential for warmth, tenderness, and vitality of a fully satisfactory sexual experience. The Court's formula thus seems to have oversimplified the problem. The Court may understand obscenity, but it does not seem to understand sex.

The oversimplification is irritating because the Court appeared unaware, as it could not have been, of the distinguished items that have been held obscene. A legal term gets its meaning from the construction put on it by the courts, and the Court's logic thus appears to lead to the conclusion that, in its view, such books as *Lady Chatterley's Lover*, *Memoirs of Hecate County*, and *Strange Fruit*, all of which have been held obscene by distinguished courts, are in the category of speech which is "utterly without redeeming social importance."

I do not think the Court meant to say this—to say, for example, that *Memoirs of Hecate County* is worthless. There is an obvious way to avoid the apparent *reductio ad absurdum*. Presumably, in the future, the Court will take it. For everything now depends on what is meant by obscene. If the Court's formula is to make any sense, it must place a heavy burden on the definition of obscenity. Obscenity must be so defined as to save any serious, complex piece of writing or art, regardless of the unconventionality of its candor. If the obscene is constitutionally subject to ban because it is worthless, it must follow that the obscene can include only that which is worthless. This approach makes sense. So-called hard-core pornography involves discussions of sex which are not integral parts of anything else. In themselves, they are, at best, fantasies of sexual prowess and response unrelated to the serious human concern that moved Lawrence and, at worst, a degrading, hostile, alien view of the sexual experience. If the so-cially worthless criterion is taken seriously, the *Roth* opinion may have made a major advance in liberating literature and art from the shadow of the censor.

The Court's approach touches another long-standing puzzle in the law of obscenity. Is there a category of privileged obscenity, using privilege in its technical legal sense? It has long been clear that certain classics—Aris-tophanes, Rabelais, Boccaccio, Shakespeare, Montaigne, Voltaire, Balzac, and, some would add, the Bible itself—have been immune from obscenity regulation. The Court has never explicitly held that the other values of a work make privileged its obscene parts; but the pattern of decision and prosecution has been clear. The abortive effort of the Postmaster a few years back to bar *Lysistrata* was greeted with, and defeated by, laughter. Judge Frank argued that the judges had written such a privilege into the law and had thereby given the game away:

> To the argument that such books (and such reproductions of fa-mous paintings and works of sculpture) fall within the statutory ban, the courts have answered that they are "classics"—books of "literary distinction" or works which have "an accepted place in the arts," in-cluding, so this court has held, Ovid's *Art of Love* and Boccaccio's *Decameron*. There is a "curious dilemma" involved in this answer that the statute condemns "only books which are dull and without merit," that in no event will the statute be applied to the "classics," i.e., books "of literary distinction." The courts have not explained how they escape that dilemma, but instead seem to have gone to sleep (although rather uncomfortably) on its horns.

> This dilemma would seem to show up the basic constitutional flaw in the statute: No one can reconcile the currently accepted test of obscenity with the immunity of such "classics" as e.g., Aristophanes' *Lysistrata*, Chaucer's *Canterbury Tales*, Rabelais' *Gargantua and Pan-tagruel*, Shakespeare's *Venus and Adonis*, Fielding's *Tom Jones*, or Balzac's *Droll Stories*. For such "obscene" writings, just because of

their greater artistry and charm, will presumably have far greater influence on readers than dull inartistic writings. . . .

The truth is that the courts have excepted the "classics" from the federal obscenity statute, since otherwise most Americans would be deprived of access to many masterpieces of literature and the pictorial arts, and a statute yielding such deprivation would not only be laughably absurd but would squarely oppose the intention of the cultivated men who framed and adopted the First Amendment.

This exception—nowhere to be found in the statute—is a judge-made device invented to avoid that absurdity. The fact that the judges have felt the necessity of seeking that avoidance, serves to suggest forcibly that the statute, in its attempt to control what our citizens may read and see, violates the First Amendment. For no one can rationally justify the judge-made exception. . . .

While the unperplexed blandness of the Court's majority opinion in *Roth* is disconcerting in the teeth of so vigorous and engaging a commentary in the court below, it is probably true that the Court has solved Judge Frank's dilemma. On the two-level theory, the classics do not need a special privilege; they fall automatically into speech on the first level, and hence automatically outside the realm of the constitutionally obscene. To put this another way, the Court is giving a constitutional privilege to all communication that has some social value. And Judge Frank's pointed query as to why obscenity embedded in a classic was less dangerous than obscenity in a book without literary distinction is not so pointed now, since the latter is banned not because it is dangerous but because it is worthless.

The Brennan opinion, however, remains curious on two grounds. The Court did not make its own best point but defined obscenity substantially in the words of the American Law Institute's model penal code: "Whether to the average person, applying contemporary community standards, the dominant theme of the material taken as a whole appeals to prurient interest." This definition has certain advantages over its predecessors. It insists on the *average* person, on the material considered *as a whole*, and on the *dominant* theme. But it shares the central weakness of all prior legal definitions of obscenity: the word is still defined in terms of itself. The key word "prurient" is defined by one dictionary in terms of "lascivious longings" and "lewd." The obscene, then, is that which appeals to an interest in the obscene. In the process of defining obscenity the Court said nothing about social worthlessness. The opinion thus failed to break sharply enough with prior definitions of obscenity, to narrow them sufficiently, to make plausible its assumption that the obscene cannot include materials of some social utility.

Moreover, it is unclear how the formula will help a future court faced with the question whether a particular item can be banned constitutionally. Everything now depends on the classification. If the item is obscene it can be banned without regard to its danger. But in any close case a court, in order to determine whether the item is "obscene enough," will have to decide first whether it can be banned. The Court's formula offers no guidance on the constitutional issue.

I suggest that the difficulties in working out the implications of the new free-speech doctrine also reflect a difficulty with the older forms of that doctrine. The classic defense of John Stuart Mill and the modern defense of Alexander Meiklejohn do not help much when the question is why the novel, the poem, the painting, the drama, or the piece of sculpture falls within the protection of the First Amendment. Nor do the famous opinions of Hand, Holmes, and Brandeis. The emphasis is all on truth winning out in a fair fight between competing ideas. The emphasis is clearest in Meiklejohn's argument that free speech is indispensable to the informed citizenry required to make democratic self-government work. The people need free speech because they vote. As a result his argument distinguishes sharply between public and private speech. Not all communications are relevant to the political process. The people do not need novels or dramas or paintings or poems because they will be called upon to vote. Art and belles-lettres do not deal in such ideas—at least not good art or belles-lettres—and it makes little sense here to talk, as Mr. Justice Brandeis did in his great opinion in *Whitney,* of whether there is still time for counter-speech. Thus there seems to be a hiatus in our basic free-speech theory.

I am not suggesting that the Court will have any hesitation in recognizing, not, as Keats would have it, that truth and beauty are one, but that beauty has constitutional status too, and that the life of the imagination is as important to the human adult as the life of the intellect. I do not think that the Court would find it difficult to protect Shakespeare, even though it is hard to enumerate the important ideas in the plays and poems. I am only suggesting that Mr. Justice Brennan might not have found it so easy to dismiss obscenity because it lacked socially useful ideas if he had recognized that as to this point, at least, obscenity is in the same position as all art and literature. . . .

CHAPTER 6

OBSCENITY REFINED

The decade following Roth was one of clarification and refinement. The ten cases included in this chapter illustrate the point. The Court ruled that booksellers cannot be expected to have knowledge of each book on their shelves (Smith v. California), that strict safeguards of search and seizure must be followed (Marcus v. Search Warrant), and that "vigilantism" and "harassment" would not be allowed (Bantam Books v. Sullivan).

Three cases decided upon together in 1966 resulted in further refinement. In Memoirs v. Massachusetts it was emphasized that the work in question must be "utterly" without redeeming social importance to be judged obscene; in Ginzburg v. United States the concept of "pandering" to erotic interests was introduced as a basis for an obscenity conviction; and in Mishkin v. New York the Court held that appealing to prurient interest of a deviant group was a basis for an obscenity conviction.

Two years later, an additional pair of far-reaching decisions handed down together led the Court for the first time to hold that state and local legislatures may enact carefully drawn laws to protect children from purchasing literature or seeing films even though those same items would be constitutionally available to adults. Ginsberg v. New York and Interstate Circuit Inc. v. Dallas, the latter a film case included in Chapter 7. The question of motion picture censorship per se is covered in Chapter 7.

In its last decision on obscenity, the Warren Court in the spring of its final term ruled that citizens are free to read and view within the privacy of their own homes obscene material. Stanley v. Georgia.

Cases of lesser importance or ones during this decade in which no opinions were written included granting access to the mails of a magazine designed for homosexuals (One, Inc. v. Olesen) and one for nudists (Sunshine Book Co. v. Summerfield), both announced in 1958. In 1964 the

Court reversed an obscenity conviction on arguments of violation of procedural safeguards and due process, but could not agree on a majority opinion despite the 7-2 reversal. A Quantity of Books v. Kansas. It also reversed per curiam the obscenity judgment against Henry Miller's Tropic of Cancer, though again the justices could not reach unanimity as to their reasons for reversal. Grove Press, Inc. v. Gerstein. In 1967 the Supreme Court emphasized in a per curiam decision that "spicy" books and "girlie" movies are not obscene per se and, therefore, are afforded the protection of the First Amendment. Redrup v. New York.

Including pertinent decisions involving motion pictures, which are covered in Chapter 7, the following ten guidelines covering obscenity were set down by the Warren Court:

1. Obscene material intended for public use does not fall within the protection of the First Amendment. (Kingsley Books, Roth)
2. Sex and obscenity are not synonymous. (Roth and Redrup)
3. Ideas may not be proscribed merely because they may be repellent to the majority. (Kingsley International Pictures)
4. Possession of obscene material within the privacy of one's own home cannot be proscribed by the state. (Stanley)
5. To be judged obscene, material must be utterly (Jacobellis and Memoirs) without redeeming social importance (Roth) and must be patently offensive (Manual Enterprises).
6. To be judged obscene, the dominant theme of the material must appeal to the prurient interest (Roth) of the average adult (Butler), applying contemporary community standards (Roth), or must appeal to the prurient interest of a clearly defined deviant group for which it is designed (Mishkin).
7. If he seeks constitutional protection for his work, the purveyor's promotional material must not pander to the salacious or the sexually provocative. (Ginzburg)
8. Swift judicial review in obscenity cases must be guaranteed (Kingsley Books and Freedman) and the burden of proof in film cases lies with the censor (Freedman).
9. Motion pictures fall under the protection of the First Amendment (Burstyn v. Wilson, a pre-Warren decision), but because of the unique nature of the medium, special safeguards (i.e. licensing) may be imposed by the state (Times Film).
10. Literature and films which are constitutionally available to adults are not necessarily constitutionally available to minors. (Ginsberg and Interstate Circuit)

The question of a bookseller's responsibility was before the Court in the 1959 case of Eleazar Smith, proprietor of a Los Angeles bookstore. He was arrested under an ordinance which forbade possession for sale of obscene materials, even though the bookseller might not have knowledge of the contents of the publication in question. The Court in a unanimous decision ruled the ordinance unconstitutional. It held that one could not expect a bookseller to have detailed knowledge of all publications on his shelves, nor could he be expected to make difficult judgments as to the obscenity of each of them. Also, the Court said that this California law would tend to restrict distribution of reading matter which was protected by the Constitution and important to a free society. The bookseller, the Court held, probably would tend to restrict sales only to those volumes he felt were "safe." This reduction in the public's access to reading matter was judged unwise and unconstitutional.

SMITH V. CALIFORNIA
361 U.S. 147 (1959)

MR. JUSTICE BRENNAN *delivered the opinion of the Court.*

Appellant, the proprietor of a bookstore, was convicted in a California Municipal Court under a Los Angeles City ordinance which makes it unlawful "for any person to have in his possession any obscene or indecent writing, [or] book . . . [i]n any place of business where . . . books . . . are sold or kept for sale." The offense was defined by the Municipal Court, and by the Appellate Department of the Superior Court, which affirmed the Municipal Court judgment imposing a jail sentence on appellant, as consisting solely of the possession, in the appellant's bookstore, of a certain book found upon judicial investigation to be obscene. The definition included no element of scienter—knowledge by appellant of the contents of the book—and thus the ordinance was construed as imposing a "strict" or "absolute" criminal liability. The appellant made timely objection below that if the ordinance were so construed it would be in conflict with the Constitution of the United States. . . .

Almost 30 years ago, Chief Justice Hughes declared for this Court:

"It is no longer open to doubt that the liberty of the press, and of speech, is within the liberty safeguarded by the due process clause of the Fourteenth Amendment from invasion by state action. It was found impossible to conclude that this essential personal liberty of a citizen was left unprotected by the general guaranty of fundamental rights of person and property. . . ." *Near v. Minnesota.* It is too familiar for citation that such has been the doctrine of this Court, in respect of these freedoms, ever since. And it also requires no elaboration that the free publication and dissemination of books and other forms of the printed word furnish very familiar applications of these constitutionally protected freedoms. It is of course no matter that the dissemination takes place under commercial auspices. See *Joseph Burstyn, Inc. v. Wilson. Grosjean v. American Press Co.* Certainly a retail book seller plays a most significant role in the process of the distribution of books.

California here imposed a strict or absolute criminal responsibility on appellant not to have obscene books in his shop. . . . [T]he question here is as to the validity of this ordinance . . . which may tend to work as substantial restriction on the freedom of speech and of the press. . . .

. . . We have held that obscene speech and writings are not protected by the constitutional guarantees of freedom of speech and the press. *Roth v. United States.* The ordinance here in question, to be sure, only imposes criminal sanctions on a bookseller if in fact there is to be found in his shop an obscene book. But our holding in *Roth* does not recognize any state power to restrict the dissemination of books which are not obscene; and we think this ordinance's strict liability feature would tend seriously to have that effect, by penalizing booksellers, even though they had not the slightest notice of the character of the books they sold. . . . By dispensing with any requirement of knowledge of the contents of the book on the part of the seller, the ordinance tends to impose a severe limitation on the public's access to constitutionally protected matter. For if the bookseller is criminally liable without knowledge of the contents, and the ordinance fulfills its purpose, he will tend to restrict the books he sells to those he has inspected; and thus the State will have imposed a restriction upon the distribution of constitutionally protected as well as obscene literature. . . . And the bookseller's burden would become the public's burden, for by restricting him the public's access to reading matter would be restricted. If the contents of bookshops and periodical stands were restricted to material of which their proprietors had made an inspection, they might be depleted indeed. The bookseller's limitation in the amount of reading material with which he could familiarize himself, and his timidity in the face of his absolute criminal liability, thus would tend to restrict the public's access to forms of the printed word which the State could not constitutionally suppress directly. The bookseller's self-censorship, compelled by the State, would be a censorship affecting the whole public, hardly less virulent for being privately administered. Through it, the distribution of all books, both obscene and not obscene, would be impeded. . . .

MR. JUSTICE BLACK, *concurring.*

The appellant was sentenced to prison for possessing in his bookstore an "obscene" book in violation of a Los Angeles City ordinance. I concur in the judgment holding that ordinance unconstitutional, but not for the reasons given in the Court's opinion. . . .

Certainly the First Amendment's language leaves no room for inference that abridgments of speech and press can be made just because they are slight. That Amendment provides, in simple words, that "Congress shall make no law . . . abridging the freedom of speech, or of the press." I read "no law . . . abridging" to mean *no law abridging*. The First Amendment, which is the supreme law of the land, has thus fixed its own value on freedom of speech and press by putting these freedoms wholly "beyond the reach" of *federal* power to abridge. No other provision of the Constitution purports to dilute the scope of these unequivocal commands of the First Amendment. Consequently, I do not believe that any federal agencies, including Congress and this Court, have power or authority to subordinate speech and press to what they think are "more important interests." . . .

If, as it seems, we are on the way to national censorship, I think it timely to suggest again that there are grave doubts in my mind as to the desirability or constitutionality of this Court's becoming a Supreme Board of Censors—reading books and viewing television performances to determine whether, if permitted, they might adversely affect the morals of the people throughout the many diversified local communities in this vast country. . . .

Censorship is the deadly enemy of freedom and progress. The plain language of the Constitution forbids it. I protest against the Judiciary giving it a foothold here.

MR. JUSTICE FRANKFURTER, *concurring.*

. . . I am no friend of deciding a case beyond what the immediate controversy requires, particularly when the limits of constitutional power are at stake. On the other hand, a case before this Court is not just a case. Inevitably its disposition carries implications and gives directions beyond its particular facts. . . . It ought at least to be made clear, and not left for future litigation, that the Court's decision in its practical effect is not intended to nullify the conceded power of the State to prohibit booksellers from trafficking in obscene literature.

. . . A bookseller may, of course, be well aware of the nature of a book and its appeal without having opened its cover, or, in any true sense, having knowledge of the book. As a practical matter therefore the exercise of the constitutional right of a State to regulate obscenity will carry with it some hazard to the dissemination by a bookseller of non-obscene literature. Such difficulties or hazards are inherent in many domains of the law for the simple reason that law cannot avail itself of factors ascertained quantitatively or even wholly impersonally. . . .

MR. JUSTICE DOUGLAS, *concurring.*

I need not repeat here all I said in my dissent in *Roth v. United States* to underline my conviction that neither the author nor the distributor of this book can be punished under our Bill of Rights for publishing or distributing it. The notion that obscene publications or utterances were not included in free speech developed in this country much later than the adoption of the First Amendment, as the judicial and legislative developments in this country show. . . .

Yet my view is in the minority; and rather fluid tests of obscenity prevail which require judges to read condemned literature and pass judgment on it. This role of censor in which we find ourselves is not an edifying one. But since by the prevailing school of thought we must perform it, I see no harm, and perhaps some good, in the rule fashioned by the Court which requires a showing of scienter. For it recognizes implicitly that these First Amendment rights, by reason of the strict command in that Amendment—a command that carries over to the States by reason of the Due Process Clause of the Fourteenth Amendment—are preferred rights. What the Court does today may possibly provide some small degree of safeguard to booksellers by making those who patrol bookstalls proceed less high handedly than has been their custom.

MR. JUSTICE HARLAN, *concurring in part and dissenting in part.*

. . . In my view . . . the scienter question involves considerations of a different order depending on whether a state or a federal statute is involved. We have here a state ordinance, and on the meager data before us I would not reach the question whether the absence of a scienter element renders the ordinance unconstitutional. I must say, however, that the generalities in the Court's opinion striking down the ordinance leave me unconvinced.

From the point of view of the free dissemination of constitutionally protected ideas, the Court invalidates the ordinance on the ground that its effect may be to induce booksellers to restrict their offerings of non-obscene literary merchandise through fear of prosecution for unwittingly having on their shelves an obscene publication. . . . A more critical appraisal of both sides of the constitutional balance, not possible on the meager material before us, seems to me required before the ordinance can be struck down on this ground. For, as the concurring opinions of my Brothers Black and Frankfurter show, the conclusion that this ordinance, but not one embodying some element of scienter, is likely to restrict the dissemination of legitimate literature seems more dialectical than real. . . .

In my opinion this conviction is fatally defective in that the trial judge, as I read the record, turned aside *every* attempt by appellant to introduce evidence bearing on community standards. The exclusionary rulings were not limited to offered expert testimony. This had the effect of depriving appellant of the opportunity to offer any proof on a constitutionally relevant issue. On this ground I would reverse the judgment below, and remand the case for a new trial.

*   *   *

Two years after Smith, the Court further restricted action taken by local authorities in dealing with obscenity. A Missouri Court authorized search and seizure of certain magazine stands for the purpose of confiscating copies of publications later judged to be obscene. The warrant was issued on the testimony of a single police officer who, after visiting the newsstands, had asserted the periodicals being sold were obscene. No judicial scrutiny was given prior to the search and seizure. Justice Brennan delivered the opinion for the unanimous Court, saying that the procedures employed lacked adequate safeguards to protect non-obscene material from unconstitutional confiscation. Procedures followed in this case should be compared with those employed and upheld by the Court in Kingsley Books, Inc. v. Brown.

MARCUS V. SEARCH WARRANT OF PROPERTY
367 U.S. 717 (1961)

MR. JUSTICE BRENNAN *delivered the opinion of the Court.*

This appeal presents the question whether due process under the Fourteenth Amendment was denied the appellants by the application in this case of Missouri's procedures authorizing the search for and seizure of allegedly obscene publications preliminarily to their destruction by burning or otherwise, if found by a court to be obscene. The procedures are statutory, but are supplemented by a rule of the Missouri Supreme Court. The warrant for search for and seizure of obscene material issues on a sworn complaint filed with a judge or magistrate. If the complainant states "positively and not upon information or belief," or states "evidential facts from which such judge or magistrate determines the existence of probable cause" to believe that obscene material "is being held or kept in any place or in any building," "such judge or magistrate shall issue a search warrant directed to any peace officer commanding him to search the place therein described and to seize and bring before such judge or magistrate the personal property therein described." The owner of the property is not afforded a hearing before the warrant issues; the proceeding is *ex parte.* However, the judge or magistrate issuing the warrant must fix a date, not less than five nor more than 20 days after the seizure, for a hearing to determine whether the seized material is obscene. The owner of the material may appear at such hearing and defend against the charge. No time limit is provided within which the judge must announce his decision. If the judge finds that the material is obscene, he is required to order it to be publicly destroyed, by burning or otherwise; if he finds that it is not obscene, he shall order its return to its owner.

The Missouri Supreme Court sustained the validity of the procedures as applied in this case. . . .

Appellant, Kansas City News Distributors, managed by appellant, Homer Smay, is a wholesale distributor of magazines, newspapers and books in the Kansas City area. The other appellants operate five retail newsstands in Kansas City. In October 1957, Police Lieutenant Coughlin of the Kansas City Police Department Vice Squad was conducting an investigation into the distribution of allegedly obscene magazines. On October 8, 1957, he visited Distributors' place of business and showed Smay a list of magazines. Smay admitted that his company distributed all but one of the magazines on the list. The following day, October 9, Lieutenant Coughlin visited the five newsstands and purchased one magazine at each. On October 10 the officer signed and filed six sworn complaints in the Circuit Court of Jackson County, stating in each complaint that "of his own knowledge" the appellant named therein, at its stated place of business, "kept for the purpose of [sale] . . . obscene . . . publications. . . ." No copy of any magazine on Lieutenant Coughlin's list, or purchased by him at the newsstands, was filed with the complaint or shown to the circircuit judge. The circuit judge issued six search warrants authorizing, as to the premises of the appellant named in each, "any peace officer in the State of Missouri . . . [to] search the said premises . . . within 10 days after the issuance of this warrant by day or night, and . . . seize . . . [obscene materials] and take same into your possession. . . ."

All of the warrants were executed on October 10, but by different law enforcement officers. Lieutenant Coughlin with two other Kansas City police officers, and an officer of the Jackson County Sheriff's Patrol, executed the warrant against Distributors. Distributors' stock of magazines runs "into hundreds of thousands . . . [p]robably closer to a million copies." The officers examined the publications in the stock on the main floor of the establishment, not confining themselves to Lieutenant Coughlin's original list. They seized all magazines which "[i]n our judgment" were obscene; when an officer thought "a magazine . . . ought to be picked up" he seized all copies of it. After three hours the examination was completed and the magazines seized were "hauled away in a truck and put on the 15th floor of the courthouse." A substantially similar procedure was followed at each of the five newsstands. Approximately 11,000 copies of 280 publications, principally magazines but also some books and photographs, were seized at the six places. . . .

The question here is whether the use by Missouri in this case of the search and seizure power to suppress obscene publications involved abuses inimical to protected expression. We held in *Roth v. United States* that "obscenity is not within the area of constitutionally protected speech or press." But in *Roth* itself we expressly recognized the complexity of the test of obscenity fashioned in that case, and the vital necessity in its application of safeguards to present denial of "the protection of freedom of speech and press for material which does not treat sex in a manner appealing to prurient interest." We have since held that a State's power to suppress obscenity is limited by the constitutional protections for free expression. . . .

We believe that Missouri's procedures as applied in this case lacked the safeguards which due process demands to assure nonobscene material the constitutional protection to which it is entitled. . . . The warrants gave the broadest discretion to the executing officers; they merely repeated the language of the statute and the complaints, specified no publications, and left to the individual judgment of each of the many police officers involved the selection of such magazines as in his view constituted "obscene . . . publications." So far as appears from the record, none of the officers except Lieutenant Coughlin had previously examined any of the publications which were subsequently seized. It is plain that in many instances, if not in all, each officer actually made *ad hoc* decisions on the spot and, gauged by the number of publications seized and the time spent in executing the warrants, each decision was made with little opportunity for reflection and deliberation. As to publications seized because they appeared on the Lieutenant's list, we know nothing of the basis for the original judgment that they were obscene. It is no reflection on the good faith or judgment of the officers to conclude that the task they were assigned was simply an impossible one to perform with any realistic expectation that the obscene might be accurately separated from the constitutionally protected. They were provided with no guide to the exercise of informed discretion, because there was no step in the procedure before seizure designed to focus searchingly on the question of obscenity. . . . Procedures which sweep so broadly and with so little discrimination are obviously deficient in techniques required by the Due Process Clause of the Fourteenth Amendment to prevent erosion of the constitutional guarantees.

*   *   *

The Rhode Island legislature in 1956 created a nine-man commission appointed by the governor to encourage morality in youth and to combat juvenile delinquency. One of the charges given this body was to "educate" the public relative to obscene literature and to investigate and recommend the prosecution of alleged violators of the state's obscenity statutes. The commission asked for bookseller "cooperation" in removing alleged objectionable publications. The appellants argued that this amounted to nothing more than "police harassment," intimidation, and "vigilantism." The Court, in another of the continuing series of obscenity opinions read by Justice Brennan, struck down the commission's actions as a thinly veiled scheme of informal censorship. Again, a comparison with Kingsley Books, Inc. would be pertinent.

BANTAM BOOKS, INC. V. SULLIVAN
372 U.S. 58 (1963)

MR. JUSTICE BRENNAN *delivered the opinion of the Court.*

. . . Appellants are four New York publishers of paperback books which have for some time been widely distributed in Rhode Island. Max Silverstein & Sons is the exclusive wholesale distributor of appellants' publications throughout most of the State. The Commission's practice has been to notify a distributor on official Commission stationery that certain designated books or magazines distributed by him had been reviewed by the Commission and had been declared by a majority of its members to be objectionable for sale, distribution or display to youths under 18 years of age. Silverstein had received at least 35 such notices at the time this suit was brought. Among the paperbook books listed by the Commission as "objectionable" were one published by appellant Dell Publishing Co., Inc., and another published by appellant Bantam Books, Inc.

The typical notice to Silverstein either solicited or thanked Silverstein, in advance, for his "cooperation" with the Commission, usually reminding Silverstein of the Commission's duty to recommend to the Attorney General prosecution of purveyors of obscenity. Copies of the lists of "objectionable" publications were circulated to local police departments, and Silverstein was so informed in the notices.

Silverstein's reaction on receipt of a notice was to take steps to stop further circulation of copies of the listed publications. He would not fill pending orders for such publications and would refuse new orders. He instructed his field men to visit his retailers and to pick up all unsold copies, and would then promptly return them to the publishers. A local police officer usually visited Silverstein shortly after Silverstein's receipt of a notice to learn what action he had taken. Silverstein was usually able to inform the officer that a specified number of the total of copies received from a publisher had been returned. According to the testimony, Silverstein acted as he did on receipt of the notice, "rather than face the possibility of some sort of a court action against ourselves, as well as the people that we supply." His "cooperation" was given to avoid becoming involved in a "court proceeding" with a "duly authorized organization." . . .

What Rhode Island has done, in fact, has been to subject the distribution of publications to a system of prior administrative restraints, since the Commission is not a judicial body and its decisions to list particular publications as objectionable do not follow judicial determinations that such publications may lawfully be banned. Any system of prior restraints of expression comes to this Court bearing a heavy presumption against its constitutional validity. . . . We have tolerated such a system only where it operated under judicial superintendence and assured an almost immediate judicial determination of the validity of the restraint. *Kingsley Books, Inc. v. Brown.* The system at bar includes no such saving features. On the contrary, its capacity for suppression of constitutionally protected publications is far in excess of that of the typical licensing scheme held constitutionally invalid by this Court. There is no provision whatever for judicial superintendence before notices issue or even for judicial review of the Commission's determinations of objectionableness. The publisher or distributor is not even entitled to notice and hearing before his publications are listed by the Commission as objectionable. Moreover, the Commission's statutory mandate is vague and uninformative, and the Commission has done nothing to make it more precise. Publications are listed as "objectionable" without further elucidation. The distributor is left to speculate whether the Commission considers his publication obscene or simply harmful to juvenile morality. For the Commission's domain is the whole of youthful morals. Finally, we note that although the Commission's supposed concern is limited to youthful readers, the "cooperation" it seeks from distributors invariably entails the complete suppression of the listed publications; adult readers are equally deprived of the opportunity to purchase the publications in the State. Cf. *Butler v. Michigan.*

The procedures of the Commission are radically deficient. They fall far short of the constitutional requirements of governmental regulation of obscenity. We hold that the system of informal censorship disclosed by this record violates the Fourteenth Amendment.

In holding that the activities disclosed on this record are constitutionally proscribed, we do not mean to suggest that private consultation between law enforcement officers and distributors prior to the institution of a judicial proceeding can never be constitutionally permissible. We do not hold that law enforcement officers must renounce all informal contacts with persons suspected of violating valid laws prohibiting obscenity. Where such consultation is genuinely undertaken with the purpose of aiding the distributor to comply with such laws and avoid prosecution under them, it need not retard the full enjoyment of First Amendment freedoms. But that is not this case. The appellees are not law enforcement officers; they do not pretend that they are qualified to give or that they attempt to give distributors only fair legal advice. Their conduct as disclosed by this record shows plainly that they went far beyond advising the distributors of their legal rights and liabilities. Their operation was in fact a scheme of state censorship effectuated by extralegal sanctions; they acted as an agency not to advise but to suppress.

MR. JUSTICE CLARK, *concurring in the result.*

As I read the opinion of the Court, it does much fine talking about freedom of expression and much condemning of the Commission's over-zealous efforts to implement the State's obscenity laws for the protection of Rhode Island's youth but, as if shearing a hog, comes up with little wool. In short, it creates the proverbial tempest in a teapot over a number of notices sent out by the Commission asking the cooperation of magazine distributors in preventing the sale of obscene literature to juveniles. . . .

In my view the Court should simply direct the Commission to abandon its delusions of grandeur and leave the issuance of "orders" to enforcement officials and "the State's criminal regulation of obscenity" to the prosecutors, who can substitute prosecution for "thinly veiled threats" in appropriate cases. . . .

MR. JUSTICE HARLAN, *dissenting.*

The Court's opinion fails to give due consideration to what I regard as the central issue in this case—the accommodation that must be made between Rhode Island's concern with the problem of juvenile delinquency and the right of freedom of expression assured by the Fourteenth Amendment. . . .

This Rhode Island Commission was formed for the laudable purpose of combatting juvenile delinquency. While there is as yet no consensus of scientific opinion on the causal relationship between youthful reading or viewing of the "obscene" and delinquent behavior, . . . Rhode Island's approach to the problem is not without respectable support. . . . The States should have a wide range of choice in dealing with such problems, . . . and this court should not interfere with state legislative judgments on them except upon the clearest showing of unconstitutionality. . . .

*　　*　　*

In the first of three major pronouncements on obscenity handed down on the same day, the Warren Court in a 6-3 decision tossed out a Massachusetts court obscenity judgment against the "erotic classic" Memoirs of a Woman of Pleasure, better known as Fanny Hill. Those in the majority, however, could not reach agreement as to the logic that led them to overrule the lower court. The effect of the ruling, however, was to emphasize the concept that material must be "utterly without social redeeming importance" in order for it to be judged obscene. The Massachusetts court had held that there might be some value, but not enough to save it from being judged obscene. This ruling, though somewhat overshadowed by the second of the trio handed down in 1966—Ginzburg—may prove to be more significant than was at first thought. Illustrating the divergence with which the Court ruled in this case, Justices Brennan, Warren, and Fortas emphasized the failure of the lower court to weigh the "redeeming social importance" of the work, Justice Black held that the court was without constitutional power to limit speech or press, Justice Douglas argued that the government has no power to limit ideas, and Justice Stewart said that the work did not constitute "hard-core pornography." Dissenting were Justice Clark, who held that the book was obscene and had no conceivable social importance, Justice Harlan, who argued that the Fourteenth Amendment says only that obscenity criteria must be applied rationally as was done by the lower court, and Justice White, who held that if the state insists on treating Memoirs as obscene, the First Amendment does not prohibit this treatment. It is interesting to note that in Memoirs there are none of the "four-letter words" which usually accompany obscenity allegations. Also, it is generally held that Fanny Hill, written in 1749, was involved in the first test of obscenity in this country. Commonwealth v. Holmes, 17 Mass. 335 (1821).

MEMOIRS V. MASSACHUSETTS
383 U.S. 413 (1966)

MR. JUSTICE BRENNAN announced the judgment of the Court and delivered an opinion in which The Chief Justice and Mr. Justice Fortas join.

. . . The sole question before the state courts was whether Memoirs satisfies the test of obscenity established in Roth v. United States.

. . . Under this definition, as elaborated in subsequent cases, three elements must coalesce: it must be established that (a) the dominant theme of the material taken as a whole appeals to a prurient interest in sex; (b) the material is patently offensive because it affronts contemporary community standards relating to the description or representation of sexual matters; and (c) the material is utterly without redeeming social value.

The [Massachusetts] Supreme Judicial Court erred in holding that a book need not be "unqualifiedly worthless before it can be deemed obscene." A book cannot be proscribed unless it is found to be *utterly* without redeeming social value. This is so even though the book is found to possess the requisite prurient appeal and to be patently offensive. Each of the three federal constitutional criteria is to be applied independently; the social value of the book can neither be weighed against nor canceled by its prurient appeal or patent offensiveness. Hence, even on the view of the court below that Memoirs possessed only a modicum of social value, its judgment must be reversed as being founded on an erroneous interpretation of a federal constitutional standard. . . .

MR. JUSTICE BLACK *and* MR. JUSTICE STEWART *concur in the reversal for the reasons stated in their respective dissenting opinions in* Ginzburg v. United States *and* Mishkin v. New York.

MR. JUSTICE DOUGLAS, *concurring.*

. . . The courts of Massachusetts found the book "obscene" and upheld its suppression. This Court reverses, the prevailing opinion having seized upon language in the opinion of the Massachusetts Supreme Judicial Court in which it is candidly admitted that *Fanny Hill* has at least "some minimal literary value." I do not believe that the Court should decide this case on so disingenuous a basis as this. I base my vote to reverse on my view that the First Amendment does not permit the censorship of expression not brigaded with illegal action. But even applying the prevailing view of the *Roth* test, reversal is compelled by this record which makes clear that *Fanny Hill* is not "obscene." The prosecution made virtually no effort to prove that this book is "utterly without redeeming social importance." The defense, on the other hand, introduced considerable and impressive testimony to the effect that this was a work of literary, historical, and social importance. . . .

Every time an obscenity case is to be argued here, my office is flooded with letters and postal cards urging me to protect the community or the Nation by striking down the publication. The messages are often identical even down to commas and semicolons. The inference is irresistible that they were all copied from a school or church blackboard. Dozens of postal cards often are mailed from the same precinct. The drives are incessant and the pressures are great. Happily we do not bow to them. I mention them only to emphasize the lack of popular understanding of our constitutional system. Publications and utterances were made immune from majoritarian control by the First Amendment, applicable to the States by reason of the Fourteenth. No exceptions were made, not even for obscenity. The Court's contrary conclusion in *Roth*, where obscenity was found to be "outside" the First Amendment, is without justification. . . .

MR. JUSTICE CLARK, *dissenting.*

It is with regret that I write this dissenting opinion. However, the public should know of the continuous flow of pornographic material reaching this Court and the increasing problem States have in controlling it. *Memoirs of a Woman of Pleasure*, the book involved here, is typical. I have "stomached" past cases for almost 10 years without much outcry. Though I am not known to be a purist—or a shrinking violet—this book is too much even for me. It is important that the Court has refused to declare it obscene and thus gives it further circulation. In order to give my remarks the proper setting I have been obliged to portray the book's contents, which gives me embarrassment. However, quotations from typical episodes would so debase our reports that I will not follow that course. . . .

In my view evidence of social importance is relevant to the determination of the ultimate question of obscenity. But social importance does not constitute a separate and distinct constitutional test. Such evidence must be considered together with evidence that the material in question appeals to prurient interest and is patently offensive. Accordingly, we must first turn to the book here under attack. . . .

. . . In my view, the book's repeated and unrelieved appeals to the prurient interest of the average person leave it utterly without redeeming social importance.

MR. JUSTICE HARLAN, *dissenting.*

The central development that emerges from the aftermath of *Roth v. United States* is that no stable approach to the obscenity problem has yet been devised by this Court. Two Justices believe that the First and Fourteenth Amendments absolutely protect obscene and nonobscene material alike. Another Justice believes that neither the States nor the Federal Government may suppress any material save for "hard-core pornography." . . .

My premise is that in the area of obscenity the Constitution does not bind the States and the Federal Government in precisely the same fashion. . . .

. . . Federal suppression of allegedly obscene matter should, in my view, be constitutionally limited to that often described as "hard-core pornography." . . .

To me it is plain, for instance, that *Fanny Hill* does not fall within this class and could not be barred from the federal mails. . . .

State obscenity laws present problems of quite a different order. The varying conditions across the country, the range of views on the need and reasons for curbing obscenity, and the traditions of local self-government in matters of public welfare all favor a far more flexible attitude in defining the bounds for the States. From my standpoint, the Fourteenth Amendment requires of a State only that it apply criteria rationally related to the accepted notion of obscenity and that it reach results not wholly out of step with current American standards. . . .

MR. JUSTICE WHITE, *dissenting.*

In my view, "social importance" is not an independent test of obscenity but is relevant only to determining the predominant prurient interest of the material, a determination which the court or the jury will make based on the material itself and all the evidence in the case, expert or otherwise.

Application of the *Roth* test, as I understand it, necessarily involves the exercise of judgment by legislatures, courts and juries. . . .

Finally, it should be remembered that if the publication and sale of *Fanny Hill* and like books are proscribed, it is not the Constitution that imposes the ban. Censure stems from a legislative act, and legislatures are constitutionally free to embrace such books whenever they wish to do so. But if a State insists on treating *Fanny Hill* as obscene and forbidding its sale, the First Amendment does not prevent it from doing so.

I would affirm the judgment below.

*   *   *

No obscenity decision following Roth created so much heated dis-cussion as did the Ginzburg decision, handed down on the same day as Memoirs, supra, and Mishkin, which follows. With Ginzburg, the Court in a 5-4 decision interjected a new element as a test for obscenity—pander-ing, i.e. openly advertising and appealing to erotic interests. This takes into account the intent of the author and apparently is to be applied in border-line cases. A publisher, the Court held, cannot plead "redeeming social importance" on the one hand and then blatantly emphasize the salacious on the other. Dissenters pointed out that the material mailed by Ginzburg was judged obscene and that the Court's action was not based upon the publications, but the manner in which they were promoted. Justice Black again took his "absolutist" view of the First Amendment. Justice Douglas did likewise, and in addition, questioned advertising in general under this ruling. Justice Harlan reiterated his view that only "hard-core pornography" should be banned. And Justice Stewart denied that Ginzburg had enjoyed due process because of the new test imposed by the Court in disapproving of his "sordid business." Ginzburg had been sentenced to a five-year prison term plus $28,000 fine.

GINZBURG V. UNITED STATES
383 U.S. 463 (1966)

MR. JUSTICE BRENNAN *delivered the opinion of the Court.*

. . . In the cases in which this Court has decided obscenity questions since *Roth*, it has regarded the materials as sufficient in themselves for the determination of the question. In the present case, however, the prosecu-tion charged the offense in the context of the circumstances of production, sale, and publicity and assumed that, standing alone, the publications themselves might not be obscene. We agree that the question of obscenity may include consideration of the setting in which the publications were presented as an aid to determining the question of obscenity, and assume without deciding that the prosecution could not have succeeded otherwise. . . . We view the publications against a background of commercial exploitation of erotica solely for the sake of their prurient appeal. The record in that regard amply supports the decision of the trial judge that the mailing of all three publications offended the statute.

The three publications were *Eros*, a hard-cover magazine of expensive format; *Liaison*, a bi-weekly newsletter; and *The Housewife's Handbook on Selective Promiscuity* (hereinafter the *Handbook*), a short book. The issue of *Eros* specified in the indictment, Vol. 1, No. 4, contains 15 articles and photo-essays on the subject of love, sex, and sexual relations. The specified issue of *Liaison*, Vol. 1, No. 1, contains a prefatory "Letter from the Editors" announcing its dedication to "keeping sex an art and preventing it from becoming a science." The remainder of the issue consists of digests of two articles concerning sex and sexual relations which had earlier appeared in professional journals and a report of an interview with a psychotherapist who favors the broadest license in sexual relationships. As the trial judge noted, "[w]hile the treatment is largely superficial, it is presented entirely without restraint of any kind. According to defendants' own expert, it is entirely without literary merit." The *Handbook* purports to be a sexual autobiography detailing with complete candor the author's sexual experiences from age 3 to age 36. The text includes, and prefatory and concluding sections of the book elaborate, her views on such subjects as sex education of children, laws regulating private consensual adult sexual practices, and the equality of women in sexual relationships. It was claimed at trial that women would find the book valuable, for example as a marriage manual or as an aid to the sex education of their children.

Besides testimony as to the merit of the material, there was abundant evidence to show that each of the accused publications was originated or sold as stock in trade of the sordid business of pandering—"the business of purveying textual or graphic matter openly advertised to appeal to the erotic interest of their customers." *Eros* early sought mailing privilege from the postmasters of Intercourse and Blue Ball, Pennsylvania. The trial court found the obvious, that these hamlets were chosen only for the value their names would have in furthering petitioners' efforts to sell their publications on the basis of salacious appeal; the facilities of the post offices were inadequate to handle the anticipated volume of mail, and the privileges were denied. Mailing privileges were then obtained from the postmaster of Middlesex, New Jersey. *Eros* and *Liaison* thereafter mailed several million circulars soliciting subscriptions from that post office; over 5,500 copies of the *Handbook* were mailed.

This evidence, in our view, was relevant in determining the ultimate question of "obscenity" and, in the context of this record, serves to resolve all ambiguity and doubt. The deliberate representation of petitioners' publications as erotically arousing, for example, stimulated the reader to accept them as prurient; he looks for titillation, not for saving intellectual content. Similarly, such representation would tend to force public confrontation with the potentially offensive aspects of the work; the brazenness of such an appeal heightens the offensiveness of the publications to those who are offended by such material. And the circumstances of presentation and dissemination of material are equally relevant to determining whether social importance claimed for material in the courtroom was, in the circumstances, pretense or reality—whether it was the basis upon which it was traded in the marketplace or a spurious claim for litigation purposes. Where the purveyor's sole emphasis is on the sexually provocative aspects of his publications, that fact may be decisive in the determination of obscenity. Certainly in a prosecution which, as here, does not necessarily imply suppression of the materials involved, the fact that they originate or are used as a subject of pandering is relevant to the application of the *Roth* test. . . .

It is important to stress that this analysis simply elaborates the test by which the obscenity *vel non* of the material must be judged. Where an exploitation of interests in titillation by pornography is shown with respect to material lending itself to such exploitation through pervasive treatment or description of sexual matters, such evidence may support the determination that the material is obscene even though in other contexts the material would escape such condemnation. . . .

MR. JUSTICE BLACK, *dissenting.*

Only one stark fact emerges with clarity out of the confusing welter of opinions and thousands of words written in this and two other cases today. That fact is that Ginzburg, petitioner here, is now finally and authoritatively condemned to serve five years in prison for distributing printed matter about sex which neither Ginzburg nor anyone else could possibly have known to be criminal. Since, as I have said many times, I believe the Federal Government is without any power whatever under the Constitution to put any type of burden on speech and expression of ideas of any kind (as distinguished from conduct), I agree with Part II of the dissent of my Brother Douglas in this case, and I would reverse Ginzburg's conviction on this ground alone. Even assuming, however, that the Court is correct in holding today that Congress does have power to clamp official censorship on some subjects selected by the Court in some ways approved by it, I believe that the federal obscenity statute as enacted by Congress and as enforced by the Court against Ginzburg in this case should be held invalid on two other grounds.

Criminal punishment by government, although universally recognized as a necessity in limited areas of conduct, is an exercise of one of government's most awesome and dangerous powers. Consequently, wise and good governments make all possible efforts to hedge this dangerous power by restricting it within easily identifiable boundaries. . . .

I agree with my Brother Harlan that the Court has in effect rewritten the federal obscenity statute and thereby imposed on Ginzburg standards and criteria that Congress never thought about, or if it did think about them certainly did not adopt them. Consequently, Ginzburg is, as I see it, having his conviction and sentence affirmed upon the basis of a statute amended by this Court for violation of which amended statute he was not charged in the courts below. Such an affirmance we have said violates due process. . . .

My conclusion is that certainly after the fourteen separate opinions handed down in these three cases today no person, not even the most learned judge much less a layman, is capable of knowing in advance of an ultimate decision in his particular case by this Court whether certain material comes within the area of "obscenity" as that term is confused by the Court today. For this reason even if, as appears from the result of the three cases today, this country is far along the way to a censorship of the subjects about which the people can talk or write, we need not commit further constitutional transgressions by leaving people in the dark as to what literature or what words or what symbols if distributed through the mails make a man a criminal. As bad and obnoxious as I believe governmental censorship is in a Nation that has accepted the First Amendment as its basic ideal for freedom, I am compelled to say that censorship that would stamp certain books and literature as illegal in advance of publication or conviction would in some ways be preferable to the unpredictable book-by-book censorship into which we have now drifted. . . .

MR. JUSTICE DOUGLAS, *dissenting.*

The use of sex symbols to sell literature, today condemned by the Court, engrafts another exception on First Amendment rights that is as unwarranted as the judge-made exception concerning obscenity. This new exception condemns an advertising technique as old as history. The advertisements of our best magazines are chock-full of thighs, ankles, calves, bosoms, eyes, and hair, to draw the potential buyers' attention to lotions, tires, food, liquor, clothing, autos, and even insurance policies. The sexy advertisement neither adds nor detracts from the quality of the merchandise being offered for sale. And I do not see how it adds to or detracts one whit from the legality of the book being distributed. A book should stand on its own, irrespective of the reasons why it was written or the wiles used in selling it. I cannot imagine any promotional effort that would make chapters 7 and 8 of the *Song of Solomon* any the less or any more worthy of First Amendment protection than does its unostentatious inclusion in the average edition of the Bible. . . .

Man was not made in a fixed mould. If a publication caters to the idiosyncrasies of a minority, why does it not have some "social importance"? Each of us is a very temporary transient with likes and dislikes that cover the spectrum. However plebeian my tastes may be, who am I to say that others' tastes must be so limited and that other tastes have no "social importance"? . . .

This leads me to the conclusion, previously noted, that the First Amendment allows all ideas to be expressed whether orthodox, popular, offbeat, or repulsive. I do not think it permissible to draw lines between the "good" and the "bad" and be true to the constitutional mandate to let all ideas alone. If our Constitution permitted "reasonable" regulations of freedom of expression, as do the constitutions of some nations, we would be in a field where the legislative and the judiciary would have much leeway. But under our charter all regulation or control of expression is barred. Government does not sit to reveal where the "truth" is. People are left to pick and choose between competing offerings. There is no compulsion to take and read what is repulsive any more than there is to spend one's time poring over government bulletins, political tracts, or theological treatises. The theory is that people are mature enough to pick and choose, to recognize trash when they see it, to be attracted to the literature that satisfies their deepest need, and, hopefully, to move from plateau to plateau and finally reach the world of enduring ideas.

I think this is the ideal of the Free Society written into our Constitution. We have no business acting as censors or endowing any group with censorship powers. It is shocking to me for us to send to prison anyone for publishing anything, especially tracts so distant from any incitement to action as the ones before us.

MR. JUSTICE HARLAN, *dissenting.*

The First Amendment, in the obscenity area, no longer fully protects material on its face nonobscene, for such material must now also be examined in the light of the defendant's conduct, attitude, motives. This seems to me a mere euphemism for allowing punishment of a person who mails otherwise constitutionally protected material just because a jury or a judge may not find him or his business agreeable. Were a State to enact a "panderer" statute under its police power, I have little doubt that—subject to clear drafting to avoid attacks on vagueness and equal protection grounds—such a statute would be constitutional. Possibly the same might be true of the Federal Government acting under its postal or commerce powers. What I fear the Court has done today is in effect to write a new statute, but without the sharply focused definitions and standards necessary in such a sensitive area. Casting such a dubious gloss over a straightforward 101-year-old statute (see 13 Stat. 507) is for me an astonishing piece of judicial improvisation. . . .

If there is anything to this new pandering dimension to the mailing statute, the Court should return the case for a new trial, for petitioners are at least entitled to a day in court on the question on which their guilt has ultimately come to depend. Compare the action of the Court in A Book Named "John Cleland's Memoirs" v. Attorney General, where the Court affords the State an opportunity to prove in a subsequent prosecution that an accused purveyor of Fanny Hill in fact used pandering methods to secure distribution of the book. . . .

MR. JUSTICE STEWART, dissenting.

The petitioner has been sentenced to five years in prison for sending through the mail copies of a magazine, a pamphlet, and a book. There was testimony at his trial that these publications possess artistic and social merit. Personally, I have a hard time discerning any. Most of the material strikes me as both vulgar and unedifying. But if the First Amendment means anything, it means that a man cannot be sent to prison merely for distributing publications which offend a judge's esthetic sensibilities, mine or any other's.

Censorship reflects a society's lack of confidence in itself. It is a hallmark of an authoritarian regime. Long ago those who wrote our First Amendment charted a different course. They believed a society can be truly strong only when it is truly free. In the realm of expression they put their faith, for better or for worse, in the enlightened choice of the people, free from the interference of a policeman's intrusive thumb or a judge's heavy hand. So it is that the Constitution protects coarse expression as well as refined, and vulgarity no less than elegance. A book worthless to me may convey something of value to my neighbor. In the free society to which our Constitution has committed us, it is for each to choose for himself. . . .

There does exist a distinct and easily identifiable class of material in which all of these elements coalesce. It is that, and that alone, which I think government may constitutionally suppress, whether by criminal or civil sanctions. I have referred to such material before as hard-core pornography, without trying further to define it. Jacobellis v. Ohio. . . .

The Court today appears to concede that the materials Ginzburg mailed were themselves protected by the First Amendment. But, the Court says, Ginzburg can still be sentenced to five years in prison for mailing them. Why? Because, says the Court, he was guilty of "commercial exploitation," of "pandering," and of "titillation." But Ginzburg was not charged with "commercial exploitation"; he was not charged with "pandering"; he was not charged with "titillation." Therefore, to affirm his conviction now on any of those grounds, even if otherwise valid, is to deny him due process of law. But those grounds are not, of course, otherwise valid. Neither the statute under which Ginzburg was convicted nor any other federal statute I know of makes "commercial exploitation" or "pandering" or "titillation" a criminal offense. And any criminal law that sought to do so in the terms so elusively defined by the Court would, of course, be unconstitutionally vague and therefore void. All of these matters are developed in the dissenting opinions of my Brethren, and I simply note here that I fully agree with them.

For me, however, there is another aspect of the Court's opinion in this case that is even more regrettable. Today the Court assumes the power to deny Ralph Ginzburg the protection of the First Amendment because it disapproves of his "sordid business." That is a power the Court does not possess. For the First Amendment protects us all with an even hand. It applies to Ralph Ginzburg with no less completeness and force than to G. P. Putnam's Sons. In upholding and enforcing the Bill of Rights, this Court has no power to pick or to choose. When we lose sight of that fixed star of constitutional adjudication, we lose our way. For then we forsake a government of law and are left with government by Big Brother. . . .

*   *   *

Another new dimension was invoked in the case of Edward Mishkin, a New York publisher of sado-masochistic material. It was claimed that Mishkin's books were of no interest to the "average person" (Roth), but were written only to certain deviant groups. Again speaking for the majority, Justice Brennan held that the "prurient interest" requirement of Roth could be met if the material in question is aimed at the prurient interest of a clearly defined deviate group, in addition to the "average person" as in Roth. In the 6-3 decision, dissents echoed previous stands: Justice Black holding that the state has no power to limit freedom of expression, Justice Douglas arguing that the First Amendment allows all ideas to be expressed, even if "offbeat," and Justice Stewart again holding that the material before the Court did not constitute "hard-core pornography."

MISHKIN V. NEW YORK
383 U.S. 502 (1966)

MR. JUSTICE BRENNAN *delivered the opinion of the Court.*

This case, like *Ginzburg v. United States*, involves convictions under a criminal obscenity statute. A panel of three judges of the Court of Special Sessions of the City of New York found appellant guilty of violating sec. 1141 of the New York Penal Law by hiring others to prepare obscene books, publishing obscene books, and possessing obscene books with intent to sell them. He was sentenced to prison terms aggregating three years and ordered to pay $12,000 in fines for these crimes. . . .

Appellant was not prosecuted for anything he said or believed, but for what he did, for his dominant role in several enterprises engaged in producing and selling allegedly obscene books. Fifty books are involved in this case. They portray sexuality in many guises. Some depict relatively normal heterosexual relations, but more depict such deviations as sado-masochism, fetishism, and homosexuality. Many have covers with drawings of scantily clad women being whipped, beaten, tortured, or abused. Many, if not most, are photo-offsets of typewritten books written and illustrated by authors and artists according to detailed instructions given by the appellant. . . .

All the books are cheaply prepared paperbound "pulps" with imprinted sales prices that are several thousand per cent above costs. All but three were printed by a photo-offset printer who was paid 40¢ or 15¢ per copy, depending on whether it was a "thick" or "thin" book. The printer was instructed by appellant not to use appellant's name as publisher but to print some fictitious name on each book, to "make up any name and address." Appellant stored books on the printer's premises and paid part of the printer's rent for the storage space. The printer filled orders for the books, at appellant's direction, delivering them to appellant's retail store, Publishers' Outlet, and, on occasion, shipping books to other places. Appellant paid the authors, artists, and printer cash for their services, usually at his book store.

Appellant attacks sec. 1141 as invalid on its face, contending that it exceeds First Amendment limitations by proscribing publications that are merely sadistic or masochistic, that the terms "sadistic" and "masochistic" are impermissibly vague, and that the term "obscene" is also impermissibly vague. . . .

. . . [A]pellant's sole contention regarding the nature of the material is that some of the books involved in this prosecution, those depicting various deviant sexual practices, such as flagellation, fetishism, and lesbianism, do not satisfy the prurient-appeal requirement because they do not appeal to a prurient interest of the "average person" in sex, that "instead of stimulating the erotic, they disgust and sicken." We reject this argument as being founded on an unrealistic interpretation of the prurient-appeal requirement.

Where the material is designed for and primarily disseminated to a clearly defined deviant sexual group, rather than the public at large, the prurient-appeal requirement of the *Roth* test is satisfied if the dominant theme of the material taken as a whole appeals to the prurient interest in sex of the members of that group. The reference to the "average" or "normal" person in *Roth* does not foreclose this holding. In regard to the prurient-appeal requirement, the concept of the "average" or "normal" person was employed in *Roth* to serve the essentially negative purpose of expressing our rejection of that aspect of the *Hicklin* test that made the impact on the most susceptible person determinative. . . .

MR. JUSTICE BLACK, *dissenting.*

. . . Neither in this case nor in *Ginzburg* have I read the alleged obscene matter. This is because I believe for reasons stated in my dissent in *Ginzburg* and in many other prior cases that this Court is without constitutional power to censor speech or press regardless of the particular subject discussed. I think the federal judiciary because it is appointed for life is the most appropriate tribunal that could be selected to interpret the Constitution and thereby mark the boundaries of what government agencies can and cannot do. But because of life tenure, as well as other reasons, the federal judiciary is the least appropriate branch of government to take over censorship responsibilities by deciding what pictures and writings people throughout the land can be permitted to see and read. When this Court makes particularized rules on what people can see and read, it determines which policies are reasonable and right, thereby performing the classical function of legislative bodies directly responsible to the people. Accordingly, I wish once more to express my objections to saddling this Court with the irksome and inevitably unpopular and unwholesome task of finally deciding by a case-by-case, sight-by-sight personal judgment of the members of this Court what pornography (whatever that means) is too hard core for people to see or read. . . .

. . . The only practical answer to these concededly almost unanswerable problems is, I think, for this Court to decline to act as a national board of censors over speech and press but instead to stick to its clearly authorized constitutional duty to adjudicate cases over things and conduct. Halfway censorship methods, no matter how laudably motivated, cannot in my judgment protect our cherished First Amendment freedoms from the destructive aggressions of both state and national government. I would reverse this case and announce that the First and Fourteenth Amendments taken together command that neither Congress nor the States shall pass laws which in any manner abridge freedom of speech and press—whatever the subjects discussed. I think the Founders of our Nation in adopting the First Amendment meant precisely that the Federal Government should pass "no law" regulating speech and press but should confine its legislation to the regulation of conduct. So too, that policy of the First Amendment made applicable to the States by the Fourteenth, leaves the States vast power to regulate conduct but no power at all, in my judgment, to make the expression of views a crime.

*　　*　　*

The inevitable question of the constitutionality of variable standards of obscenity, one standard for adults and another for children, was answered by the Warren Court in a 1968 decision, Ginsberg v. New York. The Court held that the state has the power to "protect" its children from material deemed harmful to them—in this case four "girlie" magazines— even though this same material would be constitutionally available to adults. It was the first time the Court had upheld a censorship law designed specifically to apply to minors. Justice Brennan, writing for the 6-3 majority, acknowledged that there was no scientifically demonstrated causal relationship between the reading of salacious literature and antisocial behavior, but noted also that this relationship had not been disproved either. Justice Fortas, dissenting, chastised his colleagues for not considering the alleged obscenity of the magazines in question, and Justice Douglas, also dissenting, labeled the Court the "nation's board of censors." A similar principle in relation to motion picture classification was expressed in Interstate Circuit, Inc. v. Dallas, handed down the same day. Excerpts from that decision appear in Chapter 7.

GINSBERG V. NEW YORK
390 U.S. 629 (1968)

MR. JUSTICE BRENNAN delivered the opinion of the Court.

This case presents the question of the constitutionality on its face of a New York criminal obscenity statute which prohibits the sale to minors under 17 years of age of material defined to be obscene on the basis of its appeal to them whether or not it would be obscene to adults.

Appellant and his wife operate "Sam's Stationery and Luncheonette" in Bellmore, Long Island. They have a lunch counter and, among other things, also sell magazines including some so-called "girlie" magazines. Appellant was prosecuted under two informations, each in two counts, which charged that he personally sold a 16-year-old boy two "girlie" magazines on each of two dates in October 1965, in violation of sec. 484-h of the New York Penal Law. He was tried before a judge without a jury in Nassau County District Court and was found guilty on both counts. The judge found (1) that the magazines contained pictures which depicted female "nudity" in a manner defined in subsection 1 (b), that is "the showing of . . . female . . . buttocks with less than a full opaque covering, or the showing of the female breast with less than a fully opaque covering of any portion thereof below the top of the nipple . . . ," and (2) that the pictures were "harmful to minors" in that they had, within the meaning of subsection 1 (f), ". . . that quality of . . . representation . . . of nudity . . . [which] . . . (i) predominantly appeals to the prurient, shameful or morbid interest of minors, and (ii) is patently offensive to prevailing standards in the adult community as a whole with respect to what is suitable material for minors, and (iii) is utterly without redeeming social importance for minors." . . .

The "girlie" picture magazines involved in the sales here are not obscene for adults. *Redrup v. New York.* But sec. 484-h does not bar the appellant from stocking the magazines and selling them to persons 17 years of age or older. . . .

Appellant's attack is not that New York was without power to draw the line at age 17. Rather, his contention is the broad proposition that the scope of the constitutional freedom of expression secured to a citizen to read or see material concerned with sex cannot be made to depend upon whether the citizen is an adult or a minor. He accordingly insists that the denial to minors under 17 of access to material condemned by sec. 484-h, insofar as that material is not obscene for persons 17 years of age or older, constitutes an unconstitutional deprivation of protected liberty. . . .

The well-being of its children is of course a subject within the State's constitutional power to regulate, and, in our view, two interests justify the limitations in sec. 484-h upon the availability of sex material to minors under 17, at least if it was rational for the legislature to find that the minors' exposure to such material might be harmful. . . . Indeed, subsection 1 (f) (ii) of sec. 484-h expressly recognizes the parental role in assessing sex related material harmful to minors according "to prevailing standards in the adult community as a whole with respect to what is suitable material for minors." Moreover, the prohibition against sales to minors does not bar parents who so desire from purchasing the magazines for their children.

The State also has an independent interest in the well-being of its youth. . . . In *Prince v. Massachusetts,* this Court . . . recognized that the State has an interest "to protect the welfare of children" and to see that they are "safeguarded from abuses" which might prevent their "growth into free and independent well-developed men and citizens." The only question remaining, therefore, is whether the New York Legislature might rationally conclude, as it has, that exposure to the materials proscribed by sec. 484-h constitutes such an "abuse."

Section 484-e of the law states a legislative finding that the material condemned by sec. 484-h is "a basic factor in impairing the ethical and moral development of our youth and a clear and present danger to the people of the state." It is very doubtful that this finding expresses an accepted scientific fact. But obscenity is not protected expression and may be suppressed without a showing of the circumstances which lie behind the phrase "clear and present danger" in its application to protected speech. *Roth v. United States.* . . . [T]here is no lack of "studies" which purport to demonstrate that obscenity is or is not "a basic factor in impairing the ethical and moral development of . . . youth and a clear and present danger to the people of the state." But the growing consensus of commentators is that "[w]hile these studies all agree that a causal link has not been demonstrated, they are equally agreed that a causal link has not been disproved either." We do not demand of legislatures a "scientifically certain criteria of legislation." . . .

MR. JUSTICE STEWART, *concurring in the result.*

A doctrinaire, knee-jerk application of the First Amendment would, of course, dictate the nullification of this New York statute. But that result is not required, I think, if we bear in mind what it is that the First Amendment protects.

The First Amendment guarantees liberty of human expression in order to preserve in our Nation what Mr. Justice Holmes called a "free trade in ideas." To that end, the Constitution protects more than just a man's freedom to say or write or publish what he wants. It secures as well the liberty of each man to decide for himself what he will read and to what he will listen. The Constitution guarantees, in short, a society of free choice. Such a society presupposes the capacity of its members to choose. . . .

I think a State may permissibly determine that, at least in some precisely delineated areas, a child—like someone in a captive audience—is not possessed of that full capacity for individual choice which is the presupposition of First Amendment guarantees. It is only upon such a premise, I should suppose, that a State may deprive children of other rights—the right to marry, for example, or the right to vote—deprivations that would be constitutionally intolerable for adults. . . .

MR. JUSTICE DOUGLAS, *with whom Mr. Justice Black concurs, dissenting.*

. . . The notion of censorship is founded on the belief that speech and press sometimes do harm and therefore can be regulated. I once visited a foreign nation where the regime of censorship was so strict that all I could find in the bookstalls were tracts on religion and tracts on mathematics. Today the Court determines the constitutionality of New York's law regulating the sale of literature to children on the basis of the reasonableness of the law in light of the welfare of the child. If the problem of state and federal regulation of "obscenity" is in the field of substantive due process, I see no reason to limit the legislatures to protecting children alone. The "juvenile delinquents" I have known are mostly over 50 years of age. If rationality is the measure of the validity of this law, then I can see how modern Anthony Comstocks could make out a case for "protecting" many groups in our society, not merely children.

While I find the literature and movies which come to us for clearance exceedingly dull and boring, I understand how some can and do become very excited and alarmed and think that something should be done to stop the flow. It is one thing for parents and the religious organizations to be active and involved. It is quite a different matter for the State to become implicated as a censor. As I read the First Amendment, it was designed to keep the State and the hands of all state officials off the printing presses of America and off the distribution systems for all printed literature. . . .

. . . Censors are of course propelled by their own neuroses. That is why a universally accepted definition of obscenity is impossible. Any definition is indeed highly subjective, turning on the neurosis of the censor. Those who have a deep-seated, subconscious conflict may well become either great crusaders against a particular kind of literature or avid customers of it. That, of course, is the danger of letting any group of citizens be the judges of what other people, young or old, should read. . . .

Today this Court sits as the Nation's board of censors. With all respect, I do not know of any group in the country less qualified first, to know what obscenity is when they see it, and second, to have any considered judgment as to what the deleterious or beneficial impact of a particular publication may have on minds either young or old. . . .

MR. JUSTICE FORTAS, *dissenting.*

. . . The Court avoids facing the problem whether the magazines in the present case are "obscene" when viewed by a 16-year-old boy, although not "obscene" when viewed by someone 17 years of age or older. It says that Ginsberg's lawyer did not choose to challenge the conviction on the ground that the magazines are not "obscene." He chose only to attack the statute on its face. Therefore, the Court reasons, we need not look at the magazines and determine whether they may be excluded from the ambit of the First Amendment as "obscene" for purposes of this case. But this Court has made strong and comprehensive statements about its duty in First Amendment cases—statements with which I agree.

In my judgment, the Court cannot properly avoid its fundamental duty to define "obscenity" for purposes of censorship of material sold to youths, merely because of counsel's position. . . .

I agree that the State in the exercise of its police power—even in the First Amendment domain—may make proper and careful differentiation between adults and children. But I do not agree that this power may be used on an arbitrary, free-wheeling basis. This is not a case where, on any standard enunciated by the Court, the magazines are obscene, nor one where the seller is at fault. Petitioner is being prosecuted for the sale of magazines which he had a right under the decisions of this Court to offer for sale, and he is being prosecuted without proof of "fault"—without even a claim that he deliberately, calculatedly sought to induce children to buy "obscene" material. Bookselling should not be a hazardous profession. . . .

In its final decision on obscenity, the Warren Court ruled that the state may not prohibit mere possession of obscene material within the privacy of one's home. "If the First Amendment means anything," wrote Justice Marshall in the opinion of the Court, "it means that a state has no business telling a man, sitting alone in his own house, what books he may read or what films he may watch. Our whole constitutional heritage rebels at the thought of giving government the power to control men's minds." He was careful, however, to distinguish between the conditions of the Stanley case and permissible state control of the distribution of obscene matter, such as was upheld in Roth and subsequent decisions. Stanley was sentenced to one year in prison for possession of obscene material, a violation of Georgia statutes. In a concurring opinion, Justices Stewart, Brennan and White departed from the majority by noting that their vote for reversal of Stanley's conviction was based on the conditions of the search of his home rather than on the private possession question. The decision, though it did not initially receive the notoriety of some of the earlier censorship cases, may prove to be one of the most significant of the decade. The Warren Court clearly took a final firm step in protecting man's rights under the Constitution to read or view privately what he wishes without interference from the state.

STANLEY V. GEORGIA
394 U.S. 557 (1969)

MR. JUSTICE MARSHALL *delivered the opinion of the Court.*

An investigation of appellant's alleged bookmaking activities led to the issuance of a search warrant for appellant's home. Under authority of this warrant, federal and state agents secured entrance. They found very little evidence of bookmaking activity, but while looking through a desk drawer in an upstairs bedroom, one of the federal agents, accompanied by a state officer, found three reels of eight-millimeter film. Using a projector and screen found in an upstairs living room, they viewed the films. The state officer concluded that they were obscene and seized them. Since a further examination of the bedroom indicated that appellant occupied it, he was charged with possession of obscene matter and placed under arrest. . . .

It is true that *Roth* does declare, seemingly without qualification, that obscenity is not protected by the First Amendment. That statement has been repeated in various forms in subsequent cases. However, neither *Roth* nor any subsequent decision of this Court dealt with the precise problem involved in the present case. Roth was convicted of mailing obscene circulars and advertising, and an obscene book, in violation of a federal obscenity statute. . . . None of the statements cited by the Court in *Roth* for the proposition that "this Court has always assumed that obscenity is not protected by the freedoms of speech and press" were made in the context of a statute punishing mere private possession of obscene material; the cases cited deal for the most part with use of the mails to distribute objectionable material or with some form of public distribution or dissemination. Moreover, none of this Court's decisions subsequent to *Roth* involved prosecution for private possession of obscene materials. Those cases dealt with the power of the State and Federal Governments to prohibit or regulate certain public actions taken or intended to be taken with respect to obscene matter. . . .

. . . [Appellant] is asserting the right to read or observe what he pleases—the right to satisfy his intellectual and emotional needs in the privacy of his own home. He is asserting the right to be free from state inquiry into the contents of his library. Georgia contends that appellant does not have these rights, that there are certain types of materials that the individual may not read or even possess. Georgia justifies this assertion by arguing that the films in the present case are obscene. But we think that mere categorization of these films as "obscene" is insufficient justification for such a drastic invasion of personal liberties guaranteed by the First and Fourteenth Amendments. Whatever may be the justifications for other statutes regulating obscenity, we do not think they reach into the privacy of one's own home. If the First Amendment means anything, it means that a State has no business telling a man, sitting alone in his own house, what books he may read or what films he may watch. Our whole constitutional heritage rebels at the thought of giving government the power to control men's minds.

And yet, in the face of these traditional notions of individual liberty, Georgia asserts the right to protect the individual's mind from the effects of obscenity. We are not certain that this argument amounts to anything more than the assertion that the State has the right to control the moral content of a person's thoughts. To some, this may be a noble purpose, but it is wholly inconsistent with the philosophy of the First Amendment. . . .

MR. JUSTICE STEWART, *with whom Mr. Justice Brennan and Mr. Justice White join, concurring in the result.*

. . . To condone what happened here is to invite a government official to use a seemingly precise and legal warrant only as a ticket to get into a man's home, and, once inside, to launch forth upon unconfined searches and indiscriminate seizures as if armed with all the unbridled and illegal power of a general warrant. . . .

*   *   *

Two significant decisions offering some clarification of the 1969 Stanley rule were handed down by the Supreme Court as it drew to a close its 1970–71 term. Both decisions dealt with distribution of obscene matter in light of the Stanley decision, which allowed individual citizens to possess obscene material for their private use. The first case, Thirty-Seven Photographs, involved seizure by customs officials of allegedly obscene material publisher Milton Luros was attempting to bring into the United States from Europe. Luros claimed he wanted to use the pictures in a book describing sexual positions. The lower courts, citing Stanley, found for Luros, but the Supreme Court reversed, holding that the approval of private possession of obscene matter under Stanley did not prohibit the government from removing such material intended for commercial purposes from the normal channels of commerce. Justice White's opinion was joined by Chief Justice Burger and Justices Blackmun and Brennan. Justices Black, Douglas and Marshall dissented. Justices Harlan and Stewart agreed with the first part of the White opinion setting constitutionally allowable time limits for the initiation of forfeiture proceedings, but Justice Stewart emphasized that he would support the rights of an individual citizen to bring through customs obscene matter intended for personal use.

UNITED STATES V. THIRTY-SEVEN PHOTOGRAPHS
(Announced May 3, 1971)

Mr. Justice White announced the judgment of the Court and an opinion in which The Chief Justice, Mr. Justice Brennan, and Mr. Justice Blackmun join.

When Milton Luros returned to the United States from Europe on October 24, 1969, he brought with him in his luggage the 37 photographs here involved. United States customs agents . . . seized the photographs as obscene. . . . The stipulation revealed, among other things, that some or all of the 37 photographs were intended to be incorporated in a hard cover edition of The Kama Sutra of Vatsyayana, a widely distributed book candidly describing a large number of sexual positions. . . .

 . . . On the authority of Stanley, Luros urged the trial court to construe the First Amendment as forbidding any restraints on obscenity except where necessary to protect children or where it intruded itself upon the sensitivity or privacy of an unwilling adult. Without rejecting this position, the trial court read Stanley as protecting, at the very least, the right to read obscene material in the privacy of one's own home and to receive it for that purpose. . . .

The trial court erred in reading Stanley as immunizing from seizure obscene materials possessed at a port of entry for the purpose of importation for private use. In *United States v. Reidel* we have today held that Congress may constitutionally prevent the mails from being used for distributing pornography. In this case, neither Luros nor his putative buyers have rights which are infringed by the exclusion of obscenity from incoming foreign commerce. By the same token, obscene materials may be removed from the channels of commerce when discovered in the luggage of a returning foreign traveler even though intended solely for his private use. That the private user under *Stanley* may not be prosecuted for possession of obscenity in his home does not mean that he is entitled to import it from abroad free from the power of Congress to exclude noxious articles from commerce. *Stanley's* emphasis was on the freedom of thought and mind in the privacy of the home. But a port of entry is not a traveler's home. His right to be let alone neither prevents the search of his luggage nor the seizure of unprotected, but illegal, materials when his possession of them is discovered during such a search. Customs officers characteristically inspect luggage and their power to do so is not questioned in this case; it is an old practice and is intimately associated with excluding illegal articles from the country. Whatever the scope of the right to receive obscenity adumbrated in *Stanley*, that right, as we said in *Reidel*, does not extend to one who is seeking, as was Luros here, to distribute obscene materials to the public, nor does it extend to one seeking to import obscene materials from abroad, whether for private use or public distribution. As we held in *Roth v. United States*, 354 U.S. 476 (1957), and reiterated today in *Reidel*, obscenity is not within the scope of first amendment protection. Hence Congress may declare it contraband and prohibit its importation, as it has elected to do. . . .

MR. JUSTICE STEWART, *concurring in the judgment and in Part I of Mr. Justice White's opinion.*

I agree that the First Amendment does not prevent the border seizure of obscene materials sought to be imported for commercial dissemination. For the reasons expressed in Part I of Mr. Justice White's opinion, I also agree that *Freedman v. Maryland*, 380 U.S. 1, requires that there be time limits for the initiation of forfeiture proceedings and for the completion of the judicial determination of obscenity.

But I would not in this case decide, even by way of dicta, that the Government may lawfully seize literary material intended for the purely private use of the importer. The terms of the statute appear to apply to an American tourist who, after exercising his constitutionally protected liberty to travel abroad, returns home with a single book in his luggage, with no intention of selling it or otherwise using it, except to read it. If the Government can constitutionally take the book away from him as he passes through customs, then I do not understand the meaning of *Stanley v. Georgia*, 394 U.S. 557. . . .

A second post-Stanley decision handed down the same day as Thirty-Seven Photographs emphasized the principles outlined in the landmark 1957 Roth decision, thereby ruling out the use of the mails to deliver obscene material. Using reasoning similar to that used in Thirty-Seven Photographs, the Supreme Court majority ruled that Stanley's approval of the possession of obscene matter for private use did not sanction the use of the channels of commerce to distribute obscene material nor did it sanction the government (i.e. the Postal Service) to be a party to such distribution. Normal Reidel had been indicted for mailing an illustrated publication, "The True Facts About Imported Pornography." The lower courts dismissed the indictment under the Stanley principle. A seven-man Supreme Court majority reversed. Justice White delivered the opinion of the Court. Justices Black and Douglas dissented.

UNITED STATES V. REIDEL
(Announced May 3, 1971)

MR. JUSTICE WHITE *delivered the opinion of the Court.*

. . . Reidel, like Roth, was charged with using the mails for the distribution of obscene material. His conviction, if it occurs and the materials are found in fact to be obscene, would be no more vulnerable than was Roth's.

Stanley v. Georgia, 394 U.S. 557 (1969), compels no different result. There, pornographic films were found in Stanley's home and he was convicted under Georgia statutes for possessing obscene material. This Court reversed the conviction, holding that the mere private possession of obscene matter cannot constitutionally be made a crime. But it neither overruled nor disturbed the holding in *Roth.* . . . Nothing in *Stanley* questioned the validity of *Roth* insofar as the distribution of obscene material was concerned. Clearly the Court had no thought of questioning the validity of [the law] as applied to those who, like Reidel, are routinely disseminating obscenity through the mails and who have no claim, and could make none, about unwanted governmental intrusions into the privacy of their home. . . .

The District Court ignored both *Roth* and the express limitations on the reach of the *Stanley* decision. Relying on the statement in *Stanley* that "the Constitution protects the right to receive information and ideas . . . regardless of their social worth," 394 U.S., at 564, the trial judge reasoned that "if a person has the right to receive and possess this material, then someone must have the right to deliver it to him." . . .

The District Court gave *Stanley* too wide a sweep. To extrapolate from Stanley's right to have a peruse obscene material in the privacy of his own home a First Amendment right in Reidel to sell it to him would effectively scuttle *Roth*, the precise result that the *Stanley* opinion abjured. Whatever the scope of the "right to receive" referred to in *Stanley*, it is not so broad as to immunize the dealings in obscenity in which Reidel engaged here—dealings which *Roth* held unprotected by the First Amendment. . . .

The personal constitutional rights of those like Stanley to possess and read obscenity in their homes and their freedom of mind and thought do not depend on whether the materials are obscene or whether obscenity is constitutionally protected. Their rights to have and view that material in private are independently saved by the Constitution.

Reidel is in a wholly different position. He has no complaints about governmental violations of his private thoughts or fantasies, but stands squarely on a claimed First Amendment right to do business in obscenity and use the mails in the process. But *Roth* has squarely placed obscenity and its distribution outside the reach of the First Amendment and they remain there today. *Stanley* did not overrule *Roth* and we decline to do so now.

A postscript is appropriate. *Roth* and like cases have interpreted the First Amendment not to insulate obscenity from statutory regulation. But the Amendment itself neither proscribes dealings in obscenity nor directs or suggests legislative oversight in this area. The relevant constitutional issues have arisen in the courts only because lawmakers having the exclusive legislative power have consistently insisted on making the distribution of obscenity a crime or otherwise regulating such materials and because the laws they pass are challenged as unconstitutional invasions of free speech and press.

It is urged that there is developing sentiment that adults should have complete freedom to produce, deal in, possess, and consume whatever communicative materials may appeal to them and that the law's involvement with obscenity should be limited to those situations where children are involved or where it is necessary to prevent imposition on unwilling recipients of whatever age. The concepts involved are said to be so elusive and the laws so inherently unenforceable without extravagant expenditures of time and effort by enforcement officers and the courts that basic reassessment is not only wise but essential. This may prove to be the desirable and eventual legislative course. But if it is, the task of restructuring the obscenity laws lies with those who pass, repeal, and amend statutes and ordinances. *Roth* and like cases pose no obstacle to such developments. . . .

MR. JUSTICE BLACK, *with whom Mr. Justice Douglas joins, dissenting.*

. . . I particularly regret to see the Court revive the doctrine of *Roth v. United States*, 354 U.S. 476 (1957), that "obscenity" is speech for some reason unprotected by the First Amendment. As the Court's many decisions in this area demonstrate, it is extremely difficult for judges or any other citizens to agree on what is "obscene." Since the distinctions between protected speech and "obscenity" are so elusive and obscure almost every "obscenity" case involves difficult constitutional issues. After *Roth* our docket and those of other courts have constantly been crowded with cases where judges are called upon to decide whether a particular book, magazine, or movie may be banned. I have expressed before my view that I can imagine no task for which this Court of lifetime judges is less equipped to deal.

. . . Despite the proven shortcomings of *Roth*, the majority today reaffirms the validity of that dubious decision. Thus, for the foreseeable future this Court must sit as a Board of Supreme Censors, sifting through books and magazines and watching movies because some official fears they deal too explicitly with sex. I can imagine no more distasteful, useless, and time-consuming task for the members of this Court than perusing this material to determine whether it has "redeeming social value." This absurd spectacle could be avoided if we would adhere to the literal command of the First Amendment that "Congress shall make no law . . . abridging the freedom of speech, or of the press. . . ."

LOOKING-GLASS LAW:
AN ANALYSIS OF THE GINZBURG CASE

By Richard B. Dyson *

. . . In evaluating the *Ginzburg* case, the question immediately arises why Mr. Justice Brennan wrote a confusing, self-contradictory opinion to announce a doctrine which, though novel, is not especially complex. Why did he need to insist that he was only "elaborating" an existing test when he was obviously treading new ground? Why try to establish by repeated assertions, contrary to common sense, that advertising crucially reduces a publication's social value, or increases its offensiveness? A more basic question is why the doctrine was found necessary at all; although the obscenity issue has caused some furor in recent years, no great pressures have appeared in the area of advertising.

The answers, it is submitted, lie in the friction between some deep moral convictions and the legal materials out of which the case was built. In previous opinions Mr. Justice Brennan made it clear that the presence of sexual themes or imagery was not enough to deprive material of first amendment protection, but the use of this sexual content to sell the material was, to him, beyond the pale. He manifested in his opinion a deep sense of outrage, a great emotional need to condemn Ralph Ginzburg's activities. The opinion rings with pejorative phrases such as "leer of the sensualist," "the sordid business of pandering," and "titillation by pornography." He was disturbed not by the fact that Ginzburg had committed a crime, which was not at all clear as the case came up, but rather that he had committed a sin—and a mortal one at that.

On the other hand, Mr. Justice Brennan was faced with facts and a statute that gave him little room to maneuver. The statute describes, by the familiar string of adjectives, obscene things, and declares them, and notices telling how to obtain them, to be non-mailable matter. The "things" in question, the two periodicals and the book, were, it seems fair to say, not really close to the outer limits of constitutional protection, and therefore not "non-mailable matter" within the prohibition of the statute as it previously had been construed. Given that Mr. Justice Brennan was aroused at the thought of selling something on the basis of its sexual content, how was he to justify its incrimination under such a statute? As Mr.

* From Richard B. Dyson. "Looking-Glass Law: An Analysis of the Ginzburg Case." *University of Pittsburgh Law Review*, Vol. 28 (October 1966), p. 1, at p. 14. Used with permission of the *University of Pittsburgh Law Review*. When the article first appeared, the author was an associate professor of law at Boston University.

Justice Stewart was to point out cogently in his dissent, no federal statute made pandering or titillating a criminal offense.

The answer was a device worthy of a seventeenth-century chancellor. Reduced to its simplest terms, which Mr. Justice Brennan sedulously avoided doing, it was, "If you say that the matter you are mailing is obscene, we will punish you under the statute barring the mailing of obscene matter, regardless of the actual nature of the matter." A statute incriminating the distribution of *obscene matter* was extrapolated to cover the *obscene distribution* of matter. He thus managed to uphold a conviction without even reaching the main argument raised by the defense, that the material in question was not obscene and therefore constitutionally protected. In justification of this line of reasoning, he mounted the collage of rather inconsistent ideas that have been discussed above, drawing from Chief Justice Warren's *Roth* concurrence, the Model Penal Code, and a 1940 Learned Hand opinion, to suggest that advertising is somehow relevant to the obscenity of the thing advertised.

As an attempt to rationalize an anomalous result, the device and its accompanying reasoning are a failure; whether they will endure is another question. In the first place, the violence done to the statute, and therefore to the defendant's right to due process of law, is notable—in Mr. Justice Harlan's words, "an astonishing piece of judicial improvisation." Ginzburg was perfectly justified in believing that the only issue raised by his activities was the obscenity of the materials he was selling, and that the chances that the issue would be decided against him were remote. To pack him off to prison for a long term on the basis of a tortured construction of a familiar statute raises grave questions of *ex post facto* justice. Our legal system is not improved by Mr. Justice Brennan's justification of the result by his opinion that Ginzburg was a nasty man in a "sordid business," an opinion that many do not share. Ginzburg was not a wretch on the fringes of society, but a well-known and successful publisher.

Furthermore, the opinion is defective even in terms of its internal logic. Its key idea is that if a seller characterizes his product as obscene, that characterization will be taken at its face value. But to say that Ginzburg's advertising implied obscenity is to ignore the definition of obscenity on which the whole doctrinal structure rests—a definition whose chief author is Mr. Justice Brennan himself. For the key test of obscenity here was not whether the material was sexually stimulating in nature ("prurient," in Brennanite terms); there was no question about that. It was, rather, whether the publications possessed redeeming social value, and here the advertisements in question loudly proclaimed the affirmative. While speaking of taking them at their face value, the opinion ignored what was plainly on their face.

Finally, the advertisements described did not fit the lurid descriptions attached to them by Mr. Justice Brennan. They invited the reader to buy publications frankly and candidly concerned with sex, which recent court decisions had rendered marketable. In his references to the courts' decisions, Ginzburg was quite correct. His felony, then, was declaring that he was doing something that the courts had said, and for the purposes of this decision we must assume, he could do. The additional matter about attemps to use towns such as Intercourse, Pa. for a mailing address is, I submit, a weak joke too trivial to merit serious discussion, not to mention five years in prison. Any suggestion that Ginzburg's advertisements were more leering than the standard Madison Avenue product in the mass media would betray a certain insulation from the product.

Beyond its obvious failures of logic and justice, the most disturbing thing about *Ginzburg* is its simplistic importation of personal values into the Constitution. The opinion has a syllogistic foundation strongly reminiscent of *Lochner v. New York*. The Constitution does not exist to protect evil activities; what he was doing was evil; therefore the Constitution cannot protect him. Value judgments are inescapable in constitutional decisions, however much we might long for purely "neutral" principles. But there is a crucial difference between making necessary choices between competing goods, such as fairness to an accused versus prosecutory effectiveness, and gratuitously taking sides, in the name of the Constitution, in a value dispute where reasonable men differ. There is a point at which a wise judge must say: Although I feel strongly about this particular value-choice (*e.g.*, whether this activity is unequivocally bad), there is a significant body of respectable opinion on the other side and I must, therefore, refrain from making my feelings on this point the basis of a constitutional rule. To fail to do so is to place the Constitution on one side or the other of contemporary disputes about economics, religion, or, heaven forbid, sex. And if the choice happens to be a bad one, the court appears not only wrong but foolish. Here there was no broadly recognized norm that Ralph Ginzburg violated; in fact, the place of sex in our current literature, art, and theater, coupled with the preponderant opposition to censorship of the academic and literary world, seems to indicate that a majority of the literate public disagrees with Mr. Justice Brennan's values. Mr. Justice Peckham in *Lochner* at least had the conventional wisdom of the day on his side.

In the long view, the *Ginzburg* case may be viewed as an expression of revulsion by the Court at the "exploitation" of its own broad interpretation of the First Amendment. The majority appears to tolerate freedom of expression, but not the attempt to popularize sex and profit by it with broad appeals through the mass media. The underlying validity of the Court's position, aside from the problems of lawmaking discussed herein, is likely to be judged by the view one takes of what Ginzburg was doing. I suggest that the majority, distracted by Ginzburg's immediate commercial goals, failed to recognize that he is in the mainstream of a broad and significant social movement. Freedom of expression is an integral part of the current drive to change freedom from a familiar slogan to an activist credo, and of the rejection of the traditional primacy, in Western society, of self-control and obedience for that of self-expression and creativity. Thus, it is inseparable from the movements for political and social freedom that are causing a notable upheaval in America today. The function of law, especially constitutional law, in the face of social upheaval should not be to enforce the personal codes, the traditional mores, that are under attack, but to limit the degree of direct impingement on person and property that such movements cause. Books, pamphlets, and magazines are among the least obnoxious channels of radicalism; once the limits of tolerance of their contents are set, there is no wisdom in further examining the methods and motives of their distributors.

OBSCENITY: RECOMMENDATIONS
OF THE PRESIDENT'S COMMISSION *

I. Non-Legislative Recommendations

The Commission believes that much of the "problem" regarding materials which depict explicit sexual activity stems from the inability or reluctance of people in our society to be open and direct in dealing with sexual matters. This most often manifests itself in the inhibition of talking openly and directly about sex. Professionals use highly technical language when they discuss sex; others of us escape by using euphemisms—or by not talking about sex at all. Direct and open conversation about sex between parent and child is too rare in our society.

Failure to talk openly and directly about sex has several consequences. It overemphasizes sex, gives it a magical, non-natural quality, making it more attractive and fascinating. It diverts the expression of sexual interest out of more legitimate channels, into less legitimate channels. Such failure makes teaching children and adolescents to become fully and adequately functioning sexual adults a more difficult task. And it clogs legitimate channels for transmitting sexual information and forces people to use clandestine and unreliable sources.

The Commission believes that interest in sex is normal, healthy, good. Interest in sex begins very early in life and continues throughout the life cycle although the strength of this interest varies from stage to stage. With the onset of puberty, physiological and hormonal changes occur which both quicken interest and make the individual more responsive to sexual interest. The individual needs information about sex in order to understand himself, place his new experiences in a proper context, and cope with his new feelings.

The basic institutions of marriage and the family are built in our society primarily on sexual attraction, love, and sexual expression. These institutions can function successfully only to the extent that they have a healthy base. Thus the very foundation of our society rests upon healthy sexual attitudes grounded in appropriate and accurate sexual information.

Sexual information is so important and so necessary that if people cannot obtain it openly and directly from legitimate sources and through accurate and legitimate channels, they will seek it through whatever channels and sources are available. Clandestine sources may not only be inaccurate but may also be distorted and provide a warped context.

---

* From the Report of the Commission on Obscenity and Pornography. Washington, D.C.: Government Printing Office, 1970, at p. 47.

The Commission believes that accurate, appropriate sex information provided openly and directly through legitimate channels and from reliable sources in healthy contexts can compete successfully with potentially distorted, warped, inaccurate, and unreliable information from clandestine, illegitimate sources; and it believes that the attitudes and orientations toward sex produced by the open communication of appropriate sex information from reliable sources through legitimate channels will be normal and healthy, providing a solid foundation for the basic institutions of our society.

The Commission, therefore, presents the following positive approaches to deal with the problem of obscenity and pornography.

1. The Commission recommends that a massive sex education effort be launched. This sex education effort should be characterized by the following:

   a) its purpose should be to contribute to healthy attitudes and orientations to sexual relationships so as to provide a sound foundation for our society's basic institutions of marriage and family;
   b) it should be aimed at achieving an acceptance of sex as a normal and natural part of life and of oneself as a sexual being;
   c) it should not aim for orthodoxy; rather it should be designed to allow for a pluralism of values;
   d) it should be based on facts and encompass not only biological and physiological information but also social, psychological, and religious information;
   e) it should be differentiated so that content can be shaped appropriately for the individual's age, sex, and circumstances;
   f) it should be aimed, as appropriate, to all segments of our society, adults as well as children and adolescents;
   g) it should be a joint function of several institutions of our society: family, school, church, etc.;
   h) special attention should be given to the training of those who will have central places in the legitimate communication channels—parents, teachers, physicians, clergy, social service workers, etc.;
   i) it will require cooperation of private and public organizations at local, regional, and national levels with appropriate funding;
   j) it will be aided by the imaginative utilization of new educational technologies for example, educational television could be used to reach several members of a family in a family context.

The Commission feels that such a sex education program would provide a powerful positive approach to the problems of obscenity and pornography. By providing accurate and reliable sex information through legitimate sources, it would reduce interest in and dependence upon clandestine and less legitimate sources. By providing healthy attitudes and orientations toward sexual relationships, it would provide better protection for the individual against distorted or warped ideas he may encounter regarding sex. By providing greater ease in talking about sexual matters in appropriate contexts, the shock and offensiveness of encounters with sex would be reduced.

2. The Commission recommends continued open discussion, based on factual information, on the issues regarding obscenity and pornography.

Discussion has in the past been carried on with few facts available and the debate has necessarily reflected, to a large extent, prejudices and fears. Congress asked the Commission to secure more factual information before making recommendations. Some of the facts developed by the Commission are contrary to widely held assumptions. These findings provide new perspectives on the issues.

The information developed by the Commission should be given wide distribution, so that it may sharpen the issues and focus the discussion.

3. The Commission recommends that additional factual information be developed.

The Commission's effort to develop information has been limited by time, financial resources, and the paucity of previously existing research. Many of its findings are tentative and many questions remain to be answered. We trust that our modest pioneering work in empirical research into several problem areas will help to open the way for more extensive and long-term research based on more refined methods directed to answering more refined questions. We urge both private and public sources to provide the financial resources necessary for the continued development of factual information so that the continuing discussion may be further enriched.

The Federal Government has special responsibilities for continuing research in these areas and has existing structures which can facilitate further inquiry. Many of the questions raised about obscenity and pornography have direct relevance to already existing programs in the National Institute of Mental Health, the National Institute of Child Health and Human Development, and the United States Office of Education. The Commission urges these agencies to broaden their concerns to include a wider range of topics relating to human sexuality, specifically including encounters with explicit sexual materials.

4. The Commission recommends that citizens organize themselves at local, regional, and national levels to aid in the implementation of the foregoing recommendations.

The sex education effort recommended by the Commission can be achieved only with broad and active citizen participation. Widespread discussion of the issues regarding the availability of explicit sexual materials implies broad and active citizen participation. A continuing research program aimed at clarifying factual issues regarding the impact of explicit sexual materials on those who encounter them will occur only with the support and cooperation of citizens.

Organized citizen groups can be more constructive and effective if they truly represent a broad spectrum of the public's thinking and feeling. People tend to assume, in the absence of other information, that most peoples' opinions are similar to their own. However, we know that opinions in the sexual realm vary greatly—that there is no unanimity of values in this area. Therefore, every group should attempt to include as wide a variety of opinion as is possible.

The aim of citizen groups should be to provide a forum whereby all views may be presented for thoughtful consideration. We live in a free, pluralistic society which places its trust in the competition of ideas in a free market place. Persuasion is a preferred technique. Coercion, repression and censorship in order to promote a given set of views are not tolerable in our society.

II. Legislative Recommendations

On the basis of its findings, the Commission makes the following legislative recommendations. The disagreements of particular Commissioners with aspects of the Commission's legislative recommendations are noted below, where the recommendations are discussed in detail. Commissioners Link, Hill, and Keating have filed a joint dissenting statement. In addition, Commissioners Keating and Link have submitted separate remarks. Commissioners Larsen and Wolfgang have filed statements explaining their dissent from certain Commission recommendations. A number of other Commissioners have filed short separate statements.

In general outline, the Commission recommends that federal, state, and local legislation should not seek to interfere with the right of adults who wish to do so to read, obtain, or view explicit sexual materials. On the other hand, we recommend legislative regulations upon the sale of sexual materials to young persons who do not have the consent of their parents, and we also recommend legislation to protect persons from having sexual materials thrust upon them without their consent through the mails or through open public display.

The Commission's specific legislative recommendations and the reasons underlying these recommendations are as follows:

A. Statutes Relating to Adults

The Commission recommends that federal, state, and local legislation prohibiting the sale, exhibition, or distribution of sexual materials to consenting adults should be repealed. Twelve of the 17 participating members of the Commission join in this recommendation. Two additional Commissioners subscribe to the bulk of the Commission's Report, but do not believe that the evidence presented at this time is sufficient to warrant the repeal of all prohibitions upon what adults may obtain. Three Commissioners dissent from the recommendation to repeal adult legislation and would retain existing laws prohibiting the dissemination of obscene materials to adults.

The Commission believes that there is no warrant for continued governmental interference with the full freedom of adults to read, obtain or view whatever such material they wish. Our conclusion is based upon the following considerations:

1. Extensive empirical investigation, both by the Commission and by others, provides no evidence that exposure to or use of explicit sexual materials play a significant role in the causation of social or individual harms such as crime, delinquency, sexual or nonsexual deviancy or severe emotional disturbances. This research and its results are described in detail in the Report of the Effects Panel of the Commission and are summarized above in the Overview of Commission findings. Empirical investigation thus supports the opinion of a substantial majority of persons professionally engaged in the treatment of deviancy, delinquency and antisocial behavior, that exposure to sexually explicit materials has no harmful causal role in these areas.

Studies show that a number of factors, such as disorganized family relationships and unfavorable peer influences, are intimately related to harmful sexual behavior or adverse character development. Exposure to sexually explicit materials, however, cannot be counted as among these determinative factors. Despite the existence of widespread legal prohibitions upon the dissemination of such materials, exposure to them appears to be a usual and harmless part of the process of growing up in our society and a frequent and nondamaging occurrence among adults. Indeed, a few Commission studies indicate that a possible distinction between sexual offenders and other people, with regard to experience with explicit sexual materials, is that sex offenders have seen markedly *less* of such materials while maturing.

This is not to say that exposure to explicit sexual materials has no effect upon human behavior. A prominent effect of exposure to sexual materials is that persons tend to talk more about sex as a result of seeing such materials. In addition, many persons become temporarily sexually aroused upon viewing explicit sexual materials and the frequency of their sexual activity may, in consequence, increase for short periods. Such behavior, however, is the type of sexual activity already established as usual activity for the particular individual.

In sum, empirical research designed to clarify the question has found no evidence to date that exposure to explicit sexual materials plays a significant role in the causation of delinquent or criminal behavior among youth or adults.

2. On the positive side, explicit sexual materials are sought as a source

of entertainment and information by substantial numbers of American adults. At times, these materials also appear to serve to increase and facilitate constructive communication about sexual matters within marriage. The most frequent purchaser of explicit sexual materials is a college-educated, married male, in his thirties or forties, who is of above average socioeconomic status. Even where materials are legally available to them, young adults and older adolescents do not constitute an important portion of the purchases of such materials.

3. Society's attempts to legislate for adults in the area of obscenity have not been successful. Present laws prohibiting the consensual sale or distribution of explicit sexual materials to adults are extremely unsatisfactory in their practical application. The Constitution permits material to be deemed "obscene" for adults only if, as a whole, it appeals to the "prurient" interest of the average person, is "patently offensive" in light of "community standards," and lacks "redeeming social value." These vague and highly subjective aesthetic, psychological and moral tests do not provide meaningful guidance for law enforcement officials, juries or courts. As a result, law is inconsistently and sometimes erroneously applied and the distinctions made by courts between prohibited and permissible materials often appear indefensible. Errors in the application of the law and uncertainty about its scope also cause interference with the communication of constitutionally protected materials.

4. Public opinion in America does not support the imposition of legal prohibitions upon the right of adults to read or see explicit sexual materials. While a minority of Americans favors such prohibitions, a majority of the American people presently are of the view that adults should be legally able to read or see explicit sexual materials if they wish to do so.

5. The lack of consensus among Americans concerning whether explicit sexual materials should be available to adults in our society, and the significant number of adults who wish to have access to such materials, pose serious problems regarding the enforcement of legal prohibitions upon adults, even aside from the vagueness and subjectivity of present law. Consistent enforcement of even the clearest prohibitions upon consensual adult exposure to explicit sexual materials would require the expenditure of considerable law enforcement resources. In the absence of a persuasive demonstration of damage flowing from consensual exposure to such materials, there seems no justification for thus adding to the overwhelming tasks already placed upon the law enforcement system. Inconsistent enforcement of prohibitions, on the other hand, invites discriminatory action based upon considerations not directly relevant to the policy of the law. The latter alternative also breeds public disrespect for the legal process.

6. The foregoing considerations take on added significance because of the fact that adult obscenity laws deal in the realm of speech and communication. Americans deeply value the right of each individual to deter-

mine for himself what books he wishes to read and what pictures or films he wishes to see. Our traditions of free speech and press also value and protect the right of writers, publishers, and booksellers to serve the diverse interests of the public. The spirit and letter of our Constitution tell us that government should not seek to interfere with these rights unless a clear threat of harm makes that course imperative. Moreover, the possibility of the misuse of general obscenity statutes prohibiting distributions of books and films to adults constitutes a continuing threat to the free communication of ideas among Americans—one of the most important foundations of our liberties.

7. In reaching its recommendation that government should not seek to prohibit censensual distributions of sexual materials to adults, the Commission discussed several arguments which are often advanced in support of such legislation. The Commission carefully considered the view that adult legislation should be retained in order to aid in the protection of young persons from exposure to explicit sexual materials. We do not believe that the objective of protecting youth may justifiably be achieved at the expense of denying adults materials of their choice. It seems to us wholly inappropriate to adjust the level of adult communication to that considered suitable for children. Indeed, the Supreme Court has unanimously held that adult legislation premised on this basis is a clearly unconstitutional interference with liberty.

8. There is no reason to suppose that elimination of governmental prohibitions upon the sexual materials which may be made available to adults would adversely affect the availability to the public of other books, magazines, and films. At the present time, a large range of very explicit textual and pictorial materials are available to adults without legal restrictions in many areas of the country. The size of this industry is small when compared with the overall industry in books, magazines, and motion pictures, and the business in explicit sexual materials is insignificant in comparison with other national economic enterprises. Nor is the business an especially profitable one; profit levels are, on the average, either normal as compared with other businesses or distinctly below average. The typical business entity is a relatively small entrepreneurial enterprise. The long-term consumer interest in such materials has remained relatively stable in the context of the economic growth of the nation generally, and of the media industries in particular.

9. The Commission has also taken cognizance of the concern of many people that the lawful distribution of explicit sexual materials to adults may have a deleterious effect upon the individual morality of American citizens and upon the moral climate in America as a whole. This concern appears to flow from a belief that exposure to explicit materials may cause moral confusion which, in turn, may induce antisocial or criminal behavior. As noted above, the Commission has found no evidence to support such

a contention. Nor is there evidence that exposure to explicit sexual materials adversely affects character or moral attitudes regarding sex and sexual conduct.

The concern about the effect of obscenity upon morality is also expressed as a concern about the impact of sexual materials upon American values and standards. Such values and standards are currently in a process of complex change, in both sexual and nonsexual areas. The open availability of increasingly explicit sexual materials is only one of these changes. The current flux in sexual values is related to a number of powerful influences, among which are the ready availability of effective methods of contraception, changes of the role of women in our society, and the increased education and mobility of our citizens. The availability of explicit sexual materials is, the Commission believes, not one of the important influences on sexual morality.

The Commission is of the view that it is exceedingly unwise for government to attempt to legislate individual moral values and standards independent of behavior, especially by restrictions upon consensual communication. This is certainly true in the absence of a clear public mandate to do so, and our studies have revealed no such mandate in the area of obscenity.

The Commission recognizes and believes that the existence of sound moral standards is of vital importance to individuals and to society. To be effective and meaningful, however, these standards must be based upon deep personal commitment flowing from values instilled in the home, in educational and religious training, and through individual resolutions of personal confrontations with human experience. Governmental regulation of moral choice can deprive the individual of the responsibility for personal decision which is essential to the formation of genuine moral standards. Such regulation would also tend to establish an official moral orthodoxy, contrary to our most fundamental constitutional traditions.

Therefore, the Commission recommends the repeal of existing federal legislation which prohibits or interferes with consensual distribution of "obscene" materials to adults. These statutes are: 18 U.S.C. sec. 1461, 1462, 1464, and 1465; 19 U.S.C. sec. 1305; and 39 U.S.C. sec. 3006. The Commission also recommends the repeal of existing state and local legislation which may similarly prohibit the consensual sale, exhibition, or the distribution of sexual materials to adults.

B. *Statutes Relating to Young Persons*

The Commission recommends the adoption by the States of legislation set forth in the Drafts of Proposed Statutes in Section III of this Part of the Commission's Report prohibiting the commercial distribution or display for sale of certain sexual materials to young persons. Similar legislation might also be adopted, where appropriate, by local governments and by the Federal Government for application in areas, such as the District of Columbia, where it has primary jurisdiction over distributional conduct.

The Commission's recommendation of juvenile legislation is joined in by 14 members of the Commission. Two of these feel the legislation should be drawn so as to include appropriate descriptions identifying the material as being unlawful for sale to children. Three members disagree. Other members of the Commission, who generally join in its recommendation for juvenile legislation, disagree with various detailed aspects of the Commission's legislative proposal. These disagreements are noted in the following discussion.

The Commission's recommendation of juvenile legislation flows from these findings and considerations:

A primary basis for the Commission's recommendation for repeal of adult legislation is the fact that extensive empirical investigations do not indicate any causal relationship between exposure to or use of explicit sexual materials and such social or individual harms such as crime, delinquency, sexual or nonsexual deviancy, or severe emotional disturbances. The absence of empirical evidence supporting such a causal relationship also applies to the exposure of children to erotic materials. However, insufficient research is presently available on the effect of the exposure of children to sexually explicit materials to enable us to reach conclusions with the same degree of confidence as for adult exposure. Strong ethical feelings against experimentally exposing children to sexually explicit materials considerably reduced the possibility of gathering the necessary data and information regarding young persons.

In view of the limited amount of information concerning the effects of sexually explicit materials on children, other considerations have assumed primary importance in the Commission's deliberations. The Commission has been influenced, to a considerable degree, by its finding that a large majority of Americans believe that children should not be exposed to certain sexual materials. In addition, the Commission takes the view that parents should be free to make their own conclusions regarding the suitability of explicit sexual materials for their children and that it is appropriate for legislation to aid parents in controlling the access of their children to such materials during their formative years. The Commission recognizes that legislation cannot possibly isolate children from such materials entirely; it also recognizes that exposure of children to sexual materials may not only do no harm but may, in certain instances, actually facilitate much needed communication between parent and child over sexual matters. The Commission is aware, as well, of the considerable danger of creating an unnatural attraction or an enhanced interest in certain materials by making them "forbidden fruit" for young persons. The Commission believes, however, that these considerations can and should be weighed by individual parents in determining their attitudes toward the exposure of their children to sexual materials, and that legislation should aid, rather than undermine, such parental choice.

Taking account of the above considerations, the modern juvenile legislation recommended by the Commission applies only to distributions to children made without parental consent. The recommended legislation applies only to commercial distributions and exhibitions; in the very few instances where noncommercial conduct in this area creates a problem it can be dealt with under existing legal principles for the protection of young persons, such as prohibitions upon contributing to the delinquency of minors. The model legislation also prohibits displaying certain sexual materials for sale in a manner which permits children to view materials which cannot be sold to them. Two members of the Commission, who recommend legislation prohibiting sales to juveniles, do not join in recommending this regulation upon display; one member of the Commission recommends only this display provision, and does not recommend a special statute prohibiting sales to young persons.

The Commission, pursuant to Congressional direction, has given close attention to the definitions of prohibited material included in its recommended model legislation for young persons. A paramount consideration in the Commission's deliberations has been that definitions of prohibited material be as specific and explicit as possible. Such specificity aids law enforcement and facilitates and encourages voluntary adherence to law on the part of retail dealers and exhibitors while causing as little interference as possible with the proper distribution of materials to children and adults. The Commission's recommended legislation seeks to eliminate subjective definitional criteria insofar as that is possible and goes further in that regard than existing state legislation.

The Commission believes that only pictorial material should fall within prohibitions upon sale or commercial display to young persons. An attempt to define prohibited textual materials for young persons with the same degree of specificity as pictorial materials would, the Commission believes, not be advisable. Many worthwhile textual works containing considerable value for young persons, treat sex in an explicit manner and are presently available to young persons. There appears to be no satisfactory way to distinguish, through a workable legal definition, between these works and those which may be deemed inappropriate by some persons for commercial distribution to young persons. As a result, the inclusion of textual material within juvenile legislative prohibitions would pose considerable risks for dealers and distributors in determining what books might legally be sold or displayed to young persons and would thus inhibit the entire distribution of verbal materials by those dealers who do not wish to expose themselves to such risks. The speculative risk of harm to juveniles from some textual material does not justify these dangers. The Commission believes, in addition, that parental concern over the material commercially available to children most often applies to pictorial matter.

The definition recommended by the Commission for inclusion in juvenile legislation covers a range of explicit pictorial and three-dimensional depictions of sexual activity. It does not, however, apply to depictions of nudity alone, unless genital areas are exposed and emphasized. The definition is applicable only if the explicit pictorial material constitutes a dominant part of a work. An exception is provided for works of artistic or anthropological significance.

Seven Commissioners would include verbal materials within the definition of materials prohibited for sale to young persons. They would, however, also include a broad exception for such textual materials when they bear literary, historical, scientific, educational, or other similar social value for young persons.

Because of changing standards as to what material, if any, is inappropriate for sale or display to children, the Commission's model statute contains a provision requiring legislative reconsideration of the need for, and scope of, such legislation at six-year intervals.

The model statute also exempts broadcast or telecast activity from its scope. Industry self-regulation in the past has resulted in little need for governmental intervention. If a need for governmental regulation should arise, the Commission believes that such regulations would be most appropriately prepared in this specialized area through the regulating power of the Federal Communications Commission, rather than through diverse state laws.

The Commission has not fixed upon a precise age limit for inclusion in its recommended juvenile legislation, believing that such a determination is most appropriately made by the States and localities which enact such provisions in light of local standards. All States now fix the age in juvenile obscenity statutes at under 17 or under 18 years. The recommended model statute also excludes married persons, whatever their age, from the category of juveniles protected by the legislation.

The Commission considered the possibility of recommending the enactment of uniform federal legislation requiring a notice or label to be affixed to materials by their publishers, importers or manufacturers, when such materials fall within a definitional provision identical to that included within the recommended state or local model juvenile statute. Under such legislation, the required notice might be used by retail dealers and exhibitors, in jurisdictions which adopt the recommended juvenile legislation, as a guide to what material could not be sold or displayed to young persons. The Commission concluded, however, that such a federal notice or labeling provision would be unwise. So long as definitional provisions are drafted to be as specific as possible, and especially if they include only pictorial material, the Commission believes that the establishment of a federal regulatory notice system is probably unnecessary; specific definitions of pictorial material, such as the Commission recommends, should themselves enable retail dealers and exhibitors to make accurate judgments regarding the status of particular magazines and films. The Commission is also extremely reluctant to recommend imposing any federal system for labeling reading or viewing matter on the basis of its quality or content. The precedent of such required labeling would pose a serious potential threat to First Amendment liberties in other areas of communication. Labels indicating sexual content might also be used artificially to enhance the appeal of certain materials. Two Commissioners favor federally imposed labeling in order to advise dealers as clearly and accurately as possible about what material is forbidden for sale to young persons, placing the responsibility for judging whether material falls within the statute on the publisher or producer who is completely aware of its contents and who is in a position to examine each item individually.

Finally, the Commission considered, but does not affirmatively recommend, the enactment by the Federal Government of juvenile legislation which would prohibit the sale of certain explicit materials to juveniles through the mails. Such federal legislation would, the Commission believes, be virtually unenforceable since the constitutional requirement of proving the defendant's guilty knowledge means that a prosecution could be successful only if proof were available that the vendor knew that the purchaser was a minor. Except in circumstances which have not been found to be prevalent, as where a sale might be solicited through a mailing list composed of young persons, mail order purchases are made without any knowledge by the vendor of the purchaser's age. Certificates of age by the purchaser would be futile as an enforcement device and to require notarized affidavits to make a purchase through the mails would unduly interfere with purchase by adults. The Commission has found, moreover, that at present juveniles rarely purchase sexually explicit materials through the mail, making federal legislative machinery in this area apparently unnecessary.

C. *Public Display and Unsolicited Mailing*

The Commission recommends enactment of state and local legislation prohibiting public displays of sexually explicit pictorial materials, and approves in principle of the federal legislation, enacted as part of the 1970 Postal Reorganization Act, regarding the mailing of unsolicited advertisements of a sexually explicit nature. The Commission's recommendations in this area are based upon its finding, through its research, that certain explicit sexual materials are capable of causing considerable offense to numerous Americans when thrust upon them without their consent. The Commission believes that these unwanted intrusions upon individual sensibilities warrant legislative regulation and it further believes that such intrusions can be regulated effectively without any significant interference with consensual communication of sexual material among adults.

PUBLIC DISPLAY

The Commission's recommendations in the public display area have been formulated into a model state public display statute which is reproduced in the Drafts of Proposed Statutes in Section III of this Part of the Commission Report. Three Commissioners dissent from this recommendation.

The model statute recommended by the Commission (which would also be suitable for enactment in appropriate instances by local government units and by the Federal Government for areas where it has general legislative jurisdiction) prohibits the display of certain potentially offensive sexually explicit pictorial materials in places easily visible from public thoroughfares or the property of others. Verbal materials are not included within the recommended prohibition. There appears to be no satisfactory way to define "offensive" words in legislation in order to make the parameters of prohibition upon their display both clear and sufficiently limited so as not to endanger the communication of messages of serious social concern. In addition, the fact that there are few, if any, "dirty" words which do not already appear fairly often in conversation among many Americans and in some very widely distributed books and films indicates that such words are no longer capable of causing the very high degree of offense to a large number of persons which would justify legislative interference. Five Commissioners disagree and would include verbal materials in the display prohibition because they believe certain words cause sufficient offense to warrant their inclusion in display prohibitions.

Telecasts are exempted from the coverage of the statute for the same reasons set forth above in connection with discussion of the Commission's recommendation of juvenile legislation.

The recommended model legislation defines in specific terms the explicit sexual pictorial materials which the Commission believes are capable of causing offense to a substantial number of persons. The definition covers a range of explicit pictorial and three-dimensional depictions of sexual activity. It does not apply to depictions of nudity alone, unless genital areas are exposed and emphasized. An exception is provided for works of artistic or anthropological significance. The Commission emphasizes that this legislation does not prohibit the sale or advertisement of any materials, but does prohibit the public display of potentially offensive pictorial matter. While such displays have not been found by the Commission to be a serious problem at the present time, increasing commercial distribution of explicit materials to adults may cause considerable offense to others in the future unless specific regulations governing public displays are adopted.

UNSOLICITED MAILING

The Commission, with three dissents, also approves of federal legislation to prevent unsolicited advertisements containing potentially offensive sexual material from being communicated through the mails to persons who do not wish to receive such advertisements. The Federal Anti-Pandering Act, which went into effect in 1968, imposes some regulation in this area, but it permits a mail recipient to protect himself against such mail only after he has received at least one such advertisement and it protects him only against mail emanating from that particular source. The Commission believes it more appropriate to permit mail recipients to protect themselves against all such unwanted mail advertisements from any source. Federal legislation in this area was enacted just prior to the date of this report as part of the 1970 Postal Reorganization Act.

The Commission considered two possible methods by which persons might be broadly insulated from unsolicited sexual advertisements which they do not wish to receive. One approach, contained in the 1970 Postal Reorganization Act, authorizes the Post Office to compile and maintain current lists of persons who have stated that they do not wish to receive certain defined materials, makes these lists available at cost to mailers of unsolicited advertisements, and prohibits sending the defined material to persons whose names appear on the Post Office lists. A second approach, described in detail in the Commission's Progress Report of July, 1969, would require all mailers of unsolicited advertisements falling within the statutory definition to place a label or code on the envelope. Mail patrons would then be authorized to direct local postal authorities not to deliver coded mail to their homes or offices.

In principle, the Commission favors the first of these approaches employed by Congress in the 1970 Postal Reorganization Act. The Commission takes this view because it believes that the primary burden of regulating the flow of potentially offensive unsolicited mail should appropriately fall upon the mailers of such materials and because of its reluctance to initiate required federal labeling of reading or viewing matter because of its sexual content. The Commission believes, however, that under current mail-order practices it may prove financially unfeasible for many smaller mailers to conform their mailing lists to those compiled by the Post Office. Use of computers to organize and search mailing lists will apparently be required by the new law; few, if any, small mailers utilize computers in this way today. If the current lists maintained by the Post Office came to contain a very large number of names—perhaps one million or more—even a computer search of these names, to discover any that were also present on a mailing list sought to be used by a mailer, might be prohibitively expensive. If such were the case, the Commission would believe the second possible approach to regulation to be more consistent with constitutional rights.

This approach, however, might place serious burdens upon Post Office personnel. The Commission was not able to evaluate the practical significance of these burdens.

In considering the definition appropriate to legislation regulating unsolicited sexual advertisements, the Commission examined a large range of unsolicited material which has given rise to complaints to the Post Office Department in recent years. A definition was then formulated which quite specifically describes material which has been deemed offensive by substantial numbers of postal patrons. This definition is set forth in the footnote. The Commission prefers this definitional provision to the less precise definitional provision in the 1970 Postal Reorganization Act.

D. *Declaratory Judgment Legislation*

The Commission recommends the enactment, in all jurisdictions which enact or retain provisions prohibiting the dissemination of sexual materials to adults or young persons, of legislation authorizing prosecutors to obtain declaratory judgments as to whether particular materials fall within existing legal prohibitions and appropriate injunctive relief. A model statute embodying this recommendation is presented in the Drafts of Proposed Statutes in Section III of this Part of the Commission Report. All but two of the Commissioners concur in the substance of this recommendation. The Commission recognizes that the particular details governing the institution and appeal of declaratory judgment actions will necessarily vary from State to State depending upon local jurisdictional and procedural provisions. The Commission is about evenly divided with regard to whether local prosecutors should have authority to institute such actions directly, or whether the approval of an official with state-wide jurisdiction, such as the State Attorney General, should be required before an action for declaratory judgment is instituted.

A declaratory judgment procedure such as the Commission recommends would permit prosecutors to proceed civilly, rather than through the criminal process, against suspected violations of obscenity prohibition. If such civil procedures are utilized, penalties would be imposed for violation of the law only with respect to conduct occurring after a civil declaration is obtained. The Commission believes this course of action to be appropriate whenever there is any existing doubt regarding the legal status of materials; where other alternatives are available, the criminal process should not ordinarily be invoked against persons who might have reasonably believed, in good faith, that the books or films they distributed were entitled to constitutional protection, for the threat of criminal sanctions might otherwise deter the free distribution of constitutionally protected material. The Commission's recommended legislation would not only make a declaratory judgment procedure available, but would require prosecutors to utilize this process instead of immediate criminal prosecution in all cases except those where the materials in issue are unquestionably within the applicable statutory definitional provisions.

WITHDRAWAL OF APPELLATE JURISDICTION

The Commission recommends against the adoption of any legislation which would limit or abolish the jurisdiction of the Supreme Court of the United States or of other federal judges and courts in obscenity cases. Two Commissioners favor such legislation; one deems it inappropriate for the Commission to take a position on this issue.

Proposals to limit federal judicial jurisdiction over obscenity cases arise from disagreement over resolution by federal judges of the question of obscenity in litigation. The Commission believes that these disagreements flow in largest measure from the vague and subjective character of the legal tests for obscenity utilized in the past; under existing legal definitions, courts are required to engage in subjective decision making and their results may well be contrary to the subjective analyses of many citizens. Adoption of specific and explicit definitional provisions in prohibitory and regulatory legislation, as the Commission recommends, should eliminate most or all serious disagreements over the application of these definitions and thus eliminate the major source of concern which has motivated proposals to limit federal judicial jurisdiction.

More fundamentally, the Commission believes that it would be exceedingly unwise to adopt the suggested proposal from the point of view of protection of constitutional rights. The Commission believes that disagreements with court results in particular obscenity cases, even if these disagreements are soundly based in some instances, are not sufficiently important to justify tampering with existing judicial institutions which are often required to protect constitutional rights. Experience shows that while courts may sometimes reverse convictions on a questionable basis, juries and lower courts also on occasion find guilt in cases involving books and films which are entitled to constitutional protection, and state appeals courts often uphold such findings. These violations of First Amendment rights would go uncorrected if such decisions could not be reversed at a higher court level.

The Commission also recommends against the creation of a precedent in the obscenity area for the elimination by Congress of federal judicial jurisdiction in other areas whenever a vocal majority or minority of citizens disagrees strongly with the results of the exercise of that jurisdiction. Freedom in many vital areas frequently depends upon the ability of the judiciary to follow the Constitution rather than strong popular sentiment. The problem of obscenity, in the absence of any indication that sexual materials cause societal harm, is not an appropriate social phenomenon upon which to base a precedent for removing federal judicial jurisdiction to protect fundamental rights guaranteed by the Bill of Rights. . . .

CHAPTER 7

MOTION PICTURE CENSORSHIP

Motion pictures as a means of mass communication are in their infancy when compared with the print media, but the film medium has
grown rapidly and has demonstrated massive impact over its first half-
century. The Supreme Court has noted that films have a "greater capacity
for evil" than do the print media and, as such, are held in a unique position
relative to First Amendment protection. It was first ruled, in a 1915 case,
that motion pictures did not fall under First Amendment safeguards because they were considered diversionary entertainment only and a "business
pure and simple." Mutual Film Corp. v. Ohio.

It was not until the 1950s that the Court reversed itself and firmly
granted motion pictures constitutional recognition along with speech and
press. Burstyn v. Wilson. A change in the 1915 Mutual Film philosophy,
however, was hinted at in 1948 when Justice Douglas in his opinion dealing
with a Sherman Act question wrote, "We have no doubt that motion pictures, like newspapers and radio, are included in the press whose freedom
is guaranteed by the First Amendment." United States v. Paramount. This
was the first indication that the Court might depart from its "business
only" position in Mutual Film. While that single statement was all the
Court said at the time about films and the First Amendment, the apparent
leaning of the Court did not go unnoticed by those interested in freedom
of expression for motion pictures, and before long the Warren Court was to
be presented with the opportunity to explain more fully the hint given by
Justice Douglas in 1948.

The philosophy of the Mutual Film decision was finally overturned in
1952 with Burstyn v. Wilson, in which the Supreme Court, for the first
time, firmly held that motion pictures are to be included within the protective scope of the First Amendment. 343 U.S. 495. It left to another day,

however, the broader questions of film censorship and licensing, restricting itself only to the specific question at hand, i.e. the New York law as related to the sacrilegious. At question was the film "The Miracle," the showing of which brought cries of outrage from various religious and private pressure groups. The 9-0 decision, in addition to placing films within the First Amendment, struck a philosophic blow at those private groups which attempt to impose their beliefs on the general viewing public. While Justice Clark's opinion of the Court did note unique characteristics which set films aside from other forms of expression under constitutional protection, it held that it was not the intent of the Constitution to protect the "religious sensitivities" of some at the expense of freedom of expression.

JOSEPH BURSTYN, INC. V. WILSON
343 U.S. 495 (1952)

MR. JUSTICE CLARK *delivered the opinion of the Court.*

The issue here is the constitutionality, under the First and Fourteenth Amendments, of a New York statute which permits the banning of motion picture films on the grounds that they are "sacrilegious." That statute makes it unlawful "to exhibit, or to sell, lease or lend for exhibition at any place of amusement for pay or in connection with any business in the state of New York, any motion picture film or reel (with specified exceptions not relevant here), unless there is at the time in full force and effect a valid license or permit therefor of the education department. . . ."

Appellant is a corporation engaged in the business of distributing motion pictures. It owns the exclusive rights to distribute throughout the United States a film produced in Italy entitled "The Miracle." On November 30, 1950, after having examined the picture, the motion picture division of the New York education department, acting under the statute quoted above, issued to appellant a license authorizing exhibition of "The Miracle," with English subtitles, as one part of a trilogy called "Ways of Love." Thereafter, for a period of approximately eight weeks, "Ways of Love" was exhibited publicly in a motion picture theater in New York City under an agreement between appellant and the owner of the theater whereby appellant received a stated percentage of the admission price.

During this period, the New York State Board of Regents, which by statute is made the head of the education department, received "hundreds of letters, telegrams, post cards, affidavits and other communications" both protesting against and defending the public exhibition of "The Miracle." The Chancellor of the Board of Regents requested three members of the Board to view the picture and to make a report to the entire Board. After viewing the film, this committee reported to the Board that in its opinion there was basis for the claim that the picture was "sacrilegious." Thereafter, on January 19, 1951, the Regents directed appellant to show cause, at a hearing to be held on January 30, why its license to show "The Miracle" should not be rescinded on that ground. Appellant appeared at this hearing, which was conducted by the same three-member committee of the Regents which had previously viewed the picture, and challenged the jurisdiction of the committee and of the Regents to proceed with the case. With the consent of the committee, various interested persons and organizations submitted to it briefs and exhibits bearing upon the merits of the picture and upon the constitutional and statutory questions involved. On February 16, 1951, the Regents, after viewing "The Miracle," determined that it was "sacrilegious" and for that reason ordered the Commissioner of Education to rescind appellant's license to exhibit the picture. The Commissioner did so. . . .

In a series of decisions beginning with *Gitlow v. New York*, 268 U.S. 652, this Court held that the liberty of speech and of the press which the First Amendment guarantees against abridgment by the federal government is within the liberty safeguarded by the Due Process Clause of the Fourteenth Amendment from invasion by state action. That principle has been followed and reaffirmed to the present day. . . .

The present case is the first to present squarely to us the question whether motion pictures are within the ambit of protection which the First Amendment, through the Fourteenth, secures to any form of "speech" or "the press."

It cannot be doubted that motion pictures are a significant medium for the communication of ideas. They may affect public attitudes and behavior in a variety of ways, ranging from direct espousal of a political or social doctrine to the subtle shaping of thought which characterizes all artistic expression. The importance of motion pictures as an organ of public opinion is not lessened by the fact that they are designed to entertain as well as to inform. As was said in *Winters v. New York*, 333 U.S. 507:

> "The line between the informing and the entertaining is too elusive for the protection of that basic right [a free press]. Everyone is familiar with instances of propaganda through fiction. What is one man's amusement, teaches another's doctrine."

It is urged that motion pictures do not fall within the First Amendment's aegis because their production, distribution, and exhibition is a large-scale business conducted for private profit. We cannot agree. That books, newspapers, and magazines are published and sold for profit does not prevent them from being a form of expression whose liberty is safeguarded by the First Amendment. We fail to see why operation for profit should have any different effect in the case of motion pictures.

It is further urged that motion pictures possess a greater capacity for evil, particularly among the youth of a community, than other modes of expression. Even if one were to accept this hypothesis, it does not follow that motion pictures should be disqualified from First Amendment protection. If there be capacity for evil it may be relevant in determining the permissible scope of community control, but it does not authorize substantially unbridled censorship such as we have here.

For the foregoing reasons, we conclude that expression by means of motion pictures is included within the free speech and free press guarantee of the First and Fourteenth Amendments. To the extent that language in the opinion in *Mutual Film Corp. v. Industrial Commission*, 236 U.S. 230, is out of harmony with the views here set forth, we no longer adhere to it.

To hold that liberty of expression by means of motion pictures is guaranteed by the First and Fourteenth Amendments, however, is not the end of our problem. It does not follow that the Constitution requires absolute freedom to exhibit every motion picture of every kind at all times and all places. That much is evident from the series of decisions of this Court with respect to other media of communication of ideas. Nor does it follow that motion pictures are necessarily subject to the precise rules governing any other particular method of expression. Each method tends to present its own peculiar problems. But the basic principles of freedom of speech and the press, like the First Amendment's command, do not vary. Those principles, as they have frequently been enunciated by this Court, make freedom of expression the rule. There is no justification in this case for making an exception to that rule.

The statute involved here does not seek to punish, as a past offense, speech or writing falling within the permissible scope of subsequent punishment. On the contrary, New York requires that permission to communicate ideas be obtained in advance from state officials who judge the content of the words and pictures sought to be communicated. This Court recognized many years ago that such a previous restraint is a form of infringement upon freedom of expression to be especially condemned. *Near v. Minnesota*, 283 U.S. 697. The Court there recounted the history which indicates that a major purpose of the First Amendment guarantee of a free press was to prevent prior restraints upon publication, although it was carefully pointed out that the liberty of the press is not limited to that protection. It was further stated that "the protection even as to previous restraint is not absolutely unlimited. But the limitation has been recognized only in exceptional cases." In the light of the First Amendment's history and of the *Near* decision, the State has a heavy burden to demonstrate that the limitation challenged here presents such an exceptional case.

New York's highest court says there is "nothing mysterious" about the statutory provision applied in this case: "It is simply this: that no religion, as that word is understood by the ordinary, reasonable person, shall be treated with contempt, mockery, scorn and ridicule. . . ." This is far from the kind of narrow exception to freedom of expression which a state may carve out to satisfy the adverse demands of other interests of society. In seeking to apply the broad and all-inclusive definition of "sacrilegious" given by the New York courts, the censor is set adrift upon a boundless sea amid a myriad of conflicting currents of religious views, with no charts but those provided by the most vocal and powerful orthodoxies. New York cannot vest such unlimited restraining control over motion pictures in a censor. Under such a standard the most careful and tolerant censor would find it virtually impossible to avoid favoring one religion over another, and he would be subject to an inevitable tendency to ban the expression of unpopular sentiments sacred to a religious minority. Application of the "sacrilegious" test, in these or other respects, might raise substantial questions under the First Amendment's guarantee of separate church and state with freedom of worship for all. However, from the standpoint of freedom of speech and the press, it is enough to point out that the state has no legitimate interest in protecting any or all religions from views distasteful to them which is sufficient to justify prior restraints upon the expression of those views. It is not the business of government in our nation to suppress real or imagined attacks upon a particular religious doctrine, whether they appear in publications, speeches, or motion pictures.

Since the term "sacrilegious" is the sole standard under attack here, it is not necessary for us to decide, for example, whether a state may censor motion pictures under a clearly drawn statute designed and applied to prevent the showing of obscene films. That is a very different question from the one now before us. We hold only that under the First and Fourteenth Amendments a state may not ban a film on the basis of a censor's conclusion that it is "sacrilegious." . . .

*　　*　　*

Film censorship through the late 1940s and into the early 1950s was based on the judgment of isolated scenes rather than on the context of the work as a whole. This approach was similar to the one used in early literary censorship. Scene-by-scene inspection often was made by state and local licensing agencies. Nakedness was limited to travelogue-like pictures of African or South Sea natives or to blurred suggestions in more commercial ventures. It was standard practice during these years to film sexually frank scenes twice, once for domestic exhibition and again for foreign showing, the latter allowing greater sexual latitude.

Following the unanimous 1952 landmark Burstyn decision granting First Amendment protection to motion pictures, the Supreme Court began to hit hard at film censorship practices in a number of controversial areas.

The Court also lifted bans against "Pinky," the interracial story of a girl who "passed for white" (Gelling v. Texas); two films, the American "Native Son," which dealt with racial frictions, and the French "La Ronde," which included the question of promiscuity (Superior Films, Inc. v. Ohio); and the French film "Game of Love," which also dealt with sex in an explicit manner (Times Film Corp. v. Chicago). This latter case, decided in 1957, should not be confused with a major decision of the same title handed down in 1961.

In the 1961 Times Film case, the Court faced the question of prior restraint per se by acknowledging the unique characteristic of motion pictures. In a heated exchange of opinions, the Court ruled 5-4 that licensing and "prior screening" requirements involving motion pictures did not violate the constitutional guarantees of free speech and press. Chief Justice Warren issued one of his strongest dissents in which he enumerated incident after incident which clearly pointed to the dangers inherent in government censorship of films. Most of his citations dealt with political and moral questions rather than with sex and obscenity and clearly left the impression that a little censorship often leads to more. Censorship of motion pictures, he concluded, was not in the best interests of a free society.

It was left for the Warren Court of the 1960s, then, to interpret and clarify the Times Film ruling. The Court responded by placing tight restrictions on the licensing practices rather than by overturning its 1961 Times Film ruling.

Three decisions stand out in this period, Jacobellis v. Ohio, Freedman v. Maryland and Interstate Circuit v. Dallas. In the first, Justice Brennan, in announcing the judgment of the Court, argued that national standards must be used in judging obscenity since the courts are dealing with concepts guaranteed by a national constitution. He also emphasized that the work must be utterly without redeeming social importance to be judged obscene. In Freedman, the Court ruled that while licensing boards were constitutional, their decision censoring films must be given swift judicial review in courts of law and that the burden of proof in these cases must lie with the censor rather than with the exhibitor. Finally, in the Interstate Circuit case of 1968, the final film censorship decision announced by the Warren Court, the justices suggested they would accept state and local motion picture classification laws (e.g., "adults only") if these laws were drawn carefully.

Clearly, these major decisions all but eliminated the Times Film rule as a meaningful and practical pronouncement. In all cases except those dealing with hard-core pornography, the Court apparently eliminated film censorship for adult viewers. These decisions did not put the censor out of business, however. The Interstate Circuit decision can be said to give new life to the few state jurisdictions which have continued to exercise prior restraint through licensing and certainly will encourage legislation establishing others.

In addition, it has been argued that more restraint is practiced by non-government groups than by "official" censors. These censorial pressures, familiar to all producers, come from magazines and newspapers, parent-teacher organizations, civic betterment clubs and church groups, to name a few. Classification by these groups has continued or intensified in spite of—or because of—court decisions. Also, the industry itself is not without restraints. Fearing Federal control, producers in the 1930s drew a self-regulatory code for the industry. As years progressed, however, the code became less and less a force in guiding the industry. The competition of television made demands for "bolder" movies in order to "pry" audiences from their easy chairs in front of television sets. The increasing popularity of more realistic foreign films (even though customs censorship continued largely unchecked), and the rise of the American independent filmmaker also made the code more hypothetical than effective. Indeed, producers who subscribed to the code sometimes subverted the intent of the agreement by releasing "adult" films under different company names. In addition, producers sometimes found that controversy or lack of code approval were financially more beneficial than was simple code approval.

The motion picture production code was altered twice in the mid-1960s in hopes of heading off governmental restrictions on attendance, i.e. legal classification of films. But by the end of the Warren Court, state legislatures, with Supreme Court sanction through the Interstate decision, had begun to write film classification systems into law and thereby to determine to a large extent the future of the motion picture industry—both as a commercial venture and as an artistic medium free to express itself.

The state of New York, seven years after the Burstyn decision granting films First Amendment protection, was the scene of the first major debate for the Warren Court regarding censorship of motion pictures. The Court was unanimous in affirming the 1952 Burstyn decision, but failed to come to grips with the fundamental question of the right of state and local governments to pre-screen, license and censor films prior to their public showing. At issue here was a film version of the D. H. Lawrence novel, Lady Chatterley's Lover, a story of love between a woman of wealth and her husband's gamekeeper. The famed novel itself had had its own skirmishes with censorship. The film was refused a license until three isolated scenes were cut, these scenes judged to be "immoral." Justice Stewart wrote the opinion of the Court in which it was pointed out that a film may not be censored merely because it portrays ideas that are rejected by the majority, in this case that adultery might for some persons and under some circumstances be desirable. The Court noted that the censoring of an idea, such as was done in the immediate case, struck at the very heart of the Constitution. Justices Douglas and Black, as they had argued with literary censorship, took the position that any form of motion picture censorship violates the First and Fourteenth Amendments.

KINGSLEY INTERNATIONAL PICTURES CORP. V. REGENTS
360 U.S. 684 (1959)

MR. JUSTICE STEWART *delivered the opinion of the Court.*

Once again the Court is required to consider the impact of New York's motion picture licensing law upon First Amendment liberties, protected by the Fourteenth Amendment from infringement by the States.

The New York statute makes it unlawful "to exhibit, or to sell, lease or lend for exhibition at any place of amusement for pay or in connection with any business in the state of New York, any motion picture film or reel [with certain exceptions not relevant here], unless there is at the time in full force and effect a valid license or permit therefore of the education department. . . ." The law provides that a license shall issue "unless such film or a part thereof is obscene, indecent, immoral, inhuman, sacrilegious, or is of such character that its exhibition would tend to corrupt morals or incite to crime. . . ." A recent statutory amendment provides that, "the term 'immoral' and the phrase 'of such a character that its exhibition would tend to corrupt morals' shall denote a motion picture film or part thereof, the dominant purpose or effect of which is erotic or pornographic; or which portrays acts of sexual immorality, perversion, or lewdness, or which expressly or impliedly presents such acts as desirable, acceptable or proper patterns of behavior." . . .

What New York has done, therefore, is to prevent the exhibition of a motion picture because that picture advocates an idea—that adultery under certain circumstances may be proper behavior. Yet the First Amendment's basic guarantee is of freedom to advocate ideas. The State, quite simply, has thus struck at the very heart of constitutionally protected liberty.

It is contended that the State's action was justified because the motion picture attractively portrays a relationship which is contrary to the moral standards, the religious precepts, and the legal code of its citizenry. This argument misconceives what it is that the Constitution protects. Its guarantee is not confined to the expression of ideas that are conventional or shared by a majority. It protects advocacy of the opinion that adultery may sometimes be proper, no less than advocacy of socialism or the single tax. And in the realm of ideas it protects expression which is eloquent no less than that which is unconvincing. . . .

The inflexible command which the New York Court of Appeals has attributed to the State Legislature thus cuts so close to the core of constitutional freedom as to make it quite needless in this case to examine the periphery. Specifically, there is no occasion to consider the appellant's contention that the State is entirely without power to require films of any kind to be licensed prior to their exhibition. Nor need we here determine whether, despite problems peculiar to motion pictures, the controls which a State may impose upon this medium of expression are precisely coextensive with those allowable for newspapers, books, or individual speech. It is enough for the present case to reaffirm that motion pictures are within the First and Fourteenth Amendments' basic protection. *Joseph Burstyn, Inc. v. Wilson.*

MR. JUSTICE BLACK, *concurring.*

I concur in the Court's opinion and judgment but add a few words because of concurring opinions by several Justices who rely on their appraisal of the movie "Lady Chatterley's Lover" for holding that New York cannot constitutionally bar it. Unlike them, I have not seen the picture. My view is that stated by Mr. Justice Douglas, that prior censorship of moving pictures like prior censorship of newspapers and books violates the First and Fourteenth Amendments. If despite the Constitution, however, this Nation is to embark on the dangerous road of censorship, my belief is that this Court is about the most inappropriate Supreme Board of Censors that could be found. So far as I know, judges possess no special expertise providing exceptional competency to set standards and to supervise the private morals of the Nation. In addition, the Justices of this Court seem especially unsuited to make the kind of value judgments—as to what movies are good or bad for local communities—which the concurring opinions appear to require. We are told that the only way we can decide whether a State or municipality can constitutionally bar movies is for this Court to view and appraise each movie on a case-by-case basis. Under these circumstances, every member of the Court must exercise his own judgment as to how bad a picture is, a judgment which is ultimately based at least in large part on his own standard of what is immoral. The end result of such decisions seems to me to be a purely personal determination by individual Justices as to whether a particular picture viewed is too bad to allow it to be seen by the public. Such an individualized determination cannot be guided by reasonably fixed and certain standards. Accordingly, neither States nor moving picture makers can possibly know in advance, with any fair degree of certainty, what can or cannot be done in the field of movie making and exhibiting. This uncertainty cannot easily be reconciled with the rule of law which our Constitution envisages.

The different standards which different people may use to decide about the badness of pictures are well illustrated by the contrasting standards mentioned in the opinion of the New York Court of Appeals and the concurring opinion of Mr. Justice Frankfurter here. As I read the New York court's opinion this movie was held immoral and banned because it makes adultery too alluring. Mr. Justice Frankfurter quotes Mr. Lawrence, author of the book from which the movie was made, as believing censorship should be applied only to publications that make sex look ugly, that is, as I understand it, less alluring.

In my judgment, this Court should not permit itself to get into the very center of such policy controversies, which have so little in common with lawsuits.

MR. JUSTICE FRANKFURTER, *concurring in the result.*

As one whose taste in art and literature hardly qualifies him for the avant-garde, I am more than surprised, after viewing the picture, that the New York authorities should have banned "Lady Chatterley's Lover." To assume that this motion picture would have offended Victorian moral sensibilities is to rely only on the stuffiest of Victorian conventions. . . .

Even the author of "Lady Chatterley's Lover" did not altogether rule out censorship, nor was his passionate zeal on behalf of society's profound interest in the endeavors of true artists so doctrinaire as to be unmindful of the facts of life regarding the sordid exploitation of man's nature and impulses. He knew there was such a thing as pornography, dirt for dirt's sake, or, to be more accurate, dirt for money's sake. This is what D. H. Lawrence wrote:

> But even I would censor genuine pornography, rigorously. It would not be very difficult. In the first place, genuine pornography is almost always underworld, it doesn't come into the open. In the second, you can recognize it by the insult it offers invariably, to sex, and to the human spirit.
>
> Pornography is the attempt to insult sex, to do dirt on it. This is unpardonable. Take the very lowest instance, the picture post-card sold underhand, by the underworld, in most cities. What I have seen of them have been of an ugliness to make you cry. The insult to the human body, the insult to a vital human relationship! Ugly and cheap they make the human nudity, ugly and degraded they make the sexual act, trivial and cheap and nasty. (D. H. Lawrence, *Pornography and Obscenity*, pp. 12–13.) . . .

It is not our province to meet these recalcitrant problems of legislative drafting. Ours is the vital but very limited task of scrutinizing the work of the draftsmen in order to determine whether they have kept within the narrow limits of the kind of censorship which even D. H. Lawrence deemed necessary. The legislation must not be so vague, the language so loose, as to leave to those who have to apply it too wide a discretion for sweeping within its condemnation what is permissible expression as well as what society may permissibly prohibit. Always remembering that the widest scope of freedom is to be given to the adventurous and imaginative exercise of the human spirit, we have struck down legislation phrased in language intrinsically vague, unless it be responsive to the common understanding of men even though not susceptible of explicit definition. The ultimate reason for invalidating such laws is that they lead to timidity and inertia and thereby discourage the boldness of expression indispensable for a progressive society. . . .

Unless I misread the opinion of the Court, it strikes down the New York legislation in order to escape the task of deciding whether a particular picture is entitled to the protection of expression under the Fourteenth Amendment. Such an exercise of the judicial function, however onerous or ungrateful, inheres in the very nature of the judicial enforcement of the Due Process Clause. We cannot escape such instance-by-instance, case-by-case application of that clause in all the varieties of situation that come before this Court. . . . *Davidson v. New Orleans*, 96 U.S. 97, 104. The task is onerous and exacting, demanding as it does the utmost discipline in objectivity, the severest control of personal predilections. But it cannot be escaped, not even by disavowing that such is the nature of our task.

MR. JUSTICE DOUGLAS, *with whom Mr. Justice Black joins, concurring.*

While I join in the opinion of the Court, I adhere to the views I expressed in *Superior Films v. Department of Education* that censorship of movies is unconstitutional, since it is a form of "previous restraint" that is as much at war with the First Amendment, made applicable to the States through the Fourteenth, as the censorship struck down in *Near v. Minnesota.* If a particular movie violates a valid law, the exhibitor can be prosecuted in the usual way. I can find in the First Amendment no room for any censor whether he is scanning an editorial, reading a news broadcast, editing a novel or a play, or previewing a movie. . . .

Happily government censorship has put down few roots in this country. The American tradition is represented by *Near v. Minnesota.* We have in the United States no counterpart of the Lord Chamberlain who is censor over England's stage. As late as 1941 only six States had systems of censorship for movies. Chafee, *Free Speech in the United States* (1941), p. 540. That number has now been reduced to four—Kansas, Maryland, New York, and Virginia—plus a few cities. . . . And from what information is available, movie censors do not seem to be very active. Deletion of the residual part of censorship that remains would constitute the elimination of an institution that intrudes on First Amendment rights.

MR. JUSTICE CLARK, *concurring in the result.*

. . . [A]s my Brother Harlan points out, "each time such a statute is struck down, the State is left in more confusion." This is true where broad grounds are employed leaving no indication as to what may be necessary to meet the requirements of due process. I see no grounds for confusion, however, were a statute to ban "pornographic" films, or those that "portray *acts* of sexual immorality, perversion or lewdness." If New York's statute had been so construed by its highest court I believe it would have met the requirements of due process. Instead, it placed more emphasis on what the film teaches than on what it depicts. There is where the confusion enters. For this reason, I would reverse on the authority of *Burstyn*.

*   *   *

The Court in 1961 finally faced the question of the constitutionality of motion picture censorship with a 5-4 decision that cities and states do have the right to pre-screen and to issue permits for public exhibition. At issue was the film "Don Juan," a version of the Mozart opera "Don Giovanni," which admittedly would have received a permit had one been applied for. The critical issue was one of prior restraint. The five-man majority, Justices Clark, Frankfurter, Harlan, Whittaker and Stewart, held that free speech is not absolute and that it was within the constitutional framework for Chicago to protect its citizens from the dangers of obscenity by licensing films, although warning that it was not the intent of the Court to give carte blanche to local government censors. The decision brought heated dissents, with Chief Justice Warren's being the most memorable as he outlines past film censorship battles.

TIMES FILM CORP. V. CHICAGO
365 U.S. 43 (1961)

MR. JUSTICE CLARK *delivered the opinion of the Court.*

. . . We are satisfied that a justiciable controversy exists. The section of Chicago's ordinance in controversy specifically provides that a permit for the public exhibition of a motion picture must be obtained; that such "permit shall be granted only after the motion picture film for which said permit is requested has been produced at the office of the commissioner of police for examination"; that the commissioner shall refuse the permit if the picture does not meet certain standards; and that in the event of such refusal the applicant may appeal to the mayor for a *de novo* hearing and his action shall be final. Violation of the ordinance carries certain punishments. The petitioner complied with the requirements of the ordinance, save for the production of the film for examination. The claim is that this concrete and specific statutory requirement, the production of the film at the office of the Commissioner for examination, is invalid as a previous restraint on freedom of speech. In *Joseph Burstyn, Inc. v. Wilson* we held that motion pictures are included "within the free speech and free press guarantee of the First and Fourteenth Amendments." Admittedly, the challenged section of the ordinance imposes a previous restraint, and the broad justiciable issue is therefore present as to whether the ambit of constitutional protection includes complete and absolute freedom to exhibit, at least once, any and every kind of motion picture. It is that question alone which we decide. We have concluded that sec. 155-4 of Chicago's ordinance requiring the submission of films prior to their public exhibition is not, on the grounds set forth, void on its face. . . .

[T]here is not a word in the record as to the nature and content of "Don Juan." We are left entirely in the dark in this regard, as were the city officials and the other reviewing courts. Petitioner claims that the nature of the film is irrelevant, and that even if this film contains the basest type of pornography, or incitement to riot, or forceful overthrow of orderly government, it may nonetheless be shown without prior submission for examination. The challenge here is to the censor's basic authority; it does not go to any statutory standards employed by the censor or procedural requirements as to the submission of the film. . . .

Petitioner would have us hold that the public exhibition of motion pictures must be allowed under any circumstances. The State's sole remedy, it says, is the invocation of criminal process under the Illinois pornography statute, and then only after a transgression. But this position . . . is founded upon the claim of absolute privilege against prior restraint under the First Amendment—a claim without sanction in our cases. To illustrate its fallacy, we need only point to one of the "exceptional cases" which Chief Justice Hughes enumerated in *Near v. Minnesota,* namely, "the primary requirements of decency [that] may be enforced against obscene publications." Moreover, we later held specifically "that obscenity is not within the area of constitutionally protected speech or press." *Roth v. United States.* Chicago emphasizes here its duty to protect its people against the dangers of obscenity in the public exhibition of motion pictures. To this argument petitioner's only answer is that regardless of the capacity for, or extent of, such an evil, previous restraint cannot be justified. With this we cannot agree. We recognized in *Burstyn* that "capacity for evil . . . may be relevant in determining the permissible scope of community control" and that motion pictures were not "necessarily subject to the precise rules governing any other particular method of expression. Each method," we said, "tends to present its own peculiar problems."

Certainly petitioner's broadside attack does not warrant, nor could it justify on the record here, our saying that—aside from any consideration of the other "exceptional cases" mentioned in our decisions—the State is stripped of all constitutional power to prevent, in the most effective fashion, the utterance of this class of speech. It is not for this Court to limit the State in its selection of the remedy it deems most effective to cope with such a problem, absent, of course, a showing of unreasonable strictures on individual liberty resulting from its application in particular circumstances. *Kingsley Books, Inc. v. Brown.* We, of course, are not holding that city officials may be granted the power to prevent the showing of any motion picture they deem unworthy of a license. *Joseph Burstyn, Inc. v. Wilson.*

As to what may be decided when a concrete case involving a specific standard provided by this ordinance is presented, we intimate no opinion. The petitioner has not challenged all—or for that matter, any—of the ordinance's standards. Naturally we could not say that every one of the standards, including those which Illinois' highest court has found sufficient, is so vague on its face that the entire ordinance is void. At this time we say no more than this—that we are dealing with motion pictures and, even as to them, only in the context of the broadside attack presented on this record.

MR. CHIEF JUSTICE WARREN, *with whom Mr. Justice Black, Mr. Justice Douglas and Mr. Justice Brennan join, dissenting.*

I cannot agree either with the conclusion reached by the Court or with the reasons advanced for its support. To me, this case clearly presents the question of our approval of unlimited censorship of motion pictures before exhibition through a system of administrative licensing. Moreover, the decision presents a real danger of eventual censorship for every form of communication, be it newspapers, journals, books, magazines, television, radio or public speeches. The Court purports to leave these questions for another day, but I am aware of no constitutional principle which permits us to hold that the communication of ideas through one medium may be censored while other media are immune. Of course each medium presents its own peculiar problems, but they are not of the kind which would authorize the censorship of one form of communication and not the others. I submit that in arriving at its decision the Court has interpreted our cases contrary to the intention at the time of their rendition and, in exalting the censor of motion pictures, has endangered the First and Fourteenth Amendment rights of all others engaged in the dissemination of ideas. . . .

Let it be completely clear what the Court's decision does. It gives official license to the censor, approving a grant of power to city officials to prevent the showing of any moving picture these officials deem unworthy of a license. It thus gives formal sanction to censorship in its purest and most far-reaching form, to a classical plan of licensing that, in our country, most closely approaches the English licensing laws of the seventeenth century which were commonly used to suppress dissent in the mother country and in the colonies. . . .

Perhaps today's surrender was forecast by *Kingsley Books, Inc. v. Brown.* But, that was obviously not this case, and accepting *arguendo* the correctness of that decision, I believe that it leads to a result contrary to that reached today. The statute in *Kingsley* authorized "the chief executive, or legal officer, of a municipality to invoke a 'limited injunctive remedy,' under closely defined procedural safeguards, against the sale and distribution of written and printed matter found after due trial [by a court] to be obscene. . . ." The Chicago scheme has no procedural safeguards; there is no trial of the issue before the blanket injunction against exhibition becomes effective. In *Kingsley*, the grounds for the restraint were that the written or printed matter was "obscene, lewd, lascivious, filthy, indecent, or disgusting . . . or immoral. . . ." The Chicago objective is to capture much more. The *Kingsley* statute required the existence of some cause to believe that the publication was obscene before the publication was put on trial. The Chicago ordinance requires no such showing.

The booklets enjoined from distribution in *Kingsley* were concededly obscene. There is no indication that this is true of the moving picture here. This was treated as a particularly crucial distinction. Thus, the Court has suggested that, in times of national emergency, the Government might impose a prior restraint upon "the publication of the sailing dates of transports or the number and location of troops." *Near v. Minnesota*. But, surely this is not to suggest that the Government might require that all newspapers be submitted to a censor in order to assist it in preventing such information from reaching print. Yet in this case the Court gives its blessing to the censorship of all motion pictures in order to prevent the exhibition of those it feels to be constitutionally unprotected.

The statute in *Kingsley* specified that the person sought to be enjoined was to be entitled to a trial of the issues within one day after joinder and a decision was to be rendered by the Court within two days of the conclusion of the trial. The Chicago plan makes no provision for prompt judicial determination. In *Kingsley*, the person enjoined had available the defense that the written or printed matter was not obscene if an attempt was made to punish him for disobedience of the injunction. The Chicago ordinance admits no defense in a prosecution for failure to procure a license other than that the motion picture was submitted to the censor and a license was obtained.

Finally, the Court in *Kingsley* painstakingly attempted to establish that that statute, in its effective operation, was no more a previous restraint on, or interference with, the liberty of speech and press than a statute imposing criminal punishment for the publication of pornography. In each situation, it contended, the publication may have passed into the hands of the public. Of course, this argument is inadmissible in this case and the Court does not purport to advance it. . . .

A revelation of the extent to which censorship has recently been used in this country is indeed astonishing. The Chicago licensors have banned newsreel films of Chicago policemen shooting at labor pickets and have ordered the deletion of a scene depicting the birth of a buffalo in Walt Disney's "Vanishing Prairie." . . . Before World War II, the Chicago censor denied licenses to a number of films portraying and criticizing life in Nazi Germany including the March of Time's "Inside Nazi Germany."

. . . Recently, Chicago refused to issue a permit for the exhibition of the motion picture "Anatomy of a Murder" based upon the best-selling novel of the same title, because it found the use of the words "rape" and "contraceptive" to be objectionable. . . . The Chicago censor bureau excised a scene in "Street With No Name" in which a girl was slapped because this was thought to be a "too violent" episode. . . . "It Happened in Europe" was severely cut by the Ohio censors who deleted scenes of war orphans resorting to violence. The moral theme of the picture was that such children could even then be saved by love, affection and satisfaction of their basic needs for food. . . . The Memphis censors banned "The Southerner" which dealt with poverty among tenant farmers because "it reflects on the south." "Brewster's Millions," an innocuous comedy of fifty years ago, was recently forbidden in Memphis because the radio and film character Rochester, a Negro, was deemed "too familiar." . . . Maryland censors restricted a Polish documentary film on the basis that it failed to present a true picture of modern Poland. . . . "No Way Out," the story of a Negro doctor's struggle against race prejudice, was banned by the Chicago censor on the ground that "there's a possibility it could cause trouble." The principal objection to the film was that the conclusion showed no reconciliation between blacks and whites. The ban was lifted after a storm of protest and later deletion of a scene showing Negroes and whites arming for a gang fight. . . . Memphis banned "Curley" because it contained scenes of white and Negro children in school together. . . . Atlanta barred "Lost Boundaries," the story of a Negro physician and his family who "passed" for white, on the ground that the exhibition of said picture "will adversely affect the peace, morals and good order" in the city. . . . "Witchcraft," a study of superstition through the ages, was suppressed for years because it depicted the devil as a genial rake with amorous leanings, and because it was feared that certain historical scenes, portraying the excesses of religious fanatics, might offend religion. "Scarface," thought by some as the best of the gangster films, was held up for months; then it was so badly mutilated that retakes costing a hundred thousand dollars were required to preserve continuity. The New York censors banned "Damaged Lives," a film dealing with venereal disease, although it treated a difficult theme with dignity and had the sponsorship of the Amercian Social Hygiene Society. The picture of Lenin's tomb bearing the inscription "Religion is the opiate of the people" was excised from "Potemkin." From "Joan of Arc" the Maryland board eliminated Joan's exclamation as she stood at the stake: "Oh, God, why hast thou forsaken me?" and from "Idiot's Delight," the sentence: "We, the workers of the world, will take care of that." "Professor Mamlock" was produced in Russia and portrayed the persecution of the Jews by Nazis. The Ohio censors condemned it as "harmful" and calculated to "stir up hatred and ill will and gain nothing." It was released only after substantial deletions were made. The police refused to permit its showing in Providence, Rhode Island, on the ground that it was communistic propaganda. "Millions of Us," a strong union propaganda film, encountered trouble in a number of jurisdictions. "Spanish Earth," a pro-Loyalist documentary picture, was banned by the board in Pennsylvania. . . . During the year ending June 30, 1938, the New York board censored, in one way or another, over five per cent of the moving pictures it reviewed. . . . Charlie Chaplin's satire on Hitler, "The Great Dictator," was banned in Chicago, apparently out of deference to its large German population. . . . Ohio and Kansas banned newsreels considered pro-labor. Kansas ordered a speech by Senator Wheeler opposing the bill for enlarging the Supreme Court to be cut from the "March of Time" as "partisan and biased." . . . An early version of "Carmen" was condemned on several different grounds. The Ohio censor objected because cigarette-girls smoked cigarettes in public. The Pennsylvania censor disapproved the duration of a kiss. . . . The New York censors forbade the discussion in films of pregnancy, venereal disease, eugenics, birth control, abortion, illegitimacy, prostitution, miscegenation and divorce. . . . A member of the Chicago censor board explained that she rejected a film because "it was immoral, corrupt, indecent, against my . . . religious principles." . . . A police sergeant attached to the censor board explained, "Coarse language or anything that would be derogatory to the Government—propaganda" is ruled out of foreign films. "Nothing pink or red is allowed," he added. *Chicago Daily News*, Apr. 7, 1959, p. 3, cols. 7–8. The police sergeant in charge of the censor unit has said: "Children should be allowed to see any movie that plays in Chicago. If a picture is objectionable for a child, it is objectionable period." *Chicago Tribune*, May 24, 1959, p. 8, col. 3. And this is but a smattering produced from limited research. Perhaps the most powerful indictment of Chicago's licensing device is found in the fact that between the Court's decision in 1952 in *Joseph Burstyn, Inc. v. Wilson* and the filing of the petition for *certiorari* in 1960 in the present case, not once have the state courts upheld the censor when the exhibitor elected to appeal. Brief of American Civil Liberties Union as *amicus curiae*, pp. 13–14.

This is the regimen to which the Court holds that all films must be submitted. It officially unleashes the censor and permits him to roam at will, limited only by an ordinance which contains some standards that, although concededly not before us in this case, are patently imprecise. . . .

Moreover, more likely than not, the exhibitor will not pursue judicial remedies. His inclination may well be simply to capitulate rather than initiate a lengthy and costly litigation. In such case, the liberty of speech and press, and the public, which benefits from the shielding of that liberty, are, in effect, at the mercy of the censor's whim. This powerful tendency to restrict the free dissemination of ideas calls for reversal.

Freedom of speech and freedom of the press are further endangered by this "most effective" means for confinement of ideas. It is axiomatic that the stroke of the censor's pen or the cut of his scissors will be a less contemplated decision than will be the prosecutor's determination to prepare a criminal indictment. The standards of proof, the judicial safeguards afforded a criminal defendant and the consequences of bringing such charges will all provoke the mature deliberation of the prosecutor. None of these hinder the quick judgment of the censor, the speedy determination to suppress. Finally, the fear of the censor by the composer of ideas acts as a substantial deterrent to the creation of new thoughts. This is especially true of motion pictures due to the large financial burden that must be assumed by their producers. The censor's sword pierces deeply into the heart of free expression. . . .

. . . The Court, in no way, explains why moving pictures should be treated differently than any other form of expression, why moving pictures should be denied the protection against censorship—"a form of infringement upon freedom of expression to be *especially* condemned." *Joseph Burstyn, Inc. v. Wilson.* (Emphasis added.) When pressed during oral argument, counsel for the city could make no meaningful distinction between the censorship of newspapers and motion pictures. In fact, the percentage of motion pictures dealing with social and political issues is steadily rising. The Chicago ordinance makes no exception for newsreels, documentaries, instructional and educational films or the like. All must undergo the censor's inquisition. Nor may it be suggested that motion pictures may be treated differently from newspapers because many movies are produced essentially for purposes of entertainment. As the Court said in *Winters v. New York:*

> We do not accede to appellee's suggestion that the constitutional protection for a free press applies only to the exposition of ideas. The line between the informing and the entertaining is too elusive for the protection of that basic right. Everyone is familiar with instances of propaganda through fiction. What is one man's amusement, teaches another's doctrine. . . .

The Court, not the petitioner, makes the "broadside attack." I would reverse the decision below.

*   *   *

The first major qualification of the Times Film precedent came three years later when the Supreme Court suggested that the concept of "contemporary community standards" in dealing with obscenity (Roth) might be interpreted as "national standards" because of the application of a national constitution. The six justices who voted for reversal, however, could not reach agreement for an opinion of the Court. Five separate opinions were expressed by the nine justices in their 6-3 decision. Also of significance was the extension of the Roth concept to protect all material unless utterly without redeeming social importance. At issue was the French film "The Lovers," in which there was a brief but explicit love scene. Justice Brennan joined by Justice Goldberg argued the points mentioned above. Justices Douglas and Black argued, in addition, that any such restraint upon an exhibitor is in violation of his First Amendment guarantees. Justice Stewart, as he had done before, "held out" for hard-core pornography, noting that this wasn't it. He also issued his oft-quoted line regarding a definition of obscenity: "I know it when I see it."

JACOBELLIS V. OHIO
378 U.S. 184 (1964)

MR. JUSTICE BRENNAN *announced the judgment of the Court and delivered an opinion in which Mr. Justice Goldberg joins.*

Appellant, Nico Jacobellis, manager of a motion picture theater in Cleveland Heights, Ohio, was convicted on two counts of possessing and exhibiting an obscene film. . . . The dispositive question is whether the state courts properly found that the motion picture involved, a French film called "Les Amants" ("The Lovers"), was obscene and hence not entitled to the protection of free expression that is guaranteed by the First and Fourteenth Amendments. We conclude that the film is not obscene and that the judgment must accordingly be reversed.

Motion pictures are within the ambit of the constitutional guarantees of freedom of speech and of the press. *Joseph Burstyn, Inc. v. Wilson.* But in *Roth v. United States* and *Alberts v. California* we held that obscenity is not subject to those guarantees. Application of an obscenity law to suppress a motion picture thus requires ascertainment of the "dim and uncertain line" that often separates obscenity from constitutionally protected expression. . . . It has been suggested that this is a task in which our Court need not involve itself. We are told that the determination whether a particular motion picture, book, or other work of expression is obscene can be treated as a purely factual judgment on which a jury's verdict is all but conclusive, or that in any event the decision can be left essentially to state and lower federal courts, with this Court exercising only a limited review such as that needed to determine whether the ruling below is supported by "sufficient evidence." The suggestion is appealing, since it would lift from our shoulders a difficult, recurring, and unpleasant task. But we cannot accept it. Such an abnegation of judicial supervision in this field would be inconsistent with our duty to uphold the constitutional guarantees. Since it is only "obscenity" that is excluded from the constitutional protection, the question whether a particular work is ob-scene necessarily implicates an issue of constitutional law. . . .

It has been suggested that the "contemporary community standards" aspect of the *Roth* test implies a determination of the constitutional ques-tion of obscenity in each case by the standards of the particular local com-munity from which the case arises. This is an incorrect reading of *Roth*. The concept of "contemporary community standards" was first expressed by Judge Learned Hand in *United States v. Kennerley*. . . .

We do not see how any "local" definition of the "community" could properly be employed in delineating the area of expression that is pro-tected by the Federal Constitution. Mr. Justice Harlan pointed out in *Manual Enterprises Inc. v. Day*, that a standard based on a particular local community would have "the intolerable consequence of denying some sections of the country access to material, there deemed acceptable, which in others might be considered offensive to prevailing community standards of decency." It is true that *Manual Enterprises* dealt with the Federal statute banning obscenity from the mails. But the mails are not the only means by which works of expression cross local-community lines in this country. It can hardly be assumed that all the patrons of a particu-lar library, bookstand, or motion picture theater are residents of the small-est local "community" that can be drawn around that establishment. Fur-thermore, to sustain the suppression of a particular book or film in one locality would deter its dissemination in other localities where it might be held not obscene, since sellers and exhibitors would be reluctant to risk criminal conviction in testing the variation between the two places. It would be a hardy person who would sell a book or exhibit a film anywhere in the land after this Court has sustained the judgment of one "commu-nity" holding it to be outside the constitutional protection. The result would thus be "to restrict the public's access to forms of the printed word which the State could not constitutionally suppress directly." *Smith v. California.*

It is true that local communities throughout the land are in fact di-verse, and that in cases such as this one the Court is confronted with the task of reconciling the rights of such communities with the rights of in-dividuals. Communities vary, however, in many respects other than their toleration of alleged obscenity, and such variances have never been con-sidered to require or justify a varying standard for application of the Fed-eral Constitution. The Court has regularly been compelled, in reviewing criminal convictions challenged under the Due Process Clause of the Four-teenth Amendment, to reconcile the conflicting rights of the local com-munity which brought the prosecution and of the individual defendant. Such a task is admittedly difficult and delicate, but it is inherent in the Court's duty of determining whether a particular conviction worked a deprivation of rights guaranteed by the Federal Constitution. The Court has not shrunk from discharging that duty in other areas, and we see no reason why it should do so here. The Court has explicitly refused to tolerate a result whereby "the constitutional limits of free expression in the Nation would vary with state lines," *Pennekamp v. Florida*; we see even less justification for allowing such limits to vary from town or county lines. We thus reaffirm the position taken in *Roth* to the effect that the constitutional status of an allegedly obscene work must be determined on the basis of a national standard. It is, after all, a national Constitution we are expounding. . . .

We have applied that standard to the motion picture in question. "The Lovers" involves a woman bored with her life and marriage who abandons her husband and family for a young archaeologist with whom she has suddenly fallen in love. There is an explicit love scene in the last reel of the film, and the State's objections are based almost entirely upon that scene. The film was favorably reviewed in a number of national publications, although disparaged in others, and was rated by at least two critics of national stature among the best films of the year in which it was produced. It was shown in approximately 100 of the larger cities in the United States, including Columbus and Toledo, Ohio. We have viewed the film, in the light of the record made in the trial court, and we conclude that it is not obscene within the standards enunciated in *Roth v. United States* and *Alberts v. California*, which we reaffirm here.

Opinion of MR. JUSTICE BLACK *with whom Mr. Justice Douglas joins.*

I concur in the reversal of this judgment. My belief, as stated in *Kingsley International Pictures Corp. v. Regents*, is that "If despite the Constitution . . . this Nation is to embark on the dangerous road of censorship, . . . this Court is about the most inappropriate Supreme Board of Censors that could be found." My reason for reversing is that I think the conviction of appellant or anyone else for exhibiting a motion picture abridges freedom of the press as safeguarded by the First Amendment, which is made obligatory on the States by the Fourteenth. . . .

MR. JUSTICE STEWART, *concurring.*

It is possible to read the Court's opinion in *Roth v. United States* and *Alberts v. California* in a variety of ways. In saying this, I imply no criticism of the Court, which in those cases was faced with the task of trying to define what may be indefinable. I have reached the conclusion, which I think is confirmed at least by negative implication in the Court's decisions since *Roth* and *Alberts*, that under the First and Fourteenth Amendments criminal laws in this area are constitutionally limited to hardcore pornography. I shall not today attempt further to define the kinds of material I understand to be embraced within that shorthand description; and perhaps I could never succeed in intelligibly doing so. But I know it when I see it, and the motion picture involved in this case is not that.

MR. JUSTICE GOLDBERG, *concurring.*

The question presented is whether the First and Fourteenth Amendments permit the imposition of criminal punishment for exhibiting the motion picture entitled "The Lovers." I have viewed the film and I wish merely to add to my Brother Brennan's description that the love scene deemed objectionable is so fragmentary and fleeting that only a censor's alert would make an audience conscious that something "questionable" is being portrayed. Except for this rapid sequence, the film concerns itself with the history of an ill-matched and unhappy marriage—a familiar subject in old and new novels and in current television soap operas. . . .

THE CHIEF JUSTICE, *with whom Mr. Justice Clark joins, dissenting.*

In this and other cases in this area of the law, which are coming to us in ever-increasing numbers, we are faced with the resolution of rights basic both to individuals and to society as a whole. Specifically, we are called upon to reconcile the right of the Nation and of the States to maintain a decent society and, on the other hand, the right of individuals to express themselves freely in accordance with the guarantes of the First and Fourteenth Amendments. Although the Federal Government and virtually every State has had laws proscribing obscenity since the Union was formed, and although this Court has recently decided that obscenity is not within the protection of the First Amendment, neither courts nor legislatures have been able to evolve a truly satisfactory definition of obscenity. In other areas of the law, terms like "negligence," although in common use for centuries, have been difficult to define except in the most general manner. Yet the Courts have been able to function in such areas with a reasonable degree of efficiency. The obscenity problem, however, is aggravated by the fact that it involves the area of public expression, an area in which a broad range of freedom is vital to our society and is constitutionally protected. . . .

For all the sound and fury that the *Roth* test has generated, it has not been proved unsound, and I believe that we should try to live with it—at least until a more satisfactory definition is evolved. No government —be it federal, state, or local—should be forced to choose between repressing all material, including that within the realm of decency, and allowing unrestrained license to publish any material, no matter how vile. There must be a rule of reason in this as in other areas of the law, and we have attempted in the *Roth* case to provide such a rule.

It is my belief that when the Court said in *Roth* that obscenity is to be defined by reference to "community standards," it meant community standards—not a national standard, as is sometimes argued. I believe that there is no provable "national standard," and perhaps there should be none. At all events, this Court has not been able to enunciate one, and it would be unreasonable to expect local courts to divine one. It is said that such a "community" approach may well result in material being proscribed as obscene in one community but not in another, and, in all probability, that is true. But communities throughout the Nation are in fact diverse, and it must be remembered that, in cases such as this one, the Court is confronted with the task of reconciling conflicting rights of the diverse communities within our society and of individuals.

We are told that only "hard-core pornography" should be denied the protection of the First Amendment. But who can define "hard-core pornography" with any greater clarity than "obscenity"? And even if we were to retreat to that position, we would soon be faced with the need to define that term just as we now are faced with the need to define "obscenity." Meanwhile, those who profit from the commercial exploitation of obscenity would continue to ply their trade unmolested. . . .

MR. JUSTICE HARLAN, *dissenting.*

While agreeing with my Brother Brennan's opinion that the responsibilities of the Court in this area are no different from those which attend the adjudication of kindred constitutional questions, I have heretofore expressed the view that the States are constitutionally permitted greater latitude in determining what is bannable on the score of obscenity than is so with the Federal Government. . . .

The more I see of these obscenity cases the more convinced I become that in permitting the States wide, but not federally unrestricted, scope in this field, while holding the Federal Government with a tight rein, lies the best promise for achieving a sensible accommodation between the public interest sought to be served by obscenity laws . . . and protection of genuine rights of free expression. . . .

*   *   *

A second major qualification of the Times Film decision occurred in 1965 with Freedman v. Maryland. The Court unanimously reversed a conviction of Ronald Freedman, Baltimore theater owner, for showing the film "Revenge at Daybreak" without a license. This case was similar to Times Film in that the motion picture admittedly could have received a license if one had been sought. What makes this case of more than passing interest are two conditions set by the Court in dealing with film licensing and censorship. First, the Court said in a unanimous opinion delivered by Justice Brennan, the burden of proof lies with the censor rather than with the exhibitor, and second, the question of denial of a license to an exhibitor must move swiftly to the courts of law, which are to have the ultimate decision on questions of prior restraint. On the point of swift judicial review, Justice Brennan used as a model the Kingsley Books case. Still, the Court reaffirmed its view that motion pictures are a unique form of expression which require unique safeguards, i.e. pre-screening, censorship and licensing. The imposition of the two new conditions to granting film review and licensing, however, has apparently and for all practical purposes eliminated state and local film censoring bodies as serious threats to freedom of expression.

FREEDMAN V. MARYLAND
380 U.S. 51 (1965)

MR. JUSTICE BRENNAN *delivered the opinion of the Court.*

Appellant sought to challenge the constitutionality of the Maryland motion picture censorship statute . . . and exhibited the film "Revenge at Daybreak" at his Baltimore theatre without first submitting the picture to the State Board of Censors as required. . . . The State concedes that the picture does not violate the statutory standards and would have received a license if properly submitted, but the appellant was convicted . . . despite his contention that the statute in its entirety unconstitutionally impaired freedom of expression. . . .

In *Times Film Corp. v. City of Chicago*, we considered and upheld a requirement of submission of motion pictures in advance of exhibition. . . .

Unlike the petitioner in *Times Film*, appellant does not argue that sec. 2 (of the Maryland statute) is unconstitutional simply because it may prevent even the first showing of a film whose exhibition may legitimately be the subject of an obscenity prosecution. He presents a question quite distinct from that passed on in *Times Film*; accepting the rule in *Times Film*, he argues that sec. 2 constitutes an invalid prior restraint because, in the context of the remainder of the statute, it presents a danger of unduly suppressing protected expression. He focuses particularly on the procedure for an initial decision by the censorship board, which, without any judicial participation, effectively bars exhibition of any disapproved film, unless and until the exhibitor undertakes a time-consuming appeal to the Maryland courts and succeeds in having the Board's decision reversed. Under the statute, the exhibitor is required to submit the film to the Board for examination, but no time limit is imposed for completion of Board action, sec. 17. . . .

Thus there is no statutory provision for judicial participation in the procedure which bars a film, nor even assurance of prompt judicial review.

Risk of delay is built into the Maryland procedure, as is borne out by experience; in the only reported case indicating the length of time required to complete an appeal, the initial judicial determination has taken four months and final vindication of the film on appellate review, six months. . . .

. . . In substance his argument is that, because the apparatus operates in a statutory context in which judicial review may be too little and too late, the Maryland statute lacks sufficient safeguards for confining the censor's action to judicially determined constitutional limits, and therefore contains the same vice as a statute delegating excessive administrative discretion.

Although the Court has said that motion pictures are not "necessarily subject to the precise rules governing any other particular method of expression," *Joseph Burstyn, Inc. v. Wilson,* it is as true here as of other forms of expression that "[a]ny system of prior restraints of expression comes to this Court bearing a heavy presumption against its constitutional validity." *Bantam Books, Inc. v. Sullivan.* ". . . [U]nder the Fourteenth Amendment, a State is not free to adopt whatever procedures it pleases for dealing with obscenity . . . without regard to the possible consequences for constitutionally protected speech." *Marcus v. Search Warrant.* The administration of a censorship system for motion pictures presents peculiar dangers to constitutionally protected speech. Unlike a prosecution for obscenity, a censorship proceeding puts the initial burden on the exhibitor or distributor. Because the censor's business is to censor, there inheres the danger that he may well be less responsive than a court—part of an independent branch of government—to the constitutionally protected interests in free expression. And if it is made unduly onerous, by reason of delay or otherwise, to seek judicial review, the censor's determination may in practice be final.

Applying the settled rule of our cases, we hold that a noncriminal process which requires the prior submission of a film to a censor avoids constitutional infirmity only if it takes place under procedural safeguards designed to obviate the dangers of a censorship system. First, the burden of proving that the film is unprotected expression must rest on the censor. As we said in *Speiser v. Randall,* "Where the transcendent value of speech is involved, due process certainly requires . . . that the State bear the burden of persuasion to show that the appellants engaged in criminal speech." Second, while the State may require advance submission of all films, in order to proceed effectively to bar all showings of unprotected films, the requirement cannot be administered in a manner which would lend an effect of finality to the censor's determination whether a film constitutes protected expression. . . . To this end, the exhibitor must be assured, by statute or authoritative judicial construction, that the censor will, within a specified brief period, either issue a license or go to court to restrain showing the film. Any restraint imposed in advance of a final judicial determination on the merits must similarly be limited to preservation of the status quo for the shortest fixed period compatible with sound judicial resolution. Moreover, we are well aware that, even after expiration of a temporary restraint, an administrative refusal to license, signifying the censor's view that the film is unprotected, may have a discouraging effect on the exhibitor. See *Bantam Books, Inc. v. Sullivan.* Therefore, the procedure must also assure a prompt final judicial decision, to minimize the deterrent effect of an interim and possibly erroneous denial of a license. . . .

It is readily apparent that the Maryland procedural scheme does not satisfy these criteria. First, once the censor disapproves the film, the exhibitor must assume the burden of instituting judicial proceedings and of persuading the courts that the film is protected expression. Second, once the Board has acted against a film, exhibition is prohibited pending judicial review, however protracted. Under the statute, appellant could have been convicted if he had shown the film after unsuccessfully seeking a license, even though no court had ever ruled on the obscenity of the film. Third, it is abundantly clear that the Maryland statute provides no assurance of prompt judicial determination. We hold, therefore, that the appellant's conviction must be reversed. The Maryland scheme fails to provide adequate safeguards against undue inhibition of protected expression, and this renders the sec. 2 requirement of prior submission of films to the Board an invalid previous restraint.

How or whether Maryland is to incorporate the required procedural safeguards in the statutory scheme is, of course, for the State to decide. But a model is not lacking: In *Kingsley Books, Inc. v. Brown* we upheld a New York injunctive procedure designed to prevent the sale of obscene books. That procedure postpones any restraint against sale until a judicial determination of obscenity following notice and an adversary hearing. The statute provides for a hearing one day after joinder of issue; the judge must hand down his decision within two days after termination of the hearing. The New York procedure operates without prior submission to a censor, but the chilling effect of a censorship order, even one which requires judicial action for its enforcement, suggests all the more reason for expeditious determination of the question whether a particular film is constitutionally protected.

The requirement of prior submission to a censor sustained in *Times Film* is consistent with our recognition that films differ from other forms of expression. Similarly, we think that the nature of the motion picture industry may suggest different time limits for a judicial determination. It is common knowledge that films are scheduled well before actual exhibition, and the requirement of advance submission in sec. 2 recognizes this. One possible scheme would be to allow the exhibitor or distributor to submit his film early enough to ensure an orderly final disposition of the case before the scheduled exhibition date—far enough in advance so that the exhibitor could safely advertise the opening on a normal basis. . . .

MR. JUSTICE DOUGLAS, *whom Mr. Justice Black joins, concurring.*

On several occasions I have indicated my view that movies are entitled to the same degree and kind of protection under the First Amendment as other forms of expression. . . .

As I see it, a pictorial presentation occupies as preferred a position as any other form of expression. If censors are banned from the publishing business, from the pulpit, from the public platform—as they are—they should be banned from the theater. I would not admit the censor even for the limited role accorded him in *Kingsley Books, Inc. v. Brown.* I adhere to my dissent in that case. Any authority to obtain a temporary injunction gives the State "the paralyzing power of a censor." The regime of *Kingsley Books* "substitutes punishment by contempt for punishment by jury trial." I would put an end to all forms and types of censorship and give full literal meaning to the command of the First Amendment.

*　　*　　*

In 1968 the Court for the first time faced the question of the constitutionality of motion picture classification. While tossing out a Dallas classification system as too vague, the Court nonetheless endorsed in Interstate Circuit, Inc. v. Dallas *the principle of movie classification relating to minors. After warning of the dangers inherent in a loosely drawn classification law, Justice Marshall, writing for the 8-1 majority, emphasized that a state "may regulate the dissemination to juveniles of, and their access to, material objectionable as to them, but which a state clearly could not regulate as to adults." This echoes the sentiments of the Court in relation to printed matter as expressed in* Ginsberg v. New York, *announced the same day and given in Chapter 6.*

INTERSTATE CIRCUIT, INC. V. DALLAS

UNITED ARTISTS CORP. V. DALLAS
390 U.S. 676 (1968)

MR. JUSTICE MARSHALL *delivered the opinion of the Court.*

Appellants are an exhibitor and the distributor of a motion picture named "Viva Maria," which, pursuant to a city ordinance, the Motion

Picture Classification Board of the respondent City of Dallas classified as
"not suitable for young persons." A county court upheld the Board's determination and enjoined exhibition of the film without acceptance by appellants of the requirements imposed by the restricted classification. The
Texas Court of Civil Appeals affirmed, and we noted probable jurisdiction,
387 U.S. 903, to consider the First and Fourteenth Amendment issues
raised by appellants with respect to respondent's classification ordinance.

That ordinance, adopted in 1965, may be summarized as follows. It
establishes a Motion Picture Classification Board, composed of nine appointed members, all of whom serve without pay. The Board classifies films
as "suitable for young persons" or as "not suitable for young persons," and
defines young persons as children who have not reached their 16th birthday.
An exhibitor must be specially licensed to show "not suitable" films. . . .

The substantive standards governing classification are as follows:

"Not suitable for young persons" means:

"(1) Describing or portraying brutality, criminal violence or de-
pravity in such a manner as to be, in the judgment of the Board, likely
to incite or encourage crime or delinquency on the part of young persons; or

"(2) Describing or portraying nudity beyond the customary limits
of candor in the community, or sexual promiscuity or extra-marital or
abnormal sexual relations in such a manner as to be, in the judgment
of the Board, likely to incite or encourage delinquency or sexual promiscuity on the part of young persons or to appeal to their prurient interest.

"A film shall be considered 'likely to incite or encourage' crime
delinquency or sexual promiscuity on the part of young persons, if, in
the judgment of the Board, there is a substantial probability that it
will create the impression on young persons that such conduct is profitable, desirable, acceptable, respectable, praiseworthy or commonly
accepted. A film shall be considered as appealing to 'prurient interest'
of young persons if in the judgment of the Board, its calculated or
dominant effect on young persons is substantially to arouse sexual desire. In determining whether a film is 'not suitable for young persons,'
the Board shall consider the film as a whole, rather than isolated portions, and shall determine whether its harmful effects outweigh artistic
or educational values such film may have for young persons."

Appellants attack those standards as unconstitutionally vague. We
agree. Motion pictures are, of course, protected by the First Amendment,
Joseph Burstyn, Inc. v. Wilson, and thus we start with the premise that
"[p]recision of regulation must be the touchstone." *NAACP v. Button*.
And while it is true that this Court refused to strike down, against a broad
and generalized attack, a prior restraint requirement that motion pictures

be submitted to censors in advance of exhibition, *Times Film Corp v. City of Chicago*, there has been no retreat in this area from rigorous insistence upon procedural safeguards and judicial superintendence of the censor's action. See *Freedman v. Maryland*. . . .

The vice of vagueness is particularly pronounced where expression is sought to be subjected to licensing. It may be unlikely that what Dallas does in respect to the licensing of motion pictures would have a significant effect upon film makers in Hollywood or Europe. But what Dallas may constitutionally do, so may other cities and States. Indeed, we are told that this ordinance is being used as a model for legislation in other localities. Thus, one who wishes to convey his ideas through that medium, which of course includes one who is interested not so much in expression as in making money, must consider whether what he proposes to film, and how he proposes to film it, is within the terms of classification schemes such as this. If he is unable to determine what the ordinance means, he runs the risk of being foreclosed, in practical effect, from a significant portion of the movie-going public. Rather than running that risk, he might choose nothing but the innocuous, perhaps save for the so-called "adult" picture. Moreover, a local exhibitor who cannot afford to risk losing the youthful audience when a film may be of marginal interest to adults—perhaps a "Viva Maria"—may contract to show only the totally inane. The vast wasteland that some have described in reference to another medium might be a verdant paradise in comparison. The First Amendment interests here are, therefore, broader than merely those of the film maker, distributor, and exhibitor, and certainly broader than those of youths under 16. . . .

The dangers inherent in vagueness are strikingly illustrated in this case. . . . The Board gave no reasons for its determination. The Board alleged in its petition for an injunction that the classification was warranted because the film portrayed "sexual promiscuity in such a manner as to be in the judgment of the Board likely to incite or encourage delinquency or sexual promiscuity on the part of young persons or to appeal to their prurient interests." Two Board members, a clergyman and a lawyer, testified at the hearing. Each adverted to several scenes in the film which, in their opinion, portrayed male-female relationships in a way contrary to "acceptable and approved behavior." Each acknowledged, in reference to scenes in which clergymen were involved in violence, most of which was farcical, that "sacrilege" might have entered into the Board's determination. And both conceded that the asserted portrayal of "sexual promiscuity" was implicit rather that explicit, *i.e.*, that it was a product of inference by, and imagination of, the viewer.

So far as "judicial superintendence" and *de novo* review is concerned, the trial judge, after viewing the film and hearing argument, stated merely: "Oh, I realize you gentlemen may be right. There are two or three features in the picture that look to me would be unsuitable to young people. . . .

So I enjoin the exhibitor . . . from exhibiting it." Nor did the Court of Civil Appeals provide much enlightenment or a narrowing definition of the ordinance. . . .

Thus, we are left merely with the film and directed to the words of the ordinance. The term "sexual promiscuity" is not there defined and was not interpreted in the state courts. It could extend, depending upon one's moral judgment, from the obvious to any sexual contacts outside a marital relationship. . . .

It is not our province to draft legislation. Suffice it to say that we have recognized that some believe "motion pictures possess a greater capacity for evil, particularly among the youth of a community, than other modes of expression," *Joseph Burstyn, Inc. v. Wilson,* and we have indicated more generally that because of its strong and abiding interest in youth, a State may regulate the dissemination to juveniles of, and their access to, material objectionable as to them, but which a State clearly could not regulate as to adults. *Ginsberg v. New York.* Here we conclude only that "the absence of narrowly drawn, reasonable and definite standards for the officials to follow," *Niemotko v. Maryland,* is fatal. . . .

MORALS AND THE CONSTITUTION

By Louis Henkin *

. . . If I am correct about the origins and purposes of obscenity legislation, much of the constitutional discussion about the control of obscenity seems out of focus. Concentration on whether obscenity may—or may not—incite to unlawful acts aims beside the mark. The question, rather, is whether the state may suppress expression it deems immoral, may protect adults as well as children from voluntary exposure to that which may "corrupt" them, may preserve the community from public, rampant "immorality." This different question may receive the same or a different answer; clearly, the path and the guide posts, the facts sought, the issues considered and the doctrine applied may be very different. Indeed, this inquiry might today command attention even to a question that must have appeared insubstantial earlier in the history of the Constitution: the authority of government under the Constitution to adopt "morals legislation," to suppress private, individual indulgence which does no harm to others, in the name of traditional notions of morality. . . .

. . . The accepted definition of obscenity, as that which "appeal[s] . . . to prurient interest," makes no assumption that it will incite to any action. The history of obscenity legislation points, rather, to origins in aspirations to holiness and propriety. Laws against obscenity have appeared conjoined and cognate to laws against sacrilege and blasphemy, suggesting concern for the spiritual welfare of the person exposed to it and for the moral well-being of the community. Metaphors of "poison" and "filth" also emphasize concern for the welfare of the one exposed and for the atmosphere of the community. A "decent" community does not tolerate obscenity. A "decent" man does not indulge himself with obscene materials.

The moral concern of the community may consist of several different strands frequently entangled beyond separation. Obscenity is immoral, an individual should not indulge it, and the community should not tolerate it. In addition, obscenity, like other immoral acts and expressions, has a deleterious effect on the individual from which the community should protect him. Obscenity is bad for a man, and the concern is not for his "psyche," his mental health. Obscenity is bad for character. It "corrupts" morals, it

---

* From Louis Henkin. "Morals and the Constitution: The Sin of Obscenity." *Columbia Law Review*, Vol. 63 (March, 1963), p. 391. Used with permission of the *Columbia Law Review* and the author, a professor of law at Columbia University.

corrupts character. Character, of course, bears on behavior, but the corruption feared, it should be emphasized, has a very unclear, very remote, and problematic relation to a likelihood that he will commit any particular unlawful act or indeed any unlawful act at all, immediately or in the future.

This concern of the state for the "character" and "morals" of the person exposed is particularly evident in the plethora of laws designed to prevent the "corruption of youth." Among other evil influences, obscenity, it is assumed, may "corrupt" a child. The state assists parents who seek to prevent this corruption, or may even act in loco of those parents who are remiss in protecting their own children. The Supreme Court built constitutional doctrine on these assumptions when it held that Michigan could not "reduce the adult population of Michigan to reading only what is fit for children." Again, the corruption of youth by obscenity is deemed to have some immeasurable effect on character and personality; it is not believed to "incite" to any particular actions now or in the future. While in regard to youth it has always been assumed that government has special responsibility and authority, laws adopted for their protection reflect assumptions and attitudes about obscenity not inapplicable to the regulation of obscenity for adults. . . .

If obscenity laws are seen primarily as "morals legislation," if a principal purpose of these laws is to protect, from himself, the person who wishes to indulge, and to maintain the moral "tone" of a community, constitutional discussion of such laws would seem to deserve emphasis different from that which has preoccupied the judges and the writers. . . .

As was perhaps inevitable, this preoccupation with the relation between speech, and action, and undeniably unlawful consequences, led lawyers as well as Justices carelessly to impose this context upon the problem of obscenity when it finally forced itself upon the Supreme Court's attention. If in fact the state's concern with obscenity has little to do with incitement to action, constitutional discussion based on the link between obscenity and unlawful action seems far beside the point. If unlawful action is not the evil at which the state aims, whether obscenity creates a "clear and present" danger of an unlawful action is not the relevant concern. The evils at which the state aims are not unlawful action, but indecency and corruption of morals. . . .

The need for facing the questions here suggested may be emphasized by reference to a unanimous decision of the Supreme Court that does not deal with obscenity at all. In *Kingsley Int'l Pictures Corp. v. Regents of the Univ. of the State of N.Y.*, the state had refused to license the film "Lady Chatterley's Lover" on the ground that it was "immoral," or "of such a character that its exhibition would tend to corrupt morals." The legislature had defined these terms to apply to any film "which portrays acts of sexual immorality . . . or which . . . presents such acts as desirable, acceptable or proper patterns of behavior." The New York courts affirmed the denial of a license for the film "because its subject matter is adultery presented as being right and desirable for certain people under certain circumstances."

The Supreme Court of the United States was agreed in reversing the state's judgment below, though hardly in the reasons for doing so. The majority recognized—as some writers have not—that this was not an obscenity case, that there was nothing in the film that appealed to prurient interests, that the case could not be decided on the basis of some special exception to the freedom of speech enjoyed by "obscenity laws." Yet the Court's opinion, too, did not wrestle with what, I believe, is the real issue. It did not consider that while this was not an obscenity case, it was a "morals" case. The Court stated that New York was censoring the advocacy of an idea, whereas the Constitution, the opinion said, guarantees freedom to advocate ideas. "It protects advocacy of the opinion that adultery may sometimes be proper, no less than advocacy of socialism or the single tax." But ideas promoting adultery—unlike those urging the single tax—impinge on traditional morality. The state, indeed, did not claim that the film incited to adultery; it found the film to be immoral and tending to corrupt morals. Incitement to action, one might urge, is as irrelevant here as it is to obscenity cases in which, in effect, the state bars the obscene because it is immoral and tends to corrupt morals.

Recognition that laws against "obscenity" and laws against "immorality" are equally "morals" legislation would have required a very different opinion from the Court, if not a different result. The Court would have had to recognize that legislation against the "immoral" had historical credentials similar to, if not better than, obscenity laws, that the common obscenity statute indeed also forbade the "immoral"; legislation against the "immoral," then, might have as good a claim as obscenity legislation to historical exception from the freedom of speech. The result in the case could have been reached only by distinguishing, in some relevant way, this "morals legislation" from obscenity laws. An acceptable distinction does not readily appear. Somehow, the Court seemed to be denying to the state the assumption that ideas can be immoral or can corrupt morals, even though it had permitted to the state, in effect, the assumption that obscenity is immoral or can corrupt morals. (Would the Court hold that a child also is deprived of his liberty without due process of law if the state keeps from him materials expressing ideas that may "corrupt morals" without inciting to action?) Or did the Court silently measure and conclude that freedom for "ideas," any ideas, inevitably outweighs the state's interest in preventing "immorality by idea" or corruption of morals by ideas?

The confusion remains. Nothing we have said suggests that any of the obscenity cases before the Court was wrongly decided, or that the dissenters, pursuing the analysis urged, could not again find themselves in dissent. The questions suggested may well reconfirm a majority in the conclusion that "obscenity is not within the area of constitutionally protected speech or press." Dissenting Justices may yet conclude that although a state may legislate against certain acts on the ground that they are immoral, it cannot constitutionally suppress expression on the ground that it is immoral or that it corrupts morals. On any view, the recognition of the moral foundations of obscenity laws may suggest that proper differentiation might bring different constitutional results in different cases. It may be that the Constitution regards state concern with private morality privately indulged differently from state protection of the sensibilities of others against offensive public display, or state prohibition of commercial exploitation and promotion of obscenity. It may be that however much one questions the authority of the state to impose morals, even on children, our society recognizes the authority of parents to educate their children, and the state may protect and support the right of parents to impose their morality on their children.

Courts and lawyers, it seems to me, must face the problem of obscenity on the terms in which society has framed it. Laws against obscenity are rooted in traditional notions of morality and decency; the moral foundations of these laws cannot be disregarded in re-assessing their constitutional validity today. It should not be assumed, without re-examination, that the morality of another day remains between the lines of the Constitution. Nor should it be assumed, without re-examination, that the morality of an older day remains a legitimate aim of government with social import outweighing growing claims of individual freedom.

It has been suggested that the Supreme Court has read obscenity out of the protection for expression in the First and Fourteenth Amendments without asking whether the "moral" character of obscenity laws continues to justify that historical exception today, or whether the moral aims of these laws may properly outweigh the freedoms suppressed. I venture now to suggest that the moral purpose and motive of obscenity legislation—and of other prevalent laws aimed at private indulgence in "immoral" activity—may invite inquiry of yet a different, fundamental order.

We lay aside now claims of freedom to communicate, even the obscene; we are concerned, instead, with claims of the "consumer" to freedom and privacy to indulge in what others may deem immoral. The authority of the state, under the Constitution, to enact "morals legislation"—laws reflecting some traditional morality having no authentic social purpose to protect other persons or property—has always been assumed; it has deep roots, and it has seemed obvious and beyond question. It may now be respectable to ask whether indeed the state may adopt any "morals legislation." And if it be concluded that morals legislation is not ipso facto beyond the state's power, can one avoid asking: what morality the state may enforce; what limitations there are on what the state may deem immoral; how these limitations are to be determined?

In doctrinal terms, one may present these as several constitutional questions, not wholly discrete. For the sake of clarity, I declare them as hypotheses to be examined:

First: even if the "freedom of speech" protected by the First and Fourteenth Amendments does not include a freedom to communicate obscene speech, suppression of obscenity is still a deprivation of liberty or property—of the person who would indulge in it, at least—which requires due process of law. Due process of law demands that legislation have a proper public purpose; only an apparent, rational, utilitarian social purpose satisfies due process. A state may not legislate merely to preserve some traditional or prevailing view of private morality.

Second: due process requires, as well, that means be reasonably related to proper public ends. Legislation cannot be based on unfounded hypotheses and assumptions about character and its corruption.

Third: morals legislation is a relic in the law of our religious heritage; the Constitution forbids such establishment of religion.

The inquiry urged can only be suggested here. I would attempt to state the principal issues. I would underscore the complexity of the questions involved. I would urge, too, that the questions suggested are not clearly insubstantial.

The relation of law to morals has been a favored preoccupation of legal philosophers for a thousand years; in the history of American law the relevance of that relation to constitutional limitations has lain unexamined behind discussions of the scope and the limits of government. That morals were the concern of government was assumed, not explored, in discussions of the reaches of the "police power" limited by substantive "due process of law."

May the state, under our Constitution, legislate in support of "morals"? The question may take us back to another: What are the purposes for which the state may legislate under the Constitution? That question, in other contexts, once deeply troubled the Supreme Court. Not too many years ago the Court seemed to assume that by the law of nature and by social contract government was given limited powers for limited purposes. Freedom was the rule; government had to justify itself, and the justifications had to satisfy the Constitution. . . .

Today, a court would probably not begin with the assumption that government has defined purposes and corresponding "inherent," "natural" limitations. The only limitations on the state, a court might say, are the prohibitions of the Constitution—specific, like those few in the original Constitution, or more general, like those in the Civil War amendments. If one would today examine embedded assumptions about morals legislation, the question, then, is not whether legislation for decency and morality is within the accepted powers of government; we must ask, rather, whether such legislation deprives one to whom it applies of "liberty or property" without due process of law. But if that question looks very different from the one that might have been asked in the nineteenth century, it may be less different than it looks. For some of the "inherent" limitations on the police power may still be with us in notions that the state may legislate only for a "public purpose." And "due process" still requires some link in reason between purpose and the means selected by the legislature to achieve that purpose. We may state the question, then, as whether morality legislation deprives one of liberty or property without due process of law. The subsidiary questions may still be: Is the state's purpose in "morality legislation" a proper public purpose? Are the means used to achieve it "reasonable"?

Emphasis on "public purpose" has usually been intended to exclude legislation for the special interest of some private person or group. Morals legislation presumably does not serve a strictly "private purpose," even if some groups seem more concerned about morals legislation than is the community at large. The beneficiaries of this legislation, it is assumed, are each citizen and the whole community. But is every "nonprivate" purpose a proper public purpose of government? Can the state legislate, not to protect the person or property of others or to promote general economic or social welfare, but to protect and promote "morals," particularly morals reflected—or violated—in private activity?

Perhaps the question can have no provable answer. Supporters of legislation like obscenity laws may urge that government has always legislated in support of accepted morality, and may challenge those who would deny the authority of government to find anything in the Constitution that would take it away. But supporters of the past do not have the only word. Others will stress that the due process clause has intervened, and that it requires government to be reasonable, in purpose as well as in means to achieve the purpose. One may even accept the right of the state to impose restrictions on the individual for his own good—by preventing his suicide, or forcing medical aid, or compelling education; in the context of society, these are "rational" ends, reasonably achieved. But how can "morals," a nonutilitarian, nonrational purpose, be "reasonable"? Could government conjure up some new (or old), nonsocial principle of morality and impose it by law? Could a state forbid me to go to an astrologer—or require me to go to one or abide by his conclusions? And if history is invoked, does the fact that some behavior has been deemed "immoral" in the past—by some, even a violation of "natural law"—render it forever a proper object of legislative prohibition? Is it sufficient to justify legislation that such acts continue to be regarded as "immoral," "sinful," "offensive" by large segments of the community? Or does the due process clause, in this context too, serve to protect individuals from the irrationalities of the majority and of its representatives?

One may ask, it is suggested, whether any nonutilitarian morality can be a reasonable public purpose of legislation. But purpose aside, due process requires also that the means to achieve that purpose be not unreasonable.

Of course, means and purposes are not discrete categories, and purposes may themselves be means to other purposes. But assuming that the preservation of private morals continues to be a proper purpose of government, obscenity legislation, in particular, raises the further question whether suppression of obscenity is reasonably related to the morality that the state seeks to preserve.

The question may be clarified if one compares obscenity laws to other morals legislation, *e.g.*, laws against incest. Incestual relations have indubitably been deemed "immoral," at least since Biblical times. If the state may suppress what is immoral, there can be no doubt about the validity of laws against incest. Exposure to obscenity, on the other hand, is at most a derivative, secondary "immorality." In itself, it has no ancient roots; presumably, it would have been condemned, or frowned on, as inconsistent with admonitions to be holy and to avoid pagan abominations. In modern times, obscenity has been condemned in large part because it corrupts morals or character. Since, I have said, corruption of morals or character has no clear relation to any unlawful acts, or even acts that could be made unlawful, what evidence is required of the state, or what assumptions permitted to it, to support the conclusion that obscenity corrupts morals? What are these "morals" and this "character," and what does their corruption mean? And if we accept the concept of "morals" as well as their corruption, how does one decide whether the state is reasonable in its conclusion that indulgence in obscenity does or does not effect this "corruption" of these "morals"?

The Constitution does not enact legal positivism; it does not enact natural law. Due process, I hypothesize, requires that the state deal with the area of the reasonable and deal with it reasonably. It is proper to ask whether the preservation of a nonsocial morality is within the realm of the reasonable, whether concepts like "private morality" and its corruption are subject to logic and proof inherent in reasonableness and rationality. These, of course, are not merely technical requirements of constitutional jurisprudence. They suggest that the Constitution renders unto government the rational governance of the affairs of man in relation to his neighbor; only if government is kept within this domain can it be limited government, subject to constitutional requirements of rational, reasonable action administered by an impartial judiciary. It is only by confining government to what is reasonable that the Constitution and the courts can protect the individual against the unreasonable. Private "morals," and their "corruption," and what "corrupts" them, as differently conceived, have profound significance in the life of a nation and of its citizens. But they are not in the realm of reason and cannot be judged by standards of reasonableness; they ought not, perhaps, to be in the domain of government.

Civilized societies, including ours, have increased the area of government responsibility to protect one against his neighbor. The authority of government to protect us from ourselves is less clearly recognized today,

except when injury to ourselves may in turn have undesirable social consequences; although, we have suggested, one may justify—within the limits
of the "rational"—governmental efforts to prevent suicide, or compel
health measures, "for the individual's own good." When we deal not with
physical injury to ourselves but with "sin," respectable and authoritative
voices are increasingly heard that there exists "a realm of private morality
and immorality which is, in brief and crude terms, not the law's business." Should not the Supreme Court today, or tomorrow, consider whether
under the Constitution some morality, at least, may be not the law's business and not appropriate support for legislation consistent with due process
of law? . . .

CHAPTER **8**

LIBEL

Concern over a good reputation is as old as society itself. On the tablets brought down from Mount Sinai by Moses was inscribed, "Thou shalt not bear false witness against thy neighbor." And Shakespeare in "Othello" wrote, "Who steals my purse steals trash . . . But he that filches from me my good name robs me of that which not enriches him, and makes me poor indeed."

The theory behind the laws of libel, then, is to protect a man's good name and reputation until such time as it comes under legitimate question. Libel most often is a civil action, i.e. a contest in which one party attempts to recover damages for alleged harm done him by the acts of another.

The person defamed, the plaintiff, must establish that the statement was published, was defamatory and was taken by the reader to refer to the plaintiff. The defendant then is called upon to justify the use of the statement in question. Common defenses include the truth of the statement, the right of fair comment and criticism on matters before the public, and the right to publish privileged material such as that found in legal and governmental documents and actions. The Warren Court gave increasingly wide latitude to the press in fulfilling its function as "watchdog" of the public's business and, consequently, has made it increasingly difficult for public figures to collect damages in libel suits against the media.

The Warren Court in a 1964 landmark decision held that debate on public issues should be "uninhibited" and "robust" and that with such free and wide open debate error would be inevitable. Thus, the Court sided with the New York Times in its defense against libel charges brought by Commissioner of Public Affairs L. B. Sullivan of Montgomery, Alabama. It held that a public official cannot collect damages for a defamatory false-hood relating to his official capacity unless he is able to prove actual malice, i.e. that the statement was made with knowledge of its falsity or with reck-less disregard of its truth or falsity. Also, the fact that the defamation might be contained in a paid advertisement did not exempt it from constitutional protection. The Court noted that public officials themselves enjoy immu-nity for their statements where no actual malice is shown. The unanimous opinion was read by Justice Brennan. Justices Goldberg, Black, and Douglas would have gone one step further by ruling out any suit by a public official, whether malice is proven or not. The case involved an advertisement, in which certain errors of fact appeared, placed in the New York Times by civil rights advocates.

NEW YORK TIMES CO. V. SULLIVAN
376 U.S. 254 (1964)

MR. JUSTICE BRENNAN *delivered the opinion of the Court.*

We are required in this case to determine for the first time the extent to which the constitutional protections for speech and press limit a State's power to award damages in a libel action brought by a public official against critics of his official conduct.

Respondent L. B. Sullivan is one of the three elected Commissioners of the City of Montgomery, Alabama. He testified that he was "Commis-sioner of Public Affairs and the duties are supervision of the Police Depart-ment, Fire Department, Department of Cemetery and Department of Scales." He brought this civil libel action against the four individual peti-tioners, who are Negroes and Alabama clergymen, and against petitioner the New York Times Company, a New York corporation which publishes The *New York Times,* a daily newspaper. A jury in the Circuit Court of Montgomery County awarded him damages of $500,000, the full amount claimed, against all the petitioners, and the Supreme Court of Alabama affirmed.

Respondent's complaint alleged that he had been libeled by state-ments in a full-page advertisement that was carried in the *New York Times* on March 29, 1960. Entitled "Heed Their Rising Voices," the advertise-ment began by stating that "As the whole world knows by now, thousands of Southern Negro students are engaged in widespread non-violent demon-strations in positive affirmation of the right to live in human dignity as guaranteed by the U. S. Constitution and the Bill of Rights." It went on to charge that "in their efforts to uphold these guarantees, they are being met by an unprecedented wave of terror by those who would deny and negate that document which the whole world looks upon as setting the pattern for modern freedom. . . ." Succeeding paragraphs purported to illustrate the "wave of terror" by describing certain alleged events. The text concluded with an appeal for funds for three purposes: support of the student movement, "the struggle for the right-to-vote," and the legal defense of Dr. Martin Luther King, Jr., leader of the movement, against a perjury indictment then pending in Montgomery.

The text appeared over the names of 64 persons, many widely known for their activities in public affairs, religion, trade unions, and the performing arts. Below these names, and under a line reading "We in the south who are struggling daily for dignity and freedom warmly endorse this appeal," appeared the names of the four individual petitioners and of 16 other persons, all but two of whom were identified as clergymen in various Southern cities. The advertisement was signed at the bottom of the page by the "Committee to Defend Martin Luther King and the Struggle for Freedom in the South," and the officers of the Committee were listed.

Of the 10 paragraphs of text in the advertisement, the third and a portion of the sixth were the basis of respondent's claim of libel. They read as follows:

Third paragraph:
"In Montgomery, Alabama, after students sang 'My Country, 'Tis of Thee' on the State Capitol steps, their leaders were expelled from school, and truckloads of police armed with shotguns and tear-gas ringed the Alabama State College Campus. When the entire student body protested to state authorities by refusing to re-register, their dining hall was padlocked in an attempt to starve them into submission."

Sixth paragraph:
"Again and again the Southern violators have answered Dr. King's peaceful protests with intimidation and violence. They have bombed his home almost killing his wife and child. They have assaulted his person. They have arrested him seven times—for 'speeding,' 'loitering' and similar 'offenses.' And now they have charged him with 'perjury'— a *felony* under which they could imprison him for *ten years*. . . ."

Although neither of these statements mentions respondent by name, he contended that the word "police" in the third paragraph referred to him as the Montgomery Commissioner who supervised the Police Department, so that he was being accused of "ringing" the campus with police. He further claimed that the paragraph would be read as imputing to the police, and hence to him, the padlocking of the dining hall in order to starve the students into submission. As to the sixth paragraph, he contended that since arrests are ordinarily made by the police, the statement "They have arrested [Dr. King] seven times" would be read as referring to him; he further contended that the "They" who did the arresting would be equated with the "They" who committed the other described acts and with the "Southern violators." Thus, he argued, the paragraph would be read as accusing the Montgomery police, and hence him, of answering Dr. King's protests with "intimidation and violence," bombing his home, assaulting his person, and charging him with perjury. Respondent and six other Montgomery residents testified that they read some or all of the statements as referring to him in his capacity as Commissioner.

It is uncontroverted that some of the statements contained in the two paragraphs were not accurate descriptions of events which occurred in Montgomery. Although Negro students staged a demonstration on the State Capitol steps, they sang the National Anthem and not "My Country, 'Tis of Thee." Although nine students were expelled by the State Board of Education, this was not for leading the demonstration at the Capitol, but for demanding service at a lunch counter in the Montgomery County Courthouse on another day. Not the entire student body, but most of it, had protested the expulsion, not by refusing to register, but by boycotting classes on a single day; virtually all the students did register for the ensuing semester. The campus dining hall was not padlocked on any occasion, and the only students who may have been barred from eating there were the few who had neither signed a preregistration application nor requested temporary meal tickets. Although the police were deployed near the campus in large numbers on three occasions, they did not at any time "ring" the campus, and they were not called to the campus in connection with the demonstration on the State Capitol steps, as the third paragraph implied. Dr. King had not been arrested seven times, but only four; and although he claimed to have been assaulted some years earlier in connection with his arrest for loitering outside a courtroom, one of the officers who made the arrest denied that there was such an assault.

On the premise that the charges in the sixth paragraph could be read as referring to him, respondent was allowed to prove that he had not participated in the events described. Although Dr. King's home had in fact been bombed twice when his wife and child were there, both of these occasions antedated respondent's tenure as Commissioner, and the police were not only not implicated in the bombings, but had made every effort to apprehend those who were. Three of Dr. King's four arrests took place before respondent became Commissioner. Although Dr. King had in fact been indicted (he was subsequently acquitted) on two counts of perjury, each of which carried a possible five-year sentence, respondent had nothing to do with procuring the indictment.

Respondent made no effort to prove that he suffered actual pecuniary loss as a result of the alleged libel. One of his witnesses, a former employer, testified that if he had believed the statements, he doubted whether he "would want to be associated with anybody who would be a party to such things that are stated in that ad," and that he would not re-employ respondent if he believed "that he allowed the Police Department to do the things that the paper say he did." But neither this witness nor any of the others testified that he had actually believed the statements in their supposed reference to respondent.

The cost of the advertisement was approximately $4800, and it was published by the *Times* upon an order from a New York advertising agency acting for the signatory Committee. The agency submitted the advertisement with a letter from A. Philip Randolph, Chairman of the Committee, certifying that the persons whose names appeared on the advertisement had given their permission. Mr. Randolph was known to the *Times*' Advertising Acceptability Department as a responsible person, and in accepting the letter as sufficient proof of authorization it followed its established practice. . . .

Alabama law denies a public officer recovery of punitive damages in a libel action brought on account of a publication concerning his official conduct unless he first makes a written demand for a public retraction and the defendant fails or refuses to comply. Respondent served such a demand upon each of the petitioners. None of the individual petitioners responded to the demand, primarily because each took the position that he had not authorized the use of his name on the advertisement and therefore had not published the statements that respondent alleged had libeled him. The *Times* did not publish a retraction in response to the demand, but wrote respondent a letter stating, among other things, that "we . . . are somewhat puzzled as to how you think the statements in any way reflect on you," and "you might, if you desire, let us know in what respect you claim that the statements in the advertisement reflect on you." Respondent filed this suit a few days later without answering the letter. . . .

The trial judge submitted the case to the jury under instructions that the statements in the advertisement were "libelous *per se*" and were not privileged, so that petitioners might be held liable if the jury found that they had published the advertisement and that the statements were made "of and concerning" respondent. The jury was instructed that, because the statements were libelous *per se*, "the law . . . implies legal injury from the bare fact of publication itself," "falsity and malice are presumed," "general damages need not be alleged or proved but are presumed," and "punitive damages may be awarded by the jury even though the amount of actual damages is neither found nor shown." An award of punitive damages—as distinguished from "general" damages, which are compensatory in nature—apparently requires proof of actual malice under Alabama law, and the judge charged that "mere negligence or carelessness is not evidence of actual malice or malice in fact, and does not justify an award of exemplary or punitive damages." He refused to charge, however, that the jury must be "convinced" of malice, in the sense of "actual intent" to harm or "gross negligence and recklessness," to make such an award, and he also refused to require that a verdict for respondent differentiate between compensatory and punitive damages. The judge rejected petitioners' contention that his rulings abridged the freedoms of speech and of the press that are guaranteed by the First and Fourteenth Amendments.

In affirming the judgment, the Supreme Court of Alabama sustained the trial judge's rulings and instructions in all respects. . . .

. . . We reverse the judgment. We hold that the rule of law applied by the Alabama courts is constitutionally deficient for failure to provide the safeguards for freedom of speech and of the press that are required by the First and Fourteenth Amendments in a libel action brought by a public official against critics of his official conduct. We further hold that under the proper safeguards the evidence presented in this case is constitutionally insufficient to support the judgment for respondent. . . .

I

The . . . contention is that the constitutional guarantees of freedom of speech and of the press are inapplicable here, at least so far as the *Times* is concerned, because the allegedly libelous statements were published as part of a paid, "commercial" advertisement. . . .

The publication here was not a "commercial" advertisement [because it] . . . communicated information, expressed opinion, recited grievances, protested claimed abuses, and sought financial support on behalf of a movement whose existence and objectives are matters of the highest public interest and concern. That the *Times* was paid for publishing the advertisement is as immaterial in this connection as is the fact that newspapers and books are sold. Any other conclusion would discourage newspapers from carrying "editorial advertisements" of this type, and so might shut off an important outlet for the promulgation of information and ideas by persons who do not themselves have access to publishing facilities—who wish to exercise their freedom of speech even though they are not members of the press. The effect would be to shackle the First Amendment in its attempt to secure "the widest possible dissemination of information from diverse and antagonistic sources." *Associated Press v. United States*. To avoid placing such a handicap upon the freedoms of expression, we hold that if the allegedly libelous statements would otherwise be constitutionally protected from the present judgment, they do not forfeit that protection because they were published in the form of a paid advertisement.

II

. . . Once "libel *per se*" has been established, the defendant has no defense as to stated facts unless he can persuade the jury that they were true in all their particulars. His privilege of "fair comment" for expressions of opinion depends on the truth of the facts upon which the comment is based. . . .

The question before us is whether this rule of liability, as applied to an action brought by a public official against critics of his official conduct, abridges the freedom of speech and of the press that is guaranteed by the First and Fourteenth Amendments. . . .

. . . Like insurrection, contempt, advocacy of unlawful acts, breach of the peace, obscenity, solicitation of legal business, and the various other formulae for the repression of expression that have been challenged in this Court, libel can claim no talismanic immunity from constitutional limitations. It must be measured by standards that satisfy the First Amendment.

The general proposition that freedom of expression upon public questions is secured by the First Amendment has long been settled by our decisions. The constitutional safeguard, we have said, "was fashioned to assure unfettered interchange of ideas for the bringing about of political and social changes desired by the people." *Roth v. United States.* . . .

Thus we consider this case against the background of a profound national commitment to the principle that debate on public issues should be uninhibited, robust, and wide-open, and that it may well include vehement, caustic, and sometimes unpleasantly sharp attacks on government and public officials. The present advertisement, as an expression of grievance and protest on one of the major public issues of our time, would seem clearly to qualify for the constitutional protection. The question is whether it forfeits that protection by the falsity of some of its factual statements and by its alleged defamation of respondent . . .

. . . Erroneous statement is inevitable in free debate, and . . . it must be protected if the freedoms of expression are to have the "breathing space" that they "need . . . to survive," *N.A.A.C.P. v. Button.* . . .

A rule compelling the critic of official conduct to guarantee the truth of all his factual assertions—and to do so on pain of libel judgments virtually unlimited in amount—leads to a comparable "self-censorship." Allowance of the defense of truth, with the burden of proving it on the defendant, does not mean that only false speech will be deterred. Even courts accepting this defense as an adequate safeguard have recognized the difficulties of adducing legal proofs that the alleged libel was true in all its factual particulars. . . . Under such a rule, would-be critics of official conduct may be deterred from voicing their criticism, even though it is believed to be true and even though it is in fact true, because of doubt whether it can be proved in court or fear of the expense of having to do so. They tend to make only statements which "steer far wider of the unlawful zone." *Speiser v. Randall.* The rule thus dampens the vigor and limits the variety of public debate. It is inconsistent with the First and Fourteenth Amendments.

The constitutional guarantees require, we think, a federal rule that prohibits a public official from recovering damages for a defamatory falsehood relating to his official conduct unless he proves that the statement was made with "actual malice"—that is, with knowledge that it was false or with reckless disregard of whether it was false or not. . . .

III

We hold today that the Constitution delimits a State's power to award damages for libel in actions brought by public officials against critics of their official conduct. Since this is such an action, the rule requiring proof of actual malice is applicable. While Alabama law apparently requires proof of actual malice for an award of punitive damages, where general damages are concerned malice is "presumed." Such a presumption is inconsistent with the federal rule. . . .

. . . The *Times'* failure to retract upon respondent's demand, although it later retracted upon the demand of Governor Patterson, is likewise not adequate evidence of malice for constitutional purposes. Whether or not a failure to retract may ever constitute such evidence, there are two reasons why it does not here. *First,* the letter written by the *Times* reflected a reasonable doubt on its part as to whether the advertisement could reasonably be taken to refer to respondent at all. *Second,* it was not a final refusal, since it asked for an explanation on this point—a request that respondent chose to ignore. . . .

Finally, there is evidence that the *Times* published the advertisement without checking its accuracy against the news stories in the *Times'* own files. The mere presence of the stories in the files does not, of course, establish that the *Times* "knew" the advertisement was false, since the state of mind required for actual malice would have to be brought home to the persons in the *Times'* organization having responsibility for the publication of the advertisement. With respect to the failure of those persons to make the check, the record shows that they relied upon their knowledge of the good reputation of many of those whose names were listed as sponsors of the advertisement, and upon the letter from A. Philip Randolph, known to them as a responsible individual, certifying that the use of the names was authorized. There was testimony that the persons handling the advertisement saw nothing in it that would render it unacceptable under the *Times'* policy of rejecting advertisements containing "attacks of a personal character"; their failure to reject it on this ground was not unreasonable. We think the evidence against the *Times* supports at most a finding of negligence in failing to discover the misstatements, and is constitutionally insufficient to show the recklessness that is required for a finding of actual malice.

We also think the evidence was constitutionally defective in another respect: it was incapable of supporting the jury's finding that the allegedly libelous statements were made "of and concerning" respondent. Respondent relies on the words of the advertisement and the testimony of six witnesses to establish a connection between it and himself. . . .

The judgment of the Supreme Court of Alabama is reversed and the case is remanded to that court for further proceedings not inconsistent with this opinion.

MR. JUSTICE BLACK, *with whom Mr. Justice Douglas joins, concurring.*

I concur in reversing this half-million-dollar judgment against the New York Times Company and the four individual defendants. In reversing the Court holds that "the Constitution delimits a State's power to award damages for libel in actions brought by public officials against critics of their official conduct." I base my vote to reverse on the belief that the First and Fourteenth Amendments not merely "delimit" a State's power to award damages to "public officials against critics of their official conduct" but completely prohibit a State from exercising such a power. The Court goes on to hold that a State can subject such critics to damages if "actual malice" can be proved against them. "Malice," even as defined by the Court, is an elusive, abstract concept, hard to prove and hard to disprove. The requirement that malice be proved provides at best an evanescent protection for the right critically to discuss public affairs and certainly does not measure up to the sturdy safeguard embodied in the First Amendment. Unlike the Court, therefore, I vote to reverse exclusively on the ground that the *Times* and the individual defendants had an absolute, unconditional constitutional right to publish in the *Times* advertisement their criticisms of the Montgomery agencies and officials. . . .

We would, I think, more faithfully interpret the First Amendment by holding that at the very least it leaves the people and the press free to criticize officials and discuss public affairs with impunity. . . . This Nation, I suspect, can live in peace without libel suits based on public discussions of public affairs and public officials. But I doubt that a country can live in freedom where its people can be made to suffer physically or financially for criticizing their government, its actions, or its officials. . . .

MR. JUSTICE GOLDBERG, *with whom Mr. Justice Douglas joins, concurring in the result.*

The Court today announces a constitutional standard which prohibits "a public official from recovering damages for a defamatory falsehood relating to his official conduct unless he proves that the statement was made with 'actual malice'—that is, with knowledge that it was false or with reckless disregard of whether it was false or not." The Court thus rules that the Constitution gives citizens and newspapers a "conditional privilege" immunizing nonmalicious misstatements of fact regarding the official conduct of a government officer. The impressive array of history and precedent marshaled by the Court, however, confirms my belief that the Constitution affords greater protection than that provided by the Court's standard to citizen and press in exercising the right of public criticism.

In my view, the First and Fourteenth Amendments to the Constitution afford to the citizen and to the press an absolute, unconditional privilege to criticize official conduct despite the harm which may flow from excesses and abuses. . . . The theory of our Constitution is that every citizen may speak his mind and every newspaper express its view on matters of public concern and may not be barred from speaking or publishing because those in control of government think that what is said or written is unwise, unfair, false or malicious. In a democratic society, one who assumes to act for the citizens in an executive, legislative, or judicial capacity must expect that his official acts will be commented upon and criticized. Such criticism cannot, in my opinion, be muzzled or deterred by the courts at the instance of public officials under the label of libel. . . .

This is not to say that the Constitution protects defamatory statements directed against the private conduct of a public official or private citizen. Freedom of press and of speech insures that government will respond to the will of the people and that changes may be obtained by peaceful means. Purely private defamation has little to do with the political ends of a self-governing society. . . .

*   *   *

Eight months after the 1964 New York Times decision, Justice Brennan again spoke for the Court in a libel case, Garrison v. Louisiana. The significance of the Garrison decision is in its application of New York Times civil libel principles to cases of criminal libel, i.e. that actual malice must be proven in order to sustain criminal sanctions for a defamatory falsehood against a public official. As in the New York Times case, Justices Douglas, Black, and Goldberg, concurring with the results, argued that the Constitution prohibits prosecution for seditious libel, knowingly making falsehoods and reckless disregard for truth notwithstanding. The case revolved around a New Orleans district attorney who severely criticized the bench, charging laziness and inefficiency. The Supreme Court reversed his conviction without dissent.

GARRISON V. LOUISIANA
379 U.S. 64 (1964)

MR. JUSTICE BRENNAN delivered the opinion of the Court.

Appellant is the District Attorney of Orleans Parish, Louisiana. During a dispute with the eight judges of the Criminal District Court of the Parish, he held a press conference at which he issued a statement disparaging their judicial conduct. As a result, he was tried without a jury before a judge from another parish and convicted of criminal defamation under the Louisiana Criminal Defamation Statute. The principal charges alleged to be defamatory were his attribution of a large backlog of pending criminal cases to the inefficiency, laziness, and excessive vacation of the judges, and his accusation that, by refusing to authorize disbursements to cover the expenses of undercover investigations of vice in New Orleans, the judges had hampered his efforts to enforce the vice laws. In impugning their motives, he said:

> The judges have now made it eloquently clear where their sympathies lie in regard to aggressive vice investigations by refusing to authorize use of the DA's funds to pay for the costs of closing down the Canal Street clip joints. . . .
> . . . This raises interesting questions about the racketeer influences on our eight vacation-minded judges.

The Supreme Court of Louisiana affirmed the conviction, 244 LA 787, 154 So 2d 400. The trial court and the State Supreme Court both rejected appellant's contention that the statute unconstitutionally abridged his freedom of expression. . . .

In *New York Times Co. v. Sullivan* we held that the Constitution limits state power, in a civil action brought by a public official for criticism of his official conduct, to an award of damages for a false statement "made with 'actual malice'—that is, with knowledge that it was false or with reckless disregard of whether it was false or not." At the outset, we must decide whether, in view of the differing history and purposes of criminal libel, the *New York Times* rule also limits state power to impose criminal sanctions for criticism of the official conduct of public officials. We hold that it does.

Where criticism of public officials is concerned, we see no merit in the argument that criminal libel statutes serve interests distinct from those secured by civil libel laws, and therefore should not be subject to the same limitations. . . .

We . . . consider whether the historical limitation of the defense of truth in criminal libel to utterances published "with good motives and for justifiable ends" should be incorporated into the *New York Times* rule as it applies to criminal libel statutes; in particular, we must ask whether this history permits negating the truth defense, as the Louisiana statute does, on a showing of malice in the sense of ill-will. . . . [W]here the criticism is of public officials and their conduct of public business, the interest in private reputation is overborne by the larger public interest, secured by the Constitution, in the dissemination of truth. In short, we agree with the New Hampshire court in *State v. Burnham:*

If upon a lawful occasion for making a publication, he has published the truth, and no more, there is no sound principle which can make him liable, even if he was actuated by express malice. . . .

It has been said that it is lawful to publish truth from good motives, and for justifiable ends. But this rule is too narrow. If there is a lawful occasion—a legal right to make a publication—and the matter true, the end is justifiable, and that, in such case, must be sufficient.

Moreover, even where the utterance is false, the great principles of the Constitution which secure freedom of expression in this area preclude attaching adverse consequences to any except the knowing or reckless falsehood. Debate on public issues will not be uninhibited if the speaker must run the risk that it will be proved in court that he spoke out of hatred; even if he did speak out of hatred, utterances honestly believed contribute to the free interchange of ideas and the ascertainment of truth. . . .

We held in *New York Times* that a public official might be allowed the civil remedy only if he establishes that the utterance was false and that it was made with knowledge of its falsity or in reckless disregard of whether it was false or true. The reasons which led us so to hold in *New York Times* apply with no less force merely because the remedy is criminal. . . .

MR. JUSTICE BLACK, *with whom Mr. Justice Douglas joins, concurring.*

For reasons stated at greater length in my opinions concurring in *New York Times Co. v. Sullivan*, and dissenting in *Beauharnais v. Illinois*, as well as in the opinion of Mr. Justice Douglas in this case, I concur in reversing the conviction of appellant Garrison, based as it is purely on his public discussion and criticism of public officials. I believe that the First Amendment, made applicable to the States by the Fourteenth, protects every person from having a State or the Federal Government fine, imprison, or assess damages against him when he has been guilty of no conduct other than expressing an opinion, even though others may believe that his views are unwholesome, unpatriotic, stupid or dangerous. . . . Fining men or sending them to jail for criticizing public officials not only jeopardizes the free, open public discussion which our Constitution guarantees, but can wholly stifle it. I would hold now and not wait to hold later, . . . that under our Constitution there is absolutely no place in this country for the old, discredited English Star Chamber law of seditious criminal libel.

MR. JUSTICE DOUGLAS, *whom Mr. Justice Black joins, concurring.*

I am in hearty agreement with the conclusion of the Court that this prosecution for a seditious libel was unconstitutional. Yet I feel that the gloss which the Court has put on "the freedom of speech" in the First Amendment to reach that result (and like results in other cases) makes that basic guarantee almost unrecognizable.

Recently in *New York Times Co. v. Sullivan,* a majority of the Court held that criticism of an official for official conduct was protected from state civil libel laws by the First and Fourteenth Amendments, unless there was proof of actual malice. We now hold that proof of actual malice is relevant to seditious libel—that seditious libel will lie for a knowingly false statement or one made with reckless disregard of the truth. . . .

While the First Amendment remains the same, the gloss which the Court has written on it in this field of the discussion of public issues robs it of much vitality.

Why does "the freedom of speech" that the Court is willing to protect turn out to be so pale and tame?

It is because, as my Brother Black has said, the Bill of Rights is constantly watered down through judicial "balancing" of what the Constitution says and what judges think is needed for a well-ordered society. . . .

The philosophy of the Sedition Act of 1798 which punished "false, scandalous and malicious" writings (1 Stat 596) is today allowed to be applied by the States. Yet Irving Brant has shown that seditious libel was "entirely the creation of the Star Chamber." It is disquieting to know that one of its instruments of destruction is abroad in the land today.

*   *   *

A second post-New York Times decision was handed down early in 1966. As with New York Times and Garrison, Justice Brennan wrote the opinion of the Court in the 8-1 decision. The lone dissent came from Justice Fortas, who noted that the Rosenblatt-Baer trial in 1960 was prior to the Court's 1964 New York Times decision. The majority, however, elaborated on the New York Times decision in overturning a libel judgment against Alfred D. Rosenblatt, a Laconia (N.H.) columnist. He was charged with libeling a former supervisor of a county recreation area. The major significance was an extension and further refinement of the New York Times' "public official" concept. The Court held that at least those who have substantial responsibility for the conduct of government affairs should be included. Disagreement erupted over the majority's view that the trial judge should make the first determination of whether one is a "public official" in the New York Times sense. In addition, Justice Douglas urged a wider interpretation of the "public official" interpretation.

ROSENBLATT V. BAER
383 U.S. 75 (1966)

MR. JUSTICE BRENNAN *delivered the opinion of the Court.*

A jury in New Hampshire Superior Court awarded respondent damages in this civil libel action based on one of petitioner's columns in the *Laconia Evening Citizen*. Respondent alleged that the column contained defamatory falsehoods concerning his performance as Supervisor of the Belknap County Recreation Area, a facility owned and operated by Belknap County Recreation Area, a facility owned and operated by Belknap County. In the interval between the trial and the decision of petitioner's appeal by the New Hampshire Supreme Court, we decided *New York Times Co. v. Sullivan*. We there held that under the First and Fourteenth Amendments a State cannot award damages to a public official for defamatory falsehood relating to his official conduct unless the official proves actual malice—that the falsehood was published with knowledge of its falsity or with reckless disregard of whether it was true or false. . . .

Petitioner regularly contributed an unpaid column to the *Laconia Evening Citizen*. In it he frequently commented on political matters. As an outspoken proponent of the change in operations at the Recreation Area, petitioner's views were often sharply stated, and he had indicated disagreement with the actions taken by respondent and the County Commissioners. In January 1960, during the first ski season under the new management, some six months after respondent's discharge, petitioner published the column that respondent alleges libeled him. In relevant part, it reads:

> Been doing a little listening and checking at Belknap Recreation Area and am thunderstruck by what am learning.
>
> This year, a year without snow till very late, a year with actually few very major changes in procedure; difference in cash income simply fantastic, almost unbelievable.
>
> On any sort of comparative basis, the Area this year is doing literally hundreds of per cent BETTER than last year.
>
> When consider that last year was excellent snow year, that season started because of more snow, months earlier last year, one can only ponder following question:
>
> What happened to all the money last year? and every other year? What magic has Dana Beane [Chairman of the new commission] and rest of commission, and Mr. Warner [respondent's replacement as supervisor] wrought to make such tremendous difference in net cash results?

I

The column on its face contains no clearly actionable statement. Although the questions "What happened to all the money last year? and every other year?" could be read to imply peculation, they could also be read, in context, merely to praise the present administration. The only persons mentioned by name are officials of the new regime; no reference is made to respondent, the three elected commissioners, or anyone else who had a part in the administration of the Area during respondent's tenure. Persons familiar with the controversy over the Area might will read it as complimenting the luck or skill of the new management in attracting increased patronage and producing a "tremendous difference in net cash results" despite less favorable snow; indeed, witnesses for petitioner testified that they so read the column. . . .

II

Turning . . . to the question whether respondent was a "public official" within *New York Times*, we reject at the outset his suggestion that it should be answered by reference to state-law standards. States have developed definitions of "public official" for local administrative purposes, not the purposes of a national constitutional protection. If existing state-law standards reflect the purposes of *New York Times*, this is at best accidental. Our decision in *New York Times*, moreover, draws its force from the constitutional protections afforded free expression. The standards that set the scope of its principles cannot therefore be such that "the constitutional limits of free expression in the Nation would vary with state lines." *Pennekamp v. Florida.*

We remarked in *New York Times* that we had no occasion "to determine how far down into the lower ranks of government employees the 'public official' designation would extend for purposes of this rule, or otherwise to specify categories of persons who would or would not be included." No precise lines need be drawn for the purposes of this case. The motivating force for the decision in *New York Times* was twofold. We expressed "a profound national commitment to the principle that debate on public issues should be uninhibited, robust, and wide-open *and* that [such debate] may well include vehement, caustic, and sometimes unpleasantly sharp attacks on government and public officials." (Emphasis supplied.) There is, first, a strong interest in debate on public issues, and second, a strong interest in debate about those persons who are in a position significantly to influence the resolution of those issues. Criticism of government is at the very center of the constitutionally protected area of free discussion. Criticism of those responsible for government operations must be free, lest criticism of government itself be penalized. It is clear, therefore, that the "public official" designation applies at the very least to those among the hierarchy of government employees who have, or appear to the public to have, substantial responsibility for or control over the conduct of governmental affairs. . . .

MR. JUSTICE DOUGLAS, *concurring.*

In *New York Times Co. v. Sullivan* we dealt with elected officials. We now have the question as to how far its principles extend or how far down the hierarchy we should go.

The problems presented are considerable ones. Maybe the key man in a hierarchy is the night watchman responsible for thefts of state secrets. Those of us alive in the 1940s and 1950s witnessed the dreadful ordeal of people in the public service being pummelled by those inside and outside government, with charges that were false, abusive, and damaging to the extreme. Many of them, unlike the officials in *New York Times* who ran for election, rarely had opportunity for rejoinder.

Yet if free discussion of public issues is the guide, I see no way to draw lines that exclude the night watchman, the file clerk, the typist, or, for that matter, anyone on the public payroll. And how about those who contract to carry out governmental missions? Some of them are as much in the public domain as any so-called officeholder. And how about the dollar-a-year man, whose prototype was publicized in *United States v. Mississippi Valley Generating Co.?* And the industrialists who raise the price of a basic commodity? Are not steel and aluminum in the public domain? And the labor leader who combines trade unionism with bribery and racketeering? Surely the public importance of collective bargaining puts labor as well as management into the public arena so far as the present constitutional issue is concerned. . . .

If the term "public official" were a constitutional term, we would be stuck with it and have to give it content. But the term is our own; and so long as we are fashioning a rule of free discussion of public issues, I cannot relate it only to those who, by the Court's standard, are deemed to hold public office. . . .

MR. JUSTICE STEWART, *concurring.*

The Constitution does not tolerate actions for libel on government. State defamation laws, therefore, whether civil or criminal, cannot constitutionally be converted into laws against seditious libel. Our decisions in the *New York Times* and *Garrison* cases turned upon that fundamental proposition. What the Court says today seems to me fully consonant with those decisions, and I join the Court's opinion and judgment. . . .

We use misleading euphemisms when we speak of the *New York Times* rule as involving "uninhibited, robust, and wide-open" debate, or "vehement, caustic, and sometimes unpleasantly sharp" criticism. What the *New York Times* rule ultimately protects is defamatory falsehood. No matter how gross the untruth, the *New York Times* rule deprives a defamed public official of any hope for legal redress without proof that the lie was a knowing one, or uttered "in reckless disregard of the truth." . . .

Moreover, the preventive effect of liability for defamation serves an important public purpose. For the rights and values of private personality far transcend mere personal interests. Surely if the 1950s taught us anything, they taught us that the poisonous atmosphere of the easy lie can infect and degrade a whole society.

MR. JUSTICE BLACK, *with whom Mr. Justice Douglas joins, concurring and dissenting.*

. . . I concur in the reversal but dissent from leaving the case open for a new trial, believing that for reasons stated in the concurring opinions of Mr. Justice Douglas and myself in the *New York Times* and *Garrison* cases a libel judgment against Rosenblatt is forbidden by the First Amendment which the Fourteenth made applicable to the States. . . .

This case illustrates, I think, what a short and inadequate step this Court took in the *New York Times* case to guard free press and free speech against the grave dangers to the press and the public created by libel actions. Half-million dollar judgments for libel damages like those awarded against the *New York Times* will not be stopped by requirements that "malice" be found, however that term is defined. Such a requirement is little protection against high emotions and deep prejudices which frequently pervade local communities where libel suits are tried. And this Court cannot and should not limit its protection against such press-destroying judgments by reviewing the evidence, findings, and court rulings only on a case-by-case basis. The only sure way to protect speech and press against these threats is to recognize that libel laws are abridgments of speech and press and therefore are barred in both federal and state courts by the First and Fourteenth Amendments. I repeat what I said in the *New York Times* case that "An unconditional right to say what one pleases about public affairs is what I consider to be the minimum guarantee of the First Amendment." . . .

*   *   *

A major extension of libel protection for the press was handed down by the Court in June 1967 as it applied the 1964 New York Times rule to "public figures" as well as "public officials." The Court, considering together two widely publicized libel cases, upheld 5-4 Wallace Butts' judgment against Curtis Publishing Co., but reversed unanimously Edwin Walker's judgment against the Associated Press. In reaching these decisions, the Court laid down the test of "accepted publishing standards."

Unintentional error spawned by the need for immediacy in covering fast-breaking news stories, the Court ruled, cannot be the basis for libel judgments awarded to "public figures." The Walker suit was based upon the 1962 AP account of his role in the rioting which surrounded the entry of Negro James Meredith into the University of Mississippi. The 1963 Saturday Evening Post story involving Wallace Butts, former director of athletics at the University of Georgia, was entitled "The Story of a Football Fix." The Court held that the urgency of the AP news account was missing from the Post "exposé" and that the Post ignored "elementary precautions" of good publication practice. Walker had sued AP and more than a dozen other publications for a total of $33 million. His suit against AP was for $2 million, which lower courts had reduced to $500,000. Butts had sued Curtis for $10 million, but eventually was awarded $460,000. The majority opinion, covering both cases, was written by Justice Harlan. Dissenters in the 5-4 Curtis case were Justices Black, Douglas, Brennan, and White. Justice Black, joined by Justice Douglas, warned the Court that it was "getting itself into the same quagmire" with libel as it had with obscenity. He reaffirmed his "absolutist" interpretation of the First Amendment and urged the Court to free the press altogether from the "harassment" of libel actions.

CURTIS PUBLISHiNG CO. V. BUTTS

ASSOCIATED PRESS V. WALKER
388 U.S. 130 (1967)

MR. JUSTICE HARLAN announced the judgment of the Court and delivered an opinion in which Mr. Justice Clark, Mr. Justice Stewart, and Mr. Justice Fortas join.

In New York Times Co. v. Sullivan, this Court held that "[t]he constitutional guarantees [of freedom of speech and press] require . . . a federal rule that prohibits a public official from recovering damages for a defamatory falsehood relating to his official conduct unless he proves that the statement was made with 'actual malice'—that is, with knowledge that it was false or with reckless disregard of whether it was false or not." We brought these two cases here to consider the impact of that decision on libel actions instituted by persons who are not public officials, but who are "public figures" and involved in issues in which the public has a justified and important interest. . . .

I

Curtis Publishing Co. v. Butts stems from an article published in petitioner's *Saturday Evening Post* which accused respondent of conspiring to "fix" a football game between the University of Georgia and the University of Alabama, played in 1962. At the time of the article, Butts was the athletic director of the University of Georgia and had overall responsibility for the administration of its athletic program. Georgia is a state university, but Butts was employed by the Georgia Athletic Association, a private corporation, rather than by the State itself. Butts had previously served as head football coach of the University and was a well-known and respected figure in coaching ranks. He had maintained an interest in coaching and was negotiating for a position with a professional team at the time of publication.

The article was entitled "The Story of a College Football Fix" and prefaced by a note from the editors stating: "Not since the Chicago White Sox threw the 1919 World Series has there been a sports story as shocking as this one. . . . Before the University of Georgia played the University of Alabama . . . Wally Butts . . . gave [to its coach] . . . Georgia's plays, defensive patterns, all the significant secrets Georgia's football team possessed." The text revealed that one George Burnett, an Atlanta insurance salesman, had accidentally overheard, because of electronic error, a telephone conversation between Butts and the head coach of the University of Alabama, Paul Bryant, which took place approximately one week prior to the game. Burnett was said to have listened while "Butts outlined Georgia's offensive plays . . . and told . . . how Georgia planned to defend. . . . Butts mentioned both players and plays by name." The readers were told that Burnett had made notes of the conversation, and specific examples of the divulged secrets were set out.

The article went on to discuss the game and the players' reaction to the game, concluding that "[t]he Georgia players, their moves analyzed, and forecast like those of rats in a maze, took a frightful physical beating," and said that the players, and other sideline observers, were aware that Alabama was privy to Georgia's secrets. It set out the series of events commencing with Burnett's later presentation of his notes to the Georgia head coach, Johnny Griffith, and culminating in Butts' resignation from the University's athletic affairs, for health and business reasons. The article's conclusion made clear its expected impact:

> The chances are that Wally Butts will never help any football team again. . . . The investigation by university and Southeastern Conference officials is continuing; motion pictures of other games are being scrutinized; where it will end no one so far can say. But careers will be ruined, that is sure.

Butts brought this diversity libel action in the federal courts in Georgia seeking $5,000,000 compensatory and $5,000,000 punitive damages. The complaint was filed, and the trial completed, before this Court handed down its decision in *New York Times,* and the only defense raised by petitioner Curtis was one of substantial truth. No constitutional defenses were interposed although Curtis' counsel were aware of the progress of the *New York Times* case, and although general constitutional defenses had been raised by Curtis in a libel action instituted by the Alabama coach who was a state employee.

Evidence at trial was directed both to the truth of the article and to its preparation. . . . The evidence showed that Burnett had indeed overheard a conversation between Butts and the Alabama coach, but the content of that conversation was hotly disputed. It was Butts' contention that the conversation had been general football talk and that nothing Burnett had overheard would have been of any particular value to an opposing coach. Expert witnesses supported Butts by analyzing Burnett's notes and the films of the game itself. The *Saturday Evening Post's* version of the game and of the players' remarks about the game was severely contradicted.

The evidence on the preparation of the article . . . cast serious doubt on the adequacy of the investigation underlying the article. It was Butts' contention that the magazine had departed greatly from the standards of good investigation and reporting and that this was especially reprehensible, amounting to reckless and wanton conduct, in light of the devastating nature of the article's assertions. . . .

The jury returned a verdict for $60,000 in general damages and for $3,000,000 punitive damages. The trial court reduced the total to $460,000 by remittitur. Soon thereafter we handed down our decision in *New York Times* and Curtis immediately brought it to the attention of the trial court by a motion for new trial. The trial judge rejected Curtis' motion on two grounds. He first held that *New York Times* was inapplicable because Butts was not a public official. He also held that "there was ample evidence from which a jury could have concluded that there was reckless disregard by defendant of whether the article was false or not."

Curtis appealed to the Court of Appeals for the Fifth Circuit which affirmed the judgment of the District Court by a two-to-one vote. . . .

II

Associated Press v. Walker arose out of the distribution of a news dispatch giving an eyewitness account of events on the campus of the University of Mississippi on the night of September 30, 1962, when a massive riot erupted because of federal efforts to enforce a court decree ordering the enrollment of a Negro, James Meredith, as a student in the University.

The dispatch stated that respondent Walker, who was present on the campus, had taken command of the violent crowd and had personally led a charge against federal marshals sent there to effectuate the court's decree and to assist in preserving order. It also described Walker as encouraging rioters to use violence and giving them technical advice on combating the effects of tear gas.

Walker was a private citizen at the time of the riot and publication. He had pursued a long and honorable career in the United States Army before resigning to engage in political activity, and had, in fact, been in command of the federal troops during the school segregation confrontation at Little Rock, Arkansas, in 1957. He was acutely interested in the issue of physical federal intervention, and had made a number of strong statements against such action which had received wide publicity. Walker had his own following, the "Friends of Walker," and could fairly be deemed a man of some political prominence.

Walker initiated this libel action in the state courts of Texas, seeking a total of $2,000,000 in compensatory and punitive damages. Associated Press raised both the defense of truth and constitutional defenses. At trial both sides attempted to reconstruct the stormy events on the campus of the University of Mississippi. Walker admitted his presence on the campus and conceded that he had spoken to a group of rioters. He claimed, however, that he had counseled restraint and peaceful protest, and exercised no control whatever over the crowd which had rejected his plea. He denied categorically taking part in any charge against the federal marshals.

There was little evidence relating to the preparation of the news dispatch. It was clear, however, that the author of this dispatch, Van Savell, was actually present during the events described and had reported them almost immediately to the Associated Press office in Atlanta. A discrepancy was shown between an oral account given the office and a later written dispatch, but it related solely to whether Walker had spoken to the group before or after approaching the marshals. No other showing of improper preparation was attempted, nor was there any evidence of personal prejudice or incompetency on the part of Savell or the Associated Press. . . .

A verdict of $500,000 compensatory damages and $300,000 punitive damages was returned. The trial judge, however, found that there was "no evidence to support the jury's answers that there was actual malice" and refused to enter the punitive award. . . . The trial judge also noted that this lack of "malice" would require a verdict for the Associated Press if *New York Times* were applicable. But he rejected its applicability since there were "no compelling reasons of public policy requiring additional defenses to suits for libel. Truth alone should be an adequate defense."

Both sides appealed and the Texas Court of Civil Appeals affirmed both the award of compensatory damages and the striking of punitive damages. . . .

III

We thus turn to a consideration, on the merits, of the constitutional claims raised by Curtis in *Butts* and by the Associated Press in *Walker*. Powerful arguments are brought to bear for the extension of the *New York Times* rule in both cases. In *Butts* it is contended that the facts are on all fours with those of *Rosenblatt v. Baer*, since Butts was charged with the important responsibility of managing the athletic affairs of a state university. It is argued that while the Athletic Association is financially independent from the State and Butts was not technically a state employee, as was Baer, his role in state administration was so significant that this technical distinction from *Rosenblatt* should be ignored. Even if this factor is to be given some weight, we are told that the public interest in education in general, and in the conduct of the athletic affairs of educational institutions in particular, justifies constitutional protection of discussion of persons involved in it equivalent to the protection afforded discussion of public officials.

A similar argument is raised in the *Walker* case where the important public interest in being informed about the events and personalities involved in the Mississippi riot is pressed. In that case we are also urged to recognize that Walker's claims to the protection of libel laws are limited since he thrust himself into the "vortex" of the controversy. . . .

The history of libel law leaves little doubt that it originated in soil entirely different from that which nurtured these constitutional values. Early libel was primarily a criminal remedy, the function of which was to make punishable any writing which tended to bring into disrepute the state, established religion, or any individual likely to be provoked to a breach of the peace because of the words. Truth was no defense in such actions and while a proof of truth might prevent recovery in a civil action, this limitation is more readily explained as a manifestation of judicial reluctance to enrich an undeserving plaintiff than by the supposition that the defendant was protected by the truth of the publication. The same truthful statement might be the basis of a criminal libel action. . . .

The law of libel has, of course, changed substantially since the early days of the Republic. . . . The emphasis has shifted from criminal to civil remedies, from the protection of absolute social values to the safe-guarding of valid personal interests. Truth has become an absolute defense in almost all cases, and privileges designed to foster free communication are almost universally recognized. . . .

While the truth of the underlying facts might be said to mark the line between publications which are of significant social value and those which might be suppressed without serious social harm and thus resolve the antithesis on a neutral ground, we have rejected, in prior cases involving materials and persons commanding justified and important public interest, the argument that a finding of falsity alone should strip protections from the publisher. *New York Times Co. v. Sullivan.* We have recognized that "putting to the pre-existing prejudices of a jury the determination of what is 'true' may effectively institute a system of censorship," and "the inevitability of some error in the situation presented in free debate," *Time, Inc. v. Hill.*

In the cases we decide today none of the particular considerations involved in *New York Times* is present. These actions cannot be analogized to persecutions for seditious libel. Neither plaintiff has any position in government which would permit a recovery by him to be viewed as a vindication of governmental policy. Neither was entitled to a special privilege protecting his utterances against accountability in libel. We are prompted, therefore, to seek guidance from the rules of liability which prevail in our society with respect to compensation of persons injured by the improper performance of a legitimate activity by another. . . . In defining these rules, and especially in formulating the standards for determining the degree of care to be expected in the circumstances, courts have consistently given much attention to the importance of defendants' activities. The courts have also, especially in libel cases, investigated the plaintiff's position to determine whether he has a legitimate call upon the court for protection in light of his prior activities and means of self-defense. We note that the public interest in the circulation of the materials here involved, and the publisher's interest in circulating them, is not less than that involved in *New York Times.* And both Butts and Walker commanded a substantial amount of independent public interest at the time of the publication; both, in our opinion, would have been labeled "public figures" under ordinary tort rules. See *Spahn v. Julian Messner, Inc.* . . .

These similarities and differences between libel actions involving persons who are public officials and libel actions involving those circumstanced as were Butts and Walker, viewed in light of the principles of liability which are of general applicability in our society, lead us to the conclusion that libel actions of the present kind cannot be left entirely to state libel laws, unlimited by any overriding constitutional safeguard, but that the rigorous federal requirements of *New York Times* are not the only appropriate accommodation of the conflicting interests at stake. We consider and would hold that a "public figure" who is not a public official may also recover damages for a defamatory falsehood whose substance makes substantial danger to reputation apparent, on a showing of highly unreasonable conduct constituting an extreme departure from the standards of investigation and reporting ordinarily adhered to by responsible publishers.

Nothing in this opinion is meant to affect the holdings in *New York Times* and its progeny, including our recent decision in *Time, Inc. v. Hill.*

IV

Having set forth the standard by which we believe the constitutionality of the damage awards in these cases must be judged, we turn now, as the Court did in *New York Times*, to the question whether the evidence and findings below meet that standard. We find the standard satisfied in *Butts*, and not satisfied by either the evidence or the findings in *Walker*. . . .

The evidence showed that the Butts story was in no sense "hot news" and the editors of the magazine recognized the need for a thorough investigation of the serious charges. Elementary precautions were, nevertheless, ignored. The *Saturday Evening Post* knew that Burnett had been placed on probation in connection with bad check charges, but proceeded to publish the story on the basis of his affidavit without substantial independent support. Burnett's notes were not even viewed by any of the magazine's personnel prior to publication. John Carmichael who was supposed to have been with Burnett when the phone call was overheard was not interviewed. No attempt was made to screen the films of the game to see if Burnett's information was accurate, and no attempt was made to find out whether Alabama had adjusted its plans after the alleged divulgence of information.

The *Post* writer assigned to the story was not a football expert and no attempt was made to check the story with someone knowledgeable in the sport. At trial such experts indicated that the information in the Burnett notes was either such that it would be evident to any opposing coach from game films regularly exchanged or valueless. Those assisting the *Post* writer in his investigation were already deeply involved in another libel action, based on a different article, brought against Curtis Publishing Co. by the Alabama coach and unlikely to be the source of a complete and objective investigation. The *Saturday Evening Post* was anxious to change its image by instituting a policy of "sophisticated muckraking," and the pressure to produce a successful exposé might have induced a stretching of standards. In short, the evidence is ample to support a finding of highly unreasonable conduct constituting an extreme departure from the standards of investigation and reporting ordinarily adhered to by responsible publishers.

The situation in *Walker* is considerably different. There the trial court found the evidence insufficient to support more than a finding of even ordinary negligence and the Court of Civil Appeals supported the trial court's view of the evidence.

In contrast to the *Butts* article, the dispatch which concerns us in *Walker* was news which required immediate dissemination. The Associated Press received the information from a correspondent who was present at the scene of the events and gave every indication of being trustworthy and competent. His dispatches in this instance, with one minor exception, were internally consistent and would not have seemed unreasonable to one familiar with General Walker's prior publicized statements on the underlying controversy. Considering the necessity for rapid dissemination, nothing in this series of events gives the slightest hint of a severe departure from accepted publishing standards. We therefore conclude that General Walker should not be entitled to damages from the Associated Press.

V

We come finally to Curtis' contention that whether or not it can be required to compensate Butts for any injury it may have caused him, it cannot be subjected to an assessment for punitive damages limited only by the "enlightened conscience" of the community. Curtis . . . contends that an unlimited punitive award against a magazine publisher constitutes an effective prior restraint by giving the jury the power to destroy the publisher's business. We cannot accept this reasoning. Publishers like Curtis engage in a wide variety of activities which may lead to tort suits where punitive damages are a possibility. To exempt a publisher, because of the nature of his calling, from an imposition generally exacted from other members of the community, would be to extend a protection not required by the constitutional guarantee. We think the constitutional guarantee of freedom of speech and press is adequately served by judicial control over excessive jury verdicts, manifested in this instance by the trial court's remittitur, and by the general rule that a verdict based on jury prejudice cannot be sustained even when punitive damages are warranted. . . .

Where a publisher's departure from standards of press responsibility is severe enough to strip from him the constitutional protection our decision acknowledges, we think it entirely proper for the State to act not only for the protection of the individual injured but to safeguard all those similarly situated against like abuse. Moreover, punitive damages require a finding of "ill will" under general libel law and it is not unjust that a publisher be forced to pay for the "venting of his spleen" in a manner which does not meet even the minimum standards required for constitutional protection. . . . We would hold, therefore, that misconduct sufficient to justify the award of compensatory damages also justifies the imposition of a punitive award, subject of course to the limitation that such award is not demonstrated to be founded on the mere prejudice of the jury. . . .

MR. CHIEF JUSTICE WARREN, *concurring in the result.*

While I agree with the results announced by Mr. Justice Harlan in both of these cases, I find myself in disagreement with his stated reasons for reaching those results. Our difference stems from his departure from the teaching of *New York Times v. Sullivan,* to which we both subscribed only three years ago. . . .

To me, differentiation between "public figures" and "public officials" and adoption of separate standards of proof for each has no basis in law, logic, or First Amendment policy. Increasingly in this country, the distinctions between governmental and private sectors are blurred. Since the depression of the 1930s and World War II there has been a rapid fusion of economic and political power, a merging of science, industry, and government, and a high degree of interaction between the intellectual, governmental, and business worlds. Depression, war, international tensions, national and international markets, and the surging growth of science and technology have precipitated national and international problems that demand national and international solutions. While these trends and events have occasioned a consolidation of governmental power, power has also become much more organized in what we have commonly considered to be the private sector. . . .

Viewed in this context then, it is plain that although they are not subject to the restraints of the political process, "public figures," like "public officials," often play an influential role in ordering society. And surely as a class these "public figures" have as ready access as "public officials" to mass media of communication, both to influence policy and to counter criticism of their views and activities. Our citizenry has a legitimate and substantial interest in the conduct of such persons, and freedom of the press to engage in uninhibited debate about their involvement in public issues and events is as crucial as it is in the case of "public officials." . . .

I therefore adhere to the *New York Times* standard in the case of "public figures" as well as "public officials." It is a manageable standard, readily stated and understood, which also balances to a proper degree the legitimate interests traditionally protected by the law of defamation. Its definition of "actual malice" is not so restrictive that recovery is limited to situations where there is "knowing falsehood" on the part of the publisher of false and defamatory matter. "Reckless disregard" for the truth or falsity, measured by the conduct of the publisher, will also expose him to liability for publishing false material which is injurious to reputation. More significantly, however, the *New York Times* standard is an important safeguard for the rights of the press and public to inform and be informed on matters of legitimate interest. Evenly applied to cases involving "public men"—whether they be "public officials" or "public figures"—it will afford the necessary insulation for the fundamental interests which the First Amendment was designed to protect. . . .

MR. JUSTICE BLACK, *with whom Mr. Justice Douglas joins, concurring.*

I concur in reversal of the judgment in *The Associated Press v. Walker,* based on the grounds and reasons stated in [p]arts . . . of The

Chief Justice's opinion. I do this, however, as in *Time, Inc. v. Hill* "in order for the Court to be able at this time to agree on an opinion in this important case based on the prevailing constitutional doctrine expressed in *New York Times v. Sullivan.* . . . In agreeing to . . . [that] opinion, I do not recede from any of the views I have previously expressed about the much wider press and speech freedoms I think the First and Fourteenth Amendments were designed to grant to the people of the Nation. . . .

MR. JUSTICE BLACK, *with whom Mr. Justice Douglas concurs, dissenting.*

I would reverse this case [*Curtis*] first for the reasons given in my concurring opinion in *New York Times v. Sullivan* and my concurring and dissenting opinion in *Rosenblatt v. Baer*, but wish to add a few words.

This case illustrates, I think, the accuracy of my prior predictions that the *New York Times* constitutional rule concerning libel is wholly inadequate to save the press from being destroyed by libel judgments. Here the Court reverses the case of *Associated Press v. Walker*, but affirms the judgment of *Curtis Publishing Co. v. Butts.* The main reason for this quite contradictory action, so far as I can determine, is that the Court looks at the facts in both cases as though it were a jury and reaches the conclusion that the *Saturday Evening Post*, in writing about Butts, was so abusive that its article is more of a libel at the constitutional level than is the one by the Associated Press. That seems a strange way to erect a constitutional standard for libel cases. If this precedent is followed, it means that we must in all libel cases hereafter weigh the facts and hold that all papers and magazines guilty of gross writing or reporting are constitutionally liable, while they are not if the quality of the reporting is approved by a majority of us. In the final analysis, what we do in these circumstances is to review the factual questions in cases decided by juries—a review which is a flat violation of the Seventh Amendment.

It strikes me that the Court is getting itself in the same quagmire in the field of libel in which it is now helplessly struggling in the field of obscenity. No one, including this Court, can know what is and what is not constitutionally obscene or libelous under this Court's rulings. . . .

I think it is time for this Court to abandon *New York Times v. Sullivan* and adopt the rule to the effect that the First Amendment was intended to leave the press free from the harassment of libel judgments.

*   *   *

In the last of the Warren Court's series of post-New York Times decisions, handed down in 1968, the Court continued to tighten the conditions under which a public official could collect damages for libel. The Court said if the attacker has good reason to believe the damaging statements to be true, mere failure to thoroughly investigate their veracity does not in itself constitute "reckless disregard" as defined in Times. "Reckless disregard," wrote Justice White for the 8-1 majority, "is not measured by whether a reasonably prudent man would have published, or would have investigated before publishing. There must be sufficient evidence to permit the conclusion that the defendant in fact entertained serious doubts as to the truth of his publication." Justice Fortas, the lone dissenter, decried the interpretation by noting that the First Amendment should not be a "shelter for the character assassinator" nor should it authorize "virtually unlimited open-season" on public servants. The St. Amant decision, however, emphasized the importance the Court places in public discussions of the public's business.

ST. AMANT V. THOMPSON
390 U.S. 727 (1968)

MR. JUSTICE WHITE *delivered the opinion of the Court.*

The question presented by this case is whether the Louisiana Supreme Court, in sustaining a judgment for damages in a public official's defamation action, correctly interpreted and applied the rule of *New York Times Co. v. Sullivan* that the plaintiff in such an action must prove that the defamatory publication "was made with 'actual malice'—that is, with knowledge that it was false or with reckless disregard of whether it was false or not."

On June 27, 1962, petitioner St. Amant, a candidate for public office, made a televised speech in Baton Rouge, Louisiana. In the course of this speech, St. Amant read a series of questions which he had put to J. D. Albin, a member of a Teamsters Union local, and Albin's answers to those questions. The exchange concerned the allegedly nefarious activities of E. G. Partin, the president of the local, and the alleged relationship between Partin and St. Amant's political opponent. One of Albin's answers concerned his efforts to prevent Partin from secreting union records; in this answer Albin referred to Herman A. Thompson, an East Baton Rouge Parish deputy sheriff and respondent here:

> "Now, we knew that this safe was gonna be moved that night, but imagine our predicament, knowing of Ed's connections with the Sheriff's office through Herman Thompson, who made recent visits to the Hall to see Ed. We also knew of money that had passed hands between Ed and Herman Thompson . . . from Ed to Herman. We also knew of his connections with State Trooper Lieutenant Joe Green. We knew we couldn't get any help from there and we didn't know

how far that he was involved in the Sheriff's office or the State Police office through that, and it was out of the jurisdiction of the City Police."

Thompson promptly brought suit for defamation, claiming that the publication had "impute[d] . . . gross misconduct" and "inter[red] conduct of the most nefarious nature." The case was tried prior to the decision in *New York Times Co. v. Sullivan.* The trial judge ruled in Thompson's favor and awarded $5,000 in damages. . . .

For purposes of this case we accept the determinations of the Louisiana courts that the material published by St. Amant charged Thompson with criminal conduct, that the charge was false, and that Thompson was a public official and so had the burden of proving that the false statements about Thompson were made with actual malice as defined in *New York Times v. Sullivan* and later cases. We cannot, however, agree with either the Supreme Court of Louisiana or the trial court that Thompson sustained this burden.

Purporting to apply the *New York Times* malice standard, the Louisiana Supreme Court ruled that St. Amant had broadcast false information about Thompson recklessly, though not knowingly. Several reasons were given for this conclusion. St. Amant had no personal knowledge of Thompson's activities; he relied solely on Albin's affidavit although the record was silent as to Albin's reputation for veracity; he failed to verify the information with those in the union office who might have known the facts; he gave no consideration to whether or not the statements defamed Thompson and went ahead heedless of the consequences; and he mistakenly believed he had no responsibility for the broadcast because he was merely quoting Albin's words.

These considerations fall short of proving St. Amant's reckless disregard for the accuracy of his statements about Thompson. "Reckless disregard," it is true, cannot be fully encompassed in one infallible definition. Inevitably its outer limits will be marked out by case-to-case adjudication, as is true with so many legal standards for judging concrete cases, whether the standard is provided by the Constitution, statutes, or case law. Our cases, however, have furnished meaningful guidance for the further definition of a reckless publication. In *New York Times* the plaintiff did not satisfy his burden because the record failed to show that the publisher was aware of the likelihood that he was circulating false information. In *Garrison v. Louisiana,* also decided before the decision of the Louisiana Supreme Court in this case, the opinion emphasized the necessity for a showing that a false publication was made with a "high degree of awareness of . . . probable falsity." Mr. Justice Harlan's opinion in *Curtis Publishing Co. v. Butts* stated that evidence of either deliberate falsification or reckless publication "despite the publisher's awareness of probable falsity" was essential to recovery by public officials in defamation actions. These cases are clear that reckless conduct is not measured by whether a reasonably prudent man would have published, or would have investigated before publishing. There must be sufficient evidence to permit the conclusion that the defendant in fact entertained serious doubts as to the truth of his publication. Publishing with such doubts shows reckless disregard for truth or falsity and demonstrates actual malice.

It may be said that such a test puts a premium on ignorance, encourages the irresponsible publisher not to inquire, and permits the issue to be determined by the defendant's testimony that he published the statement in good faith and unaware of its probable falsity. Concededly the reckless disregard standard may permit recovery in fewer situations than would a rule that publishers must satisfy the standard of the reasonable man or the prudent publisher. But *New York Times* and succeeding cases have emphasized that the stake of the people in public business and the conduct of public officials is so great that neither the defense of truth nor the standard of ordinary case would protect against self-censorship and thus adequately implement First Amendment policies. Neither lies nor false communications serve the ends of the First Amendment, and no one suggests their desirability or further proliferation. But to insure the ascertainment and publication of the truth about public affairs, it is essential that the First Amendment protect some erroneous publications as well as true ones. . . .

The defendant in a defamation action brought by a public official cannot, however, automatically insure a favorable verdict by testifying that he published with a belief that the statements were true. The finder of fact must determine whether the publication was indeed made in good faith. Professions of good faith will be unlikely to prove persuasive, for example, where a story is fabricated by the defendant, is the product of his imagination, or is based wholly on an unverified anonymous telephone call. Nor will they be likely to prevail when the publisher's allegations are so inherently improbable that only a reckless man would have put them in circulation. Likewise, recklessness may be found where there are obvious reasons to doubt the veracity of the informant or the accuracy of his reports.

By no proper test of reckless disregard was St. Amant's broadcast a reckless publication about a public officer. Nothing referred to by the Louisiana courts indicates an awareness by St. Amant of the probable falsity of Albin's statement about Thompson. Failure to investigate does not in itself establish bad faith. . . .

MR. JUSTICE FORTAS, *dissenting.*

I do not believe that petitioner satisfied the minimal standards of care specified by *New York Times v. Sullivan*. The affidavit that petitioner broadcast contained a seriously libelous statement directed against respondent. Respondent was a public official. He was not petitioner's adversary in the political contest. His casual, careless, callous use of the libel cannot be rationalized as resulting from the heat of a campaign. . . .

The First Amendment is not so fragile that it requires us to immunize this kind of reckless, destructive invasion of the life, even of public officials, heedless of their interests and sensitivities. The First Amendment is not a shelter for the character assassinator, whether his action is heedless and reckless or deliberate. The First Amendment does not require that we license shotgun attacks on public officials in virtually unlimited open-season. The occupation of public officeholder does not forfeit one's membership in the human race. The public official should be subject to severe scrutiny and to free and open criticism. But if he is needlessly, heedlessly, falsely accused of crime, he should have a remedy in law. *New York Times* does not preclude this minimal standard of civilized living. . . .

*　　*　　*

The Supreme Court continued its commitment to "uninhibited, robust, and wide-open" debate on public issues following the retirement of Chief Justice Warren. In May of 1970 the Court unanimously reversed a $17,500 libel judgment won by Charles S. Bresler against the Greenbelt (Md.) News Review. Greenbelt Publishing Assn. v. Bresler, 398 U.S. 6. The controversy centered around the use of the word "blackmail" in the news columns of the weekly newspaper. The term had been used in heated public debates before the city council. These debates had been covered by the News Review. Justice Stewart, writing the opinion of the Court, noted that the news stories were accurate accounts of the public debates and referred to New York Times and Curtis as precedents. He noted, however, that if the stories had been "truncated" or "distorted," different results might have been forthcoming.

GREENBELT PUBLISHING ASS'N V. BRESLER
398 U.S. 6 (1970)

MR. JUSTICE STEWART *delivered the opinion of the Court.*

The petitioners are the publishers of a small weekly newspaper, the *Greenbelt News Review*, in the City of Greenbelt, Maryland. The respondent Bresler is a prominent local real estate developer and builder in Greenbelt, and was, during the period in question, a member of the Maryland House of Delegates from a neighboring district. In the autumn of

1965 Bresler was engaged in negotiations with the Greenbelt City Council to obtain certain zoning variances that would allow the construction of high density housing on land owned by him. At the same time the city was attempting to acquire another tract of land owned by Bresler for the construction of a new high school. Extensive litigation concerning compensation for the school site seemed imminent, unless there should be an agreement on its price between Bresler and the city authorities, and the concurrent negotiations obviously provided both parties considerable bargaining leverage.

These joint negotiations evoked substantial local controversy, and several tumultuous city council meetings were held at which many members of the community freely expressed their views. The meetings were reported at length in the news columns of the *Greenbelt News Review*. Two news articles in consecutive weekly editions of the paper stated that at the public meetings some people had characterized Bresler's negotiating position as "blackmail." The word appeared several times, both with and without quotation marks, and was used once as a subheading within a news story.

Bresler reacted to these news articles by filing the present lawsuit for libel, seeking both compensatory and punitive damages. The primary thrust of his complaint was that the articles, individually and along with other items published in the petitioners' newspaper, imputed to him the crime of blackmail. The case went to trial, and the jury awarded Bresler $5,000 in compensatory damages and $12,500 in punitive damages. The Maryland Court of Appeals affirmed the judgment. We granted certiorari to consider the constitutional issues presented.

In *New York Times Co. v. Sullivan*, 376 U.S. 254, we held that the Constitution permits a "public official" to recover money damages for libel only if he can show that the defamatory publication was not only false but was uttered with " 'actual malice'—that is, with knowledge that it was false or with reckless disregard of whether it was false or not." In *Curtis Publishing Co. v. Butts*, 388 U.S. 130, we dealt with the constitutional restrictions upon a libel suit brought by a "public figure."

In the present case Bresler's counsel conceded in his opening statement to the jury that Bresler was a public figure in the community. This concession was clearly correct. Bresler was deeply involved in the future development of the City of Greenbelt. He had entered agreements with the city for zoning variances in the past, and was again seeking such favors to permit the construction of housing units of a type not contemplated in the original city plan. At the same time the city was trying to obtain a tract of land owned by Bresler for the purpose of building a school. Negotiations of significant public concern were in progress, both with school officials and the city council. Bresler's status thus clearly fell within even the most restrictive definition of a "public figure." . . .

It is not disputed that the articles published in the petitioners' newspaper were accurate and truthful reports of what had been said at the public hearings before the city council. In this sense, therefore, it cannot even be claimed that the petitioners were guilty of any "departure from the standards of investigation and reporting ordinarily adhered to by responsible publishers," *Curtis Publishing Co. v. Butts,* much less the knowing use of falsehood or a reckless disregard of whether the statements made were true or false. *New York Times Co. v. Sullivan.*

The contention is, rather, that the speakers at the meeting, in using the word "blackmail," and the petitioners in reporting the use of that word in the newspaper articles, were charging Bresler with the crime of blackmail, and that since the petitioners knew that Bresler had committed no such crime, they could be held liable for the "knowing use of falsehood." It was upon this theory that the case was submitted to the jury, and upon this theory that the judgment was affirmed by the Maryland Court of Appeals. For the reasons that follow, we hold that the imposition of liability on such a basis was constitutionally impermissible—that as a matter of constitutional law, the word "blackmail" in these circumstances was not slander when spoken, and not libel when reported in the *Greenbelt News Review.*

There can be no question that the public debates at the sessions of the city council regarding Bresler's negotiations with the city were a subject of substantial concern to all who lived in the community. The debates themselves were heated, as debates about controversial issues usually are. During the course of the arguments Bresler's opponents characterized the position he had taken in his negotiations with the city officials as "blackmail." The *Greenbelt News Review* was performing its wholly legitimate function as a community newspaper when it published full reports of these public debates in its news columns. If the reports had been truncated or distorted in such a way as to extract the word "blackmail" from the context in which it was used at the public meetings, this would be a different case. But the reports were accurate and full. Their headlines, "School Site Stirs Up Council—Rezoning Deal Offer Debated" and "Council Rejects By 4-1 High School Site Deal," made it clear to all readers that the paper was reporting the public debates on the pending land negotiations. Bresler's proposal was accurately and fully described in each article, along with the accurate statement that some people at the meetings had referred to the proposal as blackmail, and others had indicated they thought Bresler's position not unreasonable.

It is simply impossible to believe that a reader who reached the word "blackmail" in either article would not have understood exactly what was meant: it was Bresler's public and wholly legal negotiating proposals that were being criticized. No reader could have thought that either the speakers at the meetings or the newspaper articles reporting their words were charging Bresler with the commission of a criminal offense. On the contrary, even the most careless reader must have perceived that the word was no more than rhetorical hyperbole, a vigorous epithet used by those who considered Bresler's negotiating position extremely unreasonable. Indeed, the record is completely devoid of evidence that anyone in the city of Greenbelt or anywhere else thought Bresler had been charged with a crime.

To permit the infliction of financial liability upon the petitioners for publishing these two news articles would subvert the most fundamental meaning of a free press, protected by the First and Fourteenth Amendments. Accordingly, we reverse the judgment and remand the case to the Court of Appeals of Maryland for further proceedings not inconsistent with this opinion.

*   *   *

The Court in 1971 continued to restrict libel judgments involving public persons. In three decisions handed down February 24, 1971, the Court emphasized that libel actions dealing with public figures must be accompanied by evidence of actual malice, i.e. knowingly printing a falsehood or exhibiting reckless disregard for truth or falsity.

In the first of the three cases, Monitor Patriot Co. v. Roy, a jury had awarded libel judgments of $10,000 against the Concord (N.H.) Monitor and the North American Newspaper Alliance syndicate because of a Drew Pearson column published in 1960. The column described Alphonse Roy, a former New Hampshire congressman who was running for the United States Senate, as a "former small-time bootlegger." Roy lost in the Democratic primary. It was argued that since the alleged criminal conduct had occurred in the 1920s and had involved the candidate's private life rather than his performance as a public servant, the newspaper and the syndicate were vulnerable to a possible libel judgment. The Supreme Court in a unanimous decision disagreed. Justices Black and Douglas concurred in the judgment, but dissented in part, arguing against sending the case back for possible retrial.

MONITOR PATRIOT CO. V. ROY
401 U.S. 265 (1971)

MR. JUSTICE STEWART delivered the opinion of the Court.

. . . The principal activity of a candidate in our political system, his "office," so to speak, consists in putting before the voters every conceivable aspect of his public and private life which he thinks may lead the electorate to gain a good impression of him. A candidate who, for example, seeks to further his cause through the prominent display of his wife and children can hardly argue that his qualities as a husband or father remain of "purely private" concern. And the candidate who vaunts his spotless record and sterling integrity cannot convincingly cry "Foul!" when an opponent or an industrious reporter attempts to demonstrate the contrary. Any test adequate to safeguard First Amendment guarantees in this area must go far beyond the customary meaning of the phrase "official conduct." . . .

We therefore hold as a matter of constitutional law that a charge of criminal conduct, no matter how remote in time or place, can never be irrelevant to an official's or a candidate's fitness for office for purposes of application of the "knowing falsehood or reckless disregard" rule of *New York Times v. Sullivan*. Since the jury in this case was permitted to make its own unguided determination that the charge of prior criminal activity was not "relevant," and that the *New York Times* standard was thus inapplicable, the judgment must be reversed. . . .

*   *   *

Justice Stewart also wrote the second libel opinion in Ocala Star-Banner Co. v. Damron. The newspaper in 1966 had charged that the mayor of Ocala, Florida, Leonard Damron, who was a candidate for county tax assessor, had been charged in Federal Court with perjury in a civil rights case. It was, in fact, Damron's brother who had been accused of perjury. An editor who was unfamiliar with the background of the story had changed the first name in the story to that of the mayor. Damron lost the election, which was held two weeks after the story appeared.

The trial judge had instructed the jury that the New York Times rule did not apply since the error did not involve Damron's official conduct, that the story constituted libel per se and that the mayor could be awarded damages. The jury awarded Damron $22,000 in compensatory damages. The Supreme Court, as in Monitor Patriot Co., reached a unanimous decision supporting the newspaper, but with Justices Black and Douglas again dissenting in part. In his brief opinion, Justice Stewart noted the wide latitude of the New York Times rule and referred to the Monitor Patriot decision handed down earlier in the day.

In the third libel decision that day, Time, Inc. v. Pape, the question was whether the failure of Time magazine to use the word "alleged" constituted actual malice. The magazine in 1961 carried a report of the findings of the U.S. Commission on Civil Rights in which charges of brutality were made against Chicago police. Detective Frank Pape was one of those involved. The allegations in the Commission's report were not proven and Time failed to make clear it was reporting mere allegations.

The opinion, reflecting the 8-1 decision, was again written by Justice

Stewart. Much of the opinion reflected dissatisfaction with the Commission's report, but it did warn the media that the judgment in this case was not to be taken as authorizing careless reporting. Time's writer and researcher admitted at the trial that the wording of the report had been changed significantly, but that the changes did not alter the true meaning of the report. Justice Stewart noted that the Time article reflected, at worst, an error in judgment, but went on to say that media which maintain professional standards should not be subject to financial liability for non-malicious errors in judgment.

TIME, INC. V. PAPE
401 U.S. 279 (1971)

MR. JUSTICE STEWART *delivered the opinion of the Court.*

. . . [A] vast amount of what is published in the daily and periodical press purports to be descriptive of what somebody *said* rather than of what anybody *did*. Indeed, perhaps the largest share of news concerning the doings of government appears in the form of accounts of reports, speeches, press conferences, and the like. The question of the "truth" of such an indirect newspaper report presents rather complicated problems.

A press report of what someone has said about an underlying event of news value can contain an almost infinite variety of shadings. Where the source of the news makes bald assertions of fact—such as that a policeman has arrested a certain man on a criminal charge—there may be no difficulty. But where the source itself has engaged in qualifying the information released, complexities ramify. Any departure from full direct quotation of the words of the source, with all its qualifying language, inevitably confronts the publisher with a set of choices.

The Civil Rights Commission's *Justice* report is a typical example of these problems. The underlying story which gave the report newsworthiness was the picture of police violence against citizens. Many of the incidents were quite clearly designed to shock, anger, and alarm the reader, indeed to move him into a position of support for specific legislative recommendations of the Commission. Yet the attitude of the Commission toward the factual verity of the episodes recounted was anything but straightforward. . . .

Time's omission of the word "alleged" amounted to the adoption of one of a number of possible rational interpretations of a document that bristled with ambiguities. The deliberate choice of such interpretation, though arguably reflecting a misconception, was not enough to create a jury issue of "malice" under *New York Times*. To permit the malice issue to go to the jury because of the omission of a word like "alleged," despite the context of that word in the Commission Report and the external evidence of the Report's overall meaning, would be to impose a much stricter standard of liability on errors of interpretation or judgment than on errors of historic fact. . . .

These considerations apply with even greater force to the situation where the alleged libel consists in the claimed misinterpretation of the gist of a lengthy government document. Where the document reported on is so ambiguous as this one was, it is hard to imagine a test of "truth" that would not put the publisher virtually at the mercy of the unguided discretion of a jury.

In certain areas of the law of defamation, *New York Times* added to the tort law of the individual States a constitutional zone of protection for errors of fact caused by negligence. The publisher who maintains a standard of care such as to avoid knowing falsehood or reckless disregard of the truth is thereby given assurance that those errors that nonetheless occur will not lay him open to an indeterminable financial liability. . . .

. . . Given the ambiguities of the Commission Report as a whole, and the testimony of the *Time* author and researcher, *Time's* conduct reflected at most an error of judgment. We have held that if "freedoms of expression are to have the breathing space that they need to survive" misstatements of this kind must have the protection of the First and Fourteenth Amendments.

We would add, however, a final cautionary note. Nothing in this opinion is to be understood as making the word "alleged" a superfluity in published reports of information damaging to reputation. Our decision today is based on the specific facts of this case, involving as they do a news report of a particular government publication that purported to describe the specific grounds for perceiving in 1961 "a serious problem in the United States." "Neither lies nor false communications serve the ends of the First Amendment, and no one suggests their desirability or further proliferation. But to insure the ascertainment and publication of the truth about public affairs, it is essential that the First Amendment protect some erroneous publications as well as true ones." *St. Amant v. Thompson.* . . .

*   *   *

In the most significant libel decision since the landmark 1964 New York Times ruling, the Supreme Court in June of 1971 handed down a 5-3 judgment which held that no person—public or private—involved in an event of public interest could collect libel damages unless he could prove actual malice on the part of the publisher or broadcaster. This decision, if it withstands future challenges, appears to make it almost impossible for any person to successfully sue a newspaper or news broadcaster for libel. Malice, extremely difficult to prove, was defined in New York Times as publishing a defamatory falsehood with knowledge of its falsity or with reckless disregard as to its truth or falsity. This broad media protection previously had applied only to "public officials" or "public figures." The Rosenbloom decision, in addition to extending media immunity from libel suit to private citizens who are involved in an event of "general concern," also firmly establishes news broadcasters as falling under First Amendment protection. George A. Rosenbloom, a Philadelphia magazine distributor, had filed libel action against radio station WIP, which in its accounts of the arrest of Rosenbloom on obscenity charges used the terms "smut distributor" and "girlie-book peddler." Rosenbloom was aquitted of the obscenity charges. In his suit against WIP he claimed he was neither a public official (under New York Times) nor a public figure (under Curtis Publishing Co.), but a private person conducting a private business when he was falsely defamed. The trial court agreed, awarding him $275,000 in damages. The Court of Appeals reversed the decision, and the Supreme Court upheld that reversal. Justice Brennan, in announcing the judgment of the Court, emphasized the hazy distinction today between public and private persons. "We honor," he wrote, "the commitment to robust debate on public issues, which is embodied in the First Amendment, by extending constitutional protection to all discussion and communication involving matters of public or general concern, without regard to whether the persons involved are famous or anonymous." He was joined by Chief Justice Burger and Justice Blackmun. Justices Black and White concurred in the judgment, but not in Justice Brennan's written opinion. Dissenting were Justices Harlan, Marshall and Stewart. Justice Douglas did not participate.

ROSENBLOOM V. METROMEDIA, INC.
(Announced June 7, 1971)

MR. JUSTICE BRENNAN announced the judgment of the Court and an opinion in which The Chief Justice and Mr. Justice Blackmun join.

. . . Self-governance in the United States presupposes far more than knowledge and debate about the strictly official activities of various levels of government. The commitment of the country to the institution of private property, protected by the Due Process and Just Compensation Clauses in the Constitution, places in private hands vast areas of economic and social power that vitally affect the nature and quality of life in the nation. Our efforts to live and work together in a free society not completely dominated by governmental regulation necessarily encompass far more than politics in a narrow sense. . . . .

If a matter is a subject of public or general interest, it cannot suddenly become less so merely because a private individual is involved, or because in some sense the individual did not "voluntarily" choose to become involved. The public's primary interest is in the event; the public focus is on the conduct of the participant and the content, effect, and significance of the conduct, not the participant's prior anonymity or notoriety. The present case illustrates the point. The community has a vital interest in the proper enforcement of its criminal laws, particularly in an area such as obscenity where a number of highly important values are potentially in conflict: the public has an interest both in seeing that the criminal law is adequately enforced and in assuring that the law is not used unconstitutionally to suppress free expression. Whether the person involved is a famous large scale magazine distributor or a "private" businessman running a corner newsstand has no relevance in ascertaining whether the public has an interest in the issue. We honor the commitment to robust debate on public issues, which is embodied in the First Amendment, by extending constitutional protection to all discussion and communication involving matters of public or general concern, without regard to whether the persons involved are famous or anonymous. . . .

. . . Drawing a distinction between "public" and "private" figures makes no sense in terms of the First Amendment guarantees. The *New York Times* standard was applied to libel of a public official or public figure to give effect to the Amendment's function to encourage ventilation of public issues, not because the public official has any less interest in protecting his reputation than an individual in private life. While the argument that public figures need less protection because they can command media attention to counter criticism may be true for some very prominent people, even then it is the rare case where the denial overtakes the original charge. Denials, retractions, and corrections are not "hot" news, and rarely receive the prominence of the original story. When the public official or public figure is a minor functionary, or has left the position which put him in the public eye, see *Rosenblatt v. Baer*, the argument loses all of its force. In the vast majority of libels involving public officials or public figures, the ability to respond through the media will depend on the same complex factor on which the ability of a private individual depends: the unpredictable event of the media's continuing interest in the story. Thus the unproven, and highly improbable, generalization that an as yet undefined class of "public figures" involved in matters of public concern will be better able to respond through the media than private individuals also involved in such matters seems too insubstantial a reed on which to rest a constitutional distinction. Furthermore, in First Amendment terms, the cure seems far worse than the disease. If the states fear that private citizens will not be able to respond adequately to publicity involving them, the solution lies in the direction of ensuring their ability to respond, rather than in stifling public discussion of matters of public concern.

Further reflection over the years since *New York Times* was decided persuades us that the view of the "public official" or "public figure" as assuming the risk of defamation by voluntarily thrusting himself into the public eye bears little relationship either to the values protected by the First Amendment or to the nature of our society. We have recognized that "[e]xposure of the self to others in varying degrees is a concomitant of life in a civilized community." *Time, Inc. v. Hill*, 385 U.S. 374, 388 (1967). Voluntarily or not, we are all "public" men to some degree. Conversely, some aspects of the lives of even the most public men fall outside the area of matters of public or general concern. Thus, the idea that certain "public" figures have voluntarily exposed their entire lives to public inspection, while private individuals have kept theirs carefully shrouded from public view is, at best, a legal fiction. In any event, such a distinction could easily produce the paradoxical result of dampening discussion of issues of public or general concern because they happen to involve private citizens while extending constitutional encouragement to discussion of aspects of the lives of "public figures" which are not in the area of public or general concern.

General references to the values protected by the law of libel conceal important distinctions. Traditional arguments suggest that libel law protects two separate interests of the individual: first, his desire to preserve a certain privacy around his personality from unwarranted intrusion, and, second a desire to preserve his public good name and reputation. The individual's interest in privacy—in preventing unwarranted intrusion upon the private aspects of his life—is not involved in this case, or even in the class of cases under consideration, since, by hypothesis, the individual is involved in matters of public or general concern. In the present case, however, petitioner's business reputation is involved, and thus the relevant interests protected by state libel law are petitioner's public reputation and good name.

These are important interests. Consonant with the libel laws of most of the states, however, Pennsylvania's libel law subordinates these interests of the individual in a number of circumstances. Thus, high government officials are immune from liability—absolutely privileged—even if they publish defamatory material from an improper motive, with actual malice, and with knowledge of its falsity. This absolute privilege attaches to judges, attorneys at law in connection with a judicial proceeding, parties and witnesses to judicial proceedings, Congressmen and state legislators, and high national and state executive officials. Moreover, a conditional privilege allows newspapers to report the false defamatory material originally published under the absolute privileges listed above, if done accurately.

Even without the presence of a specific constitutional command, therefore, Pennsylvania libel law recognizes that society's interest in protecting individual reputation often yields to other important social goals. In this case, the vital needs of freedom of the press and freedom of speech persuade us that allowing private citizens to obtain damage judgments on the basis of a jury determination that a publisher probably failed to use reasonable care would not provide adequate "breathing space" for these great freedoms. Reasonable care is an "elusive standard" which "would place on the press the intolerable burden of guessing how a jury might assess the reasonableness of steps taken by it to verify the accuracy of every reference to a name, picture or portrait." *Time, Inc. v. Hill,* 385 U.S. at 389. Fear of guessing wrong must inevitably cause self-censorship and thus create the danger that the legitimate utterance will be deterred.

Moreover, we ordinarily decide civil litigation by the preponderance of the evidence. Indeed, the judge instructed the jury to decide the present case on that standard. . . . In libel cases, however, we view an erroneous verdict for the plaintiff as most serious. Not only does it mulct the defendant for an innocent misstatement—the three-quarter-million-dollar jury verdict in this case could rest on such an error—but the possibility of such error, even beyond the vagueness of the negligence standard itself, would create a strong impetus toward self-censorship, which the First Amendment cannot tolerate. These dangers for freedom of speech and press led us to reject the reasonable-man standard of liability as "simply inconsistent" with our national commitment under the First Amendment when sought to be applied to the conduct of a political campaign. *Monitor Patriot Co. v. Roy.* The same considerations lead us to reject that standard here.

We are aware that the press has, on occasion, grossly abused the freedom it is given by the Constitution. All must deplore such excesses. In an ideal world, the responsibility of the press would match the freedom and public trust given it. But from the earliest days of our history, this free society, dependent as it is for its survival upon a vigorous free press, has tolerated some abuse. . . .

LIBEL AND THE SUPREME COURT

By Jerome Lawrence Merin [*]

. . . The proposition that "[w]hatever is added to the field of libel is taken from the field of free debate" is not necessarily true. Free debate is not a simple phenomenon but is the result of many interrelated factors; it should not be an absolute end; it should be a means toward the end of a free and democratic society. Free debate may aid in achieving and maintaining a democratic society; but freedom cannot be equated with anarchy, since anarchy results in freedom only for the strongest, the richest, the loudest, or the most numerous. Freedom flourishes when it is limited by the boundaries of self-restraint and the rights of others. Free debate cannot be achieved merely by removing all barriers to public speech and writings because true debate also depends on the willingness of men to enter the public arena, on the presence of, and belief in, the presence of credible statements, and on a responsive, educated, and unintimidated populace.

Zechariah Chafee, Jr. wrote that

> [o]ne of the most important purposes of society and government is the discovery and spread of truth on subjects of general concern. This is possible only through absolutely unlimited discussion, for, as Bagehot points out, once force is thrown into the argument, it becomes a matter of chance whether it is thrown on the false side or the true, and truth loses all its natural advantage in the contest.

This is the Holmensian "marketplace of ideas" view derived, in large measure, from the philosophy of John Stuart Mill. The concept of a clash of conflicting ideas resulting in the truth, however, depends upon a prior assumption that all ideas will be presented in good faith and in a straightforward manner without the use of force or guile. If truth is to emerge from a free clash of ideas, all ideas must reach all citizens, and each citizen must be both interested in weighing the ideas presented and educated enough to evaluate them. The "marketplace of ideas" theory is a philosophic equivalent of the economic theory of laissez-faire which also developed in the nineteenth century. Like a laissez-faire economic marketplace, the "marketplace of ideas" theory is postulated upon an ideological abstrac-

* From Jerome Lawrence Merin. "Libel and the Supreme Court," *William and Mary Law Review*, Vol. 11 (1969), p. 371, at p. 415. Used with permission of the *William and Mary Law Review*. The author received his J. D. from Harvard Law School in 1969.

tion—a perfect, frictionless society where all entrants in the market are equally powerful and honest and are dealing with a citizenry that will behave in an intelligent, rational manner. It is ironic that the very people who have rejected the theory of laissez-faire economics have feverishly embraced the theory of laissez-faire civil liberties.

Chafee did not, however, view a free press and free speech as unlimited; he believed that though the spread of truth was important,

> there are other purposes of government, such as order, the training of the young, protection against external aggression. Unlimited discussion sometimes interferes with these purposes, which must then be balanced against freedom of speech, but freedom of speech ought to weigh heavily in the scales.

Balancing values and rights requires a prior determination of what the conflicting interests are and the importance of those interests. Fixed abstract doctrines and popular clichés are injurious to consideration of even everyday problems; but they are disastrous when used to deal with problems of civil rights. Doctrinaire formulas lead to a substitution of words for thought and of easy platitudes for the difficult solutions and unsatisfying compromises that allow democracies to function.

The value of free expression, according to one authority, is that it assures individual self-fulfillment, provides a means of attaining the truth, creates a method of securing the participation of the members of a society in political and social decision-making, and serves as a means of maintaining the balance between stability and change in a society. Limiting ourselves to the area of libel and freedom of the press, let us weigh these functions against the interest of the individual in his good name and sound reputation. Granting that man's ability to reason, to feel, and to think in abstract terms distinguishes him from other animals, it does not follow that *any* limitation on the public expression of a man's opinions and beliefs is a denial of his humanity. A statement which jeopardizes others' lives or property or quality of living carries the ideal of individual self-fulfillment beyond the individual by affecting other individuals. In doing so, it also limits other individuals' right to self-fulfillment. A verbal trespass, to use a term from torts, can be just as injurious as a physical trespass. Indeed, it injures one more if he loses his job because someone falsely accused him of theft than if that person physically injures him and thus keeps him away from work for a week. Limitation of free speech becomes harmful only when it is broadly and thoughtlessly applied.

Having considered the ideal of free expression as a means to arrive at truth in the discussion of Holmes' marketplace theory, let us consider the role free expression plays in bringing people into the decision-making process. A lack of free expression will either turn people against a government or, as is more often the case, make citizens apathetic and docile in their dealings with the government. In a system where free expression is not allowed, decisions are made by the few and obeyed by the masses. Unlimited freedom of expression, however, may well result in the same situation if it allows the powerful, the unscrupulous, or the careless to defame those they oppose, shout into silence those who disagree, distort the truth to a guileless population, and make an interested citizenry cynical and jaded. Under such circumstances, unlimited debate may become the province of the few and potential debaters representing different points of view can be discouraged or intimidated from entering the decision-making process. One of the functions of the first amendment is to protect the press, but the first amendment must also protect the weak, the unpopular, and the isolated. The society's needs in the abstract ought not to preempt the individual's actual needs.

Freedom of expression is an agent of peaceful change. Expression is also an agent of violence. Both of these statements have a bearing on the establishment of certain limits of expression, but the allowance of libel suits is not tantamount to foreclosure of freedom of expression. The same reasons advanced to justify safeguarding individual reputations and preventing verbal mudslinging and journalistic carelessness also apply here. A person who is afraid to express himself publicly because he may be defamed or ridiculed is as much the victim of suppression as the person who avoids proposing a reform because he fears the secret police.

Unfortunately, the Supreme Court's decisions, beginning with *New York Times v. Sullivan,* have steadily moved away from a flexible balancing test. The Court has not adopted the Black-Douglas test, but it has come to view the first amendment in a doctrinaire fashion that fails to take accurately into account either the intentions of the framers or the needs of individuals in a modern society. The Supreme Court has overemphasized society's commitment to free speech and has underemphasized the commitment of our scheme of government to the protection of the individual. The Court's opinions since *New York Times* have barred public officials, and quite possibly all public figures, from suing for libel unless the defendant used the libel knowing that it was false. At least five members of the Warren Court considered the *New York Times* test (which has been greatly broadened by subsequent decisions) to extend to *any* member of the public who becomes of general interest. The malice test exception in the original *New York Times* rule has been truncated so that malice is now limited to cases where a defendant knows that a statement is false and prints it anyway. Such personal knowledge is almost impossible to prove. A minority of Justices on the Warren Court would distinguish between public figures and public officials and would hold publishers to a higher standard of responsibility when dealing with the former.

The decisions of the Supreme Court since *New York Times v. Sullivan* have radically modified the traditional law of libel. The Supreme Court has not made the crooked way straight, but has taken a tangled area of the law and rendered it almost impenetrable. The *New York Times* rule, when first announced, was merely the elevation of a minority view of the fair comment rule to constitutional status. The fair comment rule itself allowed a newspaper to comment on a public figure or event or work of public interest if the statement of fact, and if the facts of the opinion, were truly stated. The opinion, furthermore, had to be fair and could not have been made with ill will or malice. The minority view extended the fair comment protection beyond opinions to statements of fact but restricted such comment to matters within the realm of government (although *Coleman v. McLennan* would have extended the fair comment privilege to statements about the managers of all public institutions and corporations dealing with the public). The Supreme Court has gone well beyond either version of the fair comment rule and has cast aside the general requirement of reasonableness of behavior which marked the outer limits of all qualified privileges in the law of libel. The Court has eliminated the fair comment requirement that the statements deal with persons who in some way have political or economic control over the public.

Having raised the fair comment rule to the level of a constitutional right, and having broadened it to protect not only opinions but also facts, the Court has cut loose the fair comment privilege from libel law and allowed it to float into the rarified heights of "free communication." Disregarding the conflicts which created the need for protection against defamation, Justices Brennan, White, Black, and Douglas, and Chief Justice Warren have viewed libelous comments in the light of principles that were formulated by Justices Holmes and Brandeis to deal with prosecutions for seditious speech or writings. Perhaps the Court has equated seditious libel with civil libel?

Justice Brennan, who has written the most important decisions in this area, has further complicated matters by apparently importing the concept of redeeming social value from the Court's decisions in the area of obscenity and introducing them into libel law. Such a test is as meaningless when applied to libels as it is when applied to obscenities, since it bars almost nothing and never fully considers the problem of conflicting interests. The test has been tacitly incorporated into the decisions following *Garrison* and has moved the Court farther and farther along the road to barring libel suits in the name of a societal commitment to free debate. By invoking this commitment to free debate and protecting all statements that have some value, the Court has failed to balance clashing values or even to ascertain what those values are. A commitment to free debate is meaningless in itself and a statement's social value is a function of the time, the circumstances, and the countervailing interests existing at the time the statement is made. Socially redeeming value, like clear and present danger, is a meaningless test in the context of defamation. Society's valuation of free speech cannot utterly disregard the needs of the sum of the individuals who make up that society. An individual's good name and reputation determine, in large part, where that individual will live, where he will work, and whether or not he will be accepted as a member in good standing in the community. These are real needs; they are necessary to both the individual and the society.

The Supreme Court would not deny redress to a man against whom a newspaper arranged a boycott, nor would it consider it legal for a mob to drive a man from his home or from his town. Yet, if the same results are accomplished by the use of speech or newspapers or radio and television, they are considered privileged. This result is both unjust and unsound. There is undoubtedly a great interest and necessity for public comment about and public scrutiny of government officials and the heads of public institutions, as well as of the institutions themselves since they greatly affect the public. Likewise, certain private corporations and institutions deserve public scrutiny because they too play a great role in shaping public life. Being a public servant, however, should not mean that a man's private and public life is fair game for the vicious, the ignorant, and the self-interested. The malice test in the original *New York Times* rule recognized this and provided some limitation on the press, but this check has been all but removed. Whatever the reasons for subjecting public officials to uncontrolled abuse, there is no reason not to provide some remedy to a "public figure" since his prominence generally does not affect the public, even though he may be of public interest.

The Court speaks of the need for "breathing space" for First Amendment rights, but "breathing space," like "Lebensraum," is a limitless concept. The term "breathing space" is meaningless. If the Court fears that a deterrent effect on expression might result from either vague or Draconian laws, it is difficult to see how a clearly defined and liberally interpreted fair comment rule would have that effect on newspapers today. A much harsher rule failed to stifle comment prior to 1964.

The *New York Times* rule, it seems, is unwieldy and unsound because it results in legal overkill. The rule fails even to ask the questions: why is debate necessary, and, what kind of debate is useful? The Court confuses debate with cacophony. We live in a democracy, yet the Court has failed to ask what the needs of democratic government are and now free expression meets these needs. Is completely free expression necessary or even desirable? Does free expression conflict with and jeopardize other values? If so, what are the other values and how important are they in furthering the ideal of a democracy of individuals, for individuals, and by individuals? What harms can result from free expression? What harms can result from the allowance of civil libel suits? The Court has not answered these questions; it has apparently not even considered them. Granting that the public must be able to criticize and scrutinize those persons controlling public or quasi-public institutions which affect the public's life, who are these persons and how far ought the public scrutiny go? Is there a strong social benefit in dissecting a public official's past, his private life, or the past of his associates and family? How vital is such exposure if it is accurate, and how damaging will it be if it is reckless? The Supreme Court seems to adopt the position that exposures of public officials are positive blessings no matter how recklessly inaccurate, and stops there. What about public figures and persons who have not chosen to enter the public arena? How relevant to the public welfare is the private life of an artist? Is there a public interest in allowing critics to make broad charges about an author's life if such charges are inaccurate? How vital are such exposures to the workings of a democracy? How harmful is such publicity to the individual? These questions have been ignored. The Court has likewise failed to ask whether its goals can be accomplished within the law of libel.

Professor Paul Freund has suggested that the fair comment rule provides an adequate safeguard if it is liberally interpreted. He would differentiate between private citizens and the heads of public institutions such as government officials, heads of universities, and presidents of banks, but he states that

> even public officers who find themselves defamed and who, under the *New York Times* decision must show malice, ought to be able to have the judge instruct that what is malice, what is recklessness, may depend on the gravity of the libelous charge. . . . [W]hat would be required to avoid a charge of recklessness in asserting that a member of Congress or an executive official is a chronic party-goer, which might be libelous, is different from what would be required to avoid the charge of recklessness if the allegation was that so-and-so was a communist party member; that one ought not make that charge as glibly as one might make a charge of a less grave offense.

Professor Freund would also allow plaintiffs to request a special verdict by which the jury could find that the utterances were untrue but not actionable because spoken without malice under the fair comment rule. The Supreme Court, were it to adopt Professor Freund's suggestion, would once again leave the courts and legislatures free to balance conflicting social interests. There may be abuses, but abuses can be corrected on appeal.

Alternatively, the distinctions made by Justice Harlan in *Curtis Publishing Co.*, if combined with the original *New York Times* rule, would mitigate the rigors of the *New York Times* rule as it stands today. The Harlan rule applies the broader test of *New York Times* to public officials and returns to the libel test of reasonable behavior in the case of public figures.

The law of libel is an imperfect tool designed to protect individuals. Practically, libel law offers less protection to the average person than he needs. A libel suit is a long and difficult process which revitalizes old lies and reopens old wounds and often ends with only minimal damage awards. It does, however, allow men to redress their injuries in the courts and not in the alleys or the dueling fields. The press may be restrained by the threat of a libel suit, but this restraint will only prompt more thorough investigation. Society has no interest in protecting lies or sheltering the character assassin or the printer who is grossly negligent. The question of whether or not libel law has a valid function cannot turn on the prejudices and ideals of one era but must be adapted to allow the greatest flexibility in dealing with future threats to the individual and the society. Indeed, a press that is in the vanguard of reform today may be in the last rank of reaction tomorrow.

We are living in an era in which newspapers and communications media are vast corporations which are unlikely to be snuffed out by a libel suit. News media have advanced far beyond the hand-press of Madison's day, and can obliterate a man's reputation within five minutes by telling the story in every state. Unlike the small, rural society of the nineteenth century, more people read or listen to the mass media and fewer people are acquainted with the person who is being discussed. The revolution in communications and the vast day-to-day power of the news media, which, in many cases, have a monopoly on the facts available because of time and space limitations, have created new problems in our mass society. In the decisions expanding the *New York Times* rule the Supreme Court has failed to recognize or to deal with these problems.

CHAPTER 9

RIGHT OF PRIVACY

The second half of the nineteenth century saw the press of America become big business. The mass appeal of Pulitzer and Hearst, the growing importance of advertising, the introduction of photojournalism, and the increasing reliance on sensationalism brought with them a new problem—the invasion of privacy. The "right to be let alone" had not been seriously challenged prior to this time.

Two Boston attorneys, Louis Brandeis (later to be appointed to the Supreme Court) and Samuel Warren, took the first significant step in recognizing this growing "invasion" by publishing in 1890 an article on the right of privacy in the Harvard Law Review. They appealed for legal remedies for what they saw as a deterioration of one of man's basic freedoms. The article received widespread comment, but the prevailing feeling at the turn of the century was that protection from unwanted and unwarranted intrusion should come from the various state legislatures rather than from the courts.

The New York Court of Appeals in 1902 rejected in a 4-3 decision the claim of a woman who sought redress for the use of her picture in the advertising and merchandising of baking flour. But in its rejection, the court suggested that action might be taken by the legislature to solve such invasions of privacy, noting that the right of privacy had "not yet found an abiding place in our jurisprudence." Roberson v. Rochester Folding Box Co. The following year the New York legislature forbade the use of a person's name or likeness for commercial purposes without consent. More than two-thirds of the states by the end of the Warren era had recognized right of privacy either through legislation or common law proceedings, though the scope of such protection varies with each jurisdiction.

Three years after the Roberson decision, a Georgia court did recognize the right of privacy by ruling in favor of a man who sought damages from an insurance company which had used his picture in its advertising. The man, in fact, did not even carry insurance from the firm in question. Pavesich v. New England Life Insurance Co. The California Constitution was used as a basis for a 1931 decision for a plaintiff who sought redress after her maiden name was used in advertising a motion picture, "The Red Kimono." The woman was a former prostitute who later had led a "normal" life. The picture was advertised as a "true story" taken from accounts of the trial. The court ruled that it was the use of the woman's name in the advertising that invaded her privacy, not the facts of the story, which were taken from public court records. Melvin v. Reid.

By the early 1940s the question concerned newsworthy figures. The courts have generally held that when a person thrusts himself—or is thrust—into the public eye he gives up much of his right of privacy. A former child prodigy who was graduated from Harvard at 16 had been featured in a New Yorker article as not fulfilling his earlier promise and living in shabby surroundings. His suit was dismissed as the court ruled that the account was substantially true and that the public had a legitimate interest in the later life of a prodigy. Certiorari was denied by the Supreme Court. Sidis v. F-R Publishing Co. There are, however, limits as to the extent of the public's right to know even when the story might be of great reader interest. A woman who had an insatiable appetite was photographed without her consent in a hospital bed. The picture was used in Time magazine accompanied by a caption entitled "Starving Glutton" and an article on the unusual medical problem. The court held for the woman. Barber v. Time, Inc.

Accidental reference to a private person was judged not to excuse an invasion of privacy in a 1942 decision in California. Hal Roach Studios, in publicizing a coming motion picture, sent through the mails 1,000 copies of a "suggestive" letter handwritten on pink stationery. The "letter" was signed "Marion Kerby." A real Marion Kerby sued for invasion of privacy and won. Innocent mistake, the court ruled, was no excuse. Kerby v. Hal Roach Studios.

The question of a "fictionalized" account of a person's biography was raised by baseball pitcher Warren Spahn in 1966. He sought and won an injunction and damages against an unauthorized publication of his life. The court found in the story a great many "factual errors, distortions and fanciful passages" and that, as such, it was proscribed by New York law dealing with right of privacy. The Court of Appeals drew a line between his actions as a public figure and the alleged "fictionalized" accounts of his private life used in a commercial venture. Spahn v. Julian Messner, Inc.

The California Supreme Court in 1971 ruled unanimously that a rehabilitated felon has the right to sue for invasion of privacy if a publication exposes his criminal record "years after the crime." He has a right to be let alone, the Court said, once he again enters the anonymity of the community and has not acted to reattract public attention. Briscoe v. Reader's Digest.

The Supreme Court actively entered the debate over right of privacy with a decision involving a $30,000 judgment against Time, Inc. In the decision the Court held that the First Amendment shields the press from invasion of privacy suits involving the public lives of newsworthy persons unless there is proof of malice, deliberate falsehood, or "reckless disregard of the truth." This philosophy had been applied earlier to libel actions by the Court in the 1964 New York Times case. In the present suit, James J. Hill had instituted legal action after Life had published a feature article based upon the play "The Desperate Hours," which, in turn, was based upon Hill's experience as a 1952 kidnap victim. He charged serious falsehood and commercial use of his name and story. The Supreme Court decision places the burden of proof upon the citizen if he is a newsworthy figure and sues on the basis of misstatement of fact.

TIME, INC. V. HILL
385 U.S. 374 (1967)

MR. JUSTICE BRENNAN *delivered the opinion of the Court.*

The question in this case is whether appellant, publisher of *Life Magazine*, was denied constitutional protections for speech and press by the application by the New York courts of sec. 50–51 of the New York Civil Rights Law to award appellee damages on allegations that *Life* falsely reported that a new play portrayed an experience suffered by appellee and his family.

The article appeared in *Life* in February 1955. It was entitled "True Crime Inspires Tense Play," with the subtitle, "The ordeal of a family trapped by convicts gives Broadway a new thriller, 'The Desperate Hours.'" The text of the article reads as follows:

> Three years ago Americans all over the country read about the desperate ordeal of the James Hill family, who were held prisoners in their home outside Philadelphia by three escaped convicts. Later they read about it in Joseph Hayes' novel, *The Desperate Hours*, inspired by the family's experience. Now they can see the story re-enacted in Hayes' Broadway play based on the book, and next year will see it in his movie, which has been filmed but is being held up until the play has a chance to pay off.
>
> The play, directed by Robert Montgomery and expertly acted, is a heart-stopping account of how a family rose to heroism in a crisis. *Life* photographed the play during its Philadelphia tryout, transported

some of the actors to the actual house where the Hills were besieged. On the next page scenes from the play are re-enacted on the site of the crime.

The pictures on the ensuing two pages included an enactment of the son being "roughed up" by one of the convicts, entitled "brutish convict," a picture of the daughter biting the hand of a convict to make him drop a gun, entitled "daring daughter," and one of the father throwing his gun through the door after a "brave try" to save his family is foiled.

The James Hill referred to in the article is the appellee. He and his wife and five children involuntarily became a front-page news story after being held hostage by three escaped convicts in their suburban, Whitemarsh, Pennsylvania, home for 19 hours on September 11–12, 1952. The family was released unharmed. In an interview with newsmen after the convicts departed, appellee stressed that the convicts had treated the family courteously, had not molested them, and had not been at all violent. The convicts were thereafter apprehended in a widely publicized encounter with the police which resulted in the killing of two of the convicts. Shortly thereafter the family moved to Connecticut. The appellee discouraged all efforts to keep them in the public spotlight through magazine articles or appearances on television.

In the spring of 1953, James Hayes' novel, *The Desperate Hours,* was published. The story depicted the experience of a family of four held hostage by three escaped convicts in the family's suburban home. But unlike Hill's experience, the family of the story suffer violence at the hands of the convicts; the father and son are beaten and the daughter subjected to a verbal sexual insult.

The book was made into a play, also entitled "The Desperate Hours," and it is *Life's* article about the play which is the subject of appellee's action. The complaint sought damages under sec. 50–51 on allegations that the *Life* article was intended to, and did, give the impression that the play mirrored the Hill family's experience, which, to the knowledge of defendant, ". . . was false and untrue." Appellant's defense was that the subject of the article was "a subject of legitimate news interest," "a subject of general interest and of value and concern to the public" at the time of publication, and that it was "published in good faith without any malice whatsoever. . . ." A motion to dismiss the complaint for substantially these reasons was made at the close of the case and was denied by the trial judge on the ground that the proofs presented a jury question as to the truth of the article.

The jury awarded appellee $50,000 compensatory and $25,000 punitive damages. On appeal the Appellate Division of the Supreme Court ordered a new trial as to damages but sustained the jury verdict of liability. The court said as to liability:

"Although the play was fictionalized, *Life's* article portrayed it as a re-enactment of the Hills' experience. It is an inescapable conclusion that this was done to advertise and attract further attention to the play, and to increase present and future magazine circulations as well. It is evident that the article cannot be characterized as a mere dissemination of news, nor even an effort to supply legitimate newsworthy information in which the public had, or might have a proper interest."

At the trial on damages, a jury was waived and the court awarded $30,000 compensatory damages without punitive damages. . . .

The guarantees for speech and press are not the preserve of political expression or comment upon public affairs, essential as those are to healthy government. One need only pick up any newspaper or magazine to comprehend the vast range of published matter which exposes persons to public view, both private citizens and public officials. Exposure of the self to others in varying degrees is a concomitant of life in a civilized community. The risk of this exposure is an essential incident of life in a society which places a primary value on freedom of speech and of press. "Freedom of discussion, if it would fulfill its historic function in this nation, must embrace all issues about which information is needed or appropriate to enable the members of society to cope with the exigencies of their period." *Thornhill v. Alabama.* "No suggestion can be found in the Constitution that the freedom there guaranteed for speech and the press bears an inverse ratio to the timeliness and importance of the ideas seeking expression." *Bridges v. California.* We have no doubt that the subject of the *Life* article, the opening of a new play linked to an actual incident, is a matter of public interest. "The line between the informing and entertaining is too elusive for the protection of . . . [freedom of the press]." *Winters v. New York.* Erroneous statement is no less inevitable in such case than in the case of comment upon public affairs, and in both, if innocent or merely negligent, ". . . it must be protected if the freedoms of expression are to have the 'breathing space' that they 'need to survive.' . . ." *New York Times Co. v. Sullivan.* As James Madison said, "Some degree of abuse is inseparable from the proper use of everything and in no instance is this more true than of the press." We create grave risk of serious impairment of the indispensable service of a free press in a free society if we saddle the press with the impossible burden of verifying to a certainty the facts associated in news articles with a person's name, picture or portrait, particularly as related to nondefamatory matter. Even negligence would be a most elusive standard, especially when the content of the speech itself affords no warning of prospective harm to another through falsity. A negligence test would place on the press the intolerable burden of guessing how a jury might assess the reasonableness of steps taken by it to verify the accuracy of every reference to a name, picture or portrait. . . .

We find applicable here the standard of knowing or reckless falsehood not through blind application of *New York Times Co. v. Sullivan*, relating solely to libel actions by public officials, but only upon consideration of the factors which arise in the particular context of the application of the New York statute in cases involving private individuals. This is neither a libel action by a private individual nor a statutory action by a public official. Therefore, although the First Amendment principles pronounced in *New York Times* guide our conclusion, we reach that conclusion only by applying these principles in this discrete context. . . .

The requirement that the jury . . . find that the article was published "for trade purposes," as defined in the charge, cannot save the charge from constitutional infirmity. "That books, newspapers and magazines are published and sold for profit does not prevent them from being a form of expression whose liberty is safeguarded by the First Amendment." *Joseph Burstyn, Inc. v. Wilson*.

The judgment of the Court of Appeals is set aside and the case is remanded for further proceedings not inconsistent with this opinion.

MR. JUSTICE BLACK, *with whom Mr. Justice Douglas joins, concurring.*

I concur in reversal of the judgment in this case based on the grounds and reasons stated in the Court's opinion. I do this, however, in order for the Court to be able at this time to agree on an opinion in this important case based on the prevailing constitutional doctrine expressed in *New York Times v. Sullivan*. The Court's opinion decides the case in accordance with this doctrine, to which the majority adhere. In agreeing to the Court's opinion, I do not recede from any of the views I have previously expressed about the much wider press and speech freedoms I think the First and Fourteenth Amendments were designed to grant to the people of the Nation. . . .

I think it not inappropriate to add that it would be difficult, if not impossible, for the Court ever to sustain a judgment against *Time* in this case without using the recently popularized weighing and balancing formula. Some of us have pointed out from time to time that the First Amendment freedoms could not possibly live with the adoption of that Constitution ignoring and destroying technique, when there are, as here, palpable penalties imposed on speech or press specifically because of the views that are spoken or printed. The prohibitions of the Constitution were written to prohibit certain specific things, and one of the specific things prohibited is a law which abridges freedom of the press. That freedom was written into the Constitution and that Constitution is or should be binding on judges as well as other officers. The "weighing" doctrine plainly encourages and actually invites judges to choose for themselves between conflicting values, even where, as in the First Amendment, the Founders made a choice of values, one of which is a free press. . . .

MR. JUSTICE DOUGLAS, *concurring.*

As intimated in my separate opinion in *Rosenblatt v. Baer* and in the opinion of my Brother Black in the same case, state action to abridge freedom of the press is barred by the First and Fourteenth Amendments where the discussion concerns matters in the public domain. The episode around which this book was written had been news of the day for some time. The most that can be said is that the novel, the play, and the magazine article revived that interest. A fictionalized treatment of the event is, in my view, as much in the public domain as would be a watercolor of the assassination of a public official. It seems to me irrelevant to talk of any right of privacy in this context. Here a private person is catapulted into the news by events over which he had no control. He and his activities are then in the public domain as fully as the matters at issue in *New York Times Co. v. Sullivan.* Such privacy as a person normally has ceases when his life has ceased to be private.

. . . A trial is a chancy thing, no matter what safeguards are provided. To let a jury on this record return a verdict or not as it chooses is to let First Amendment rights ride on capricious or whimsical circumstances, for emotions and prejudices often do carry the day. The exception for "knowing and reckless falsity" is therefore, in my view, an abridgment of speech that is barred by the First and Fourteenth Amendments. . . .

MR. JUSTICE FORTAS, *with whom the Chief Justice and Mr. Justice Clark join, dissenting.*

The Court's holding here is exceedingly narrow. It declines to hold that the New York "Right of Privacy" statute is unconstitutional. I agree. The Court concludes, however, that the instructions to the jury in this case were fatally defective because they failed to advise the jury that a verdict for the plaintiff could be predicated only on a finding of knowing or reckless falsity in the publication of the *Life* article. Presumably, the plaintiff is entitled to a new trial. If he can stand the emotional and financial burden, there is reason to hope that he will recover damages for the reckless and irresponsible assault upon himself and his family which this article represents. But he has litigated this case for 11 years. He should not be subjected to the burden of a new trial without significant cause. . . .

I fully agree with the views of my Brethren who have stressed the need for a generous construction of the First Amendment. I, too, believe that freedom of the press, of speech, assembly, and religion, and the freedom to petition are of the essence of our liberty and fundamental to our values. . . . But I do not believe that whatever is in words, however much of an aggression it may be upon individual rights, is beyond the reach of the law, no matter how heedless of others' rights—how remote from public purpose, how reckless, irresponsible, and untrue it may be. I do not believe that the

First Amendment precludes effective protection of the right of privacy—or, for that matter, an effective law of libel. . . . In 1890, Warren and Brandeis published their famous article "The Right to Privacy," in which they eloquently argued that the "excesses" of the press in "overstepping in every direction the obvious bounds of propriety and decency" made it essential that the law recognize a right to privacy, distinct from traditional remedies for defamation, to protect private individuals against the unjustifiable infliction of mental pain and distress. A distinct right of privacy is now recognized, either as a "common-law" right or by statute, in at least 35 States. Its exact scope varies in the respective jurisdictions. It is, simply stated, the right to be let alone; to live one's life as one chooses, free from assault, intrusion or invasion except as they can be justified by the clear needs of community living under a government of law. . . .

The Court today does not repeat the ringing words of so many of its members on so many occasions in exaltation of the right of privacy. Instead, it reverses a decision under the New York "Right of Privacy" statute because of the "failure of the trial judge to instruct the jury that a verdict of liability could be predicated only on a finding of knowing or reckless falsity in the publication of the *Life* article." In my opinion, the jury instructions, although they were not a text-book model, satisfied this standard. . . .

The courts may not and must not permit either public or private action that censors or inhibits the presss. But part of this responsibility is to preserve values and procedures which assure the ordinary citizen that the press is not above the reach of the law—that its special prerogatives, granted because of its special and vital functions, are reasonably equated with its needs in the performance of these functions. For this Court totally to immunize the press—whether forthrightly or by the subtle indirection—in areas far beyond the needs of news, comment on public persons and events, discussion of public issues and the like would be no service to freedom of the press, but an invitation to public hostility to that freedom. This Court cannot and should not refuse to permit under state law the private citizen who is aggrieved by the type of assault which we have here and which is not within the specially protected core of the First Amendment to recover compensatory damages for recklessly inflicted invasions of his rights. . . .

PRIVACY: THE RIGHT THAT FAILED

By Donald L. Smith *

In a sense, the right of privacy is like Miniver Cheevy, who "wept that he was ever born, and he had his reasons." It seemed like a good idea at the time it was introduced into tort law, a concept filled with great promise for soothing abrasions caused by friction between the sensibilities of many citizens and the probings of a press becoming more pervasive through industrialization. But its development has been so uneven and its performance so unsatisfactory that, if torts had tear ducts, it might weep that it was ever born.

The right, as is well known, grew out of an article by Samuel D. Warren and Louis D. Brandeis published in the *Harvard Law Review* in 1890. Writing as an era of yellow journalism dawned, they wanted the law to afford relief to people who were victims of unwanted or embarrassing publicity. The influence of the article has been enormous. It is "the outstanding example of the influence of legal periodicals upon the American law," according to William L. Prosser, and it did "nothing less than add a chapter to our law," according to Roscoe Pound.

Some experts wish that that chapter had never been written. Others, disagreeing as to just what privacy involves, wish that it had turned out better. Still others, believing that it was basically well executed, wish that the United States Supreme Court had not recently found a new meaning in its pages.

Among those who think tort law could do without a right of privacy are Frederick Davis and Harry Kalven, Jr., both professors of law. Davis has complained that "one can logically argue that the concept of a right to privacy was never required in the first place." And Kalven, although he says "privacy is for me a great and important value," has called it "a mistake" and a "petty" tort.

Some other commentators have trouble agreeing on just what the right encompasses. The leading modern article on privacy, by Prosser, appeared in the August, 1960, issue of the *California Law Review*. After surveying a slew of privacy cases (he said some 300 were on the books at the time), Prosser concluded that privacy "is not one tort, but a complex of four."

* From Donald L. Smith. "Privacy: The Right That Failed." *Columbia Journalism Review*, Vol. 8, No. 1 (Spring 1969), p. 18. Used with permission of the *Columbia Journalism Review* and the author, an associate professor of journalism at Pennsylvania State University.

A major challenge to this interpretation has been issued by Edward J. Bloustein, who complains that Prosser has in effect repudiated Warren and Brandeis "by suggesting that privacy is not an independent value at all but a composite of the interests of reputation, emotional tranquillity and intangible property." For Bloustein, privacy is a dignitary tort; that is, the interest protected concerns individual dignity.

Although Prosser's analysis has not gone unchallenged, it has been very influential and will serve nicely here as a summary of the kinds of cases involving the mass media that arise in privacy law. The four torts he distinguishes are:

⟨ Intrusion upon a plaintiff's seclusion or solitude, or into his private affairs. The main risk for the media lies in such acts as photographing people without their consent in their home or in a hospital bed.

⟨ Public disclosure of embarrassing private facts about a plaintiff. This is what chiefly concerned Warren and Brandeis. But suits for such invasions generally fail, because the law recognizes a broad privilege to report news.

⟨ Publicity that places a plaintiff in a false light in the public eye. False-light invasion has two main consequences for the media. First, it is important as an independent principle. Examples of cases involving it are: pictures of people used to illustrate books or articles about things with which they have no reasonable connection; books and articles, or ideas expressed in either, spuriously attributed to people; and fictitious testimonials used in advertising and attributed to real people. Second, it has often been used to defeat the media's privilege to report news and matters of public interest.

There has been a rather widespread overlapping with defamation in the false-light cases, and this has worried some authorities. For example, in his 1960 article, Prosser wondered if this branch of privacy might not be capable of "swallowing up and engulfing" the whole law of public defamation and if there were any false libel that might not be redressed on false-light grounds.

⟨ Appropriation, for a defendant's advantage, of a plaintiff's name or likeness. Many cases on the books concern appropriation; the number is large partly because the nation's oldest privacy law deals mainly with this tort. It was enacted by the New York legislature in 1903. Similar statutes have been approved in Oklahoma, Virginia, and Utah. Some thirty other states have recognized a right of privacy at common law. . . .

One criticism of *Hill*, made by several dissenting justices as well as by other persons, is that the court has cavalierly undercut a basic right—an action especially disturbing to many observers because it comes at a time when privacy is being increasingly threatened in a "naked society." Such complaints usually point out that the court itself as recently as 1965 had found a right of privacy in "penumbras" of five amendments to the Constitution. (The case was *Griswold v. Connecticut*; the court voided a state law against disseminating information about birth control.) But this overlooks an important point made by Dana Bullen, then Supreme Court reporter for the *Washington Star,* in an interpretive story printed shortly after *Hill* was decided. He wrote:

> Recognizing the toughness of the [actual malice] test, three of the four dissenting justices accused the majority of giving only "lip service" to rights of privacy that the court has backed in other types of cases.
>
> The difference, of course, is that the other situations involved contests between an individual and a government agency [as in *Griswold*] or between an individual and the police.

Although he did not spell it out, the difference referred to by Bullen concerns the fact that the tort of privacy does not enjoy constitutional status. "It is statutes and the law of torts—not constitutional guaranties—which forbid invasions of privacy by private individuals," Bernard Schwartz recently wrote in his monumental commentary on the Constitution. "The constitutional guaranties, from which a constitutional right of privacy may be derived, are directed against government action alone. To the extent that the Constitution does confer a right of privacy, it is a right against governmental invasions."

Some critics of *Hill* assert that the court's extension of the actual malice rule from libel to privacy was an illogical leap. They seem to assume that libel and privacy are very distinct torts—from which it follows that a defense originated in libel cannot be legitimately used in privacy as well. If the court's "leap" is not completely defensible, it may at least be seen as an understandable one.

First, libel and privacy are not always readily distinguishable. Although libel concerns one's reputation and privacy concerns one's peace of mind, the two have always overlapped somewhat. And increasingly, as noted earlier, there has been a tendency for defamations to be absorbed into false-light privacy, where newsworthiness, a broad defense to many privacy actions, has no privileged status. The decided cases, wrote John W. Wade in the October, 1962, issue of the *Vanderbilt Law Review,* indicate that "the 'privilege' of publishing matters of public interest does not extend to false statements, so that even a public personage or a person connected with a newsworthy event can maintain an action if the false statement is one which would offend a person of ordinary sensibilities."

Second, it is clear that in a string of decisions going back to *Times* in 1964, the Supreme Court has been reducing the threat to the media of defamation actions in an effort to encourage "debate on public issues" that is "uninhibited, robust, and wide open." And it is also clear that the creation of the actual malice test in *Times* was partly related to the Court's commitment to the Negro rights movement. At a time when the nation is experiencing the worst crises in a century, the Court understandably wishes to facilitate peaceful social change by encouraging wide discussion of controversial questions. (Of course, the court is undoubtedly naïve to suppose that the media will indulge in robust discussion now that the threat of lawsuits has been reduced; it seems unaware of the fact that their status as businesses appealing to mass audiences often softens the media's spines.)

Third, in its efforts to facilitate peaceful change by promoting public debate, the Court has been greatly influenced by the First Amendment theory of the late Alexander Meiklejohn. His key ideas are that the people are both the governors and the governed, and that the intent of the First Amendment is to prohibit all subordinate agencies from abridging the freedom of the electoral power of the people. Speech is free not because an individual desires to speak, but because the people as governors need to hear.

When *Hill* is judged against this background, one can imagine that the court saw that its efforts to foster debate could be frustrated if there was any chance that people no longer able to sue for libel without proof of actual malice could collect for false-light invasion of privacy. And any tendency for the court to think this way may have been reinforced by a long-held interest in protecting expression for the civil rights movement.

That some such link connected the *Times* test to *Hill* was divined by Dana Bullen. In the story mentioned earlier, he noted that some recent Supreme Court decisions bolstering the constitutional guarantees of expression had occurred in the context of the civil rights movement. Then he concluded in regard to *Hill:* "In most purely private lawsuits, it seems, the developing remedy for invasion of privacy simply lost out. It may be yet another unintended victim of the civil rights struggle." Also important to note is the influence of Meiklejohn (whose ideas were relied on by counsel for Time Inc. in their brief for reargument), an influence made clear by striking parallels in language between Justice William J. Brennan's opinion and Meiklejohn's writings. . . .

Meantime, one should not conclude that the Court has destroyed the tort of privacy. It has simply ruled that damages will not be awarded for false-light actions unless plaintiffs prove knowing or reckless falsehood. Nor should one conclude that much has been lost, or will have been lost in the future if the Court undercuts privacy still more.

For regardless of how noble the interest may be that the right seeks to protect, the tort of privacy has not been a notable success. This seems especially true of the kind of interests Warren and Brandeis wished to see protected because, as Harry Kalven has said, the "generous privilege to serve the public interest in news" is so great as to virtually swallow the public-disclosure tort. And even the tort aimed at affording relief in instances of commercial appropriation—a tort that most experts agree makes sense—leaves much to be desired. As Frederick Davis has said of the New York statute, it "excludes almost as many deserving plaintiffs as it covers."

Given the slowness of the law to change, it is hard to believe that privacy will soon vanish from the tort scene. But given the checkered history of the right, it is easy to agree with Zechariah Chafee, Jr. He said:

> Times have changed since Brandeis wrote in 1890. Seeing how society dames and damsels sell their faces for cash in connection with cosmetics, cameras, and cars, one suspects that the right to publicity is more highly valued than any right to privacy. . . . *So I recommend that respect for privacy be left to public opinion and the conscience of owners and editors.*

PRIVACY, DEFAMATION, AND THE FIRST AMENDMENT: THE IMPLICATIONS OF TIME, INC. V. HILL *

III. THE HILL CASE AND DR. MEIKLEJOHN'S THEORY OF THE FIRST AMENDMENT

The most significant element in the *Hill* decision is its extension of First Amendment protections to privacy suits involving published matter which is "of public interest." The "public interest" standard is intended to be wide-reaching; Justice Brennan stated emphatically that "public interest" encompasses more than "political expression or comment upon public affairs." It is true that broad application of the first amendment is hardly novel; the "redeeming social importance" test, for example, assures first amendment protection to all but a narrow range of utterances. But such liberal standards were intended to foreclose attempts to suppress expression on the ground that it is dangerous to society at large; none dealt with publications which directly affected the feelings or reputation of particular individuals. In this respect, the closest analogue to the privacy suit is the defamation action. In libel cases, however, the Supreme Court thus far has limited the constitutional requirement of actual malice to cases in which the challenged statements are relevant to the conduct of "public officials." While the actual malice rule has been extended to other sorts of libel cases by some lower courts, the broad "public interest" standard has rarely been employed.

The greater deference shown by the Court to speech and press in privacy, as opposed to libel, cases might be explained on a number of grounds. As the Court noted, nondefamatory falsehoods carry no inherent warning to the publisher of the possible harm to another. Furthermore, it might be thought that damage to feelings and sensibilities is less serious than harm to reputation. Finally, in recognizing an "additional state interest in the protection of the individual against damage to his reputation," the Court may have been expressing an awareness of the different historical development of the two torts. The cause of action for defamation has deep common law roots and fairly clear boundaries, while the privacy suit is relatively new, amorphous, and not universally recognized. These suggested distinctions may, however, prove insubstantial; the privacy test of today could become the libel test of tomorrow. Assessment of both the likelihood

* From "Privacy, Defamation, and the First Amendment: The Implications of Time, Inc. v. Hill." *Columbia Law Review*, Vol. 67 (May 1967), p. 926, at p. 937. Used with permission of the *Columbia Law Review*.

of this development and the significance of the *Hill* case for the law of privacy requires analysis of the first amendment theory underlying the *Hill* decision.

Although the works of Alexander Meiklejohn were not cited in *Hill*, it is clear that his ideas significantly influenced the Court. Certain passages of the opinion closely parallel Meiklejohn's theory; moreover, his views were specifically relied upon by the appellant in its brief, and Justice Brennan, author of the opinion, had previously spoken of Meiklejohn's influence on the Court in first amendment cases.

The first premise of the Meiklejohn theory is that the people of the United States are both the governors and the governed. Through a written constitution they have delegated some powers to subordinate agencies and reserved others—notably the right to vote—to themselves. The first amendment was intended to protect this reserved power by denying "to all subordinate agencies authority to abridge the freedom of the electoral power of the people." Thus, "those activities of thought and communication by which we 'govern' " must be free from interference. This protected class of expression which has "governing" or "social" importance is not limited to communication of a political nature. Knowledge of literature and the arts and of the achievements of philosophy and the sciences is also necessary to acquire the intelligence, integrity, and sensitivity required for effective self-government. In short, speech is free, according to Meiklejohn, not because persons "desire to speak" but because the people "need to hear."

Meiklejohn, then, does not balance individual interests against the First Amendment; instead, he attempts to define speech as public or private. Once an expression is found to have "governing" importance it is absolutely protected by the First Amendment. Thus, the reasoning in the *New York Times* and *Hill* cases is consistent with his views, except insofar as the Court established a qualified rather than absolute privilege. However, Meiklejohn's theory is not entirely consistent with the views of the leading exponent of the "definitional" approach on the Supreme Court; in contrast to Justice Black, he would permit recovery for purely private defamation and presumably for invasions of privacy where public interest was not involved.

The influence of Meiklejohn's thinking is evident throughout the Court's opinion in *Hill*. Justice Brennan employed the term "public interest" to define protected expression; Meiklejohn used "governing importance." Moreover, in emphasizing both the public need for information on a wide variety of subjects, political and nonpolitical, and the interests of the hearer rather than the speaker, the Court followed the arguments of Dr. Meiklejohn. Under either formulation, this approach to the first amendment makes the scope of protection given to speech and press dependent upon verbal formulae that may be difficult to apply. In many situations, the meaning of "public interest" or "governing importance" is uncertain. Defining the scope of these critical terms is likely to remain a prime task of the courts in future applications of the *Hill* doctrine.

IV. The Implications of Time, Inc. v. Hill

A. *Impact on the Law of Privacy*

The impact of the *Hill* decision is, by its terms, expressly limited to the sphere of publications in which the public has a legitimate interest. Formerly, most jurisdictions permitted recovery in such cases whenever the account was false or fictionalized; the defendant's liability was not, however, dependent upon the degree of care he exercised in verifying the accuracy of his statements. Hence, the requirement in *Hill* that the plaintiff prove knowing or reckless falsehood on the part of the defendant substantially reduces the scope of protection accorded by the privacy action in "public interest" cases.

It remains unclear whether a requirement of malice, or even of mere falsity, will also be extended to privacy actions not involving matters in the public interest. In this category are suits based on commercial exploitation or involving unjustified revelation of embarrassing or offensive details of a person's life. The Meiklejohn theory would impose no First Amendment limits on such actions, for they do not affect capacity for self-government. Under Justice Black's approach, however, the defendant's activity might be regarded as "speech" entitled to absolute protection.

Where the *Hill* standard concededly applies—reports of public interest which contain false statements—it may be argued that the actual malice test does not provide sufficient protection for First Amendment freedoms. Even as strict a requirement as proof of calculated falsehood or reckless disregard of the truth may operate to stifle the dissemination of legitimate information in some cases. Recklessness has always been a particularly amorphous concept used to stigmatize all types of conduct which are not intentional but are more objectionable than mere negligence. And while the Court was certainly correct in declaring that the substantial deliberate lie in a purportedly factual presentation has no informative value, it must be remembered that calculated falsehoods and recklessly published untruths are likely to constitute only part of larger works which contain a good deal of worthwhile information. The recent case of *Spahn v. Julian Messner, Inc.* provides an example. Defendants published an unauthorized juvenile biography of baseball pitcher Warren Spahn which contained descriptions of some incidents which never took place and distorted accounts of other episodes. Dialogue was fabricated and imaginary thoughts were attributed to Spahn. Nonetheless the book undoubtedly contained much accurate information and apparently was faithful to the outline of plaintiff's career, departing from the truth only to fill gaps or to embellish plaintiff's achievements in order to inspire the youthful reader. It may be argued that damages are awarded only for the fictionalized portions; in practice, however, the damage sanction—or, more obviously, the injunction—will have a "chilling effect" upon the dissemination of an entire work. Therefore it is naive to assume that when recovery is permitted for knowing or reckless falsehood, publication of legitimate information will not suffer. The expense of expunging the offensive material may be so great that a publisher will decide not to republish at all. Unfortunately, this effect appears to be an inevitable aspect of any system which imposes liability for false statements about matters of public interest.

A second objection to the knowing or reckless falsehood standard is that it seems too narrow when the alleged invasion of privacy occurs in a creative rather than a reportorial work. Meiklejohn and others have recognized the need to protect novels, poems, and the like not only because they convey information but also because exposure to them will "lead the way toward sensitive and informed appreciation and response to the values out of which the riches of the general welfare are created." Although the persons portrayed in many literary works enjoy no independent existence, the content or style of the work can make a significant contribution to educational development. Problems arise, however, where an actual person or event is portrayed in a partly fictional, partly factual manner. If the figures portrayed are deceased, as in the historical novel, ordinarily no privacy questions arise. But where a living figure is depicted in a nonfactual work, the actual malice standard may break down.

The *Youssoupoff* litigation provides an example of the problems encountered in creative portraits of living persons. Defendants in that case were producers of a television play which dealt with the murder of Rasputin. An actor portrayed plaintiff—whose role in the assassination was conceded—and fictional dialogue was used. The case involved, for the most part, the question whether the inaccuracies were "substantial" enough to result in liability. More importantly, however, it illustrates the inappositeness of the actual malice test to works in which actual events and creative elements are intertwined. To speak of calculated falsehood with reference to such works is artificial, for they do not purport to be objectively reportorial; a dramatic presentation of an historical event does not seek to be judged by the standards of truth and falsity. It may be that a broader privilege is required when creative works are involved. A privilege to portray a public figure so long as the words or actions attributed to him do not constitute an "outrage to decency" might best protect the information-providing function of the first amendment while preserving the essence of the right to privacy. Yet this solution would require judges to employ still another fine distinction, for creative and reportorial works would have to be separated. Spectres of the "redeeming social utility" test in obscenity cases haunt even the contemplation of such a distinction; judges would be required to become literary critics.

In addition to these difficulties posed by the actual malice test, the *Hill* decision presents the troublesome problem of defining "public interest," a task previous encountered on many occasions by the state and lower federal courts. At least one state court has tried "to steer far wider" of First Amendment thickets in privacy cases and thus to avoid uncertainties inherent in present approaches. The Utah Supreme Court has ruled that the state's privacy statute—identical in most material respects to the New York statute—applies only to actual advertising or sales promotion of collateral commodities. While the statutory language and the legislative history clearly support this construction, the court was motivated in part by First Amendment considerations. Upon analysis, however, it appears that this Utah rule may be both too broad and too narrow. With its emphasis on advertising of collateral products, the rule might not provide a cause of action in the case of a magazine which published a picture of plaintiff that was either offensive or totally unrelated to the matter reported. On the other hand, it is not clear that limiting the privacy action to references in advertisements of collateral commodities will avoid all First Amendment questions. For example, the innocent or negligent publication of a public figure's false endorsement of a biography which concerns matters in the public interest would appear to be actionable under the Utah statute. Under *Hill*, however, the publication should be protected notwithstanding the fact that it is in the form of an advertisement.

B. *Effect on the Law of Defamation*

If the Supreme Court has adopted the Meiklejohn conception of the First Amendment without reservation, rejection of the *New York Times* "public official" test awaits only an appropriate case before the Court. Under that theory, the First Amendment is viewed as a means of safeguarding the interests of the hearer, and the same protection must be accorded publications of "public interest" irrespective of whether recovery is sought for injury to feelings or harm to reputation. However, the Court has noted distinctions, expressed caveats, and suggested alternative theories—both in the *Hill* decision and elsewhere—which make it difficult to predict with certainty what the mature theory of the First Amendment, where it conflicts with private interests, will be.

As one justification for applying an actual malice rule in all privacy cases involving matters in the public interest, the Court noted that a privacy-invading statement, in contrast to libelous material, "affords no warning" of the possible harm to the individual. This distinction seems inadequate since many libelous statements may seem perfectly innocuous on their face. For example, "Sam smokes cigars and wears overalls" looks harmless enough but may be very destructive if Sam is a girl. Since the Court in *Hill* specifically left open the rule to be applied in libel cases, the "warning" factor did not rise to the level of a distinction. In view of the deficiencies discussed above, however, it is unlikely that the Court will rely in the future on the availability of a warning from the nature of the material published to distinguish privacy and defamation.

A more significant source of doubt concerning the applicability of the *Hill* rule to defamation is evidence, in the *Hill* opinion and a recent libel decision, that the Court has not forsaken the balancing approach. After noting the "tension" between society's "strong interest in preventing and redressing attacks upon reputation" and "the values nurtured by" the first amendment, the Court in *Rosenblatt* summed up the "thrust" of the *New York Times* case as follows: "when interests in public discussion are particularly strong as they were in that case, the Constitution limits the protections afforded by the law of defamation." While this statement is not free from ambiguity, it apparently contemplates a "weighing" of the competing interests. Similarly, Justice Brennan's opinion in *Hill* mentioned "the additional state interest in the protection of the individual against damage to his reputation" when it listed the different factors which would be present in a libel case. Even if "additional" was not meant to imply that the state interest in protecting reputation is stronger than the interest in protecting feelings and sensibilities, this differentiation could be relevant only if these interests were to be "balanced" against First Amendment values. In sum, the Court has refused to commit itself to an extension of the *New York Times* doctrine in libel, and has been careful to leave open other alternatives.

Nevertheless, expansion of the strict "public official" rule seems inevitable for several reasons. Even under a balancing approach it would seem unreasonable to distinguish between two actions based upon injurious falsehood merely because one asserted a harm to reputation while the other was based upon invasion of privacy. The difference in the importance of the two interests is not great enough to justify such an anomaly. Second, the history of libel is conducive to application of a *Hill* standard. What little protection the common law gave to the publisher was based upon the "public interest"; the privilege of fair comment protected honest comment or criticism based upon true (or privileged) facts as long as it concerned matters of "legitimate public interest." While this privilege extended only to opinion, not fact, and while it was otherwise narrower than the corresponding "public interest" privilege in privacy law, it certainly extends to a much broader class of plaintiffs than the Supreme Court's "public official" test.

Finally, the lower court decisions subsequent to the *New York Times* opinion have made it clear that the "public official" concept is an impossible stopping place; the rationale of the rule is simply too broad to be confined by the phrase. For example, several cases have arisen in which the relationship between a public official and a private citizen has engendered criticism. *Gilberg v. Goffi* is representative. A local political candidate made statements in a speech, subsequently published in the local newspaper, which referred to the conflict of interest created by the practice of the mayor's law firm before the city courts. The mayor's partner, a private citizen, brought suit for defamation. Should the private citizen obtain compensation without proving actual malice? Obviously not. The deterrent effect on comment relating to the official's fitness for office is the same as if the official were permitted to recover without meeting the *New York Times* standard of proof. Thus, it is not because one is a public official that one's rights in defamation are limited; rather, it is because recovery would have an inhibiting effect on discussion of a public *issue*, the fitness of a man for public office. The nature of the issue, not the characterization of the plaintiff, is determinative.

A broad range of information about the character and conduct of a person is necessary to evaluate his performance as a public official or holder of another position of public trust; where other issues are involved, however, the "public interest" extends to a narrower sphere of discussion of personal qualities and activities. Thus, the "public interest" standard should protect descriptions of an individual's activities contained in reports of newsworthy events; otherwise full reporting of such events as the University of Mississippi integration riots, in which the litigious General Walker played a role, would be discouraged. But this protection ought not extend to defamatory statements referring to characteristics or actions in no way related to the newsworthy event.

Questions of relevancy and the scope of public interest are even more difficult where a single individual is described to illustrate some aspect of a broad social problem. *Afro-American Publishing Corp. v. Jaffe* is the best example. Plaintiff, a drug store operator, cancelled his order for a Negro-oriented newspaper which subsequently published an editorial charging him with bigotry. Racial discord is a problem in the forefront of public discussion, but is there a public interest in the allegation that a particular person is a bigot? It is nearly always possible to make at least an attenuated argument of public interest. For example, the Negro patrons of Jaffe's drugstore might not wish to continue to deal with an exponent of racism, and thus would desire to know of his beliefs.

The problem of defining the scope of a qualified privilege to misstate facts about a matter of "public interest" also arises when these falsehoods are made in the course of comment and criticism directed at work submitted to the public by artists, writers, entertainers, and the like. The difficult question is determining how far the "public interest" permits one to delve into those characteristics or actions not directly related to the work or performance that is before the public. Perhaps it is clear that the "public interest" extends to the personally derogatory implications contained in the statement that columnist Drew Pearson is the "Garbage Man of the Fourth Estate" or to the charge that comic Jackie Mason made obscene

gestures on the Ed Sullivan television show. But what of the political beliefs of a folk singer or the sexual aberrations of a sports figure? Perhaps
the most perplexing problem is the determination of limitations on recovery for speech critical of those taking strong public stands on public
issues. If the critic wishes to show that the speaker's positions are not
worthy of respect or belief, he may refer to a wide range of character deficiencies having little or nothing to do with the subject matter of his
speech. Also common is the labeling of a speaker as an affiliate of a politically extreme group—either to the left or to the right depending on
the original tenor of the speech. It is difficult to say that such assertions
do not involve matters of legitimate public interest. Yet such a characterization, insofar as it imports the actual malice standard, is questionable
in light of the purposes of the *New York Times* decision. That case formulated the public official rule to avoid the chilling effect of potential liability for defamation. However, if a private individual subjects himself to
sweeping defamatory attacks by taking a stand on an issue of public concern, his desire to participate in public discussion is likely to be diminished.
Thus, the public would be deprived of the very speech which the First
Amendment is designed to protect. Unless the bold initiator of discussion
is given adequate protection, the victory of the press in *New York Times*
is an empty one.

Conclusion

Although the *Hill* case has extended a much-needed protection to the
communications media, it has not deprived the tort of privacy of its vitality. Perhaps greater inroads will be necessary, however, to assure adequate
protection of creative works. In any event, the more compelling occasions
for protection of privacy in modern society, unlike the times of Warren
and Brandeis, are found in the cases of electronic eavesdropping and other
types of secretive prying, none of which are prohibited under the New
York privacy statute.

It appears that the major impact of the *Hill* case, with its emphasis
on the informing function of the First Amendment, may be on the law of
defamation. The formulation of the "public interest" test can be viewed
as indicating the readiness of the Court to look away from the status of
the individual being defamed and to focus instead upon the legitimacy of
public interest in the subject discussed. Public interest is not an easy phrase
to define. It will be difficult, at times, to determine the relevance of the
defamatory statements to the issues of concern to the public. The matter
under discussion should determine the scope of legitimate inquiry. If a
candidate's fitness for office is the subject, the scope of inquiry should be
quite broad because decisions on questions of the qualifications of competing candidates are among the most important made under our form of
government. As the discourse turns to the merits of works of art or to the

caliber of service offered by a medical laboratory the need for debate remains, but questions of relevancy require the formation of more refined judgments. Of course, courts inevitably will disagree at times on the correct characterization of a given report. But this is the price which must be paid for any approach to the first amendment which does not give absolute protection to all expression.

CHAPTER 10

TRIAL BY NEWSPAPER

Under the law there is no priority listing among the first ten amendments, the Bill of Rights. Freedom of the press, as guaranteed in the First Amendment, is no more or no less important than the guarantee of a fair trial, covered by the Sixth Amendment. Indeed, these human rights protected by the first ten amendments are closely entwined and often interdependent. But this closeness also brings entanglements, and this is the present state of the First and Sixth Amendments—the present debate over "fair trial vs. free press," or "trial by newspaper."

Interest was focused on this apparent conflict first by the 1954 murder trial of Dr. Sam Sheppard and later by the report of the Warren Commission following the 1963 assassination of President Kennedy, the confusion that followed in Dallas and the murder of the accused assassin, Lee Harvey Oswald. The fundamental question can be simply stated: "Had he lived to face trial, could Lee Harvey Oswald have received a fair trial?"

The broad implications of "trial by newspaper" are not easily answered. Three solutions have been widely discussed since the tragedies of November 1963. The first calls for voluntary adherence by the news media to a code which would demand restrained treatment of criminal trial coverage. The press would agree to turn to the more significant aspects of American justice and away from the sensational aspects which normally are used to boost circulation or which are "knee-jerk" reactions of overenthusiasm.

Only a few members of the news media, however, have announced such voluntary restraints. There has been much serious discussion within the media, but most of it has centered on opposition to lawyers who have argued for firm control of trial news. Also, voluntary media codes of restraint have not been particularly successful in the past. The Motion Picture Production Code is an example. Finally, a voluntary code is only as effective as the members of the media want it to be, and the news profession has not seen fit to censure its members who are guilty of "trial by newspaper." Nor is there a unanimous view among editors and publishers that such a code would be desirable.

A second proposal has been to follow the lead of England by laying a heavy hand on the press through the contempt powers of the court. The Supreme Court, in this regard, has given the American press a generally free hand in discussing cases before the bar since the landmark Bridges decision of 1941. Critics of strong contempt powers also point to the shortcomings of the English system—which is far from foolproof—and to the differences between our legal systems, such as the election of judges in this country and the presence of a Constitution which protects press freedom. Also, public prosecutors are responsible to the electorate, who must be kept informed as to the condition of law enforcement and justice. It is more than mere curiosity, therefore, that motivates the press to cover and comment upon American justice and those who seek to enforce it.

Finally, a third method of controlling pre-trial publicity is to govern the flow of information at the source, i.e. at those legally under the jurisdiction of the court. This was the method approved by the House of Delegates of the American Bar Association in 1968 with the adoption of the ABA's Reardon Report. The judge, if the Reardon recommendations are followed, would limit the information available to the press from the prosecutor, the defense attorney, the police, and all others directly within his control. Principals, under threat of contempt, would be prohibited from discussing alleged confessions, prior criminal records, potential witnesses, potential pleas or other comments as to guilt or innocence of the accused.

The success of the Reardon suggestions, however, must await the test of time and trial. The press, it should be noted, is not being restrained directly. Still, members of the media generally have been opposed to the Reardon recommendations. Some point to the lack of evidence surrounding media coverage and juror reaction. Not all members of the Bar support the Reardon Report either. Nor have they been without fault in trying to win cases for their clients. Both prosecutors and defense attorneys have long "courted" the media openly when it was to their advantage to do so. Neither the Bar nor the press, in truth, is without fault in this most delicate of human considerations.

The Court in 1941 turned a significant corner in dealing with out-of-court contempt with its opinion in the California cases of Bridges v. California and Times-Mirror v. Superior Court, 314 U.S. 252 (1941), handed down together. In a 5-4 decision, the Court formally rejected the Toledo "reasonable tendency" guide and substituted the more restrictive concept of "clear and present danger," which Justice Holmes had first proposed for seditious utterances in his 1919 Schenck v. United States opinion. The

Bridges decision meant that a clear and present danger to the administration of justice—not just a possible threat—would have to be established in order for a court to substantiate out-of-court contempt. Also, comment was authorized in cases still pending, especially if they have great public interest.

The debate, of course, was between two fundamental principles that continue to this day to be in apparent philosophic and real conflict—freedom of the press to comment on public affairs and the right to administer justice without undue interference. The Bridges case resulted from a telegram attacking the judgment of the court. The Los Angeles Times contempt was based on editorials run after verdicts were announced but before sentencing, application for probation, or appeal. Both contempts were set aside by the Supreme Court. The press heralded the decisions as significant to First Amendment guarantees. The Los Angeles Times was awarded a Pulitzer Prize for Public Service in 1942 for its pursuance of the principles involved.

BRIDGES V. CALIFORNIA

TIMES-MIRROR CO. V. SUPERIOR COURT
314 U.S. 252 (1941)

MR. JUSTICE BLACK *delivered the opinion of the Court.*

These two cases, while growing out of different circumstances and concerning different parties, both relate to the scope of our national constitutional policy safeguarding free speech and a free press. All of the petitioners were adjudged guilty and fined for contempt of court by the Superior Court of Los Angeles County. Their conviction rested upon comments pertaining to pending litigation which were published in newspapers. In the Superior Court and later in the California Supreme Court, petitioners challenged the state's action as an abridgment, prohibited by the Federal Constitution, of freedom of speech and of the press, but the Superior Court overruled this contention, and the Supreme Court affirmed. The importance of the constitutional question prompted us to grant *certiorari. . . .*

We may appropriately begin our discussion of the judgments below by considering how much, as a practical matter, they would affect liberty of expression. It must be recognized that public interest is much more likely to be kindled by a controversial event of the day than by a generalization, however penetrating, of the historian or scientist. Since they punish utterances made during the pendency of a case, the judgments below therefore produce their restrictive results at the precise time when public interest in the matters discussed would naturally be at its height. Moreover, the ban is likely to fall not only at a crucial time but upon the most important topics of discussion. Here, for example, labor controversies were the topics of some of the publications. Experience shows that the more acute labor controversies are, the more likely it is that in some aspect they will get into court. It is therefore the controversies that command most interest that the decisions below would remove from the arena of public discussion. . . .

The Los Angeles Times Editorials. The Times-Mirror Company, publisher of the *Los Angeles Times,* and L. D. Hotchkiss, its managing editor, were cited for contempt for the publication of three editorials. Both found by the trial court to be responsible for one of the editorials, the company and Hotchkiss were each fined $100. The company alone was held responsible for the other two, and was fined $100 more on account of one, and $300 more on account of the other.

The $300 fine presumably marks the most serious offense. The editorial thus distinguished was entitled "Probation for Gorillas?" After vigorously denouncing two members of a labor union who had previously been found guilty of assaulting nonunion truck drivers, it closes with observation: "Judge A. A. Scott will make a serious mistake if he grants probation to Matthew Shannon and Kennan Holmes. This community needs the example of their assignment to the jute mill." Judge Scott had previously set a day (about a month after the publication) for passing upon the application of Shannon and Holmes for probation and for pronouncing sentence.

The basis for punishing the publication as contempt was by the trial court said to be its "inherent tendency" and by the Supreme Court its "reasonable tendency" to interfere with the orderly administration of justice in an action then before a court for consideration. In accordance with what we have said on the "clear and present danger" cases, neither "inherent tendency" nor "reasonable tendency" is enough to justify a restriction of free expression. But even if they were appropriate measures, we should find exaggeration in the use of those phrases to describe the facts here.

From the indications in the record of the position taken by the *Los Angeles Times* on labor controversies in the past, there could have been little doubt of its attitude toward the probation of Shannon and Holmes. In view of the paper's long-continued militancy in this field, it is inconceivable that any judge in Los Angeles would expect anything but adverse criticism from it in the event probation were granted. Yet such criticism after final disposition of the proceedings would clearly have been privileged. Hence, this editorial, given the most intimidating construction it will bear, did no more than threaten future adverse criticism which was reasonably to be expected anyway in the event of a lenient disposition of the pending case. To regard it, therefore, as in itself of substantial influence upon the course of justice would be to impute to judges a lack of firmness, wisdom, or honor, which we cannot accept as a major premise. . . .

MR. JUSTICE FRANKFURTER, *with whom concurred the Chief Justice, Mr. Justice Roberts and Mr. Justice Byrnes, dissenting.*

Our whole history repels the view that it is an exercise of one of the civil liberties secured by the Bill of Rights for a leader of a large following or for a powerful metropolitan newspaper to attempt to over-awe a judge in a matter immediately pending before him. The view of the majority deprives California of means for securing to its citizens justice according to law—means which, since the Union was founded, have been the possession, hitherto unchallenged, of all the states. This sudden break with the uninterrupted course of constitutional history has no constitutional warrant. To find justification for such deprivation of the historic powers of the states is to misconceive the idea of freedom of thought and speech as guaranteed by the Constitution. . . .

We turn to the specific cases before us:

The earliest [*Times*] editorial . . . "Sit-strikers Convicted," commented upon a case the day after a jury had returned a verdict and the day before the trial judge was to pronounce sentence and hear motions for a new trial and applications for probation. On its face the editorial merely expressed exulting approval of the verdict, a completed action of the court, and there is nothing in the record to give it additional significance. The same is true of the second editorial, "Fall of an Ex-Queen," which luridly draws a moral from a verdict of guilty in a sordid trial and which was published eight days prior to the day set for imposing sentence. In both instances imposition of sentences was immediately pending at the time of publication, but in neither case was there any declaration, direct or sly, in regard to this. As the special guardian of the Bill of Rights this Court is under the heaviest responsibility to safeguard the liberties guaranteed from any encroachment, however astutely disguised. The Due Process Clause of the Fourteenth Amendment protects the right to comment on a judicial proceeding, so long as this is not done in a manner interfering with the impartial disposition of litigation. There is no indication that more was done in these editorials; they were not close threats to the judicial function which a state should be able to restrain. We agree that the judgment of the state court in this regard should not stand.

"Probation for Gorillas?", the third editorial, is a different matter. On April 22, 1938, a Los Angeles jury found two defendants guilty of assault with a deadly weapon and of a conspiracy to violate another section of the penal code. On May 2d, the defendants applied for probation and the trial judge on the same day set June 7th as the day for disposing of this application and for sentencing the defendants. In the *Los Angeles Times* for May 5th appeared the following editorial entitled "Probation for Gorillas?":

> Two members of Dave Beck's wrecking crew, entertainment committee, goon squad or gorillas, having been convicted in Superior Court of assaulting nonunion truck drivers, have asked for probation. Presumably they will say they are 'first offenders,' or plead that they were merely indulging a playful exuberance when, with slingshots, they fired steel missiles at men whose only offense was wishing to work for a living without paying tribute to the erstwhile boss of Seattle.
>
> Sluggers for pay, like murderers for profit, are in a slightly different category from ordinary criminals. Men who commit mayhem for wages are not merely violators of the peace and dignity of the State; they are also conspirators against it. The man who burgles because his children are hungry may have some claim on public sympathy. He whose crime is one of impulse may be entitled to lenity. But he who hires out his muscles for the creation of disorder and in aid of a racket is a deliberate foe of organized society and should be penalized accordingly.
>
> It will teach no lesson to other thugs to put these men on good behavior for a limited time. Their 'duty' would simply be taken over by others like them. If Beck's thugs, however, are made to realize that they face San Quentin when they are caught, it will tend to make their disreputable occupation unpopular. Judge A. A. Scott will make a serious mistake if he grants probation to Matthew Shannon and Kennan Holmes. This community needs the example of their assignment to the jute mill.

This editorial was published three days after the trial judge had fixed the time for sentencing and for passing on an application for probation, and a month prior to the date set. It consisted of a sustained attack on the defendants, with an explicit demand of the judge that they be denied probation and be sent "to the jute mill." This meant, in California idiom, that in the exercise of his discretion the judge should treat the offense as a felony, with all its dire consequences, and not as a misdemeanor. Under the California Penal Code the trial judge had wide discretion in sentencing the defendants: he could sentence them to the county jail for one year or less, or to the state penitentiary for two years. The editorial demanded that he take the latter alternative and send the defendants to the "jute mill" of the state penitentiary. A powerful newspaper admonished a judge, who within a year would have to secure popular approval if he desired continuance in office, that failure to comply with its demands would be "a serious mistake." Clearly, the state court was justified in treating this as a threat to impartial adjudication. It is too naive to suggest that the editorial was written with a feeling of impotence and an intention to utter idle words. The publication of the editorial was hardly an exercise in futility. . . . Here there was a real and substantial manifestation of an endeavor to exert outside influence. A powerful newspaper brought its full coercive power to bear in demanding a particular sentence. If such sentence had been imposed readers might assume that the court had been influenced in its action; if lesser punishment had been imposed at least a portion of the community might be stirred to resentment. It cannot be denied that even a judge may be affected by such a quandary. We cannot say that the state court was out of bounds in concluding that such conduct offends the free course of justice. . . .

*   *   *

The Warren Court in 1961 was the first to reverse a state criminal conviction on grounds of adverse pre-trial publicity. Leslie "Mad Dog" Irvin, as he was popularly identified, was arrested in Indiana on suspicion of burglary and passing bad checks, but subsequently was connected with several murders. He was tried, convicted, and sentenced to death. He claimed—and the Supreme Court agreed—that he was denied a fair trial because of the extremely prejudicial nature of the press coverage. For example, 370 of the 430 prospective jurors admitted under voir dire they believed Irvin to be guilty. The Irvin decision acted as a prelude to the free press and fair trial argument and was followed by three additional reversals —Sheppard, Rideau, and Estes—which allowed the Justices in the final Warren years to speak out forcefully on questions of pre-trial publicity.

IRVIN V. DOWD
366 U.S. 717 (1961)

MR. JUSTICE CLARK *delivered the opinion of the Court.*

. . . It is not required . . . that the jurors be totally ignorant of the facts and issues involved. In these days of swift, wide-spread and diverse methods of communication, an important case can be expected to arouse the interest of the public in the vicinity, and scarcely any of those best qualified to serve as jurors will not have found some impression or opinion as to the merits of the case. . . . It is sufficient if the juror can lay aside his impression or opinion and render a verdict based on the evidence presented in court. . . .

Here the build-up of prejudice is clear and convincing. An examination of the then current community pattern of thought as indicated by the popular news media is singularly revealing. For example, petitioner's first motion for a change of venue from Gibson County alleged that the awaited trial of petitioner had become the *cause célèbre* of this small community—so much so that curb-stone opinions, not only as to petitioner's guilt but even as to what punishment he should receive, were solicited and recorded on the public streets by a roving reporter, and later were broadcast over the local stations. A reading of the 46 exhibits which petitioner attached to his motion indicates that a barrage of newspaper headlines, articles, cartoons and pictures was unleashed against him during the six or seven months preceding his trial. The motion further alleged that the newspapers in which the stories appeared were delivered regularly to approximately 95% of the dwellings in Gibson County and that, in addition, the Evansville radio and TV stations, which likewise blanketed that county, also carried extensive newscasts covering the same incidents. These stories revealed the details of his background, including a reference to crimes committed when a juvenile, his convictions for arson almost 20 years previously, for burglary and by a court-martial on AWOL charges during the war. He was accused of being a parole violator. The headlines announced his police line-up identification, that he faced a lie detector test, had been placed at the scene of the crime and that the six murders were solved but the petitioner refused to confess. Finally, they announced his confession to the six murders and the fact of his indictment for four of them in Indiana. They reported petitioner's offer to plead guilty if promised a 99-year sentence, but also the determination, on the other hand, of the prosecutor to secure the death penalty, and that petitioner had confessed to 24 burglaries (the *modus operandi* of these robberies was compared to that of the murders and the similarity noted). One story dramatically relayed the promise of a sheriff to devote his life to securing petitioner's execution by the State of Kentucky, where petitioner is alleged to have committed one of the six murders, if Indiana failed to do so. Another characterized petitioner as remorseless and without conscience but also having been found sane by a court-appointed panel of doctors. In many of the stories petitioner was described as the "confessed slayer of six," a parole violator and fraudulent-check artist. Petitioner's court-appointed counsel was quoted as having received "much criticism over being Irvin's counsel" and it was pointed out by way of excusing the attorney, that he would be subject to disbarment should he refuse to represent Irvin. . . .

Finally, and with remarkable understatement, the headlines reported that "impartial jurors are hard to find." . . .

MR. JUSTICE FRANKFURTER *concurring.*

. . . One of the rightful boasts of Western civilization is that the State has the burden of establishing guilt solely on the basis of evidence produced in court and under circumstances assuring an accused all the safe-guards of a fair procedure. These rudimentary conditions for determining guilt are inevitably wanting if the jury which is to sit in judgment on a fellow human being comes to its task with its mind ineradicably poisoned against him. How can fallible men and women reach a disinterested ver-dict based exclusively on what they heard in court when, before they en-tered the jury box, their minds were saturated by press and radio for months preceding by matter designed to establish the guilt of the accused. A conviction so secured obviously constitutes a denial of due process of law in its most rudimentary conception. . . .

This Court has not yet decided that the fair administration of crimi-nal justice must be subordinated to another safeguard of our Constitu-tional system—freedom of the press, properly conceived. . . .

* * *

The classic case in the debate over "trial by newspaper" involved the 1954 murder conviction of Dr. Sam Sheppard. The Supreme Court denied certiorari on the original appeal, but a decade later accepted the question of pre-trial publicity and decided 8-1 that Sheppard did not get a fair trial because of the sensational press coverage. The Court reversed the murder judgment against him and ordered him freed until such time as a new trial was sought by the prosecution. The majority opinion by Justice Clark recounts in detail the events leading to Sheppard's conviction. The Court was critical of press coverage, reporting independently discovered "evi-dence" and gossip, and assumptions of guilt. Still, the opinion appeared to be aimed more at the court for allowing the "massive, pervasive and prejudicial publicity" than directly at the media which published it. The case was given banner headline treatment not only in Cleveland, where the drama unfolded, but in media across the nation. The significance of the Sheppard decision and its influence upon press-court relations still is being felt. Sheppard, in a second trial in 1966, was acquitted. The signifi-cant and readable opinion of Justice Clark follows in its entirety except for case reference numbers.

SHEPPARD V. MAXWELL
384 U.S. 333 (1966)

MR. JUSTICE CLARK *delivered the opinion of the Court.*

This federal *habeas corpus* application involves the question whether Sheppard was deprived of a fair trial in his state conviction for the second-degree murder of his wife because of the trial judge's failure to protect Sheppard sufficiently from the massive, pervasive and prejudicial publicity that attended his prosecution. The United States District Court held that he was not afforded a fair trial and granted the writ subject to the State's right to put Sheppard to trial again, 231 F. Supp. 37 (D.C.S.D. Ohio 1964). The Court of Appeals for the Sixth Circuit reversed by a divided vote, 346 F. 2d 707 (1965). We granted *certiorari*, 382 U.S. 916 (1966). We have concluded that Sheppard did not receive a fair trial consistent with the Due Process Clause of the Fourteenth Amendment and, therefore, reverse the judgment.

I

Marilyn Sheppard, petitioner's pregnant wife, was bludgeoned to death in the upstairs bedroom of their lakeshore home in Bay Village, Ohio, a suburb of Cleveland. On the day of the tragedy, July 4, 1954, Sheppard pieced together for several local officials the following story: He and his wife had entertained neighborhood friends, the Aherns, on the previous evening at their home. After dinner they watched television in the living room. Sheppard became drowsy and dozed off to sleep on a couch. Later, Marilyn partially awoke him saying that she was going to bed. The next thing he remembers was hearing his wife cry out in the early morning hours. He hurried upstairs and in the dim light from the hall saw a "form" standing next to his wife's bed. As he struggled with the "form" he was struck on the back of the neck and rendered unconscious. On regaining his senses he found himself on the floor next to his wife's bed. He raised up, looked at her, took her pulse and "felt that she was gone." He then went to his son's room and found him unmolested. Hearing a noise he hurried downstairs. He saw a "form" running out the door and pursued it to the lake shore. He grappled with it on the beach and again lost consciousness. Upon his recovery he was laying face down with the lower portion of his body in the water. He returned to his home, checked the pulse on his wife's neck, and "determined or thought that she was gone." He then went downstairs and called a neighbor, Mayor Houk of Bay Village. The Mayor and his wife came over at once, found Sheppard slumped in an easy chair downstairs and asked, "What happened?" Sheppard replied: "I don't know but somebody ought to try to do something for Marilyn." Mrs. Houk immediately went up to the bedroom. The Mayor told Sheppard, "Get hold of yourself. Can you tell me what happened?" Sheppard then related the above-outlined events. After Mrs. Houk discovered the body, the Mayor called the local police, Dr. Richard Sheppard, petitioner's brother, and Aherns. The local police were the first to arrive. They in turn notified the Coroner and Cleveland police. Richard Sheppard then arrived, determined that Marilyn was dead, examined his brother's injuries, and removed him to the nearby clinic operated by the Sheppard family.

When the Coroner, the Cleveland police and other officials arrived, the house and surrounding area were thoroughly searched, the rooms of the house were photographed, and many persons, including the Houks and the Aherns, were interrogated. The Sheppard home and premises were taken into "protective custody" and remained so until after the trial.

From the outset officials focused suspicion on Sheppard. After a search of the house and premises on the morning of the tragedy, Dr. Gerber, the Coroner, is reported—and it is undenied—to have told his men, "Well, it is evident the doctor did this, so let's go get the confession out of him." He proceeded to interrogate and examine Sheppard while the latter was under sedation in his hospital room. On the same occasion, the Coroner was given the clothes Sheppard wore at the time of the tragedy together with the personal items in them. Later that afternoon Chief Eaton and two Cleveland police officers interrogated Sheppard at some length, confronting him with evidence and demanding explanations. Asked by Officer Shotke to take a lie detector test, Sheppard said he would if it were reliable. Shotke replied that it was "infallible" and "you might as well tell us all about it now." At the end of the interrogation Shotke told Sheppard: "I think you killed your wife." Still later in the same afternoon a physician sent by the Coroner was permitted to make a detailed examination of Sheppard. Until the Coroner's inquest on July 22, at which time he was subpoenaed, Sheppard made himself available for frequent and extended questioning without the presence of an attorney.

On July 7, the day of Marilyn Sheppard's funeral, a newspaper story appeared in which Assistant County Attorney Mahon—later the chief prosecutor of Sheppard—sharply criticized the refusal of the Sheppard family to permit his immediate questioning. From there on headline stories repeatedly stressed Sheppard's lack of cooperation with the police and other officials. Under the headline "Testify Now In Death, Bay Doctor Is Ordered," one story described a visit by Coroner Gerber and four police officers to the hospital on July 8. When Sheppard insisted that his lawyer be present, the Coroner wrote out a subpoena and served it on him. Sheppard then agreed to submit to questioning without counsel and the subpoena was torn up. The officers questioned him for several hours. On July 9, Sheppard, at the request of the Coroner, re-enacted the tragedy at his home before the Coroner, police officers, and a group of newsmen, who apparently were invited by the Coroner. The home was locked so that Sheppard was obliged to wait outside until the Coroner arrived. Sheppard's performance was reported in detail by the news media along with photographs. The newspapers also played up Sheppard's refusal to take a lie detector test and "the protective ring" thrown up by his family. Front-page newspaper headlines announced on the same day that "Doctor Balks At Lie Test; Retells Story." A column opposite that story contained an "exclusive" interview with Sheppard headlined: " 'Loved My Wife, She

Loved Me,' Sheppard Tells News Reporters." The next day, another headline story disclosed that Sheppard had "again late yesterday refused to take
a lie detector test" and quoted an Assistant County Attorney as saying that
"at the end of a nine-hour questioning of Dr. Sheppard, I felt he was now
ruling [a test] out completely." But subsequent newspaper articles reported
that the Coroner was still pushing Sheppard for a lie detector test. More
stories appeared when Sheppard would not allow authorities to inject him
with "truth serum."

On the 20th, the "editorial artillery" opened fire with a front-page
charge that somebody is "getting away with murder." The editorial attributed the ineptness of the investigation to "friendships, relationships, hired
lawyers, a husband who ought to have been subjected instantly to the same
third degree to which any person under similar circumstances is subjected. . . ." The following day, July 21, another page-one editorial was
headed: "Why No Inquest? Do It Now, Dr. Gerber." The Coroner called
an inquest the same day and subpoenaed Sheppard. It was staged the next
day in a school gymnasium; the Coroner presided with the County Prosecutor as his advisor and two detectives as bailiffs. In the front of the room
was a long table occupied by reporters, television and radio personnel, and
broadcasting equipment. The hearing was broadcast with live microphones
placed at the Coroner's seat and the witness stand. A swarm of reporters
and photographers attended. Sheppard was brought into the room by police who searched him in full view of several hundred spectators. Sheppard's
counsel were present during the three-day inquest but were not permitted
to participate. When Sheppard's chief counsel attempted to place some
documents in the record, he was forcibly ejected from the room by the
Coroner, who received cheers, hugs, and kisses from ladies in the audience.
Sheppard was questioned for five and one-half hours about his actions on
the night of the murder, his married life, and a love affair with Susan
Hayes. At the end of the hearing the Coroner announced that he "could"
order Sheppard held for the grand jury, but did not do so.

Throughout this period the newspapers emphasized evidence that
tended to incriminate Sheppard and pointed out discrepancies in his statements to authorities. At the same time, Sheppard made many public statements to the press and wrote feature articles asserting his innocence. During
the inquest on July 26, a headline in large type stated: "Kerr [Captain of
the Cleveland Police] Urges Sheppard's Arrest." In the story, Detective
McArthur "disclosed that scientific tests at the Sheppard home have defi-
nitely established that the killer washed off a trail of blood from the murder
bedroom to the downstairs section," a circumstance casting doubt on Sheppard's accounts of the murder. No such evidence was produced at trial. The
newspapers also delved into Sheppard's personal life. Articles stressed his
extra-marital love affairs as a motive for the crime. The newspapers por-

trayed Sheppard as a Lothario, fully explored his relationship with Susan Hayes, and named a number of other women who were allegedly involved with him. The testimony at trial never showed that Sheppard had any illicit relationships besides the one with Susan Hayes.

On July 28, an editorial entitled "Why Don't Police Quiz Top Suspect" demanded that Sheppard be taken to police headquarters. It described him in the following language:

> "Now proved under oath to be a liar, still free to go about his business, shielded by his family, protected by a smart lawyer who has made monkeys of the police and authorities, carrying a gun part of the time, left free to do whatever he pleases. . . ."

A front-page editorial on July 30 asked: "Why Isn't Sam Sheppard in Jail?" It was later titled "Quit Stalling—Bring Him In." After calling Sheppard "the most unusual murder suspect ever seen around these parts" the article said that "[e]xcept for some superficial questioning during Coroner Sam Gerber's inquest he has been scot-free of any official grilling. . . ." It asserted that he was "surrounded by an iron curtain of protection [and] concealment."

That night at 10 o'clock Sheppard was arrested at his father's home on a charge of murder. He was taken to the Bay Village City Hall where hundreds of people, newscasters, photographers and reporters were awaiting his arrival. He was immediately arraigned—having been denied a temporary delay to secure the presence of counsel—and bound over to the grand jury.

The publicity then grew in intensity until his indictment on August 17. Typical of the coverage during this period is a front-page interview entitled: "Dr. Sam: 'I Wish There Was Something I Could Get Off My Chest—but There Isn't.'" Unfavorable publicity included items such as a cartoon of the body of a sphinx with Sheppard's head and the legend below: " 'I Will Do Everything In My Power to Help Solve This Terrible Murder.'—Dr. Sam Sheppard." Headlines announced, *inter alia*, that: "Doctor Evidence is Ready for Jury," "Corrigan Tactics Stall Quizzing," "Sheppard 'Gay Set' Is Revealed By Houk," "Blood Is Found In Garage," "New Murder Evidence Is Found, Police Claim," "Dr. Sam Faces Quiz At Jail On Marilyn's Fear Of Him." On August 18, an article appeared under the headline "Dr. Sam Writes His Own Story." And reproduced across the entire front page was a portion of the typed statement signed by Sheppard: "I am not guilty of the murder of my wife, Marilyn. How could I, who have been trained to help people and devote my life to saving life, commit such a terrible and revolting crime?" We do not detail the coverage further. There are five volumes filled with similar clippings from each of the three Cleveland newspapers covering the period from the murder until Sheppard's conviction in December 1954. The record includes no excerpts from newscasts on radio and television but since space was reserved in the courtroom for these media we assume that their coverage was equally large.

II

With this background the case came on for trial two weeks before the November general election at which the chief prosecutor was a candidate for municipal judge and the presiding judge, Judge Blythin, was a candidate to succeed himself. Twenty-five days before the case was set, a list of 75 veniremen were called as prospective jurors. This list, including the addresses of each venireman, was published in all three Cleveland newspapers. As a consequence, anonymous letters and telephone calls, as well as calls from friends, regarding the impending prosecution were received by all of the prospective jurors. The selection of the jury began on October 18, 1954.

The courtroom in which the trial was held measured 26 by 48 feet. A long temporary table was set up inside the bar, in back of the single counsel table. It ran the width of the courtroom, parallel to the bar railing, with one end less than three feet from the jury box. Approximately 20 representatives of newspapers and wire services were assigned seats at this table by the court. Behind the bar railing there were four rows of benches. These seats were likewise assigned by the court for the entire trial. The first row was occupied by representatives of television and radio stations, and the second and third rows by reporters from out-of-town newspapers and magazines. One side of the last row, which accommodated 14 people, was assigned to Sheppard's family and the other to Marilyn's. The public was permitted to fill vacancies in this row on special passes only. Representatives of the news media also used all the rooms on the courtroom floor, including the room where cases were ordinarily called and assigned for trial. Private telephone lines and telegraphic equipment were installed in these rooms so that reports from the trial could be speeded to the papers. Station WSRS was permitted to set up broadcasting facilities on the third floor of the courthouse next door to the jury room, where the jury rested during recesses in the trial and deliberated. Newscasts were made from this room throughout the trial, and while the jury reached its verdict.

On the sidewalk and steps in front of the courthouse, television and newsreel cameras were occasionally used to take motion pictures of the participants in the trial, including the jury and the judge. Indeed, one television broadcast carried a staged interview of the judge as he entered the courthouse. In the corridors outside the courtroom there was a host of photographers and television personnel with flash cameras, portable lights and motion picture cameras. This group photographed the prospective jurors during selection of the jury. After the trial opened, the witnesses, counsel, and jurors were photographed and televised whenever they entered or left the courtroom. Sheppard was brought to the courtroom about 10 minutes before each session began; he was surrounded by reporters and extensively photographed for the newspapers and television. A rule of court prohibited picture-taking in the courtroom during the actual sessions of the court, but no restraints were put on photographers during recesses, which were taken once each morning and afternoon, with a longer period for lunch.

All of these arrangements with the news media and their massive coverage of the trial continued during the entire nine weeks of the trial. The courtroom remained crowded to capacity with representatives of news media. Their movement in and out of the courtroom often caused so much confusion that, despite the loud speaker system installed in the courtroom, it was difficult for the witnesses and counsel to be heard. Furthermore, the reporters clustered within the bar of the small courtroom made confidential talk among Sheppard and his counsel almost impossible during the proceedings. They frequently had to leave the courtroom to obtain privacy. And many times when counsel wished to raise a point with the judge out of the hearing of the jury it was necessary to move to the judge's chambers. Even then, news media representatives so packed the judge's anteroom that counsel could hardly return from the chambers to the courtroom. The reporters vied with each other to find out what counsel and the judge had discussed, and often these matters later appeared in newspapers accessible to the jury.

The daily record of the proceedings was made available to the newspapers and the testimony of each witness was printed *verbatim* in the local editions, along with objections of counsel, and rulings by the judge. Pictures of Sheppard, the judge, counsel, pertinent witnesses, and the jury often accompanied the daily newspaper and television accounts. At times the newspapers published photographs of exhibits introduced at the trial, and the rooms of Sheppard's house were featured along with relevant testimony.

The jurors themselves were constantly exposed to the news media. Every juror, except one, testified at *voir dire* to reading about the case in the Cleveland papers or to having heard broadcasts about it. Seven of the 12 jurors who rendered the verdict had one or more Cleveland papers delivered in their homes; the remaining jurors were not interrogated on the point. Nor were there questions as to radios or television sets in the talesmen's homes, but we must assume that most of them owned such conveniences. As the selection of the jury progressed, individual pictures of prospective members appeared daily. During the trial, pictures of the jury appeared over 40 times in the Cleveland papers alone. The court permitted photographers to take pictures of the jury in the box, and individual pictures of the members in the jury room. One newspaper ran pictures of the jurors at the Sheppard home when they went there to view the scene of the murder. Another paper featured the home life of an alternate juror. The day before the verdict was rendered—while the jurors were at lunch and sequestered by two bailiffs—the jury was separated into two groups to pose for photographs which appeared in the newspapers.

III

We now reach the conduct of the trial. While the intense publicity continued unabated, it is sufficient to relate only the more flagrant episodes:

1. On October 9, 1954, nine days before the case went to trial, an editorial in one of the newspapers criticized defense counsel's random poll of people on the streets as to their opinion of Sheppard's guilt or innocence in an effort to use the resulting statistics to show the necessity for change of *venue*. The article said the survey "smacks of mass jury tampering," called on defense counsel to drop it, and stated that the bar association should do something about it. It characterized the poll as "non-judicial, non-legal, and nonsense." The article was called to the attention of the court but no action was taken.

2. On the second day of *voir dire* examination a debate was staged and broadcast live over WHK radio. The participants, newspaper reporters, accused Sheppard's counsel of throwing roadblocks in the way of the prosecution and asserted that Sheppard conceded his guilt by hiring a prominent criminal lawyer. Sheppard's counsel objected to this broadcast and requested a continuance, but the judge denied the motion. When counsel asked the court to give some protection from such events, the judge replied that "WHK doesn't have much coverage," and that "[a]fter all, we are not trying this case by radio or in newspapers or any other means. We confine ourselves seriously to it in this courtroom and do the very best we can."

3. While the jury was being selected, a two-inch headline asked: "But Who Will Speak for Marilyn?" The front-page story spoke of the "perfect face" of the accused. "Study that face as long as you want. Never will you get from it a hint of what might be the answer. . . ." The two brothers of the accused were described as "Prosperous, poised. His two sisters-in-law. Smart, chic, well-groomed. His elderly father. Courtly, reserved. A perfect type for the patriarch of a staunch clan." The author then noted Marilyn Sheppard was "still off stage," and that she was an only child whose mother died when she was very young and whose father had no interest in the case. But the author—through quotes from Detective Chief James McArthur—assured readers that the prosecution's exhibits would speak for Marilyn. "Her story," McArthur stated, "will come into this courtroom through our witnesses." The article ends:

> Then you realize how what and who is missing from the perfect setting will be supplied.
> How in the Big Case justice will be done.

Justice to Sam Sheppard.
And to Marilyn Sheppard.

4. As has been mentioned, the jury viewed the scene of the murder on the first day of the trial. Hundreds of reporters, cameramen and onlookers were there, and one representative of the news media was permitted to accompany the jury while they inspected the Sheppard home. The time of the jury's visit was revealed so far in advance that one of the newspapers was able to rent a helicopter and fly over the house taking pictures of the jurors on their tour.

5. On November 19, a Cleveland police officer gave testimony that tended to contradict details in the written statement Sheppard made to the Cleveland police. Two days later, in a broadcast heard over Station WHK in Cleveland, Robert Considine likened Sheppard to a perjuror and compared the episode to Alger Hiss' confrontation with Whittaker Chambers. Though defense counsel asked the judge to question the jury to ascertain how many heard the broadcast, the court refused to do so. The judge also overruled the motion for continuance based on the same ground, saying:

> Well, I don't know, we can't stop people, in any event, listening to it. It is a matter of free speech, and the court can't control everybody. . . . We are not going to harass the jury every morning. . . . It is getting to the point where if we do it every morning, we are suspecting the jury. I have confidence in this jury. . . .

6. On November 24, a story appeared under an eight-column headline: "Sam Called A 'Jekyll-Hyde' By Marilyn, Cousin To Testify." It related that Marilyn had recently told friends that Sheppard was a "Dr. Jekyll and Mr. Hyde" character. No such testimony was ever produced at the trial. The story went on to announce: "The prosecution has a 'bombshell witness' on tap who will testify to Dr. Sam's display of fiery temper—countering the defense claim that the defendant is a gentle physician with an even disposition." Defense counsel made motions for change of venue, continuance and mistrial, but they were denied. No action was taken by the court.

7. When the trial was in its seventh week, Walter Winchell broadcasted over WXEL television and WJW radio that Carole Beasley, who was under arrest in New York City for robbery, had stated that, as Sheppard's mistress, she had borne him a child. The defense asked that the jury be queried on the broadcast. Two jurors admitted in open court that they had heard it. The judge asked each: "Would that have any effect upon your judgment?" Both replied, "No." This was accepted by the judge as sufficient; he merely asked the jury to "pay no attention whatever to that type of scavenging. . . . Let's confine ourselves to this courtroom, if you please." In answer to the motion for mistrial, the judge said:

Well, even so, Mr. Corrigan, how are you ever going to prevent those things, in any event? I don't justify them at all. I think it is outrageous, but in a sense, it is outrageous even if there were no trial here. The trial has nothing to do with it in the Court's mind, as far as its outrage is concerned, but—

Mr. Corrigan: I don't know what effect it had on the mind of any of these jurors, and I can't find out unless inquiry is made.

The Court: How would you ever, in any jury, avoid that kind of a thing?

8. On December 9, while Sheppard was on the witness stand he testified that he had been mistreated by Cleveland detectives after his arrest. Although he was not at the trial, Captain Kerr of the Homicide Bureau issued a press statement denying Sheppard's allegations which appeared under the headline: " 'Bare-faced Liar,' Kerr Says of Sam." Captain Kerr never appeared as a witness at the trial.

9. After the case was submitted to the jury, it was sequestered for its deliberations, which took five days and four nights. After the verdict, defense counsel ascertained that the jurors had been allowed to make telephone calls to their homes every day while they were sequestered at the hotel. Although the telephones had been removed from the jurors' rooms, the jurors were permitted to use the phones in the bailiff's rooms. The calls were placed by the jurors themselves; no record was kept of the jurors who made calls, the telephone numbers or the parties called. The bailiffs sat in the room where they could hear only the jurors' end of the conversation. The court had not instructed the bailiffs to prevent such calls. By a subsequent motion, defense counsel urged that this ground alone warranted a new trial, but the motion was overruled and no evidence was taken on the question.

IV

The principle that justice cannot survive behind walls of silence has long been reflected in the "Anglo-American distrust for secret trials." *In re Oliver*. A responsible press has always been regarded as the handmaiden of effective judicial administration, especially in the criminal field. Its function in this regard is documented by an impressive record of service over several centuries. The press does not simply publish information about trials but guards against the miscarriage of justice by subjecting the police, prosecutors, and judicial processes to extensive public scrutiny and criticism. This Court has, therefore, been unwilling to place any direct limitations on the freedom traditionally exercised by the news media for "[w]hat transpires in the court room is public property." *Craig v. Harney*. The "unqualified prohibitions laid down by the framers were intended to give to liberty of the press . . . the broadest scope that could be countenanced in an orderly society." *Bridges v. California.* And where there was "no threat or menace to the integrity of the trial," *Craig v. Harney,* we have consistently required that the press have a free hand, even though we sometimes deplored its sensationalism.

But the Court has also pointed out that "[l]egal trials are not like elections, to be won through the use of the meeting-hall, the radio, and the newspaper." *Bridges v. California.* And the Court has insisted that no one be punished for a crime without "a charge fairly made and fairly tried in a public tribunal free of prejudice, passion, excitement, and tyrannical power." *Chambers v. Florida.* "Freedom of discussion should be given the widest range compatible with the essential requirement of the fair and orderly administration of justice." *Pennekamp v. Florida.* But it must not be allowed to divert the trial from the "very purpose of a court system . . . to adjudicate controversies, both criminal and civil, in the calmness and solemnity of the courtroom according to legal procedures." *Cox v. Louisiana* (Black, J., dissenting). Among these "legal procedures" is the requirement that the jury's verdict be based on evidence received in open court, not from outside sources. Thus, in *Marshall v. United States,* we set aside a federal conviction where the jurors were exposed "through news accounts" to information that was not admitted at trial. We held that the prejudice from such material "may indeed be greater" than when it is part of the prosecution's evidence "for it is then not tempered by protective procedures." At the same time, we did not consider dispositive the statement of each juror "that he would not be influenced by the news articles, that he could decide the case only on the evidence of record, and that he felt no prejudice against petitioner as a result of the articles." Likewise, in *Irvin v. Dowd,* even though each juror indicated that he could render an impartial verdict despite exposure to prejudicial newspaper articles, we set aside the conviction holding:

> With his life at stake, it is not requiring too much that petitioner be tried in an atmosphere undisturbed by so huge a wave of public passion. . . .

The undeviating rule of this Court was expressed by Mr. Justice Holmes over a half a century ago in *Patterson v. Colorado:*

> The theory of our system is that the conclusions to be reached in a case will be induced only by evidence and argument in open court, and not by any outside influence, whether of private talk or public print.

Moreover, "the burden of showing essential unfairness . . . as a demonstrable reality," *Adams v. United States ex rel. McCann,* need not be undertaken when television has exposed the community "repeatedly and in depth to the spectacle of [the accused] personally confessing in detail to the crimes with which he was later to be charged." *Rideau v. Louisiana.* In *Turner v. Louisiana* two key witnesses were deputy sheriffs who doubled as jury shepherds during the trial. The deputies swore that they had not talked to the jurors about the case, but the Court nonetheless held that,

> even if it could be assumed that the deputies never did discuss the case directly with any members of the jury, it would be blinking reality not to recognize the extreme prejudice inherent in this continual association. . . .

Only last Term in *Estes v. Texas,* we set aside a conviction despite the absence of any showing of prejudice. We said there:

> It is true that in most cases involving claims of due process deprivations we require a showing of identifiable prejudice to the accused. Nevertheless, at times a procedure employed by the State involves such a probability that prejudice will result that it is deemed inherently lacking in due process.

And we cited with approval the language of Mr. Justice Black for the Court in *In re Murchison* that "our system of law has always endeavored to prevent even the probability of unfairness."

V

It is clear that the totality of circumstances in this case also warrant such an approach. Unlike Estes, Sheppard was not granted a change of venue to a locale away from where the publicity originated; nor was his jury sequestered. The *Estes* jury saw none of the television broadcasts from the courtroom. On the contrary, the Sheppard jurors were subjected to newspaper, radio and television coverage of the trial while not taking part in the proceedings. They were allowed to go their separate ways outside of the courtroom, without adequate directions not to read or listen to anything concerning the case. The judge's "admonitions" at the beginning of the trial are representative:

> I would suggest to you and caution you that you do not read any newspapers during the progress of this trial, that you do not listen to radio comments nor watch or listen to television comments, insofar as this case is concerned. You will feel very much better as the trial proceeds. . . . I am sure that we shall all feel very much better if we do not indulge in any newspaper reading or listening to any comments whatever about the matter while the case is in progress. After it is all over, you can read it all to your heart's content. . . .

At intervals during the trial, the judge simply repeated his "suggestions" and "requests" that the jury not expose themselves to comment upon the case. Moreover, the jurors were thrust into the role of celebrities by the judge's failure to insulate them from reporters and photographers. The numerous pictures of the jurors, with their addresses, which appeared in the newspapers before and during the trial itself exposed them to expressions of opinion from both cranks and friends. The fact that anonymous letters had been received by prospective jurors should have made the judge aware that this publicity seriously threatened the jurors' privacy.

The press coverage of the Estes trial was not nearly as massive and pervasive as the attention given by the Cleveland newspapers and broadcasting stations to Sheppard's prosecution. Sheppard stood indicted for the murder of his wife; the State was demanding the death penalty. For months the virulent publicity about Sheppard and the murder had made the case notorious. Charges and countercharges were aired in the news media besides those for which Sheppard was called to trial. In addition, only three months before trial, Sheppard was examined for more than five hours without counsel during a three-day inquest which ended in a public brawl. The inquest was televised live from a high school gymnasium seating hundreds of people. Furthermore, the trial began two weeks before a hotly contested election at which both Chief Prosecutor Mahon and Judge Blythin were candidates for judgeships.

While we cannot say that Sheppard was denied due process by the judge's refusal to take precautions against the influence of pretrial publicity alone, the court's later rulings must be considered against the setting in which the trial was held. In light of this background, we believe that the arrangements made by the judge with the news media caused Sheppard to be deprived of that "judicial serenity and calm to which [he] was entitled." *Estes v. Texas.* The fact is that bedlam reigned at the courthouse during the trial and newsmen took over practically the entire courtroom, hounding most of the participants in the trial, especially Sheppard. At a temporary table within a few feet of the jury box and counsel table sat some 20 reporters staring at Sheppard and taking notes. The erection of a press table for reporters inside the bar is unprecedented. The bar of the court is reserved for counsel, providing them a safe place in which to keep papers and exhibits, and to confer privately with client and co-counsel. It is designed to protect the witness and the jury from any distractions, intrusions or influences, and to permit bench discussions of the judge's rulings away from the hearing of the public and the jury. Having assigned almost all of the available seats in the courtroom to the news media the judge lost his ability to supervise that environment. The movement of the reporters in and out of the courtroom caused frequent confusion and disruption of the trial. And the record reveals constant commotion within the bar. Moreover, the judge gave the throng of newsmen gathered in the corridors of the courthouse absolute free rein. Participants in the trial, including the jury, were forced to run a gantlet of reporters and photographers each time they entered or left the courtroom. The total lack of consideration for the privacy of the jury was demonstrated by the assignment to a broadcasting station of space next to the jury room on the floor above the courtroom, as well as the fact that jurors were allowed to make telephone calls during their five-day deliberation.

VI

There can be no question about the nature of the publicity which surrounded Sheppard's trial. We agree, as did the Court of Appeals, with the findings in Judge Bell's opinion for the Ohio Supreme Court:

> Murder and mystery, society, sex and suspense were combined in this case in such a manner as to intrigue and captivate the public fancy to a degree perhaps unparalleled in recent annals. Throughout the preindictment investigation, the subsequent legal skirmishes and the nine-week trial, circulation-conscious editors catered to the insatiable interest of the American public in the bizarre. . . . In this atmosphere of a "Roman holiday" for the news media, Sam Sheppard stood trial for his life.

Indeed, every court that has considered this case, save the court that tried it, has deplored the manner in which the news media inflamed and prejudiced the public.

Much of the material printed or broadcast during the trial was never heard from the witness stand, such as the charges that Sheppard had purposely impeded the murder investigation and must be guilty since he had hired a prominent criminal lawyer; that Sheppard was a perjurer; that he had sexual relations with numerous women; that his slain wife had characterized him as a "Jekyll-Hyde"; that he was "a bare-faced liar" because of his testimony as to police treatment; and, finally, that a woman convict claimed Sheppard to be the father of her illegitimate child. As the trial progressed, the newspapers summarized and interpreted the evidence, devoting particular attention to the material that incriminated Sheppard, and often drew unwarranted inferences from testimony. At one point, a front-page picture of Mrs. Sheppard's blood-stained pillow was published after being "doctored" to show more clearly an alleged imprint of a surgical instrument.

Nor is there doubt that this deluge of publicity reached at least some of the jury. On the only occasion that the jury was queried, two jurors admitted in open court to hearing the highly inflammatory charge that a prison inmate claimed Sheppard as the father of her illegitimate child. Despite the extent and nature of the publicity to which the jury was exposed during trial, the judge refused defense counsel's other requests that the jury be asked whether they had read or heard specific prejudicial comment about the case, including the incidents we have previously summarized. In these circumstances, we can assume that some of this material reached members of the jury.

VII

The court's fundamental error is compounded by the holding that it lacked power to control the publicity about the trial. From the very inception of the proceedings the judge announced that neither he nor anyone else could restrict prejudicial news accounts. And he reiterated this view on numerous occasions. Since he viewed the news media as his target, the judge never considered other means that are often utilized to reduce the appearance of prejudicial material and to protect the jury from outside influence. We conclude that these procedures would have been sufficient to guarantee Sheppard a fair trial and so do not consider what sanctions might be available against a recalcitrant press nor the charges of bias now made against the state trial judge.

The carnival atmosphere at trial could easily have been avoided since the courtroom and courthouse premises are subject to the control of the court. As we stressed in *Estes,* the presence of the press at judicial proceedings must be limited when it is apparent that the accused might otherwise be prejudiced or disadvantaged. Bearing in mind the massive pretrial publicity, the judge should have adopted stricter rules governing the use of the courtroom by newsmen, as Sheppard's counsel requested. The number of reporters in the courtroom itself could have been limited at the first sign that their presence would disrupt the trial. They certainly should not have been placed inside the bar. Furthermore, the judge should have more closely regulated the conduct of newsmen in the courtroom. For instance, the judge belatedly asked them not to handle and photograph trial exhibits laying on the counsel table during recesses.

Secondly, the court should have insulated the witnesses. All of the newspapers and radio stations apparently interviewed prospective witnesses at will, and in many instances disclosed their testimony. A typical example was the publication of numerous statements by Susan Hayes, before her appearance in court, regarding her love affair with Sheppard. Although the witnesses were barred from the courtroom during the trial the full *verbatim* testimony was available to them in the press. This completely nullified the judge's imposition of the rule.

Thirdly, the court should have made some effort to control the release of leads, information, and gossip to the press by police officers, witnesses, and the counsel for both sides. Much of the information thus disclosed was inaccurate, leading to groundless rumors and confusion. That the judge was aware of his responsibility in this respect may be seen from his warning to Steve Sheppard, the accused's brother, who had apparently made public statements in an attempt to discredit testimony for the prosecution. The judge made this statement in the presence of the jury:

Now, the court wants to say a word. That he was told—he was not read anything about it at all—but he was informed that Dr. Steve Sheppard, who has been granted the privilege of remaining in the courtroom during the trial, has been trying the case in the newspapers and making rather uncomplimentary comments about the testimony of the witnesses for the State.

Let it be now understood that if Dr. Steve Sheppard wishes to use the newspapers to try his case while we are trying it here, he will be barred from remaining in the courtroom during the progress of the trial if he is to be a witness in the case.

The Court appreciates he cannot deny Steve Sheppard the right of free speech, but he can deny him the . . . privilege of being in the courtroom, if he wants to avail himself of that method during the progress of the trial.

Defense counsel immediately brought to the court's attention the tremendous amount of publicity in the Cleveland press that "misrepresented entirely the testimony" in the case. Under such circumstances, the judge should have at least warned the newspapers to check the accuracy of their accounts. And it is obvious that the judge should have further sought to alleviate this problem by imposing control over the statements made to the news media by counsel, witnesses, and especially the Coroner and police officers. The prosecution repeatedly made evidence available to the news media which was never offered in the trial. Much of the "evidence" disseminated in this fashion was clearly inadmissible. The exclusion of such evidence in court is rendered meaningless when a news media makes it available to the public. For example, the publicity about Sheppard's refusal to take a lie detector test came directly from police officers and the Coroner. The story that Sheppard had been called a "Jekyll-Hyde" personality by his wife was attributed to a prosecution witness. No such testimony was given. The further report that there was "a 'bombshell witness' on tap" who would testify as to Sheppard's "fiery temper" could only have emanated from the prosecution. Moreover, the newspapers described in detail clues that had been found by the police, but not put into the record.

The fact that many of the prejudicial news items can be traced to the prosecution, as well as the defense, aggravates the judge's failure to take any action. Effective control of these sources—concededly within the court's power—might well have prevented the divulgence of inaccurate information, rumors, and accusations that made up much of the inflammatory publicity, at least after Sheppard's indictment.

More specifically, the trial court might well have proscribed extra-judicial statements by any lawyer, party, witness, or court official which divulged prejudicial matters, such as the refusal of Sheppard to submit to interrogation or take any lie detector tests; any statement made by Sheppard to officials; the identity of prospective witnesses or their probable testimony; any belief in guilt or innocence; or like statements concerning the merits of the case. See *State v. Van Duyne*, in which the court interpreted Canon 20 of the American Bar Association's Canons of Professional Ethics to prohibit such statements. Being advised of the great public interest in the case, the mass coverage of the press, and the potential prejudicial impact of publicity, the court could also have requested the appropriate city and county officials to promulgate a regulation with respect to dissemination of information about the case by their employees. In addition, reporters who wrote or broadcasted prejudicial stories, could have been warned as to the impropriety of publishing material not introduced in the proceedings. The judge was put on notice of such events by defense counsel's complaint about the WHK broadcast on the second day of trial. In this manner, Sheppard's right to a trial free from outside interference would have been given added protection without corresponding curtailment of the news media. Had the judge, the other officers of the court, and the police placed the interest of justice first, the news media would have soon learned to be content with the task of reporting the case as it unfolded in the courtroom—not pieced together from extra-judicial statements.

From the cases coming here we note that unfair and prejudicial news comment on pending trials has become increasingly prevalent. Due process requires that the accused receive a trial by an impartial jury free from outside influences. Given the pervasiveness of modern communications and the difficulty of effacing prejudicial publicity from the minds of the jurors, the trial courts must take strong measures to ensure that the balance is never weighed against the accused. And appellate tribunals have the duty to make an independent evaluation of the circumstances. Of course, there is nothing that proscribes the press from reporting events that transpire in the courtroom. But where there is a reasonable likelihood that prejudicial news prior to trial will prevent a fair trial, the judge should continue the case until the threat abates, or transfer it to another county not so permeated with publicity. In addition, sequestration of the jury was something the judge should have raised *sua sponte* with counsel. If publicity during the proceedings threatens the fairness of the trial, a new trial should be ordered. But we must remember that reversals are but palliatives; the cure lies in those remedial measures that will prevent the prejudice at its inception. The courts must take such steps by rule and regulation that will protect their processes from prejudicial outside interferences. Neither prosecutors, counsel for defense, the accused, witnesses, court staff nor enforcement officers coming under the jurisdiction of the court should be permitted to frustrate its function. Collaboration between counsel and the press as to information affecting the fairness of a criminal trial is not only subject to regulation, but is highly censurable and worthy of disciplinary measures.

Since the state trial judge did not fulfill his duty to protect Sheppard from the inherently prejudicial publicity which saturated the community and to control disruptive influences in the courtroom, we must reverse the denial of the *habeas* petition. The case is remanded to the District Court with instructions to issue the writ and order that Sheppard be released from custody unless the State puts him to its charges again within a reasonable time.

It is so ordered.

CHAPTER 11

TRIAL BY TELEVISION

The presence of cameras in the courtroom has been debated since the 1935 trial of Richard Bruno Hauptmann on charges of kidnapping the baby of Charles A. Lindbergh. Judges generally have forbidden the use of cameras, following the guidance of the American Bar Association's Canon 35, adopted soon after the Hauptmann trial. The ABA argues that cameras tend to lessen the essential dignity of the court and its deliberations. Only Colorado and Texas have not been firm in adhering to the Canon 35 prohibition.

Arguments in favor of allowing cameras to record the courtroom scene include: 1) the public's right to know, 2) the constitutional guarantees of a free press, 3) the camera and resulting pictures are merely extensions of the courtroom's walls, 4) the defendant's right to a public trial, 5) the several experiments which have shown no loss of courtroom decorum when cameras have been used surreptitiously, 6) the technical improvements including miniaturization of equipment and fast film which uses natural light and 7) the lack of firm evidence that the presence of cameras is harmful to the administration of justice.

Those who argue for continuation and strengthing of a ban on cameras point to the unknown effects, including: 1) the subconscious effect on witnesses or potential witnesses, 2) the possibility of attorney theatrics, 3) the question of the concentration of jury members, 4) the microscopic probe of the camera which tends to focus on an instant out of context and in closeup, 5) the tendency for the photographer to focus on the unusual, 6) the temptation to play up the sensational rather than the significant, 7) the possibility with television of commercial interjections and 8) the general lessening of the basic dignity of the proceedings.

The fundamental question, of course, is whether justice tends to blur

on film and on the screen. And this essential question has not been adequately answered, though the prohibitive view of the ABA generally has
been opposed by professional journalism organizations. Still, there has been
serious doubt expressed over the ability to secure a fair trial for Lee Harvey
Oswald, the accused assassin of President Kennedy, who in turn was slain
before live television cameras as millions watched.

In its first opportunity to speak out on the question of television in
the courtroom, the Supreme Court in 1965 could not reach an opinion of
the Court relative to the question of cameras in the courtroom per se,
though it did decide by a 5-4 decision that Billie Sol Estes did not receive
a fair trial because of television. The future of courtroom television was
left clouded, however, when Justice Stewart announced that his vote (with
the majority) stood for the Estes trial only and that it was not to be taken
as a vote against the television of all future trials.

The Court did, however, speak with more clarity in the case of a televised pre-trial interview in Rideau v. Louisiana, which follows. Future questions almost certainly will come before the Court regarding the role of
cameras in the courtroom. Both the press and the bar will have more than a
passing interest in the decisions.

The role of a pre-trial television confession first came under Supreme
Court scrutiny with the appeal of Wilbert Rideau, charged in 1961 with
armed robbery, kidnapping and murder. Justice Stewart, in his majority
opinion, details the facts leading to the Court's findings. It was held that
Rideau was denied due process of law because the trial court failed to grant
a change of venue. The pre-trial televised "interview," which was given repeated exposure to a substantial segment of the community, contained a
personal confession of the crimes with which Rideau was later to be
charged. Justice Clark, who was joined by Justice Harlan, dissented by
claiming there was no evidence that the televised confession did in fact
result in an unfair trial for the defendant.

RIDEAU V. LOUISIANA
373 U.S. 723 (1963)

MR. JUSTICE STEWART delivered the opinion of the Court.

On the evening of February 16, 1961, a man robbed a bank in Lake
Charles, Louisiana, kidnapped three of the bank's employees, and killed
one of them. A few hours later the petitioner, Wilbert Rideau, was apprehended by the police and lodged in the Calcasieu Parish jail in Lake
Charles. The next morning a moving picture film with a sound track was
made of an "interview" in the jail between Rideau and the Sheriff of Calcasieu Parish. This "interview" lasted approximately 20 minutes. It con-

sisted of interrogation by the sheriff and admissions by Rideau that he had perpetrated the bank robbery, kidnapping, and murder. Later the same day the filmed "interview" was broadcast over a television station in Lake Charles, and some 24,000 people in the community saw and heard it on television. The sound film was again shown on television the next day to an estimated audience of 53,000 people. The following day the film was again broadcast by the same television station, and this time approximately 29,000 people saw and heard the "interview" on their television sets. Calcasieu Parish has a population of approximately 150,000 people.

Some two weeks later, Rideau was arraigned on charges of armed robbery, kidnapping, and murder, and two lawyers were appointed to represent him. His lawyers promptly filed a motion for a change of venue, on the ground that it would deprive Rideau of rights guaranteed to him by the United States Constitution to force him to trial in Calcasieu Parish after the three television broadcasts there of his "interview" with the sheriff. After a hearing, the motion for change of venue was denied, and Rideau was accordingly convicted and sentenced to death on the murder charge in the Calcasieu Parish trial court.

Three members of the jury which convicted him had stated on *voir dire* that they had seen and heard Rideau's televised "interview" with the sheriff on at least one occasion. Two members of the jury were deputy sheriffs of Calcasieu Parish. Rideau's counsel had requested that these jurors be excused for cause, having exhausted all of their peremptory challenges, but these challenges for cause had been denied by the trial judge. The judgment of conviction was affirmed by the Supreme Court of Louisiana. . . .

The record in this case contains as an exhibit the sound film which was broadcast. What the people of Calcasieu Parish saw on their television set was Rideau, in jail, flanked by the sheriff and two state troopers, admitting in detail the commission of the robbery, kidnapping, and murder, in response to leading questions by the sheriff. The record fails to show whose idea it was to make the sound film, and broadcast it over the local television station, but we know from the conceded circumstances that the plan was carried out with the active cooperation and participation of the local law enforcement officers. And certainly no one has suggested that it was Rideau's idea, or even that he was aware of what was going on when the sound film was being made. . . .

The case now before us does not involve physical brutality. The kangaroo court proceedings in this case involved a more subtle but no less real deprivation of due process of law. Under our Constitution's guarantee of due process, a person accused of committing a crime is vouchsafed basic minimal rights. Among these are the right to counsel, the right to plead not guilty, and the right to be tried in a courtroom presided over by a judge. Yet in this case the people of Calcasieu Parish saw and heard, not once but three times, a "trial" of Rideau in a jail, presided over by a sheriff, where there was no lawyer to advise Rideau of his right to stand mute. . . .

MR. JUSTICE CLARK, *with whom Mr. Justice Harlan joins, dissenting.*

. . . Having searched the Court's opinion and the record, I am unable to find any deprivation of due process under the Fourteenth Amendment and I therefore dissent. . . .

Initially, we face an obstacle in determining the pervasiveness of the televised interview, since the circulation of a television program is less susceptible of determination than that of a newspaper. The figures quoted by the Court as representing the number of people who "saw and heard" the interview were given by the Program Director of the television station and represented the typical number of viewers at the times when the interview was broadcast, as determined by a rating service which had conducted a sampling some months previous to the broadcasts. The Director testified that those figures represented "an approximate number and, as I say, there is no way you can prove this because communications is an intangible business. . . ."

The most crucial evidence relates to the composition of the 12-man jury. Of the 12 members of the panel only three had seen the televised interview which had been shown almost two months before the trial. The petitioner does not assert, and the record does not show, that these three testified to holding opinions of petitioner's guilt. . . .

*   *   *

The question of courtroom television was inevitably to come before the Supreme Court. In June of 1965 the Court handed down its first such decision on appeal by Billie Sol Estes, a much publicized Texas financier who was closely associated with Washington politics. He claimed he did not get a fair trial because of the televising and broadcasting of portions of his judicial proceedings. Justice Clark wrote the opinion of the 5-4 majority, which agreed. He was joined by Justices Warren, Douglas, Goldberg, and Harlan. But the broader question of courtroom television in general would have to await another day, for Justice Harlan was specific in pointing out in his concurrence that his agreement with the 5-4 majority applied to the Estes case only (because of Estes' nation-wide prominence) and that he did not rule out the possibility of televising proceedings of lesser notoriety. Interestingly enough, Justice Brennan, issuing a salvo foretelling future discussions pointed out in a separate dissent that only four of the nine justices favored an outright ban on courtroom television. However, Chief Justice Warren in a strongly worded concurrence to the majority opinion argued that courtroom television in a criminal trial did indeed violate the Sixth Amendment for federal courts and the Fourteenth Amendment for state courts. He was joined in this concurrence by Justices Douglas and Goldberg. The final answer, therefore, is yet to come. Estes was convicted in the District Court for the Seventh Judicial District of Texas of swindling. The judgment was affirmed by the Texas Court of Criminal Appeals. Both before and during his trial, he voiced objections to the telecasting and broadcasting of courtroom proceedings. Texas courts did not adhere to Canon 35 of the American Bar Association which recommends a ban on cameras in the courtroom.

ESTES V. TEXAS
381 U.S. 532 (1965)

MR. JUSTICE CLARK *delivered the opinion of the Court.*

The question presented here is whether the petitioner, who stands convicted in the District Court for the Seventh Judicial District of Texas at Tyler for swindling, was deprived of his right under the Fourteenth Amendment to due process by the televising and broadcasting of his trial. Both the trial court and the Texas Court of Criminal Appeals found against the petitioner. We hold to the contrary and reverse his conviction.

While petitioner recites his claim in the framework of Canon 35 of the Judicial Canons of the American Bar Association he does not contend that we should enshrine Canon 35 in the Fourteenth Amendment, but only that the time-honored principles of a fair trial were not followed in his case and that he was thus convicted without due process of law. Canon 35, of course, has of itself no binding effect on the courts but merely expresses the view of the Association in opposition to the broadcasting, televising and photographing of court proceedings. Likewise, Judicial Canon 28 of the Integrated State Bar of Texas, which leaves to the trial judge's sound discretion the telecasting and photographing of court proceedings, is of itself not law. In short, the question here is not the validity of either Canon 35 of the American Bar Association or Canon 28 of the State Bar of Texas, but only whether petitioner was tried in a manner which comports with the due process requirement of the Fourteenth Amendment.

Petitioner's case was originally called for trial on September 24, 1962, in Smith County after a change of venue from Reeves County, some 500 miles west. Massive pretrial publicity totaling 11 volumes of press clippings, which are on file with the Clerk, had given it national notoriety. All available seats in the courtroom were taken and some 30 persons stood in the aisles. However, at that time a defense motion to prevent telecasting, broadcasting by radio and news photography and a defense motion for continuance were presented, and after a two-day hearing the former was denied and the latter granted.

These initial hearings were carried live by both radio and television, and news photography was permitted throughout. The video-tapes of these hearings clearly ilustrate that the picture presented was not one of that judicial serenity and calm to which petitioner was entitled. Indeed, at least 12 cameramen were engaged in the courtroom throughout the hearing taking motion and still pictures and televising the proceedings. Cables and wires were snaked across the courtroom floor, three microphones were on the judge's bench and others were beamed at the jury box and the counsel table. It is conceded that the activities of the television crews and news photographers led to considerable disruption of the hearings. Moreover, veniremen had been summoned and were present in the courtroom during the entire hearing but were later released after petitioner's motion for continuance had been granted. The court also had the names of the witnesses called; some answered but the absence of others led to a continuance of the case until October 22, 1962. It is contended that this two-day pretrial hearing cannot be considered in determining the question before us. We cannot agree. Pretrial can create a major problem for the defendant in a criminal case. Indeed, it may be more harmful than publicity during the trial for it may well set the community opinion as to guilt or innocence. Though the September hearings dealt with motions to prohibit television coverage and to postpone the trial, they are unquestionably relevant to the issue before us. . . .

When the case was called for trial on October 22 the scene had been altered. A booth had been constructed at the back of the courtroom which was painted to blend with the permanent structure of the room. It had an aperture to allow the lens of the cameras an unrestricted view of the courtroom. All television cameras and newsreel photographers were restricted to the area of the booth when shooting film or telecasting.

Because of continual objection, the rules governing live telecasting, as well as radio and still photos, were changed as the exigencies of the situation seemed to require. As a result, live telecasting was prohibited during a great portion of the actual trial. Only the opening and closing arguments of the State, the return of the jury's verdict and its receipt by the trial judge were carried live with sound. Although the order allowed videotapes of the entire proceeding without sound, the cameras operated only intermittently, recording various portions of the trial for broadcast on regularly scheduled newscasts later in the day and evening. At the request of the petitioner, the trial judge prohibited coverage of any kind, still or television, of the defense counsel during their summations to the jury.

Because of the varying restrictions placed on sound and live telecasting the telecasts of the trial were confined largely to film clips shown on the stations' regularly scheduled news programs. The news commentators would use the film of a particular part of the day's trial activities as a backdrop for their reports. Their commentary included excerpts from testimony and the usual reportorial remarks. On one occasion the videotapes of the September hearings were rebroadcast in place of the "late movie." . . .

We start with the proposition that it is a "public trial" that the Sixth Amendment guarantees to the "accused." The purpose of the requirement of a public trial was to guarantee that the accused would be fairly dealt with and not unjustly condemned. History had proven that secret tribunals were effective instruments of oppression. . . .

It is said, however, that the freedoms granted in the First Amendment extend a right to the news media to televise from the courtroom, and that to refuse to honor this privilege is to discriminate between the newspapers and television. This is a misconception of the rights of the press.

The free press has been a mighty catalyst in awakening public interest in governmental affairs, exposing corruption among public officers and employees and generally informing the citizenry of public events and occurrences, including court proceedings. While maximum freedom must be allowed the press in carrying on this important function in a democratic society its exercise must necessarily be subject to the maintenance of absolute fairness in the judicial process. While the state and federal courts have differed over what spectators may be excluded from a criminal trial, the *amici curiae* brief of the National Association of Broadcasters and the Radio Television News Directors Association, says, as indeed it must, that "neither of these two amendments [First and Sixth] speaks of an unlimited right of access to the courtroom on the part of the broadcasting media. . . ." Moreover, they recognize that the "primary concern of all must be the proper administration of justice"; that "the life or liberty of any individual in this land should not be put in jeopardy because of actions of any news media"; and that "the due process requirements in both the Fifth and Fourteenth Amendments and the provisions of the Sixth Amendment require a procedure that will assure a fair trial. . . ."

Nor can the courts be said to discriminate where they permit the newspaper reporter access to the courtroom. The television and radio reporter has the same privilege. All are entitled to the same rights as the general public. The news reporter is not permitted to bring his typewriter or printing press. When the advances in these arts permit reporting by printing press or by television without their present hazards to a fair trial we will have another case.

The State contends that the televising of portions of a criminal trial does not constitute a denial of due process. Its position is that because no prejudice has been shown by the petitioner as resulting from the televising, it is permissible; that claims of "distractions" during the trial due to the physical presence of television are wholly unfounded; and that psychological considerations are for psychologists, not courts, because they are purely hypothetical. It argues further that the public has a right to know what goes on in the courts; that the court has no power to "suppress, edit, or censor events which transpire in proceedings before it," citing *Craig v. Harney*; and that the televising of criminal trials would be enlightening to the public and would promote greater respect for the courts. . . .

It is true that the public has the right to be informed as to what occurs in its courts, but reporters of all media, including television, are always present if they wish to be and are plainly free to report whatever occurs in open court through their respective media. This was settled in *Bridges v. California* and *Pennekamp v. Florida*, which we reaffirm. . . .

As has been said, the chief function of our judicial machinery is to ascertain the truth. The use of television, however, cannot be said to contribute materially to this objective. Rather its use amounts to the injection of an irrelevant factor into court proceedings. In addition experience teaches that there are numerous situations in which it might cause actual unfairness—some so subtle as to defy detection by the accused or control by the judge. We enumerate some in summary:

1. The potential impact of television on the jurors is perhaps of the greatest significance. They are the nerve center of the fact-finding process. It is true that in States like Texas where they are required to be sequestered in trials of this nature the jurors will probably not see any of the proceedings as televised from the courtroom. But the inquiry cannot end there. From the moment the trial judge announces that a case will be televised it becomes a *cause célèbre*. The whole community, including prospective jurors, becomes interested in all the morbid details surrounding it. The approaching trial immediately assumes an important status in the public press and the accused is highly publicized along with the offense with which he is charged. Every juror carries with him into the jury box these solemn facts and thus increases the chance of prejudice that is present in every criminal case. And we must remember that realistically it is only the notorious trial which will be broadcast, because of the necessity for paid sponsorship. The conscious or unconscious effect that this may have on the juror's judgment cannot be evaluated, but experience indicates that it is not only possible but highly probable that it will have a direct bearing on his vote as to guilt or innocence. Where pretrial publicity of all kinds has created intense public feeling which is aggravated by the telecasting or picturing of the trial the televised jurors cannot help but feel the pressures of knowing that friends and neighbors have their eyes upon them. If the community be hostile to an accused a televised juror, realizing that he must return to neighbors who saw the trial themselves, may well be led "not to hold the balance nice, clear and true between the State and the accused. . . ."

Moreover, while it is practically impossible to assess the effect of television on jury attentiveness, those of us who know juries realize the problem of jury "distraction." The State argues this is *de minimis* since the physical disturbances have been eliminated. But we know that distractions are not caused solely by the physical presence of the camera and its telltale red lights. It is the awareness of the fact of telecasting that is felt by the juror throughout the trial. We are all self-conscious and uneasy when being televised. Human nature being what it is, not only will a juror's eyes be fixed on the camera, but also his mind will be preoccupied with the telecasting rather than with the testimony.

Furthermore, in many States the jurors serving in the trial may see the broadcasts of the trial proceedings. . . . [J]urors would return home and turn on the TV if only to see how they appeared upon it. They would also be subjected to re-enactment and emphasis of the selected parts of the proceedings which the requirements of the broadcasters determined would be telecast and would be subconsciously influenced the more by that testimony. Moreover, they would be subjected to the broadcast commentary and criticism and perhaps the well-meant advice of friends, relatives and inquiring strangers who recognized them on the streets.

Finally, new trials plainly would be jeopardized in that potential jurors will often have seen and heard the original trial when it was telecast. Yet viewers may later be called upon to sit in the jury box during the new trial. . . .

2. The quality of the testimony in criminal trials will often be impaired. The impact upon a witness of the knowledge that he is being viewed by a vast audience is simply incalculable. Some may be demoralized and frightened, some cocky and given to overstatement; memories may falter, as with anyone speaking publicly, and accuracy of statement may be severely undermined. Embarrassment may impede the search for the truth, as may a natural tendency toward overdramatization. Furthermore, inquisitive strangers and "cranks" might approach witnesses on the street with jibes, advice or demands for explanation of testimony. There is little wonder that the defendant cannot "prove" the existence of such factors. Yet we all know from experience that they exist.

In addition the invocation of the rule against witnesses is frustrated. In most instances witnesses would be able to go to their homes and view broadcasts of the day's trial proceedings, notwithstanding the fact that they had been admonished not to do so. They could view and hear the testimony of preceding witnesses, and so shape their own testimony as to make its impact crucial. And even in the absence of sound, the influences of such viewing on the attitude of the witness toward testifying, his frame of mind upon taking the stand or his apprehension of withering cross-examination defy objective assessment. Indeed, the mere fact that the trial is to be televised might render witnesses reluctant to appear and thereby impede the trial as well as the discovery of the truth.

While some of the dangers mentioned above are present as well in newspaper coverage of any important trial, the circumstances and extraneous influences intruding upon the solemn decorum of court procedure in the televised trial are far more serious than in cases involving only newspaper coverage.

3. A major aspect of the problem is the additional responsibilities the presence of television places on the trial judge. His job is to make certain that the accused receives a fair trial. This most difficult task requires his undivided attention. Still when television comes into the courtroom he must also supervise it. . . .

But this is not all. There is the initial decision that must be made as to whether the use of television will be permitted. This is perhaps an even more crucial consideration. Our judges are high-minded men and women. But it is difficult to remain oblivious to the pressures that the news media can bring to bear on them both directly and through the shaping of public opinion. Moreover, where one judge in a district or even in a State permits telecasting, the requirement that the others do the same is almost mandatory. Especially is this true where the judge is selected at the ballot box.

4. Finally, we cannot ignore the impact of courtroom television on the defendant. Its presence is a form of mental—if not physical—harassment, resembling a police line-up or the third degree. The inevitable close-ups of his gestures and expressions during the ordeal of his trial might well transgress his personal sensibilities, his dignity, and his ability to concentrate on the proceedings before him—sometimes the difference between life and death—dispassionately, freely and without the distraction of wide public surveillance. A defendant on trial for a specific crime is entitled to his day in court, not in a stadium, or a city or nationwide arena. The heightened public clamor resulting from radio and television coverage will inevitably result in prejudice. Trial by television, is, therefore, foreign to our system. . . .

. . . The sole issue before the court for two days of pretrial hearing was the question now before us. The hearing was televised live and repeated on tape in the same evening, reaching approximately 100,000 viewers. In addition, the courtroom was a mass of wires, television cameras, microphones and photographers. The petitioner, the panel of prospective jurors, who were sworn the second day, the witnesses and the lawyers were all exposed to this untoward situation. The judge decided that the trial proceedings would be telecast. He announced no restrictions at the time. This emphasized the notorious nature of the coming trial, increased the intensity of the publicity on the petitioner and together with the subsequent televising of the trial beginning 30 days later inherently prevented a sober search for the truth. This is underscored by the fact that the selection of the jury took an entire week. As might be expected, a substantial amount of that time was devoted to ascertaining the impact of the pre-trial televising on the prospective jurors. As we have noted, four of the jurors selected had seen all or part of those broadcasts. The trial, on the other hand, lasted only three days.

Moreover, the trial judge was himself harassed. After the initial deci-sion to permit telecasting he apparently decided that a booth should be built at the broadcasters' expense to confine its operations; he then decided to limit the parts of the trial that might be televised live; then he decided to film the testimony of the witnesses without sound in an attempt to pro-tect those under the rule; and finally he ordered that defense counsel and their argument not be televised, in the light of their objection. Plagued by his original error—recurring each day of the trial—his day-to-day orders made the trial more confusing to the jury, the participants and to the view-ers. Indeed, it resulted in a public presentation of only the State's side of the case.

As Mr. Justice Holmes said in *Patterson v. Colorado:*

> The theory of our system is that the conclusions to be reached in a case will be induced only by evidence and argument in open court, and not by any outside influence, whether of private talk or public print.

It is said that the ever-advancing techniques of public communication and the adjustment of the public to its presence may bring about a change in the effect of telecasting upon the fairness of criminal trials. But we are not dealing here with future developments in the field of electronics. Our judgment cannot be rested on the hypothesis of tomorrow but must take the facts as they are presented today.

The judgment is therefore reversed.

MR. CHIEF JUSTICE WARREN, *whom Mr. Justice Douglas and Mr. Justice Goldberg join, concurring.*

While I join the Court's opinion and agree that the televising of criminal trials is inherently a denial of due process, I desire to express addi-tional views on why this is so. In doing this, I wish to emphasize that our condemnation of televised criminal trials is not based on generalities or abstract fears. The record in this case presents a vivid illustration of the inherent prejudice of televised criminal trials and supports our conclusion that this is the appropriate time to make a definitive appraisal of television in the courtroom. . . .

On September 24, a hearing was held to consider petitioner's motion to prohibit television, motion pictures, and still photography at the trial. The courtroom was filled with newspaper reporters and cameramen, television cameramen and spectators. At least 12 cameramen with their equipment were seen by one observer, and there were 30 or more people standing in the aisles. . . .

With photographers roaming at will through the courtroom, petitioner's counsel made his motion that all cameras be excluded. As he spoke, a cameraman wandered behind the judge's bench and snapped his picture. . . .

I believe that it violates the Sixth Amendment for federal courts and the Fourteenth Amendment for state courts to allow criminal trials to be televised to the public at large. I base this conclusion on three grounds: (1) that the televising of trials diverts the trial from its proper purpose in that it has an inevitable impact on all the trial participants; (2) that it gives the public the wrong impression about the purpose of trials, thereby detracting from the dignity of court proceedings and lessening the reliability of trials; and (3) that it singles out certain defendants and subjects them to trials under prejudicial conditions not experienced by others. . . .

In the early days of this country's development, the entertainment a trial might provide often tended to obfuscate its proper role.

> The people thought holding court one of the greatest performances in the range of their experience. . . . The country folks would crowd in for ten miles to hear these 'great lawyers' plead; and it was a secondary matter with the client whether he won or lost his case, so the 'pleading' was loud and long." [Wigmore, A *Kaleidoscope of Justice*]

> In early frontier America, when no motion pictures, no television, and no radio provided entertainment, trial day in the country was like fair day, and from near and far citizens young and old converged on the county seat. The criminal trial was the theater and spectaculum of old rural America. Applause and cat calls were not infrequent. All too easily lawyers and judges became part-time actors at the bar. . . . [Mueller, 110 Pal Rev 16]

I had thought that these days of frontier justice were long behind us, but the courts below would return the theater to the courtroom.

The televising of trials would cause the public to equate the trial process with the forms of entertainment regularly seen on television and with the commercial objectives of the television industry. In the present case, tapes of the September 24 hearing were run in place of the "Tonight Show" by one station and in place of the late night movie by another. Commercials for soft drinks, soups, eyedrops and seatcovers were inserted when there was a pause in the proceedings. In addition, if trials were televised there would be a natural tendency on the part of broadcasters to develop the personalities of the trial participants, so as to give the proceedings more of an element of drama. This tendency was noticeable in the present case. Television commentators gave the viewing audience a homey, flattering sketch about the trial judge, obviously to add an extra element of viewer appeal to the trial.

> Tomorrow morning at 9:55 the WFAA T. V. cameras will be in Tyler to telecast live [the trial judge's] decision whether or not he will permit live coverage of the Billie Sol Estes trial. If so, this will be the first such famous national criminal proceeding to be televised in its entirety live. [The trial judge] was appointed to the bench here in Tyler in 1942 by [the Governor]. The judge has served every two years since then. This *very* beautiful Smith County Courthouse was built and dedicated in 1954, but before that [the trial judge] had made a reputation for himself that reached not only throughout Texas, but throughout the United States as well. It is said that [the trial judge], who is now 53 years old, has tried more cases than any other judge during his time in office.

The television industry might also decide that the bareboned trial itself does not contain sufficient drama to sustain an audience. It might provide expert commentary on the proceedings and hire persons with legal backgrounds to anticipate possible trial strategy, as the football expert anticipates plays for his audience. . . .

Moreover, should television become an accepted part of the courtroom, greater sacrifices would be made for the benefit of broadcasters. In the present case construction of a television booth in the courtroom made it necessary to alter the physical layout of the courtroom and to move from their accustomed position two benches reserved for spectators. If this can be done in order better to accommodate the television industry, I see no reason why another court might not move a trial to a theater, if such a move would provide improved television coverage. Our memories are short indeed if we have already forgotten the wave of horror that swept over this country when Premier Fidel Castro conducted his prosecutions before 18,000 people in Havana Stadium. . . .

. . . The next logical step in this partnership might be to schedule the trial for a time that would permit the maximum number of viewers to watch and to schedule recesses to coincide with the need for station breaks. Should the television industry become an integral part of our system of criminal justice, it would not be unnatural for the public to attribute the shortcomings of the industry to the trial process itself. The public is aware of the television industry's consuming interest in ratings, and it is also aware of the steps that have been taken in the past to maintain viewer interest in television programs. Memories still recall vividly the scandal caused by the disclosure that quiz programs had been corrupted in order to heighten their dramatic appeal. Can we be sure that similar efforts would not be made to heighten the dramatic appeal of televised trials?

Can we be sure that the public would not inherently distrust our system of justice because of its intimate association with a commercial enterprise? . . .

It is argued that television not only entertains but also educates the public. But the function of a trial is not to provide an educational experience; and there is a serious danger that any attempt to use a trial as an educational tool will both divert it from its proper purpose and lead to suspicions concerning the integrity of the trial process. The Soviet Union's trial of Francis Gary Powers provides an example in point. The integrity of the trial was suspect because it was concerned not only with determining the guilt of the individual on trial but also with providing an object lesson to the public. This divided effort undercut confidence in the guilt-determining aspect of the procedure and by so doing rendered the educational aspect self-defeating. . . .

Finally, if the televising of criminal proceedings were approved, trials would be selected for television coverage for reasons having nothing to do with the purpose of trial. A trial might be televised because a particular judge has gained the fancy of the public by his unorthodox approach; or because the district attorney has decided to run for another office and it is believed his appearance would attract a large audience; or simply because a particular courtroom has a layout that best accommodates television coverage. For the most part, however, the most important factor that would draw television to the courtroom would be the nature of the case. The alleged perpetrator of the sensational murder, the fallen idol, or some other person who, like petitioner, has attracted the public interest would find his trial turned into a vehicle for television. Yet, these are the very persons who encounter the greatest difficulty in securing an impartial trial, even without the presence of television. This Court would no longer be able to point to the dignity and calmness of the courtroom as a protection from outside influences. For the television camera penetrates this protection and brings into the courtroom tangible evidence of the widespread interest in a case—an interest which has often been fanned by exhaustive reports in the newspapers, television and radio for weeks before trial. . . .

After living in the glare of this publicity for weeks, petitioner came to court for a legal adjudication of the charges against him. As he approached the courthouse he was confronted by an army of photographers, reporters and television commentators shoving microphones in his face. When he finally made his way into the courthouse it was reasonable for him to expect that he could have a respite from this merciless badgering and have his case adjudicated in a calm atmosphere. Instead, the carnival atmosphere of the September hearing served only to increase the publicity surrounding petitioner and to condition further the public's mind against him. Then, upon his entrance into the courtroom for his actual trial he was confronted with the sight of the television camera zeroed in on him and the ever-present still photographers snapping pictures of interest. As he opened a newspaper waiting for the proceedings to begin, the close-up lens of a television camera zoomed over his shoulder in an effort to find out what he was reading. . . .

So long as the television industry, like the other communications media, is free to send representatives to trials and to report on those trials to its viewers, there is no abridgment of the freedom of press. The right of the communications media to comment on court proceedings does not bring with it the right to inject themselves into the fabric of the trial process to alter the purpose of that process.

In summary, television is one of the great inventions of all time and can perform a large and useful role in society. But the television camera, like other technological innovations, is not entitled to pervade the lives of everyone in disregard of constitutionally protected rights. The television industry, like other institutions, has a proper area of activities and limitations beyond which it cannot go with its cameras. That area does not extend into an American courtroom. On entering that hallowed sanctuary, where the lives, liberty and property of people are in jeopardy, television representatives have only the rights of the general public, namely, to be present, to observe the proceedings, and thereafter, if they choose, to report them.

MR. JUSTICE HARLAN, *concurring.*

I concur in the opinion of the Court, subject, however, to the reservations and only to the extent indicated in this opinion. . . .

The probable impact of courtroom television on the fairness of a trial may vary according to the particular kind of case involved. The impact of television on a trial exciting wide popular interest may be one thing; the impact on a run-of-the-mill case may be quite another. Furthermore, the propriety of closed circuit television for the purpose of making a court recording or for limited use in educational institutions obviously presents markedly different considerations. The *Estes* trial was a heavily publicized and highly sensational affair. I therefore put aside all other types of cases; in so doing, however, I wish to make it perfectly clear that I am by no means prepared to say that the constitutional issue should ultimately turn upon the nature of the particular case involved. When the issue of television in a non-notorious trial is presented it may appear that no workable distinction can be drawn based on the type of case involved, or that the possibilities for prejudice, though less severe, are nonetheless of constitutional proportions. . . . The resolution of those further questions should await an appropriate case; the Court should proceed only step by step in this unplowed field. The opinion of the Court necessarily goes no farther, for only the four members of the majority who unreservedly join the Court's opinion would resolve those questions now. . . .

MR. JUSTICE STEWART, *whom Mr. Justice Black, Mr. Justice Brennan, and Mr. Justice White join, dissenting.*

I cannot agree with the Court's decision that the circumstances of this trial led to a denial of the petitioner's Fourteenth Amendment rights. I think that the introduction of television into a courtroom is, at least in the present state of the art, an extremely unwise policy. It invites many constitutional risks, and it detracts from the inherent dignity of a courtroom. But I am unable to escalate this personal view into a *per se* constitutional rule. And I am unable to find, on the specific record of this case, that the circumstances attending the limited televising of the petitioner's trial resulted in the denial of any right guaranteed him by the United States Constitution. . . .

What ultimately emerges from this record . . . is one bald question —whether the Fourteenth Amendment of the United States Constitution prohibits all television cameras from a state courtroom whenever a criminal trial is in progress. In the light of this record and what we now know about the impact of television on a criminal trial, I can find no such prohibition in the Fourteenth Amendment or in any other provision of the Constitution. If what occurred did not deprive the petitioner of his constitutional right to a fair trial, then the fact that the public could view the proceeding on television has no constitutional significance. The Constitution does not make us arbiters of the image that a televised state criminal trial projects to the public.

While no First Amendment claim is made in this case, there are intimations in the opinions filed by my Brethren in the majority which strike me as disturbingly alien to the First and Fourteenth Amendments' guarantees against federal or state interference with the free communication of information and ideas. The suggestion that there are limits upon the public's right to know what goes on in the courts causes me deep concern. The idea of imposing upon any medium of communications the burden of justifying its presence is contrary to where I had always thought the presumption must lie in the area of First Amendment freedoms. And the proposition that nonparticipants in a trial might get the "wrong impression" from unfettered reporting and commentary contains an invitation to censorship which I cannot accept. Where there is no disruption of the "essential requirement of the fair and orderly administration of justice," "[f]reedom of discussion should be given the widest range." *Pennekamp v. Florida.*

I do not think that the Constitution denies to the State or to individual trial judges all discretion to conduct criminal trials with television cameras present, no matter how unobtrusive the cameras may be. I cannot say at this time that it is impossible to have a constitutional trial whenever any part of the proceedings is televised or recorded on television film.

I cannot now hold that the Constitution absolutely bars television cameras from every criminal courtroom, even if they have no impact upon the jury, no effect upon any witness, and no influence upon the conduct of the judge.

For these reasons, I would affirm the judgment.

MR. JUSTICE WHITE, *with whom Mr. Justice Brennan joins, dissenting.*

. . . The opinion of the Court in effect precludes further opportunity for intelligent assessment of the probable hazards imposed by the use of cameras at criminal trials. Serious threats to constitutional rights in some instances justify a prophylactic rule dispensing with the necessity of showing specific prejudice in a particular case. *Rideau v. Louisana.* But these are instances in which there has been ample experience on which to base an informed judgment. Here, although our experience is inadequate and our judgment correspondingly infirm, the Court discourages further meaningful study of the use of television at criminal trials. Accordingly, I dissent.

MR. JUSTICE BRENNAN.

I write merely to emphasize that only four of the five Justices voting to reverse rest on the proposition that televised criminal trials are constitutionally infirm, whatever the circumstances. Although the opinion announced by my Brother Clark purports to be an "opinion of the Court," my Brother Harlan subscribes to a significantly less sweeping proposition. . . .

Thus today's decision is *not* a blanket constitutional prohibition against the televising of state criminal trials.

While I join the dissents of my Brothers Stewart and White, I do so on the understanding that their use of the expressions "the Court's opinion" or "the opinion of the Court" refers only to those views of our four Brethren which my Brother Harlan explicitly states he shares.

RESPONSIBILITY OF NEWS MEDIA

The Warren Commission *

. . . If Oswald had been tried for his murders of November 22, the effects of the news policy pursued by the Dallas authorities would have proven harmful both to the prosecution and the defense. The misinformation reported after the shootings might have been used by the defense to cast doubt on the reliability of the State's entire case. Though each inaccuracy can be explained without great difficulty, the number and variety of misstatements issued by the police shortly after the assassination would have greatly assisted a skillful defense attorney attempting to influence the attitudes of jurors.

A fundamental objection to the news policy pursued by the Dallas police, however, is the extent to which it endangered Oswald's constitutional right to a trial by an impartial jury. Because of the nature of the crime, the widespread attention which it necessarily received, and the intense public feelings which it aroused, it would have been a most difficult task to select an unprejudiced jury, either in Dallas or elsewhere. But the difficulty was markedly increased by the divulgence of the specific items of evidence with which the police linked Oswald to the two killings. The disclosure of evidence encouraged the public, from which a jury would ultimately be impaneled, to prejudge the very questions that would be raised at trial.

Moreover, rules of law might have prevented the prosecution from presenting portions of this evidence to the jury. For example, though expressly recognizing that Oswald's wife could not be compelled to testify against him, District Attorney Wade revealed to the Nation that Marina Oswald had affirmed her husband's ownership of a rifle like that found on the sixth floor of the Texas School Book Depository. Curry stated that Oswald had refused to take a lie detector test, although such a statement would have been inadmissible in a trial. The exclusion of such evidence, however, would have been meaningless if jurors were already familiar with the same facts from previous television or newspaper reports. Wade might have influenced prospective jurors by his mistaken statement that the paraffin test showed that Oswald had fired a gun. The tests merely showed that he had nitrate traces on his hands, which did not necessarily mean that he had fired either a rifle or a pistol.

---

* From the *Report of the President's Commission on the Assassination of President John F. Kennedy*. Washington, D.C.: Government Printing Office, 1964, at p. 238.

The disclosure of evidence was seriously aggravated by the statements of numerous responsible officials that they were certain of Oswald's guilt. Captain Fritz said that the case against Oswald was "cinched." Curry reported on Saturday that "we are sure of our case." Curry announced that he considered Oswald sane, and Wade told the public that he would ask for the death penalty.

The American Bar Association declared in December 1963 that "widespread publicizing of Oswald's alleged guilt, involving statements by officials and public disclosures of the details of 'evidence,' would have made it extremely difficult to impanel an unprejudiced jury and afford the accused a fair trial." Local bar associations expressed similar feelings. The Commission agrees that Lee Harvey Oswald's opportunity for a trial by 12 jurors free of preconception as to his guilt or innocence would have been seriously jeopardized by the premature disclosure and weighing of the evidence against him.

The problem of disclosure of information and its effect on trials is, of course, further complicated by the independent activities of the press in developing information on its own from sources other than law enforcement agencies. Had the police not released the specific items of evidence against Oswald, it is still possible that the other information presented on television and in the newspapers, chiefly of a biographical nature, would itself have had a prejudicial effect on the public.

In explanation of the news policy adopted by the Dallas authorities, Chief Curry observed that "it seemed like there was a great demand by the general public to know what was going on." In a prepared statement, Captain King wrote:

> At that time we felt a necessity for permitting the newsmen as much latitude as possible. We realized the magnitude of the incident the newsmen were there to cover. We realized that not only the nation but the world would be greatly interested in what occurred in Dallas. We believed that we had an obligation to make as widely known as possible everything we could regarding the investigation of the assassination and the manner in which we undertook that investigation.

The Commission recognizes that the people of the United States, and indeed the world, had a deep-felt interest in learning of the events surrounding the death of President Kennedy, including the development of the investigation in Dallas. An informed public provided the ultimate guarantee that adequate steps would be taken to apprehend those responsible for the assassination and that all necessary precautions would be taken to protect the national security. It was therefore proper and desirable that the public know which agencies were participating in the investigation and the rate at which their work was progressing. The public was also entitled to know that Lee Harvey Oswald had been apprehended and that the State had gathered sufficient evidence to arraign him for the murders of the President and Patrolman Tippit, that he was being held pending action of the grand jury, that the investigation was continuing, and that the law enforcement agencies had discovered no evidence which tended to show that any other person was involved in either slaying.

However, neither the press nor the public had a right to be contemporaneously informed by the police or prosecuting authorities of the details of the evidence being accumulated against Oswald. Undoubtedly the public was interested in these disclosures, but its curiosity should not have been satisfied at the expense of the accused's right to a trial by an impartial jury. The courtroom, not the newspaper or television screen, is the appropriate forum in our system for the trial of a man accused of a crime.

If the evidence in the possession of the authorities had not been disclosed, it is true that the public would not have been in a position to assess the adequacy of the investigation or to apply pressures for further official undertakings. But a major consequence of the hasty and at times inaccurate divulgence of evidence after the assassination was simply to give rise to groundless rumors and public confusion. Moreover, without learning the details of the case, the public could have been informed by the responsible authority of the general scope of the investigation and the extent to which State and Federal agencies were assisting in the police work.

While appreciating the heavy and unique pressures with which the Dallas Police Department was confronted by reason of the assassination of President Kennedy, primary responsibility for having failed to control the press and to check the flow of undigested evidence to the public must be borne by the police department. It was the only agency that could have established orderly and sound operating procedures to control the multitude of newsmen gathered in the police building after the assassination.

The Commission believes, however, that a part of the responsibility for the unfortunate circumstances following the President's death must be borne by the news media. The crowd of newsmen generally failed to respond properly to the demands of the police. Frequently without permission, news representatives used police offices on the third floor, tying up facilities and interfering with normal police operations. Police efforts to preserve order and to clear passageways in the corridor were usually unsuccessful. On Friday night the reporters completely ignored Curry's injunction against asking Oswald questions in the assembly room and crowding in on him. On Sunday morning, the newsmen were instructed to direct no questions at Oswald; nevertheless, several reporters shouted questions at him when he appeared in the basement.

Moreover, by constantly pursuing public officials, the news representatives placed an insistent pressure upon them to disclose information. And this pressure was not without effect, since the police attitude toward the press was affected by the desire to maintain satisfactory relations with the news representatives and to create a favorable image of themselves. Chief Curry frankly told the Commission that

> I didn't order them out of the building, which if I had it to do over I would. In the past like I say, we had always maintained very good relations with our press, and they had always respected us.

Curry refused Fritz' request to put Oswald behind the screen in the assembly room at the Friday night press conference because this might have hindered the taking of pictures. Curry's subordinates had the impression that an unannounced transfer of Oswald to the county jail was unacceptable because Curry did not want to disappoint the newsmen; he had promised that they could witness the transfer. It seemed clear enough that any attempt to exclude the press from the building or to place limits on the information disclosed to them would have been resented and disputed by the newsmen, who were constantly and aggressively demanding all possible information about anything related to the assassination.

Although the Commission has found no corroboration in the video and audio tapes, police officials recall that one or two representatives of the press reinforced their demands to see Oswald by suggesting that the police had been guilty of brutalizing him. They intimated that unless they were given the opportunity to see him, these suggestions would be passed on to the public. Captain King testified that he had been told that

> A short time after Oswald's arrest one newsman held up a photograph and said, "This is what the man charged with the assassination of the President looks like. Or at least this is what he did look like. We don't know what he looks like after an hour in the custody of the Dallas Police Department."

City Manager Elgin Crull stated that when he visited Chief Curry in his office on the morning of November 23, Curry told him that he "felt it was necessary to cooperate with the news media representatives, in order to avoid being accused of using Gestapo tactics in connection with the handling of Oswald." Crull agreed with Curry. The Commission deems any such veiled threats to be absolutely without justification.

The general disorder in the Police and Courts Building during November 22–24 reveals a regrettable lack of self-discipline by the newsmen. The Commission believes that the news media, as well as the police authorities, who failed to impose conditions more in keeping with the orderly process of justice, must share responsibility for the failure of law enforcement which occurred in connection with the death of Oswald. On previous occasions, public bodies have voiced the need for the exercise of self-restraint by the news media in periods when the demand for information must be tempered by other fundamental requirements of our society.

At its annual meeting in Washington in April 1964, the American

Society of Newspaper Editors discussed the role of the press in Dallas immediately after President Kennedy's assassination. The discussion revealed the strong misgivings among the editors themselves about the role that the press had played and their desire that the press display more self-discipline and adhere to higher standards of conduct in the future. To prevent a recurrence of the unfortunate events which followed the assassination, however, more than general concern will be needed. The promulgation of a code of professional conduct governing representatives of all news media would be welcome evidence that the press had profited by the lesson of Dallas.

The burden of insuring that appropriate action is taken to establish ethical standards of conduct for the news media must also be borne, however, by State and local governments, by the bar, and ultimately by the public. The experience in Dallas during November 22–24 is a dramatic affirmation of the need for steps to bring about a proper balance between the right of the public to be kept informed and the right of the individual to a fair and impartial trial.

CHAPTER 12

THE LEGACY OF THE
WARREN COURT

The continuing struggle for freedom of expression is neither new nor easy. An early victim was Socrates, who was condemned to death in 399 B.C. for speaking the truth as he saw it.

Freedom of expression to a democratic form of government is not a mere luxury, but a necessity. Democracy to move forward demands informed criticism. Answers to the complex problems facing free nations today are to be found in the great public debates, both spoken and written—debates that invite the tests of reflection and rebuttal.

Truth is not always found in the majority view. Indeed, much social legislation now governing the nation was first proposed by those in the minority. And many First Amendment freedoms enjoyed in this nation today were born in Supreme Court dissents of decades past.

The Supreme Court is "apolitical" in that the Justices, appointed for life, are not responsible to the electorate. But there are four built-in methods for checking the power of the Court, though three of these have rarely been used.

First, the Senate may reject a presidential Supreme Court nomination. The first such challenge—a successful one—came in 1795 with the rejection of Justice Rutledge, a former Associate Justice who had been nominated as Chief Justice by President Washington. More recent challenges by members of the Senate have been aimed at Justice Brandeis, the first Jew to sit with the High Court, and Justice Fortas, Associate Justice nominated by President Johnson to succeed Chief Justice Warren, a nomination which was later withdrawn, and rejections of two of President Nixon's nominees—Judges Clement Haynsworth and G. Harrold Carswell.

Second, a Justice may be impeached. However, no Supreme Court

Justice has been removed from the bench through impeachment and conviction.

Third, the Court's actions may checked by amendment to the Constitution. The Supreme Court, for example, held the graduated income tax to be unconstitutional, a ruling which was overturned by the passage of the Sixteenth Amendment. More recently the Court refused to strike down a poll tax only to be reversed by the passage of the Twenty-fourth Amendment. But the same "check power," it should be noted, has dangers as well. It is possible, for example, to amend the Constitution to include second-class citizenship for racial or religious minorities or to alter or dilute the role of the Court itself.

Finally, Supreme Court decisions may be overturned by later decisions of the Court itself, as was the case with public school segregation and First Amendment protection for motion pictures. The framers of the Constitution wrote in generalities. They stated principles and pointed to goals rather than to specifics. They were wise enough to prepare for unforeseen technological and social changes. So they wrote in terms of "due process" and "equal protection under the law," both imprecise terms which necessarily demand social and political interpretation. It should not come as a surprise, then, that changing times require changing interpretations by the Justices.

THE WARREN COURT AND THE PRESS

BY JOHN P. MACKENZIE *

The conventional wisdom about the relationship between the Warren Court and the news media runs something like this: With a few exceptions, the press corps is populated by persons with only a superficial understanding of the Court, its processes, and the values with which it deals. The Court has poured out pages of legal learning, but its reasoning has been largely ignored by a result-oriented news industry interested only in the superficial aspects of the Court's work. The Court can trace much of its "bad press," its "poor image," to the often sloppy and inaccurate work of news gatherers operating in mindless deadline competition. The competition to be first with the story has been the chief obstacle in these critical years to a better public understanding of the Court and of our liberties and laws.

The difficulty with this characterization is that it contains just enough truth to appear reasonably complete. This picture of the press, because it is plausible, unfortunately may actually mask difficulties that lie deeper both in the structure of complex news media and in the Court's practices as they affect both the media and the general public—difficulties which, if recognized, may provide some opportunities for better understanding of the Court. If the Warren Court has received an especially bad press, there is blame enough to go around for it; the Court and the press should each accept shares of the blame, but within each institution the blame must be reallocated.

If the ultimate history of the Warren Court includes a judgment that the press has been unfair to the institution, this surely ought to be labeled as ingratitude of the highest order. *New York Times Co. v. Sullivan* and its progeny have carved out press freedoms to print news without fear of libel judgments under standards more generous and permissive to the fourth estate than the standards set by responsible newspapers for themselves. It is well that the Court has done so, and it is especially appropriate in a period when executive officials and political candidates have expressed mounting hostility toward the news media. Not only ideas, but men dealing in ideas and words, need breathing space to survive. These great first amendment decisions contemplated that judges, like other public

* John P. MacKenzie. "The Warren Court and the Press." *Michigan Law Review*, Vol. 67, No. 2 (December 1968), p. 303. Reprinted with permission of the author, a Supreme Court reporter for the *Washington Post*.

men, would suffer considerable personal abuse and that they must be rugged enough to take most of it, but the Court surely did not mean to invite press treatment of itself that was unfair as well as highly critical.

Before discussing what the Court and the press have done to injure each other, it is worth noting that each has thrived somewhat on the developing relationships of the past decade and a half. By any definition of that elusive concept known as "news," an activist and innovative Supreme Court makes news and thus provides grist for the press. In turn, to an increasing degree, the press has been expanding its resources to cope with the flow of judicial news. Thus, the media have been giving the Court more exposure to the public.

It must be stated, however, that the relationships between press and Court have been complex and difficult. Some of the problems are built into the systems of both institutions. The Court begins as a mystery, and the reportor or editor who fails to appreciate the fact that certain things about the Supreme Court will remain unknowable and consequently unprintable simply does not understand the situation. The Court's decisions are the start of an argument more often than they are the final, definitive word on a given subject. Opinions often are written in such a way that they mask the difficulties of a case rather than illuminate them. New decisions frequently cannot be reconciled with prior rulings because "policy considerations, not always apparent on the surface, are powerful agents of decision."

Certainly not all the turmoil of the conference room spills over into the delivery of opinions. Secrecy at several levels both protects and obscures the Court and its work. The process of marshalling a Court, of compromise, of submerging dissents and concurrences, or of bringing them about, can only be imagined or deduced by the contemporary chronicler of the Court; history lags decades behind with its revelations of the Court's inner workings. This is not to say that newsmen need be privy to the Court's inner dealings, helpful as that might be, to describe its decisions accurately and well. But I would suggest that murky decision-reporting may be the reporting of murky decisions as well as the murky reporting of decisions.

The handling of petitions for certiorari—a process replete with elements of subjectivity and perhaps even arbitrariness—eludes the attempts of newsmen to fathom, much less to communicate to the general public, the sense of what the Court is doing. Certiorari action is the antithesis of what the Opinion of the Court is supposed to represent: a reasoned judicial action reasonably explained. Yet when the Court does speak through opinions, the press is frequently found lacking both in capacity for understanding and capacity for handling the material. Precious newspaper space, when it is available, often is wasted on trivia at the expense of reporting a decision's principal message and impact. Newspapers often fail to adjust to the abnormally large volume of material produced on a "decision day," or to the task of reporting the widespread implications of a landmark decision.

Some of the demands made by the flow of Supreme Court news are beyond the capabilities of all newspapers; some are beyond the capacities of all but the newspapers most dedicated to complete coverage of the institution. For example, the actions of the last two Mondays of the October 1963 term consume all of Volume 378 of the United States Reports. The decisions and orders of June 12, 1967, the final day of that term, are printed in Volume 388, which exceeds 580 pages. Many of these decisions have remained under advisement until the end of a term precisely because of their difficulty and complexity, elements that frequently correlate with newsworthiness. Many of them are sufficiently interesting to warrant substantial newspaper coverage, which often includes printing their full texts or excerpts. Many decisions generate, or should generate, "side-bar" or feature stories of their own on the same day. Supreme Court stories compete with each other for available column space, and all the Court news of a given day must in turn compete with all the others news from everywhere else in the world.

Between the Court and the press stands perhaps the most primitive arrangement in the entire communications industry for access to an important source of news material and distribution of the information generated by that source. On days of decision delivery, two dozen newsmen and newswomen gather in the press room on the ground floor of the Supreme Court Building to receive opinions in page proof form as they are delivered orally in the courtroom one floor above. Each Justice's contribution is passed out one opinion at a time, so that if there are, for example, several separate opinions in a cluster of three related cases, the news reporter will not be able to tell what has happened until he has assembled his entire bundle of opinions one by one.

Upstairs in the courtroom, at a row of desks between the high bench and the counsel's podium, sit six newsmen (several more are seated elsewhere in the audience), three of whom represent the Associated Press, United Press International, and the Dow-Jones financial ticker. As opinions are delivered orally, Court messengers deliver printed copies to the six desks. The two wire service reporters send their copies through pneumatic tubes to fellow workers waiting in cubicles below. The AP reporter there, aided by an assistant, types out his stories and dictates them over the telephone to a stenographer at the office of the service's Washington bureau. The UPI reporter does essentially the same thing, but hands his copy to a teletype operator for direct transmission to the bureau office for editing. Reporters for the major afternoon newspapers must devise methods of their own for getting copy to their main offices. Reporters for morning papers do not have "all day" to perform the same tasks, but they have a much easier time of it at the moment of decision delivery. For example, they need not resort to the device used by their more time-pressed colleagues—that of preparing "canned" stories about petitions for certiorari that are released automatically when the Court announces its action granting or denying review. Such articles are prepared so that they can be transmitted with the insertion or change of a few words depending on the Court's order.

The Court's clerical and semiclerical workings pose problems of their own. In the day-to-day coverage of the Supreme Court the reporter may encounter secrecy at every stage, not all of it necessary to the independent performance of the judicial function. There may be secret pleadings, of which one minor but colorful example will suffice. On December 4, 1967, the Court denied review to two topless, and by definition newsworthy, young ladies from Los Angeles, whose petition claimed first amendment protection for their chosen form of expression. The ladies sought relief from the toils of prosecution by means of a petition for a writ of habeas corpus—a remedy that was intriguing in itself—but had been spurned by the lower courts. Unbeknownst to the press, which was inclined to take the petition at face value, the Court was in receipt of a letter, actually a responsive pleading, notifying the Justices that the defendants were pursuing normal appellate remedies at the same time. This information made their petition much less urgent and it might well have chilled the press interest in the case as well as the Court's. Only Justice Douglas noted his vote in favor of review. The letter was lodged in a correspondence file, a fact which this reporter learned by accident after his and other news stories about the case had been printed.

There also may be secret correspondence which does not amount to a pleading but which nevertheless may shape the outcome of a case or materially affect the writing of an opinion. In *Rees v. Peyton*, a court-appointed attorney in a capital case communicated to the Court by letter the fact that his client wanted to dismiss his petition, a suicidal step which counsel was understandably resisting. Again, the communication was placed in a correspondence file apart from the remainder of the record. A request to see the correspondence was denied by the Clerk's office, initially on grounds that it might invade the lawyer-client relationship and later on no grounds at all: At length the letter was released. Similarly, it might be noted that the celebrated communication from J. Edgar Hoover, Director of the Federal Bureau of Investigation, regarding FBI interrogation practices—one which figured importantly in the Chief Justice's opinion in *Miranda v. Arizona*—has not been made public despite requests for access to it.

There may also be secret exhibits, such as the one requested from the bench by the Chief Justice in *Giles v. Maryland*, which may prove decisive in a case. There may even be secret petitions for certiorari in a controversy not involving national security; this occurred recently in a bitterly fought domestic relations case from Maryland. And, although the Court's press room is supposed to have available all briefs that are filed, the word "filed" is a term of art meaning "accepted for filing with the Court." This excludes many papers which the Justices see, including many amicus curiae briefs lodged with the Court pending its disposition of a motion for leave to file when one or both parties has objected to the filing. The "deferred appendix" method authorized by the 1967 revisions in the Supreme Court's rules means that more major briefs will be formally on file with the Court in proof form; however, the briefs, while available for inspection if the fact of filing is known to the news reporter, do not become available generally until later when printed copies are delivered to the Court.

In what way, then, have these ingredients—the nature of the Court's work, the lack of capacity on the part of the press, and the Court's own administrative habits—combined to influence the public's view of the Supreme Court? Examples abound in which the principal cause of public confusion must be laid to one or another of these elements. The examples are to be found primarily in the areas of deepest controversy: race relations, use of confessions in criminal cases, reapportionment, obscenity, and religion.

In the area of the Warren Court's central achievement, the promotion of equal treatment for racial minorities, the Court must take some share of the blame for the bad press it received. One source of difficulty was the famous footnote 11 in *Brown v. Board of Education*, which cited "modern authority" as to the state of psychological knowledge about the detrimental effects of state-imposed segregated education. The importance of the gratuitous footnote was emphasized out of all proportion by segregationists, and at least by hindsight it seems to have been inevitable that this should be so. The press contributed to the difficulty not so much by misreporting the opinion as by failing to muster the depth of understanding to place the footnote in perspective by comparing "modern authority" with the amateur sociology used by the nineteenth century Court.

In the field of criminal law, another area in which the Warren Court has made headlines, one may again see the difficulty of attributing blame. As with civil rights, it is virtually certain that most members of the general public literally know about the Supreme Court's work in this area only what they have read in the newspapers, heard on the radio, or seen on television. Mixed though the picture may be, it has become clear at least to this writer that press misinterpretation of *Escobedo, Miranda,* and *Wade,* to name several of the most controversial decisions, has not been the fault of the "regular" reporters at the Supreme Court, whether writers for wire services or daily newspapers. These decisions probably were reported more accurately under the deadline pressure of decision day than they have been reported since that time.

In *Escobedo,* for example, it was widely and correctly reported at the time of decision that the suspect's incriminating statements had been ruled inadmissible because he had been denied access to counsel who had already been retained and who was figuratively beating on the interrogation room door while the petitioner was being questioned in disregard of his express wish to consult his lawyer. Since his release from the murder charge against him, Danny Escobedo has been embroiled with the law many times; finally, in 1968, he was convicted on federal criminal charges. Yet, in most of the news accounts about the later life of Danny Escobedo, the Court's initial decision has been described as one which threw out his confession on grounds that police refused to let him see "*a lawyer.*" *Miranda* may have mooted the distinction, at least for trials starting after June 13, 1966, but surely the fact that Escobedo was denied permission to consult a previously retained attorney makes a difference to an evaluation of the situation that confronted the now-notorious petitioner. Given the actual factual setting, the ruling seems less based on a "technicality" or excessive solicitude for a criminal.

Fairness demands acknowledgment that writers of subsequent news reports dealing with any Supreme Court decision may themselves be working under considerable deadline pressure, and usually they suffer from the added handicap of not having immediate access to the written texts of the Court's opinions. An after-dinner speaker may opine that the Supreme Court would throw out the confession of a man who walked up to a policeman on a street corner and told him of a crime he had just committed. The speaker might also say, as indeed members of the United States Senate were fond of saying during the battle over the nomination of Justice Fortas to replace Chief Justice Warren, that the Court "has made it impossible to prohibit or punish the showing of indecent movies to children." What does the reporter do when confronted by such statements while on an otherwise routine assignment to cover the speech? His only source of help may be the newspaper's legal correspondent, if there is one and if he is sufficiently knowledgeable in such matters; the legal correspondent may be able to furnish information for a brief statement in the story, telling, for the benefit of the uninformed reader, what the Court actually did or said. . . .

The failure of communications, so at odds with the Court's necessary function as a constitutional teacher, had worthy origins. The school desegregation cases would doubtless have been excoriated by segregationists no matter what form of words the Court had chosen, and segregationist officials clearly would have defied the rulings just as vigorously. Perhaps *Brown v. Board of Education*, besides being a catalyst for other constitutional breakthroughs, set the pattern for the Warren Court's judicial conduct in the face of conservative hostility. The Court sent the message out that segregation was unlawful; the message came back that unlawfulness would persist in parts of the land; and the Court became determined to do whatever justice it could on its own. Similarly, in the criminal law field, Earl Warren and some of his colleagues ultimately expressed doubts that the Court could issue a constitutional exclusionary rule that would be effective in actual police practice; however, they undertook to lay down the rules anyway, although quite possibly the Justices were conditioned to some disappointment about the level of compliance.

Under Chief Justice Warren significant advances were made in the techniques of communicating the Court's work to the public, although the advances were outstripped by events. Starting soon after *Brown*, the press at its best began to reach new levels of competence. The Court made the press' job a bit easier by meeting at ten a.m. instead of at noon. The Association of American Law Schools began a helpful program of issuing background memoranda for the press on major cases which had been argued before the Court. The Court also began to space out the delivery of some of its opinions. Some often-mentioned experiments were not tried, however—most notably the proposal to supply the press with opinions a few hours in advance of delivery in order to give reporters time to compose more careful articles. Apparently the deterrent has been fear that some decisions, especially important economic ones, might be compromised by early release no matter what precautions were taken by the short-handed Court staff. The experiment should be tried anyway, if necessary with the specific exclusion of such economic cases. In the future, the Court must also seriously consider some *rapprochement* with television and re-examination of its ban on cameras in the courtroom. Television will certainly not invest money, manpower, and air time to cover a subject that will not reward the medium pictorially, and more and more Americans seem to receive all or most of their news over that medium.

During his confirmation hearings, Justice Fortas offered in broad outline a mixture of proposals for study of many of these problems. He mentioned the already-accomplished revision of the "Decision Monday" procedure and noted that the burden on the press had been relieved somewhat but perhaps could be relieved more. He suggested expanding the Association of American Law Schools' project (now supported by the American Bar Foundation), which supplies helpful memoranda about most of the argued cases to the press at the time of argument, to the post-decision phase of the Court's work. He also recommended that statistical information be compiled for newsmen; as an example of a little-reported fact, he cited the results of a survey showing that 92 or 93 per cent of all criminal cases presented to the Court for review during the October 1967 term had been rejected. He commended the formation of an organization of practitioners before the Court. And, he suggested coming to grips with the pressing problems of radio and television coverage.

. . . The cornerstone for constructing any improvements is that the Supreme Court must be an open institution—as open as is truly consistent with proper adjudication and as open as the democratic society the Warren Court sought so earnestly to fashion.

THE SUPREME COURT AND ITS CRITICS

By Anthony Lewis *

I. Result-Oriented Criticism

The body of criticism that is the largest in volume, and the loudest, is what might be termed result-oriented. The fundamental characteristic of this type of criticism is that it is more concerned with the results reached by the Court than with the reasons for those results. Thus the *Jencks* case, holding that federal criminal defendants were entitled to check pre-trial statements by government witnesses against their trial testimony, was attacked in good part because Mr. Jencks was allegedly a Communist. One wonders what the critics would have said if the principle had been laid down in the case of a criminal antitrust action against a large corporation.

Decisions involving, one way or another, Communists and suspected Communists have been a major target of vituperative, unreasoned criticism. A good example was an editorial in the *New York Daily News*, which began:

> Everywhere you go, almost everyone you know has his or her own theory as to what's wrong with the Earl Warren Supreme Court. (A handful of people—mainly Communists and fellow-travelers—think the Court is strictly okay.) [Nov. 23, 1959]

Perhaps the ultimate example of result-oriented criticism was a chart made by a United States Senator showing the number of times each member of the Court had "voted in accordance with the position advocated by Communists." The complete assumption there was that facts and law are irrelevant if Communists support the position of one side in a pending case. That side must lose, or else the Court is pro-Communist.

The school segregation cases, decided in *Brown v. Board of Education*, undoubtedly represent the single most important reason for contemporary animosity toward the Court. Southern judges and lawyers who might be expected to know better have joined Southern politicians and newspaper editors in denouncing the *Brown* decision as immoral, illegal, even unconstitutional. One of the curiosities of the attack has been the veneration paid by these Southern critics to the rule of separate but equal accommodations for Negroes which the Supreme Court abandoned in 1954. This

---

* From Anthony Lewis. "The Supreme Court and Its Critics." *Minnesota Law Review*, Vol. 45 (1960–61), p. 305, at p. 306. Used with permission of the Minnesota Law Review Foundation and the author, former Supreme Court correspondent for the *New York Times*.

veneration is a little tardy, to say the least. The South in fact made no real effort to provide equal schooling for Negroes during many decades after *Plessy v. Ferguson* established the separate but equal doctrine in 1896. As recently as 1944 the average current expenditure per pupil in six Southeastern states was less than half as much in Negro schools as in white. Figures from earlier in this century are even more shocking. It was only when the trend of Supreme Court opinions beginning in the 1930's and 1940's made it clear that the legal basis of segregation was threatened that the South began spending those vast sums on Negro education that we now hear so much about.

Although the result-oriented critics often talk about the need for "self-restraint" on the part of the Supreme Court, even self-restraint does not please them when it leads to the wrong result. An example was *Frank v. Maryland*. Over the strong protest of four dissenters, the Court held that the Federal Constitution does not compel every local health inspector in the country to obtain a warrant before gaining entry to a house which he has good reason to believe is a source of disease. Logically, one should call the decision a triumph of self-restraint, not to mention states' rights. The majority declined to put another constitutional limitation on local action. But the day after the decision Dale Alford, a segregationist Congressman from Little Rock, Arkansas, said of the decision: "Once again the oath-breaking usurpers destroyed one of our basic freedoms. . . ."

This is know-nothing criticism. It is nonintellectual, indeed anti-intellectual. It often includes the suggestion of bad motives on the part of the Justices, a suggestion conveyed by such language as "judicial usurpation" and "judicial tyranny." Robert A. Girard has said that such epithets—

> signify nothing more than that their author either agrees or does not agree with a particular decision or group of decisions by the Court. If he thinks the court should not have interfered as it did, then you have "judicial legislation" or, even worse, "judicial usurpation," depending upon the intensity of the author's conviction. If the court should have stepped in when it did not, the result is "judicial abnegation." On the other hand, if the Court's response meets his fancy, then you are blessed with "judicial restraint" or "judicial statesmanship." It has always seemed to me that if all an author has to say is that he thinks the Court is mistaken or unwise in its decisions, he would do a great service by speaking in concrete terms of mistake or absence of wisdom which are at once more meaningful and less likely to inflame than such provocative terms as "judicial usurpation," "judicial abnegation," and the rest.

But it goes without saying that Mr. Girard's plea is not likely to get very far with the know-nothing critics. Their very purpose is to inflame. Epithets are more useful for that purpose than reasoned argument.

Under the same general heading of result-oriented criticism must go some efforts which bear more impressive intellectual credentials. Among these are the 1958 report of the Conference of (State) Chief Justices' Committee on Federal-State Relationships as Affected by Judicial Decisions; the 1959 report of the American Bar Association's Committee on Communist Tactics, Strategy and Objectives; and the work of some newspaper columnists who write frequently about the Supreme Court.

The report of the chief justices' committee is a hybrid document. After a historical outline of our federal system the report cites a number of areas of the law in which Supreme Court decisions during the last few decades have altered the federal-state balance. There are lengthy discussions of cases imposing restraints on state legislative investigations, state control of admissions to the bar and state administration of criminal law. The tone is reasoned, if critical. But then comes a section labeled "Conclusions." These are, *inter alia*, that the Supreme Court "too often has tended to adopt the role of policy-maker without proper judicial restraint," that "the overall tendency" of its decisions "over the last 25 years or more has been to press the extension of federal power and to press it rapidly," that the Court "in many cases arising under the 14th amendment has assumed what seem to us primarily legislative powers," and—last but not least—that "any study of recent decisions of the Supreme Court will raise at least considerable doubt as to the validity" of the "boast that we have a Government of laws and not of men."

Preliminarily, one may raise an eyebrow at the propriety of any report by state chief justices on the behavior of the Supreme Court of the United States. The result is to make the conference of chief justices, as Paul Freund put it with characteristically gentle wit, "a corporate body one of whose functions is to vote in review of the performance of their reviewer." The conclusions, moreover, do not follow from the earlier discussion in the report and often seem to bear little relation to it. Their sweeping character and emotional tone are hardly good examples of judicial restraint. Is it helpful—or lawyerlike—to throw at the Supreme Court such slogans as a government of laws, not men? And in complaining that the Court has nibbled at states' rights the report skips lightly over highly significant areas in which the present Supreme Court has been much more deferential to the states than were its predecessors. Professor Freund points out that the Court has greatly enlarged the power of the states to impose economic regulation, to tax businesses engaged in interstate commerce, and to tax property despite a degree of federal ownership. Are those powers really not more important to state government than a right to harry a man invited to lecture at a state university about whether he once belonged to the Progressive Party?

The report of the American Bar Association committee similarly uses a broad and unlawyerlike brush, generalizing about problems that are particular and distinct. The conclusion that got the headlines was: "Many cases have been decided in such a manner as to encourage an increase in Communist activity in the United States. . . . The paralysis of our internal security grows largely from construction and interpretation centering around technicalities emanating from our judicial process which the Communists seek to destroy, yet use as a refuge to masquerade their diabolical objectives." Apart from the impenetrable syntax, it is distressing to see a group of lawyers describe statutory and constitutional guaranties of fair procedure and reasonable governmental action as "technicalities." And the contention that the Supreme Court has caused a "paralysis" of our internal security, a paralysis evidently not visible to the naked eye, was devastatingly answered in a report by a committee of the Association of the Bar of the City of New York.

Of newspaper columnists who appraise the work of the Supreme Court the most prominent is probably David Lawrence. He has had this to say about the Court:

> Traditionally, the spirit of America has been that if you do not like the rules of the game, change the rules—but don't soak the umpire.
>
> For generations the Supreme Court of the United States has been the umpire in deciding what are and what are not valid acts of the government within the meaning of the supreme law of the land—the Constitution. . . .
>
> To say that this tribunal of nine men shall not henceforth declare the supreme law of the land is to say in effect that we must change our form of government and substitute the rule of passion for the rule of reason.

If the quotation surprises those who are regular readers of Mr. Lawrence's column, it should be added hastily that he made the comment in 1937 in a book dedicated to "nine honest men." He approved, then, of the Court's intervening to protect economic rights. Today he heartily disapproves of the frequent intervention by the Court to assure fair criminal procedure, free speech, and freedom from racial discrimination.

Once again, then, the results reached by the Court appear to dictate the verdict of the critic. Many years ago Charles Warren, the historian of the Court, concluded that most of the attacks made upon it throughout its history had been based not on any consistent legal theory or philosophy but on "the particular economic, political or social legislation which the decisions of the Court happened to sustain or overthrow"—in short, on whose ox was gored. The situation today is no different. While the most highly publicized attacks have come from the right, there has also been a chorus from the left to deplore any decision sustaining governmental exercise of power against individual challenge. Henry M. Hart, Jr. has accurately parodied the typical result-oriented comment: " 'One up (or one down) for subversion,' 'One up (or one down) for civil liberties'. . . ."

II. Criticism of Judicial Review

A second category of Supreme Court criticism is assuredly not based on results. It takes the position that the Court has too broadly exercised its great power to review the constitutionality of legislation. The foremost exponent of this viewpoint is, of course, Judge Learned Hand. Disinterested, nonpolitical, intellectually the most eminent of critics, he has given his position added force by holding to it through all the changing results of the last several decades.

In his Holmes lectures, delivered at the Harvard Law School in 1958, Judge Hand examined the origins of the doctrine of judicial review and the exercise of the power over the years. He found the doctrine legitimate, but it is fair to say that his acceptance was grudging:

> The arguments deducing the court's authority from the structure of the new government, or from the implications of any government, were not valid, in spite of the deservedly revered names of their authors. . . . On the other hand it was probable, if indeed it was not certain, that without some arbiter whose decision should be final the whole system would have collapsed. . . . In construing written documents it has always been thought proper to engraft upon the text such provisions as are necessary to prevent the failure of the undertaking. That is no doubt a dangerous liberty, not lightly to be resorted to; but it was justified in this instance, for the need was compelling.

As Herbert Wechsler pointed out in his Holmes lecture of 1959, Judge Hand's views on the source of the Supreme Court's power to review legislation condition his approach to the exercise of the power. Judge Hand says it "was absolutely essential to confine the power to the need that evoked it," a need which he has described as the preservation of the government. He says the Supreme Court should intervene only to keep a governmental department within its "frontiers," not to reappraise "the propriety of its choices within those frontiers." That view is hardly self-explanatory, but Judge Hand's examples are revealing. He frowns, for example, at what must have been one of the Supreme Court's least controversial decisions of recent years, *Butler v. Michigan,* holding that a state might not prohibit the sale to adults of books found objectionable for children. Judge Hand concludes that the Court has used the power of judicial review so broadly as to become, again and again, "a third legislative chamber." For nine men in lifetime appointive positions to exercise such power, he says, is not only inconsistent with democratic government but harmful to the Court, because involvement in what are essentially political matters inevitably lessens public reverence for the judiciary.

The proper role of the Supreme Court in our system of government is too large a topic for this summary discussion. But it is necessary to indicate briefly, with all deference, where one disagrees with Judge Hand.

If his lectures are taken at large as a warning against excessive reliance on the courts to do the work of democracy, then it is difficult to quarrel with the theme. Certainly it is too easy to say, as so many libertarian observers seem to content themselves with saying, that judicial activism in behalf of property rights a generation ago was bad, but intervention in behalf of "personal rights" today is admirable. But the negative tone taken by Judge Hand really goes farther than a simple caution. It goes too far, in fact, for there are more positive values in judicial review than he would concede.

A. *The Court as a Forum for Moral Protest*

For one thing, the American tradition of courts serving as forums for moral protest may not be unhealthy. In a country as large as this one, and with legislatures—both state and national—so frozen by inertia, litigation is often the best device to focus attention on moral considerations. In considering a general immigration statute, for example, individual members of Congress are unlikely to give much thought to a provision requiring the deportation of aliens who at any time belonged to the Communist party, however long their residence here and however brief and remote their party membership. In the abstract—where it is likely to remain in the mind of the busy legislator—the provision has the appeal of being tough on communism. But as applied to a real human being, who came to the United States at the age of eight months, 50 years ago, and has known no other land, the statute's cruelty is easier to see. Of course a court is not empowered to reappraise the moral quality of every legislative decision. But is it not true that the relative remoteness of the judicial forum from political excitements, the security of federal judges' tenure, their freedom from sectional and party ties, and—most important—the slow, deliberative quality of the judicial process all tend to insure a greater concern for fairness to the individual than is ordinarily found in legislatures?

B. *The Court as a Catalyst*

Judicial review is sometimes mistakenly discussed as if it were an all-or-nothing proposition, in which statutes are either upheld or struck down. But in operation the power is much subtler, its radiations broader. For one thing, a court's attitude in construing a statute is significantly affected by existence of the authority to invalidate it. In recent years some of the Supreme Court's most significant decisions have been statutory constructions designed to avoid constitutional questions—constructions that could fairly be called strained. The effect of such decisions is to put the problem before Congress again, but to put it in such a way that Congress is more likely to be aware of the values at stake when it acts.

The Passport Cases and their aftermath provide an example of the

Court's role as a legislative catalyst. The Secretary of State had claimed broad, indeed virtually unlimited, statutory authority to prevent the travel of American citizens outside the Western Hemisphere whenever he decided—often on the basis of undisclosed information—that their "activities abroad would . . . be prejudicial to the interests of the United States." The Court found no such authority. When Congress undertook to repair the asserted breach in national security, the bill which passed the House narrowly defined the circumstances in which travel could be prohibited and required the Secretary, if sued over the denial of a passport, to disclose all information on which he relied.

The same kind of catalytic action may take place between the Supreme Court and the Executive Branch. In June, 1959, in *Greene v. McElroy*, the Court, construing the statutes and executive orders strictly in the light of constitutional problems, held that there was no authority for an industrial security program which denied suspected defense plant workers the right to confront their accusers. It took the Executive Branch eight months to draft a substitute program; for the first time its officials had to address themselves to the difficult problem of balancing the needs of security against fairness to the individual. The resulting order assured confrontation except in unusual cases and on the personal direction of a department head. Of course it was sad that it took a Supreme Court decision to make the President and his aides face up to a responsibility that had been pointed out by many critics, but surely intervention by the Court was preferable to continued inaction.

The Supreme Court may affect governmental policy by calling attention to moral considerations even when it upholds a challenged action. Examples are *Bartkus v. Illinois* and *Abbate v. United States*, in which the Court upheld the constitutionality of successive federal and state prosecutions of the same man for the same criminal act. Immediately after the decisions Attorney General Rogers, concerned by the possibility of prosecutorial abuse of this newly confirmed power, announced a policy against federal-following-state prosecutions. The next term he went so far in applying the policy as to ask the Supreme Court to set aside a conviction which resulted from a second federal prosecution of a defendant on the same facts—a conviction which apparently violated no statute or constitutional provision and which was really beyond the announced principle against successive state-federal prosecutions. Even more interesting is the fact that the Illinois legislature, a few months after *Bartkus* was decided, passed a law barring the prosecution of any person for a criminal act which had previously been the basis of a federal prosecution.

Even though the states have especially resented Supreme Court interference in the administration of state criminal law, the best of their officials might admit that the Court has inspired correction of what are, after all, not states' rights but states' wrongs. As scattered and haphazard as the cases on forced confessions and denial of counsel have been, surely they have encouraged the improvement of state criminal procedure. Even as enlightened a state as New York has been found wanting in recent years in its handling of criminal suspects. It seems beyond argument that the growth of federal habeas corpus as a remedy for constitutional flaws in state convictions has served to reduce the number of those flaws and to stimulate the development of state post-conviction procedures.

C. *The Court as a Nonpolitical Arbiter*

There are issues which are better left to the ivory tower handling of a court than thrown into political debate. Take the divisive questions of church and state, such as the extent to which the Constitution permits official assistance to religious schools. Paul Blanshard has written that Congress is happy "to have an impartial agency speaking without passion in so controversial an area." And that position has more to commend it than congressional timidity. The 1960 Presidential campaign has given us a taste, a small taste, of religion as a political issue. Would it really be wise, in a country of diverse races and creeds, to seek political decisions on such questions as the permissibility of released-time programs for religious education? The unhappy history of bitter national conflict over the church-state relationship in the countries of Europe argues strongly to the contrary. The Court's relatively remote position, protected from political pressures, may also enable it to deal more rationally and fairly with the problem of internal security measures as they affect individual rights. Louis Henkin has wisely observed that, in this security area, "one sometimes suspects many in Congress are pleased to have the Court save them from follies which they deem politically necessary."

One wonders whether race relations is not also a problem that Congress has been just as happy to leave to the Supreme Court. Certainly Congress abdicated to the Court from Reconstruction days until 1957 the responsibility for enforcing the Fourteenth and Fifteenth Amendments, and acquiesced in the long line of decisions that resulted. Perhaps issues so divisive were thought better entrusted to the Court than argued and forced to a conclusion in Congress, with all the strains the latter course would necessarily put on the legislative process. Southern Senators confide today that they would rather see the President or the Supreme Court accomplish some purpose for the Negro, however objectionable, than have the end achieved through legislation which will put them through a Senatorial replica of the War Between the States.

D. *The Court as an Instrument of National Unity*

Finally, there is the Supreme Court's vital and probably irreplaceable role as an instrument of national unity. Justice Holmes doubted that the United States could survive as a nation if the Court lost its power to in-

validate state statutes. For all the growth of federal power in recent decades, regional prejudices and parochialism have hardly disappeared. It still
takes a decision of the Supreme Court to prevent a state from changing
city boundaries so as to exclude Negro voters, or to prevent a state from
banning a film deemed "sacrilegious" by a politically powerful minority in
that state. At least it is hard to conceive of Congress playing this role. Even
Judge Hand saw possible justification, because of the dangers of sectional-
ism, for the Court's early construction of the commerce clause to permit a
judicial negative on state regulation of commerce. Nor has the need for
Supreme Court intervention in the field of state taxation and regulation of
commerce ended. Congress has certainly shown little desire or capacity to
deal with the multitudinous and subtle problems involved. One reason is
that state and sectional pressures remain powerful in Congress; the Supreme Court is freer to place national above local interests. . . .

"UNINHIBITED, ROBUST, AND WIDE-OPEN"—
A NOTE ON FREE SPEECH AND THE WARREN COURT

By Harry Kalven, Jr. *

There are several ways to give at the outset, in quick summary, an over-all impression of the Warren Court in the area of the First Amendment. The quotation in the title can for many reasons be taken as its trademark. The quotation comes, of course, from a statement about public debate made in the Court's preeminent decision, *New York Times v. Sullivan,* and it carries echoes of Alexander Meiklejohn. We have, according to Justice Brennan, "a profound national commitment to the principle that debate on public issues should be uninhibited, robust, and wide-open. . . ." What catches the eye is the daring, unconventional selection of adjectives. These words capture the special quality of the Court's stance toward First Amendment issues. They express the gusto and enthusiasm with which the Court has tackled such issues. They indicate an awareness that heresy is robust; that counterstatement on public issues, if it is to be vital and perform its function, may not always be polite. And, most significantly, they express a desire to make a fresh statement about the principles of free speech rather than simply repeat the classic phrases of Holmes in *Abrams* and Brandeis in *Whitney.* The Court is interested enough to be minting contemporary epigrams—to be making it its own.

For a further impression of the Court's work in the First Amendment field, we might turn to the 1959 case involving *Lady Chatterley's Lover* in movie form, *Kingsley Pictures Corp. v. Regents.* Chiefly because of an inability to agree on precisely how the court below had disposed of the case, the Supreme Court, although unanimous in reversing, found it necessary to produce six separate opinions. Of particular interest for the moment is Justice Stewart's opinion: he read the court below as banning the movie because it had dealt too sympathetically with adultery. In meeting this objection he was moved to restate the basic principle with notable freshness:

> It is contended that the State's action was justified because the motion picture attractively portrays a relationship which is contrary to the moral standards, the religious precepts, and the legal code of its

* Harry Kalven, Jr. " 'Uninhibited, Robust, and Wide-open'—A Note on Free Speech and The Warren Court." *Michigan Law Review,* Vol. 67 (December 1968), p. 289. Used with permission of the author, a professor of law at the Univeristy of Chicago.

citizenry. This argument misconceives what it is that the Constitution protects. Its guarantee is not confined to the expression of ideas that are conventional or shared by a majority. It protects advocacy of the opinion that adultery may sometimes be proper no less than advocacy of socialism or the single tax. And in the realm of ideas it protects expression which is eloquent no less than that which is unconvincing.

Again what strikes the special note is not just the firm grasp of the basic principle but the gallantry, if you will, of its restatement. It is easier to champion freedom for the thought we hate than for the thought that embarrasses.

Yet another way of reducing to quick summary the special quality of this Court with regard to First Amendment issues is to compare the opinions in *Curtis Publishing Company v. Butts*, decided in 1967, with the opinion in *Debs v. United States*. The *Debs* case was decided March 10, 1919, exactly one week after *Schenck* had launched the clear-and-present-danger formula. In an opinion by Justice Holmes, the Court affirmed Debs' conviction (carrying a ten-year prison sentence) for attempting to incite insubordination, disloyalty, mutiny, and refusal of duty in the armed forces and for attempting to obstruct the recruiting and enlistment service of the United States in violation of the Espionage Act of 1917. The overt conduct of Debs consisted solely in making a public speech to a general adult audience in Canton, Ohio. At the time he was a major national political figure, and in 1920 he was to run as the Socialist candidate for President from prison and receive over 900,000 votes.

The speech itself, which is summarized in Justice Holmes' opinion, involved a criticism of war in general and World War I in particular from a Socialist point of view. It asserted, for example, that "the master class has always declared the war and the subject class has always fought the battles. . . ." It expressed sympathy for several others already convicted for their opposition to the war, saying that "if they were guilty so was he." It appears that most of the speech was devoted to Socialist themes apart from the war, and it concluded with the exhortation: "Don't worry about the charge of treason to your masters; but be concerned about the treason that involves yourselves." During the trial Debs addressed the jury himself and stated: "I have been accused of obstructing the war. I admit it. Gentlemen, I abhor war. I would oppose the war if I stood alone."

The Court disposed of the case in a perfunctory two-page opinion, treating as the chief question whether a jury could find that "one purpose of the speech, whether incidental or not does not matter, was to oppose not only war in general but this war, and that the opposition was so expressed that its natural and intended effect would be to obstruct recruiting." The First Amendment defense exacted only the following sentence from Justice Holmes: "The chief defenses upon which the defendant seemed willing to rely were the denial that we have dealt with and that based upon the First Amendment to the Constitution, disposed of in *Schenck v. United States*. . . ." The decision was unanimous and without any comment from Justice Brandeis.

Let us now jump a half century to *Butts*. At issue there was a judgment under state law in a libel action brought by a noted football coach against a national magazine for an article which in effect accused him of "fixing" a college football game by giving his team's secrets in advance of the game to the opposing coach. The case produced an elaborate outpouring of opinions and an intricate pattern of votes in the five-to-four decision affirming the judgment. All Justices agreed that since Butts was a public figure, the reporting of his activities was in the public domain and therefore the state libel law was subject to the discipline of the First Amendment. The Justices divided over what level of privilege the defendant publisher must be given to satisfy the constitutional concern with freedom of speech. Three separate positions were expressed: Justices Black and Douglas would have granted an absolute or unqualified privilege not defeasible by any showing of malice. At the other extreme, Justice Harlan, joined by Justices Clark, Fortas, and Stewart, held the privilege defeated by a showing of "highly un-reasonable conduct constituting an extreme departure from the standards of investigation and reporting ordinarily adhered to by responsible journal-ists." The middle ground was occupied by Justices Brennan, White, and the Chief Justice, who would have adhered to the standards set forth in *New York Times* and thus would have held the privilege defeasible by actual malice—defined as "knowing falsehood or reckless disregard for truth." Out of this unpromising and apparently trivial factual context came deeply felt essays on freedom of speech by Justices Harlan, Black, and the Chief Justice. In wondering about all this on another occasion, I observed:

> This is perhaps the fitting moment to pause to marvel at the pat-tern of the Court's argument on this issue. The Court was divided 5 to 4 on whether the constitutional standard for the conditional privi-lege of those who libel public figures is that it be defeasible only upon a showing of reckless disregard for truth or merely on a showing of an extreme departure from professional newspaper standards! Further it was understood that the chief significance of the standard relates sim-ply to how jury instructions will be worded. Yet this nuance triggered a major debate in the court on the theory of free speech. [1967 Sup. Ct. Rev. 267]

And in speculating on why these issues held such extraordinary power to move the Supreme Court—after noting that in the sequence of cases fol-lowing *New York Times* the Court had located a novel and difficult issue involving "public speech interlaced with comments on individuals"—I could only add: "Second, it shows once again—and it is a splendid thing—

that all members of this Court care deeply about free speech values and their proper handling by law. Only a concerned Court would have worked so hard on such a problem."

The difference between *Debs* and *Butts* is a measure of how much the Court's approach to free speech has changed over the years since World War I. And it is a difference, it will be noted, in result, in theory, in style, and, above all, in concern.

But even as one acknowledges the deep concern of this Court for the First Amendment, there is need to pause at the outset for a perplexity and an irony. The perplexity is one that must have troubled all the contributors to this Symposium: What exactly is one referring to when he speaks of the Warren Court? Are we simply using the Chief Justiceship as a device to mark off a span of years? Would it have been any more arbitrary to talk of the work of the Court from, say, 1958 to 1964? If we find some distinctive traits in that work, as both friends and critics of the Court are so readily prone to do in the First Amendment area, to whom are we ascribing them? To some durable *team* of Justices? To the special influence of the Chief? The Court's roster during the Warren years has included some seventeen Justices, and the "Warren Court" has for varying periods of time numbered among its members Justices Minton, Burton, Clark, Whittaker, Reed, Jackson, Goldberg, and Frankfurter. Perhaps we should adapt the old Greek conundrum and ask if we can comment on the same Court twice.

I would hesitate to adopt the alternative and say that what unifies the topic is the distinctive influence of the Chief Justice on the Court's response to the First Amendment. This would require not only that we find a distinctive pattern of decisions, but that we connect it up somehow to the chairmanship of the Chief—which seems to me to attribute excessive power to that office.

But perhaps I am being too solemn about it all. There has indeed been a kind of First Amendment team: Black and Douglas have been on the Court during the entire tenure of the Chief Justice. Brennan and Harlan were appointed in 1956, and Stewart in 1958. And it is the analysis and response of these six Justices to the First Amendment that I have chiefly in mind in considering the Warren Court's reaction to free speech issues. At least we match here the rough unity of topic provided, say, by talk of the greatness of the New York Yankees in the middle 1920s.

. . . The wretched controversy over the Fortas appointment was interpreted widely as an attack more on the Court as a whole than on Justice Fortas. The Senate was presumably providing its own commentary on the work of the Warren Court. And for our immediate purposes, it is striking how much of the Senate's concern was with the work of the Court in the First Amendment area. There is a temptation to brood over the gap which appears to have been created between the First Amendment values the

Court has championed and those the public, or a considerable segment of the public, will tolerate. Is there, then, a *political* limit on the meaning of the First Amendment? Two offsetting considerations should, in any event, be noted. The Senate's free-speech grievances related almost exclusively, so far as I could tell, to the decisions on obscenity and did not put in issue the striking work of the Court in other areas of First Amendment concern. Further, such a gap between public and judicial attitudes may be a healthy sign. The tradition has never been that freedom of speech was a value to be left to majority vote; indeed, that may be the whole point of the First Amendment and of judicial review under it.

I

At the Museum of Science and Industry in Chicago there is a chart which occupies a long wall and which graphs over time the changes in human technology. The time span is some 50,000 years, and the introduction of each technological advance—from the first crude stone used as a tool for digging to today's latest electronic or space age wonders—is entered on the graph. The result is a stunning visual impression of the acceleration of cultural inheritance. Man has made more major technical advances in the past 100 years than in the previous 49,900!

There is a general analogy here to the making of law. Invention seems to breed invention, and precedent breeds more precedent. But I cite the Museum wall to make a specific point about the Warren Court. If one were to imagine a comparable scheme charting the incidence of First Amendment cases from 1791 to date, the parallel would be striking indeed; we would get a proper sense of the accelerated accumulation of First Amendment precedents in the past fifteen years. The point is, I think, a neutral one. It goes for the moment not to the quality of the Court's answers but to its willingness to confront First Amendment questions at an unprecedented rate. The result is that a great part of the law, and a greater part of what is of interest today to the teacher or commentator, is the work of the Warren Court.

Even the quickest survey makes the point. All of the constitutional decisions on obscenity have come from this Court, starting with *Roth* in 1957; if one is interested in law and obscenity he will perforce find himself studying essentially the work of the Warren Court. Similarly, the constitutional law on libel has—with the exception of *Beauharnais* in 1952—come from this Court, starting with *New York Times* in 1964. . . .

There is perhaps one other way of putting into perspective how much the Warren Court has enriched the constitutional doctrine of freedom of speech, press, and assembly. It is to compare the classic book in the field, Chafee's *Free Speech in the United States,* first published in 1920 and republished in elaborated form in 1941, with the current corpus of law. A book today performing the function of Chafee's volume would look notably different, deal to a considerable degree with different principles, and confront to a considerable extent different problems. If the analytic density of the Chafee book were to be maintained, the contemporary treatment would surely require two volumes; and the second volume would be devoted to the work of the Warren Court.

II

It is not feasible within the compass of this Article to attempt a systematic review of the results the Court has achieved in the various areas of First Amendment law. I should prefer, therefore, to check off briefly some of the new *ideas* the Court has introduced into the field.

New York Times may have effected a major alteration in official thinking about free speech. To begin with, the Court introduced the attractive notion that the First Amendment has a "central meaning" and thus suggested the possibility of a "core" theory of free speech. The central meaning suggested in *Times* appears to be the notion that seditious libel is not actionable.

It must be admitted that the promise of radical rethinking of the theory and rationale of the First Amendment which this invites has not as yet been judicially pursued. The Court has been careful, however, to preserve the status of *New York Times* as a key precedent. The Court has also made visible a new kind of problem in *Times* and its sequelae: the question of whether falsity in fact as contrasted with falsity in doctrine is entitled to any protection. This problem arises when discussion of issues in the public domain is interlaced with statements of fact about particular individuals. The issue is whether in protecting the individual's interest in reputation or privacy we will give him a veto power over the general discussion. This was the problem in *Times* itself and again in *Time Inc. v. Hill, Butts,* and *Associated Press v. Walker;* it looms as a large issue since much public discussion appears to have this mixed quality. The dilemma is a difficult one, but the Court has confronted it and, to my mind, has made real progress toward a satisfactory solution.

Perhaps equally important is the abrogation of outmoded ideas by the Court; the most significant step here, I suggest, has been the great reduction in the status and prestige of the clear-and-present-danger test. Immediately prior to the advent of the Warren Court, this test had a considerable claim as *the* criterion of the constitutionality of an exercise of governmental authority over communication. In limited areas the test may still be alive, but it has been conspicuous by its absence from opinions in the last decade. Since the test—whatever sense it may have made in the limited context in which it originated—is clumsy and artificial when expanded into a general criterion of permissible speech, the decline in its fortunes under the Warren Court seems to be an intellectual gain.

Another major conceptual contribution of the Warren Court has been development of the idea of self-censorship. A regulation of communication may run afoul of the Constitution not because it is aimed directly at free speech, but because in operation it may trigger a set of behavioral consequences which amount in effect to people censoring themselves in order to avoid trouble with the law. The idea has appeared in several cases, and, while the Court has not yet addressed a major opinion to it, it has all the earmarks of a seminal concept. The cases have varied in contexts from *Speiser v. Randall*, to *Smith v. California*, to *Time Inc. v. Hill*. In *Speiser* the Court invalidated a state statute requiring affidavits of non-Communist affiliation as a condition for a tax exemption. The vice was a subtle one: as the Court understood the state procedure, the affidavit was not conclusive; thus the burden of proof of nonsubversion was left on the applicant. The Court stated:

> The vice of the present procedure is that, where the particular speech falls close to the line separating the lawful and the unlawful, the possibility of mistaken factfinding—inherent in all litigation—will create the danger that the legitimate utterance will be penalized. The man who knows that he must bring forth proof and persuade another of the lawfulness of his conduct necessarily must steer far wider of the unlawful zone than if the State must bear these burdens.

In *Smith* the Court confronted an ordinance imposing strict criminal liability on the sellers of obscene books. Again, the Court found the vice in the chain of consequences such regulation might engender:

> By dispensing with any requirement of knowledge of the contents of the book on the part of the seller, the ordinance tends to impose a severe limitation on the public's access to constitutionally protected matter. For if the bookseller is criminally liable without knowledge of the contents, and the ordinance fulfills its purpose, he will tend to restrict the books he sells to those he has inspected; and thus the State will have imposed a restriction upon the distribution of constitutionally protected as well as obscene literature. . . . The bookseller's self-censorship, compelled by the State, would be a censorship affecting the whole public, hardly less virulent for being privately administered.

Finally, in the context of tort liability for "false light" privacy, the Court in *Hill* conceptualized the problem as one of triggering self-censorship; it thus would give the publisher a conditional privilege defeasible only by actual malice:

> We create grave risk of serious impairment of the indispensable service of a free press in a free society if we saddle the press with the impossible burden of verifying to a certainty the facts associated in a

news article with a person's name, picture or portrait, particularly as related to nondefamatory matter. Even negligence would be a most elusive standard especially when the content of the speech itself affords no warning of prospective harm to another through falsity. . . . Fear of large verdicts in damage suits for innocent or merely negligent misstatement, even the fear of expense involved in their defense, must inevitably cause publishers "to steer . . . wider of the unlawful zone. . . ."

The Court is thus in command of a versatile concept which represents, I think, a fascinating addition to the vocabulary of First Amendment doctrine. It should perhaps be acknowledged that the opinions in all three cases were written by Justice Brennan.

One other potentially powerful idea of the Warren Court should be noted: the principle that strict economy of means is required when communication is regulated. It is not enough that the end be legitimate; the means must not be wasteful of First Amendment values. The seeds of this notion first appeared in *Schneider v. New Jersey*, decided in 1939, which invalidated a prohibition against distributing leaflets where the governmental objective was to prevent littering the streets. But the idea was given its fullest expression by the Warren Court in *Shelton v. Tucker*, which voided a state statute requiring each school teacher as a condition of employment to file annually an affidavit listing every organization to which he had belonged or contributed in the preceding five years. The Court found that, although the state had a legitimate interest in the organizational commitments of its teachers, the statute gratuitously overshot its target. Justice Stewart stated the principle this way:

> In a series of decisions this Court has held that, even though the governmental purpose be legitimate and substantial, that purpose cannot be pursued by means that broadly stifle fundamental personal liberties when the end can more narrowly be achieved. The breadth of legislative abridgment must be viewed in the light of less drastic means for achieving the same basic purpose.

It remains to be seen whether this principle, too, will be seminal. There is more than a suggestion in it of a preferred-position thesis. Legislation regulating communication may not be presumptively unconstitutional today, but under the economy principle it will not be entitled to, in Holmes' phrase, "a penumbra" of legislative convenience.

III

The momentum of the Warren Court in other areas of constitutional law has been the source of sustained controversy and criticism. Without attempting to assess the merits of such criticism in general, I should like to explore whether in the special area of free speech the Court's work is subject to similar disapproval.

It has frequently been objected that the Court has moved too fast and in giant steps rather than with the gradual deliberation appropriate to the judicial process, that its opinions have often displayed inadequate craftsmanship, that it has failed to confront the issues and to rationalize its results with appropriate rigor. However, if we consider for a moment the work of the Court in two important areas—obscenity and the scope of the power of congressional investigating committees—these criticisms do not appear warranted. To be sure there had been, as we noted, no constitutional decisions whatsoever on the obscenity issue prior to 1957. But that was simply because such cases had not come before the Court; there was no general consensus that such regulation was constitutional. In fact, there had long been recognized a tension between obscenity regulation and the First Amendment. It is enough to cite the widespread praise of Judge Woolsey's decision and opinion in the *Ulysses* case to document the tension generally seen between the regulation of obscenity and the reach of the First Amendment; by the time the Supreme Court entered the field in the *Roth* case, judges in other courts had explicitly noted the constitutional shadows.

Moreover, in *Roth* the Court *upheld* the constitutionality of the obscenity regulation involved. In doing so, however, it recognized and attempted to define the constitutional limitations on such regulation. While in the past decade an unusual number of obscenity cases have reached the Supreme Court, the sequence of resulting decisions can fairly be characterized as involving the gradual resolution of limited and closely related problems on a case-by-case basis. Thus, *Kingsley Pictures* resolved the problems of thematic obscenity; *Butler v. Michigan* resolved the problems of regulation of general literature distribution keyed to what is suitable for children; and *Smith* dealt with permissible regulation of booksellers. Moreover, *Manual Enterprises v. Day* added the element of "patent offensiveness" to the constitutional definition of obscenity, and *Jacobellis v. Ohio* attached the element of "utterly without redeeming significance." If there has been a jarring note, it has come not in accelerating the liberation of arts and letters from obscenity censorship, but rather from the sudden move in the opposite direction in *Ginzburg v. United States* by adding the perplexing "pandering" element to the constitutional test.

It is true that the Court has been conspicuous within itself as to how to handle obscenity cases. It is possible to detect at least six different doctrinal positions among the nine Justices. But this is due, I would suggest, to the intrinsic awkwardness of the problem rather than to a judicial failure to take the cases seriously or to face the issues squarely. In any event, the Court cannot be criticized for rushing past existing precedent in order to abolish censorship altogether. . . .

We noted at the start that the topic of the Warren Court is an oblique, elusive one. Surely it would be easier to discuss straight away the substantive issues the Court has dealt with rather than to probe for some pattern of positions distinctive to the personality of this particular Court. Nevertheless, as we also said at the outset, there does seem to be a special trademark to this Court's work in the area of freedom of speech, press, and assembly. There is a zest for these problems and a creative touch in working with them. It has been noted that there are overtones of Alexander Meiklejohn in the Court's idiom. It may, therefore, not be inappropriate to turn to Mr. Meiklejohn for a final comment. Speaking of the principle of the First Amendment, he once said: "We must think for it as well as fight for it." The Warren Court in its enriching gloss on the amendment over the past fifteen years has done a good deal to help us do both.

*   *   *

Because the Constitution "is" what the Justices say it is, the Court is considered by many to be the most powerful group of men in the world. The greatest restraining influence remains the restraint of the Justices themselves. Still, the Supreme Court cannot create. As Justice Frankfurter noted, the Court acts merely as a "break" on other men's actions. It probes into government, but does not have the responsibility to govern. It merely says "yes" or "no"—and even then only when asked to do so.

The preceding chapters undoubtedly have raised as many questions as they have answered, but such is the plight of all learning. And it is from these unanswered questions that new ideas are born and new solutions honed.

Much unfinished First Amendment business remains before the post-Warren Courts. One such item is the growing debate surrounding "freedom of information." Does freedom of the press imply a public's "right to know"? Freedom of speech and press is of little value to a democracy if the media are deprived of data to transmit to a waiting electorate.

Also, the Warren Court spoke only haltingly on several basic media problems including a workable definition of obscenity, cameras in the courtroom, the public's access to the media, licensing of motion pictures and limits of allowable defamation and of privacy, to name but a few. Administrative problems also face future Courts. The sharp rise in the case-load is one, the reliance on a "book-by-book" definition of obscenity another.

But the overriding First Amendment challenge in these times of world and national conflict is for this nation to guarantee to its citizens the freedom of expression intended by the Constitution. Who but the Supreme Court can guarantee this freedom? Will it be guarded by the politicians—the government in power? Can it be maintained by the media or by the people themselves? And, finally, who but the Court will guard the guardian?

AMENDMENTS
TO THE CONSTITUTION
OF THE UNITED STATES
RELEVANT TO FREEDOM OF EXPRESSION

ARTICLE I

Congress shall make no law respecting an establishment of religion, or prohibiting the free exercise thereof; or abridging the freedom of speech, or of the press; or the right of the people peaceably to assemble, and to petition the government for a redress of grievances.

ARTICLE IV

The right of the people to be secure in their persons, houses, papers, and effects, against unreasonable searches and seizures, shall not be violated, and no warrants shall issue, but upon probable cause, supported by oath or affirmation, and particularly describing the place to be searched, and the persons or things to be seized.

ARTICLE V

No person shall be held to answer for a capital, or otherwise infamous crime, unless on a presentment or indictment of a grand jury, except in cases arising in the land or naval forces, or in the militia, when in actual service in time of war or public danger; nor shall any person be subject for the same offense to be twice put in jeopardy of life or limb; nor shall be compelled in any criminal case to be a witness against himself, nor be deprived of life, liberty, or property, without due process of law; nor shall private property be taken for public use without just compensation.

ARTICLE VI

In all criminal prosecutions, the accused shall enjoy the right to a speedy and public trial, by an impartial jury of the State and district wherein the crime shall have been committed, which district shall have been previously ascertained by law, and to be informed of the nature and cause of the accusations; to be confronted with the witnesses against him; to have compulsory process for obtaining witnesses in his favor, and to have the assistance of counsel for his defense.

ARTICLE VII

In suits at common law, where the value in controversy shall exceed twenty dollars, the right of trial by jury shall be preserved, and no fact tried by a jury shall be otherwise reexamined in any court of the United States, than according to the rules of the common law.

ARTICLE VIII

Excessive bail shall not be required, nor excessive fines imposed, nor cruel and unusual punishments inflicted.

ARTICLE X

The powers not delegated to the United States by the Constitution, nor prohibited by it to the States, are reserved to the States respectively, or to the people.

ARTICLE XIV

SECTION 1. All persons born or naturalized in the United States, and subject to the jurisdiction thereof, are citizens of the United States and of the State wherein they reside. No State shall make or enforce any law which shall abridge the privileges or immunities of citizens of the United States; nor shall any State deprive any person of life, liberty, or property, without due process of law; nor deny to any person within its jurisdiction the equal protection of the laws.

APPENDIX II

JUSTICES OF THE
UNITED STATES SUPREME COURT

JUSTICE	TERM	YRS.
*Jay, John	1789–1795	5
Rutledge, John	1789–1791	1
Cushing, William	1789–1810	20
Wilson, James	1789–1798	8
Blair, John	1789–1796	6
Harrison, Robert H.	1789–1790	—
Iredell, James	1790–1799	9
Johnson, Thomas	1791–1793	1
Paterson, William	1793–1806	13
*Rutledge, John	1795–1795	—
Chase, Samuel	1796–1811	15
*Ellsworth, Oliver	1796–1799	4
Washington, Bushrod	1798–1829	31
Moore, Alfred	1799–1804	4
*Marshall, John	1801–1835	34
Johnson, William	1804–1834	30
Livingston, Brockholst	1806–1823	16
Todd, Thomas	1807–1826	18
Story, Joseph	1811–1845	33
Duval, Gabriel	1812–1835	22
Thompson, Smith	1823–1843	20
Trimble, Robert	1826–1828	2
McLean, John	1829–1861	32
Baldwin, Henry	1830–1844	14
Wayne, James M.	1835–1867	32
*Taney, Roger B.	1836–1864	28
Barbour, Philip P.	1836–1841	4
Catron, John	1837–1865	28
McKinley, John	1837–1852	15
Daniel, Peter V.	1841–1860	19
Nelson, Samuel	1845–1872	27
Woodbury, Levi	1845–1851	5
Grier, Robert C.	1846–1870	23
Curtis, Benjamin R.	1851–1857	6
Campbell, John A.	1853–1861	8
Clifford, Nathan	1858–1881	23
Swayne, Noah H.	1862–1881	18
Miller, Samuel F.	1862–1890	28
Davis, David	1862–1877	14
Field, Stephen J.	1863–1897	34
*Chase, Salmon P.	1864–1873	8
Strong, William	1870–1880	10
Bradley, Joseph P.	1870–1892	21
Hunt, Ward	1873–1882	9
*Waite, Morrison R.	1874–1888	14
Harlan, John M.	1877–1911	34
Woods, William B.	1881–1887	6
Matthews, Stanley	1881–1889	7
Gray, Horace	1882–1902	20
Blatchford, Samuel	1882–1893	11
Lamar, Lucius	1888–1893	5
*Fuller, Melville W.	1888–1910	21
Brewer, David J.	1890–1910	20
Brown, Henry B.	1891–1906	15
Shiras, George, Jr.	1892–1903	10
Jackson, Howell E.	1893–1895	2
White, Edward D.	1894–1910	16
Peckham, Rufus W.	1896–1909	13
McKenna, Joseph	1898–1925	26
Holmes, Oliver W.	1902–1932	29
Day, William R.	1903–1922	19
Moody, William H.	1906–1910	3
Lurton, Horace H.	1910–1914	4
Hughes, Charles E.	1910–1916	5
Van Devanter, Willis	1911–1937	26
Lamar, Joseph R.	1911–1916	5
*White, Edward D.	1910–1921	10
Pitney, Mahlon	1912–1922	10
McReynolds, James C.	1914–1941	26
Brandeis, Louis D.	1916–1939	22
Clarke, John H.	1916–1922	5
*Taft, William H.	1921–1930	8

*Indicates Chief Justice

Sutherland, George	1922–1938	15
Butler, Pierce	1922–1939	16
Sanford, Edward T.	1923–1930	7
Stone, Harlan F.	1925–1941	16
*Hughes, Charles E.	1930–1941	11
Roberts, Owen J.	1930–1945	15
Cardozo, Benjamin N.	1932–1938	6
Black, Hugo L.	1937–1971	35
Reed, Stanley F.	1938–1957	19
Frankfurter, Felix	1939–1962	23
Douglas, William O.	1939	
Murphy, Frank	1940–1949	9
*Stone, Harlan	1941–1946	5
Byrnes, James F.	1941–1942	1
Jackson, Robert H.	1941–1954	12
Rutledge, Wiley B.	1943–1949	6

Burton, Harold H.	1945–1958	13
*Vinson, Fred M.	1946–1953	7
Clark, Tom C.	1949–1967	18
Minton, Sherman	1949–1956	7
*Warren, Earl	1953–1969	16
Harlan, John M.	1955–	
Brennan, William J., Jr.	1956–	
Whittaker, Charles E.	1957–1962	5
Stewart, Potter	1958–	
White, Byron R.	1962–	
Goldberg, Arthur J.	1962–1965	3
Fortas, Abe	1965–1969	4
Marshall, Thurgood	1967–	
*Burger, Warren	1969–	
Blackmun, Harry	1970–	

GLOSSARY OF MAJOR LEGAL TERMS
USED IN THE PRECEDING CASES

Acquittal. Being set free or exonerated of a criminal charge through a verdict of not guilty.

Affirm. To sustain the decision or ruling of a lower court.

Amicus curiae. A friend of the court who offers advice.

Appellant. A party who bring an appeal. Also called plaintiff-in-error.

Appellee. A party against whom an appeal is brought (usually the winner in the lower court action). Also called respondent-in-error.

Cause. Grounds for legal action.

Certiorari, writ of. A request by a higher court for the lower court to forward the record of the case in review. Also called writ of error or writ of review.

Claimant. One who makes a claim.

Complaint. A specific charge against an individual which leads to legal action.

Concur. To agree or to be in accord with, such as to share a legal opinion.

Continuance. A postponement of an action pending.

Defame. To hold a party up to public ridicule, hatred or contempt. A libel.

Defendant. The party against whom a legal action is brought.

Demurrer. A pleading by a defendant that even if the charge is true, it constitutes insufficient grounds for legal action.

De novo. From the beginning. Once more. Anew.

Dissent. To differ or to disagree.

Due process. The normal and proper administration of law.

Enjoin. To forbid or restrain through an injunction.

Error, writ of. A request by a higher court for the lower court to forward the record of the case in review. Also called writ of certiorari or writ of review.

Ex parte. In the interest of or on behalf of one party.

Ex rel. In the interest of or at the instigation of one party after which the state assumes responsibility for the case.

Habeas corpus, writ of. A requirement that the prisoner be brought before the court, which then is to determine the legality of his detention.

Indictment. A formal charge against an individual made by a grand jury.

Information. A formal charge against an individual made by a public officer, usually a district attorney.

Infra. Below.

Injunction. A court order restraining a party from committing certain acts.

In re. Concerning or in the matter of.

Inter alia. Among other things.

Judgment. A decision of the court as to the outcome of the case before it.

Jurisprudence. The science of law.

Libel. To hold a party up to public hatred, ridicule or contempt. To defame.

Litigation. A legal action.

Malfeasance. Wrongdoing or misconduct.

Malice. Intent to commit a wrongful act.

Mandamus. A court order requiring a party to fulfill some act or duty.

Memorandum case. One involving usually a brief, informal statement noting the findings of the court.

Mistrial. Termination without decision of a trial because of some legal error or because the jury could not reach agreement.

Nonfeasance. Failure to fulfill some act required by law.

Opinion. A formal statement by a court as to the outcome of the case before it.

Per curiam. An opinion delivered by the court as a whole and without reference to opinions of individual jurists.

Per quod, libel. A defamation which can be ascertained only after additional information is known.

Per se, libel. A defamation on its surface and without the need of any additional background information.

Petition. A formal written request in which specific legal action is requested.

Plaintiff. A party which brings charges in a civil action.

Plaintiff-in-error. A party appealing a lower court decision to a higher court. Also called appellant.

Remand. To send back to a lower court for specific action.

Remit. To send back to a lower court for further action.

Res judicata. A legal principle which has been settled by court action.

Respondent. A party against whom an appeal has been sought. A defendant. Also called respondent-in-error.

Reverse. To set aside or annul a decision of a lower court.

Review, writ of. A request by a higher court for the lower court to forward the record of the case in review. Also called writ of certiorari or writ of error.

Sequester. To temporarily remove property from the possession of the owner until certain legal questions are answered. Also to remove the jury from public exposure.

Show cause. To substantiate legally why a certain judgment should not take effect.

Summary judgment. A statement by the court giving the legal questions and rendering a decision without a formal trial.

Supra. Above.

Sustain. To uphold, support or confirm.

Tort. A civil wrong (or personal injury) for which damages may be recovered.

Veniremen. Those called to jury service.

Venue. The locality of the criminal act or cause of legal action, or the place where the jury is called or the trial is held.

Voir dire. The preliminary questioning of a prospective juror or witness by the court.

Writ. A formal document ordering or prohibiting some act.

INDEX

For an Index of the cases cited in this book, see Table of Cases, page viii.

Dr. KENNETH S. DEVOL is a professor and chairman of the Department of Journalism at San Fer-
nando Valley State College in California. He received
his Ph.D. from the University of Southern California
and undertook additional study in journalism law and
ethics at Stanford University under a grant from the
National Institute for the Humanities. He has worked
in the mass media with positions in television, public
relations and on newspapers and has served as a
judge in news competitions for the annual California
Press-Bar awards, the Radio-Television News Director's Association, and the National Academy of Television Arts and Sciences.

Date Due